ENCYCLOPEDIA OF THINGS THAT NEVER WERE

This book belongs to

....

....

Date ....

ENCYCLOPEDIA OF THINGS THAT NEVER WERE

CREATURES, PLACES, AND PEOPLE

MICHAEL PAGE   ROBERT INGPEN

PENGUIN STUDIO
Published by the Penguin Group
Penguin Putnam Inc., 375 Hudson Street,
New York, New York 10014, U.S.A.
Penguin Books Ltd, 27 Wrights Lane,
London W8 5TZ, England
Penguin Books Australia Ltd, Ringwood,
Victoria, Australia
Penguin Books Canada Ltd, 10 Alcorn Avenue,
Toronto, Ontario, Canada M4V 3B2
Penguin Books (N.Z.) Ltd, 182-190 Wairau Road,
Auckland 10, New Zealand

Penguin Books Ltd, Registered Offices:
Harmondsworth, Middlesex, England

First published in Great Britain by Dragons's World Ltd 1985
First published in the United States od America by Viking Penguin Inc. 1987
Published in a Penguin Studio paperback edition 1998

10 9 8 7 6 5 4 3 2 1

ISBN 0 14 01.0008 3

Library of Congress Catalog Card Number 86-40356
(CIP data available)

Printed in Slovenia

There is a world
just around the corner of your mind,
where reality is an intruder
and dreams come true...

...You may escape into it at will.
You need no secret password,
no magic wand or Aladdin's lamp;
only your own imagination
and curiosity...

... about things that never were

There are those who scoff at dreams and call them a waste of time. But dreams are as much a part of you as the beating of your heart. The gift of dreaming, of fantasising, is precious because it expands one life into countless other lives, like a myriad blossoms on a single branch. Those who cannot dream are to be pitied by those who can. They will never know the magic of slipping through from Realtime into Dreamtime: of seeing through dimension after dimension unknown to our five senses, as though one curtain after another was drawn aside to reveal a passionate world of colours, deeds, achievements and abilities.

Every people, of everytime, have known the importance of dreaming. When their dreams have been recorded we call them myths, or legends, or fairy stories. They are part of the treasure of our secret world, able to transport us instantly to Valhalla or Olympus. They explain to us everything we long to know, and give substance to our instinct that there are worlds beyond our world.

Dreaming, or fantasy, is our only escape from reality until we pass through those great gates which lead to the ultimate dream. And yet there is only a shadow curtain between reality and fantasy. The fantasies of the past are the realities of the present. In 1903, H. G. Wells wrote a book entitled *The First Men in the Moon*, and his contemporaries enjoyed it as a flight of fantasy. But, within the lifetimes of many humans born in 1903, the first men actually walked on the moon. No doubt we will see many other Wellsian fantasies change to reality, and perhaps travel through time as easily as we now travel through space.

Everything we accept as part of our lives was once a fantasy. The mythology of every race tells of cosmic beings who used the elements as their weapons, and that fantasy came dreadfully true at Hiroshima. The legendary beings of the past could travel in chariots without horses, speak to each other across the universe, make fire obey them, and cure diseases with their magical powers. We have automobiles, radio, aeroplanes, electricity, laser beams, miracle drugs and submarines. Our human ancestors would have regarded all such things as fantasies.

A scientist might deplore the notion that there is any link between science and fantasy, but fantasy always comes first. It is the creature of imagination, and without imagination there would be no science. Every invention is the result of fantasy.

This book is planned to help you release your own powers of fantasy: to show you that in slipping through the shadow curtain you are following an honourable tradition. As you read it, you will remember that research into things which never existed is by no means an exact science. One must use illogic instead of logic, illusion instead of lusion, insight rather than eyesight. The stories and illustrations of Things That Never Were may vary sometimes from others you have read or seen, but that is because the creators of the book have used it as a key to unlock their own fantasies. They have used the word 'Thing' in its broadest meaning—'Any possible object of thought'—and followed the trails of fantasy through many weird and tangled thickets of mythology, folk lore, legend, fiction, and fairy tales. If they are contradictory it is because fantasy itself is a contradiction.

The popular theory is that the earliest creators of fantasy, in its form of myths and legends, used it to explain all the wonders of the Cosmos which they could not understand. But there is a Cosmos within us as well as a Cosmos around us, and it is far greater than anything we see or hear with our outward faculties. The exquisite or fearsome pictures of our imagination, the voices and music of the mind, arise out of an immensity for which we have no name. The Cosmos within us holds all the gods and demons ever invented by mankind, with all their magical creativity compressed in mystic seeds within our hearts and minds. We are able to use their powers to achieve joy and freedom or to spread physical and spiritual devastation.

All we may do is hope to achieve some understanding of that immense Cosmos within us. That which we call fantasy is the first step towards such understanding, because it is the electricity of imagination from which all knowledge springs. As you look into the dream worlds of other men and women they may help you to understand.

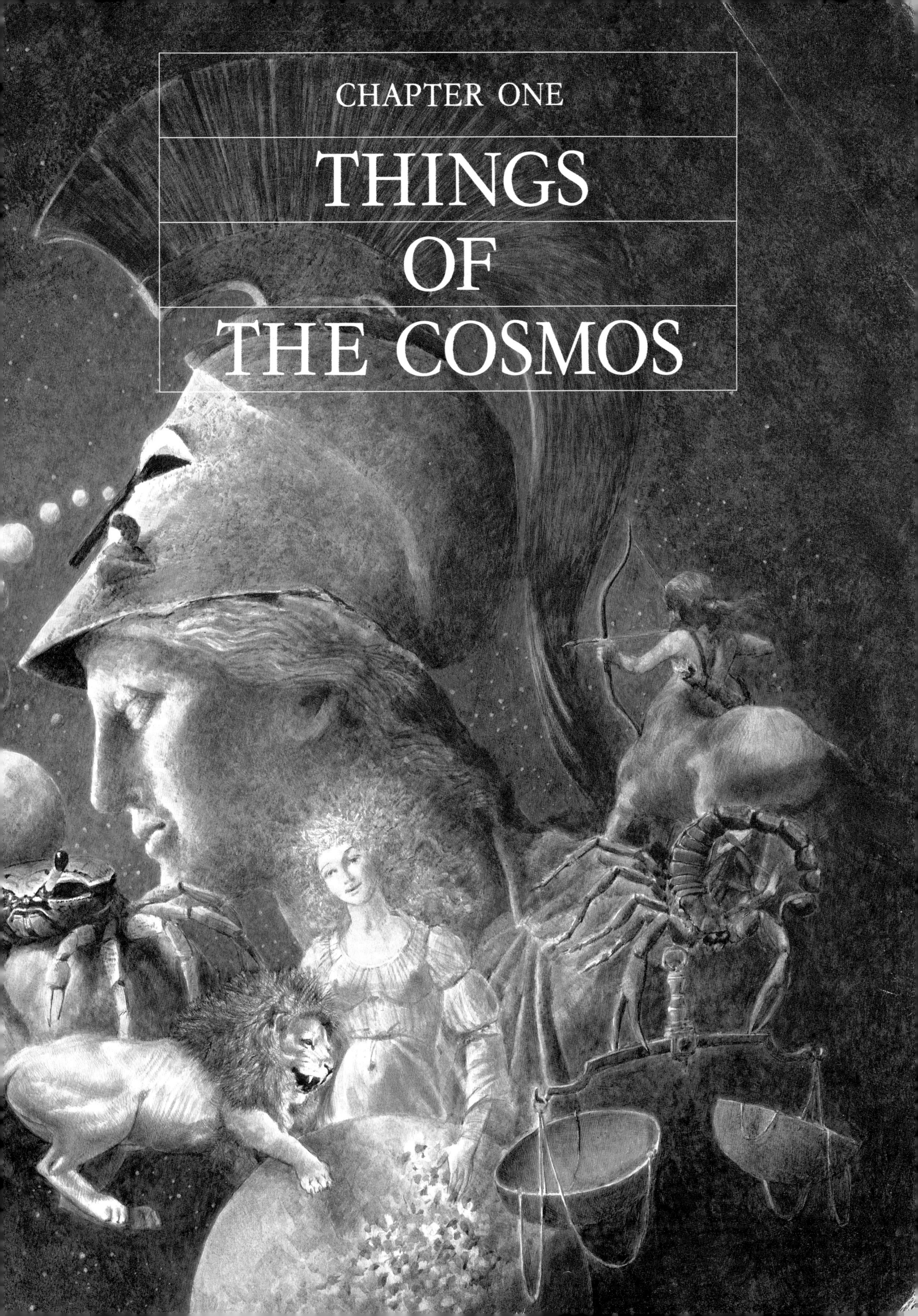

CHAPTER ONE

THINGS OF THE COSMOS

THINGS OF THE COSMOS

We of the Cosmos are eternally different and yet eternally the same. Our powers are unchanging, yet we assume so many forms that a man could not name them all in a lifetime. We exist in the countless stars of the sky, in every wave of the sea, in everything above or below the earth. Water and flame, soil and air, all hold us within themselves.

In the beginning we created the Cosmos out of Chaos. Every race and language tells our story in their own ways. When there was nothing, we came out of nowhere and separated Chaos into its innumerable elements. We set the stars in their courses and placed limits on the seas: we invented the sun and lit the lamp of the moon.

At first there were only the Sky Father and Earth Mother. Every race gives them different names but as cosmic beings they were always the same. They created the entire family of gods, and when they had built their heavens they had to battle against the forces of evil—which may also have been children of the great parents. We waged such wars above every quarter of the world you know, from Iceland to New Zealand, and when we had time we created mankind.

You humans possess all the qualities which we know as gods: courage, lust, love, avarice, despair, nobility, cowardice, and all the rest. You need not wonder why your natures are as tangled as a thornbush, mingling flowers and thorns. You inherited them from we innumerable gods, who still meddle with your destiny.

We live within the heart of a diamond and in the lightest breeze which touches your cheek. Most of all we live within the hearts of men. If you seek us you will find us there, but do not open the doors too wide. You may release Odin the Wise or Venus the Lover, or even some of our manifestations such as gallant King Arthur, but red-eyed Mars and dreadful Hades also lurk within your heart. We are you and you are we.

Perhaps you find it hard to believe in us. If so, then think about the words of one of your own wise men. He said that if you bet on the gods, and they don't exist, you lose nothing. But if you bet against them, and they do exist, you lose everything.

Remember this as you read our stories.

Aeolus

Guardian of the Winds: a son of Poseidon, Lord of the Ocean, by a mortal woman. He went to sea as a boy and eventually gained command of his own ship. As a shipmaster he realised that ships could be blown along by the winds instead of having to depend on oars, and he invented sails. After many adventurous voyages he married a princess and settled down on the island of Lipara.

As a member of the Liparan royal family he became both a judge and a priest and performed both duties so well that his immortal relations looked kindly upon him. Zeus appointed him Guardian of the Winds and put him in charge of the brothers Boreas the North Wind, Zephyrus the West Wind, Eurus the East Wind, and Notus the South Wind. He keeps them chained in a cave on Lipara and releases them only when it is necessary to make the weather.

When the great adventurer and navigator Odysseus visited Lipara, Aeolus gave him a leather bag in which he had secured all the winds which might harm his ship. Unfortunately Odysseus' crew were so curious that they opened the bag and let the winds escape, thus changing a prosperous voyage into a disaster.

Aesir

The Creators of the Cosmos and first gods of northern Europe. In the beginning there was nothing but a great wasteland of ice and snow, stretching between the Cloud Land of the north and the Land of Fire in the south. Sparks from the Land of Fire melted some of the ice and its drops formed into Ymir, father of the giants.

As he lay sleeping he gave birth to giants within his armpit. He was nourished by Audumla, a cow which appeared out of the melting ice, and as Ymir drank the milk from her udders she licked at the ice until it revealed a being named Buri. He had a son named Bor, who married Ymir's daughter Bestla and fathered the giant gods Odin, Vili, and Ve.

These Aesir battled against Ymir and his giant children and killed all of them except Bergelmir and his wife, who sailed away on the sea of blood from the battle to become the parents of a new race of giants.

The three Aesir then built the Cosmos out of the body of Ymir, using his flesh for the earth and his salty blood for the sea. They changed his hair into trees and his bones into mountains, and when this work was done they raised his skull on four pillars so that its curved interior might become the sky.

Sparks drifted over the earth from the Land of Fire, and the three Aesir caught a number of these to place within the skull of Ymir. Odin and his brothers commanded one of them to become the sun and another the moon, while the others became the stars and planets. Once in position they stayed there, obedient to the rules which the Aesir made for their duties.

When the Cosmos was ready for habitation, other Aesir appeared to join the task of creation and administration. Two of them, Hoenir and Lothur, were walking with Odin upon the earth when they saw two dead trees and changed them into the first man and the first woman.

Albion

The dominant kingdom of the Isle of Britain, named after the great white (*alba*) cliffs which soar out of the Sea of the Franks along its south-west coastline. In former times, the people of Albion consisted of fierce tribes similar to the Scots of the far north and the Cymri of the west. A race of giants, led by Gogmagog, inhabited the south of the country until they were defeated by Brutus the Trojan.

His Trojan followers, famed for their strength and courage, intermarried with the people of Albion and created a splendid new race whom they called Britons after their leader Brutus. Joseph of Arimathea converted them to Christianity, after showing the power of the new faith by thrusting his staff into the soil near Glastonbury, where it blossomed as a white thorn tree.

After their conversion, the noble descendants of the Trojans dedicated themselves to the knightly virtues of valour, charity, and the succour of the helpless, especially virgins who had been kidnapped by dragons.

Albion is a singularly beautiful country, largely covered by misty forests inhabited by fays, goblins, pixies, and similar beings. The castles of the knights stand on hilltops above the towns and villages, and from these eminences the knightly class protects the farmers and craftsmen who toil diligently in the lower lands.

The country is rich in iron and has ironworkers of great skill. They fashion weapons and armour for the knights, often with the guidance of sorcerers who help them to create swords of magical powers.

There are also mines of gold, silver, copper, tin, and precious stones. Gnomes and kobolds help the miners to find the most profitable veins of these minerals.

Albion is noted for the beauty and purity of its women, although the knights often have to protect their virtue against assault by evildoers.

Surrounding kingdoms envy the richness of Albion and make frequent attacks upon the nation. This state of almost continuous war has an unhappy effect upon its politics. The knights often quarrel about the military leadership, but the powerful Pendragon family from the far west has succeeded the descendants of Brutus and they maintain order by a mixture of force, magic, and guile.

Apples of Youth

The gods are immortal because they enjoy a diet forbidden to mankind, such as the nectar and ambrosia of Olympus. In Asgard, the Scandinavian heaven, the Aesir maintain eternal youth by eating the golden Apples of Youth. The goddess Idunn always carries them with her and makes sure that no mortal ever has a chance to sample the golden fruit.

A giant, Thjazi, knew of the apples, however, and longed for them to ensure his immortality. His chance came when he captured Loki, the youngest and most mischievous of the Aesir, and refused to let him go unless he promised to bring Idunn and her apples down to earth.

Loki never hesitated to betray his fellow-Aesir and he soon thought up a trick to lure Idunn out of Asgard. He told her he had seen golden apples in the forests of earth which were even more beautiful and powerful than the Apples of Youth.

Idunn was so curious that she followed Loki down to Thjazi's hut, where the giant locked her inside. The Aesir soon noticed her absence when they began to grow old and weak, and they knew that Loki was the only one of their number so dishonourable that he would have betrayed her. They threatened him with such savage punishment that he changed himself into a hawk and flew down to rescue Idunn and the apples.

He changed her into a nut so that he might carry her through the air, and laden with Idunn and the apples he climbed slowly up towards Asgard. Thjazi pursued him in the form of an eagle, and the Aesir watched anxiously as the giant bird soared closer and closer to Loki and his precious cargo. The eagle was about to pounce on the hawk when the Aesir built a great fire in the sky, so that it scorched the pursuer's wings and Thjazi fell back to earth.

The Apples of Youth have remained safely in Asgard ever since those days, and no mortal has ever been able to taste these or any other of the forbidden foods which preserve the youth of the gods.

Arthur

The king of England whose story shows that even the most gallant knight may fall victim to base emotions.

He was the son of a strange liaison between King Uther Pendragon and Ygerna, Duchess of Cornwall. Uther fell so violently in love with Ygerna that he persuaded Merlin the magician to change him into a replica of the Duke, so that he might enter Tintagel Castle and the bed of Ygerna.

Uther's men killed the Duke before Ygerna's son was born, but Merlin predicted an unhappy fate for the infant. He said that enemies would kill him and put an end to the rule of the Pendragons.

To avoid this fate, Ygerna surrendered her newborn son to Merlin. The magician gave him to the noble knight Sir Ector, who had the boy christened as Arthur and brought him up with his own son.

Sir Ector taught Arthur all the knightly skills and virtues and the boy grew into a splendid fair-haired youth, expert in weaponry but gracious and fair to his vassals and henchmen. England was in its usual state of perpetual war and King Uther, now old and ailing, had to fight off an alliance of northern kings. He defeated them at the battle of St Albans but the effort was too great for him, and as he lay dying Merlin called on him to declare Arthur as his successor.

King Uther's last words were 'I give him God's blessing and my own, and bid him pray for my soul and claim the crown!'

Uther's knights had never heard of Arthur and they refused to accept an unknown youth as king, especially since many of them also laid claim to the crown. Merlin tricked them by contriving the appearance of a sword thrust through a great anvil, and on the sword were written in letters of gold 'Whoso pulleth out this sword is rightwise king of all Britain.'

Each of the rebellious knights swaggered up to the anvil to strain and tug at the sword, and they guffawed when a slender youth also stepped up for his turn. When Arthur drew the sword from the anvil they roared angrily that he must be a fairy child. Rumour said that he had been cast up on the beach by a golden wave. When Arthur claimed the crown and invited them to a great feast they replied that they would give him 'gifts of hard swords betwixt the neck and shoulders.'

Arthur rose to the challenge by enlisting Sir Ector and a nucleus of faithful knights to follow him. He fought the rebels in a series of battles, and showed such strength and skill that they bowed the knee to him.

In one of the battles he broke the sword he had drawn from the anvil, but Merlin led him to a lonely lake where a hand rose from the water holding another sword. The Lady of the Lake appeared and told Arthur he might have the sword, named Excalibur, and this magical weapon always ensured victory in Arthur's defence of the realm and conquest of the pagans.

Arthur soon proved himself the greatest warrior and general in Europe. The knights who once resented him soon gloried in his victories. Under his command they fought with unbeatable strength and spirit; first in Britain where they slashed their way through invading hordes of Scots and Irish, and then in Europe where they conquered Gaul.

Arthur's magnificent court at Camelot attracted every knight in the nation, eager to prove himself in battle and tournament. The fierce young men fought each other with lance and sword on the tourney ground but accepted Arthur's rules of chivalry, in which they swore fealty to Arthur, the faith of Christendom, and the fair rules of battle.

The old magician Merlin always stood behind Arthur as his adviser, but as the young king grew in strength and power he did not always heed Merlin's warnings. He ignored Merlin's advice that he should not marry Guinevere, the most beautiful woman in Britain. Arthur's best knight and dearest friend, Sir Lancelot, was also in love with her, and Merlin foresaw that this triangle must inevitably lead to disaster. But Arthur's desire for Guinevere was so great that he refused to surrender her to his friend and they were married in a great ceremony.

Arthur was more impressed by Merlin's prediction that a man born on May Day would bring him to disaster. He ordered that all male children born on May Day should be brought to Camelot, but the ship in which they travelled was wrecked and only one survived. He was Modred, Arthur's nephew, who was washed onto the beach and brought up by a good man until he could present himself at court. Arthur received Modred gladly, ignoring Merlin's warnings that he was a traitor.

Under Arthur's rule his kingdom seemed about to enter a new Golden Age, but there was one flaw upon the contentment of his people. This was the loss of the Holy Grail, the vessel from which Christ ate at the Last Supper. Joseph of Arimathea brought the Grail to Britain but it had not been seen for many years, and there could be no lasting peace or prosperity until the Grail had been seen again.

But the Grail may be seen only by those who are flawless in soul and spirit, and Arthur doubted whether he or any of his knights might claim such perfection. While he pondered these matters a new knight, Prince Galahad, joined his court. Galahad was a young man of surpassing strength, grace, and beauty, but the other knights noticed that he carried no weapons and that his scabbard was empty.

Just as Galahad was being introduced to them, a squire brought miraculous news. A great stone floated on the river below Camelot, and in the stone was a sword with a glittering jewelled hilt. Inscribed upon it were the words 'No man shall take me hence, but only he by whose side I ought to hang, and he shall be the best knight in the world.'

Once more the knights of Britain vied with each other to release a miraculous sword, but Galahad was the only one to draw the sword from the stone. As he thrust it into his scabbard, the other knights saw the happening as a sign that they should now go forth in search of the Holy Grail.

A hundred and fifty of Arthur's great company vowed themselves to the quest, and left Camelot in a cavalcade brilliant with the flashing of their arms and armour and the colours of their shields and banners. Many died on their adventures while others grew weary and drifted back to Camelot. Sir Lancelot returned broken with sorrow, because he had just been about to see the Grail when it was shut out from his sight. The perfection of his knighthood was flawed by his secret desire for Queen Guinevere.

Only the knights Galahad, Bors, and Percival continued the search. After fearful adventures they found Joseph of Arimathea, who showed them the Holy Grail. Galahad was overcome by such joy that he prayed to be taken up to heaven, and this flawless knight was raised up by a host of angels. Percival, grieving for Galahad, died as a hermit, and Bors returned to Camelot with the news that the quest was ended. It seemed that the Golden Age might now begin, but Merlin's deadly predictions still had to be fulfilled.

Modred, the knight born on May Day, aspired to Arthur's crown, and he conspired to destroy the faith and fellowship between Arthur and the knights. He spread rumours about the relationship between Lancelot and Guinevere, and persuaded twelve knights that they must kill Lancelot to preserve the honour of the queen. The death of Lancelot, Arthur's greatest friend and supporter, would split the brotherhood of Camelot and help Modred to gain the crown.

But Lancelot slew all twelve knights in furious combat, and Modred would have been foiled if Arthur had not shown a flaw in his own nature. He was jealous of Lancelot's attraction for Guinevere and he believed Modred's gossip of an illicit liaison. In his fury at her alleged unfaithfulness he ordered the knights Gaharis and Gareth to have her burnt at the stake.

A lamenting crowd of Camelot folk saw her led forth to death, but even as the flames licked at her garments Lancelot charged to the rescue. He cut his way through the guards, killed Gareth and Gaharis, and galloped off with Guinevere to his castle of Joyous Gard.

Bloody battles between the supporters of Arthur and of Lancelot now wracked the kingdom. Those who had once feasted together at Camelot turned their swords against each other. The slaughter continued until the Pope ordered Arthur to make peace, and he might have done so if Sir Gawain, the brother of Gareth and Gaharis, had not kept Arthur's jealousy of Lancelot alive.

Lancelot left Guinevere and fled to Brittany, but Arthur followed with a great force of men-at-arms. His absence gave Modred the chance to claim the crown. He spread word that Arthur had died in battle, and demanded that Guinevere should marry him.

When Arthur heard this news he hastened back to Britain and fought two great battles with Modred. In the second of these the fighting ceased when Arthur and Modred arranged a parley, and met between the armies to discuss terms of peace.

Modred agreed to content himself with the dukedoms of Kent and Cornwall if he might succeed to the throne after the death of Arthur. The king agreed, and it seemed that peace was in sight when a snake slithered from the grass and bit the foot of one of the knights standing behind Arthur. He drew his sword to kill it, and both sides took this as a signal to renew the battle.

They fought so savagely that, in the evening, only Modred still stood among the corpses on one side and Arthur, Lucan, and Bedivere on the other. Arthur ran at Modred with his spear, but even as he ran it through his enemy he received a fatal wound.

As Arthur's strength ebbed he ordered Bedivere to throw the sword Excalibur into a nearby lake. As the sword fell towards the dark surface a hand rose out of the waters, caught Excalibur and brandished it three times, and then vanished with it into the lake.

Bedivere then carried the dying king to the edge of the sad waters, where a black-draped boat occupied by three mourning women awaited him. They took Arthur aboard and sailed with him to the isle of Avalon, where he lies until the people of Britain have need of him again.

Asgard

The heaven of the Nordic gods of Scandinavia and the Teutonic peoples. When the gods Odin, Vili, and Ve had fashioned the earth, which they called Midgard or the Middle Abode because it is halfway between heaven and hell, they set to work to construct Asgard. They were soon joined by other gods, or Aesir, and they called their heaven Asgard, meaning Place of the Aesir.

When the host of gods had completed their work, Asgard had some resemblance to the earth below. The homes of the gods provided a model for the great halls of the Vikings and other races of Midgard. A great fire burns in the centre of the hall, its smoke blackening the rafters and seeping out through the thatch. The chief gods sit around the fire, drinking mead and discussing their plans for mankind, while the lesser gods sit beyond its warmth and eat the scraps, as do the servants of earthly chieftains.

Whenever the Aesir wish to visit earth they walk down the rainbow known as Bifrost: the heavenly bridge they built to link Asgard and Midgard.

Aquarius

The waterbearer who occupies the eleventh House of the Zodiac. He pours refreshment down upon the northern hemisphere as the earth moves through the cosmic influence of his House, between January and February each year.

Aquarius was originally Ganymede, the son of King Tros of Phrygia. He was an astoundingly beautiful youth, and travellers came from all over the ancient world to watch him as he exercised naked except for the Phrygian cap upon his silken curls.

He soon attracted the attention of Zeus, the ruler of Olympus, who was an ardent lover of male and female beauty. Zeus struck a bargain with King Tros, who exchanged his son for a team of heavenly steeds, and Zeus changed himself into an eagle in order to lift the youth up to Olympus.

He appointed Ganymede as cupbearer to the gods and goddesses, and as their young servant kept their goblets filled they were all charmed by his grace and beauty. Eventually Zeus rewarded him with immortality by placing him in the heavens as a constellation.

As a servant of the gods the beautiful youth had been a chatty and gregarious companion, eager to make friends with all of them and displaying an alert and sensitive mind. Sometimes he got into trouble by talking too much, and sometimes he argued violently in order to impress them with his own ideas.

Now, when Aquarius fulfils his cosmic duty of providing refreshment for mortals instead of gods, humans born under his influence may absorb his characteristics.

Aries

This powerful creature grazes upon the spring grass of the pastures of heaven. When the creators of the Cosmos first put him out to pasture he resembled the sheep of ancient Arcady. He was coloured white and brown and black, his long tangled fleece was more like hair than wool, he was long-legged and agile and his horns were more like those of a goat than a sheep. But the eternal beings who inhabit the various Houses of the Zodiac are continuously changing, although they are forever the same, and Aries now has some resemblance to a ram of the true Merino breed such as those reared in Australia.

Aries is leader of the flock once owned by the great god Mars, who was a farmer before he took up the profession of arms, and the constellation of Aries lies close to the planet Mars.

Aries is a true ram: belligerent, lustful, and fertile in creation. He is quite placid when left in undisputed possession of his ewes but he charges furiously against any challenger. Naturally he imparts these qualities to humans born between March and April under the sign of the Ram.

Bacchus

Originally known as Dionysus, he is the god who brought the double-edged gift of wine and its festivals to mankind. He is one of the many sons of Zeus born to mortal women, and as a baby he had narrow escapes from death because of the jealousy of Zeus' wife Hera.

Zeus protected him by giving him into the care of the nymphs of Mount Nysa,

where he enjoyed a carefree youth. The nymphs made him their brother, the Muses taught him to sing and dance, and old Silenus inspired him with a love of glory. The nymphs crowned him with myrtle and laurel and he spent his days frolicking with them on the slopes of Mount Nysa.

As a young man he experimented with the grapes which grew on Mount Nysa, and made a drink previously unknown to god or man. He sampled it so freely that the nymphs thought he had been stricken with madness, and when he experienced the world's first hangover he visited an oracle to be cured. She told him that his sufferings were a punishment for enjoying a pleasure unknown even to the gods, but he replied that the pleasure had been worth the pain. On the way home he caught a wild ass, which became his eternal mount and companion.

With unselfish ardour he set out to spread the news of wine among the whole of mankind, but his gift often had unhappy results. When he taught King Icarius how to make wine the king gave some to his shepherds, and as they became drunk they thought their king had poisoned them and put him to death.

Dionysus was determined that men should accept his gift, even when he had to force it upon them. He used both human and magical powers to overcome his opponents, including the pirates who captured him and tied him to the mast of their ship. He made the sea around the ship turn into wine and a great vine grow up the mast, while he turned himself into a lion. The pirates were so terrified that they jumped overboard and became dolphins.

His mission had unfortunate effects on his character. The young man who had delighted in the glory of wine developed into a violent and surly toper, accompanied by a crowd of centaurs, satyrs, nymphs and Bacchantes who capered around him as he rode on his wild ass. The Bacchantes, a throng of drunken and immoral men and women, forced innocent youths and virgins to swallow their first taste of wine and join the frenzied Bacchanals.

Dionysus, or Bacchus, still wanders the world with his boozy mob of followers. They sing, spew, caper and hiccup their way from one community to another, supporting the gross form of Bacchus as he waves his winecup and croaks some ancient drinking-song. The battles and arguments about the gift of Bacchus still continue but even the strictest laws have never prevented the Bacchantes from holding their rowdy festivals and tempting youths and virgins to follow them. Wise men have learned that the gift of Bacchus can bring them deep contentment, but they rarely allow themselves to be dragged into the revels.

Bumba

The creator of all the animals, including man, who inhabit the region of the Congo. Only the witch doctors of certain tribes have seen Bumba and they give conflicting reports of his appearance, possibly to confuse the uninitiated. It seems that he may resemble a chieftain of one of the forest tribes, although he is of immensely greater stature, and that he may carry similar weapons and adornments.

Bumba appeared magically at the beginning of the world. When he saw that the earth had nothing but plants upon it he decided to create the animals of the water, earth, and air, by vomiting up nine creatures which became the ancestors of fish, birds, reptiles, and mammals.

He examined these creatures, felt they all lacked some special quality, and vomited once more. This time he produced a two-legged animal which had powers denied to all the others.

He made strict rules for the behaviour of all his creatures but one of them, the female Tsetse Bumba, refused to obey them. Bumba banished her from earth to sky, and although he could destroy her he allows her to exist because she caused the lightning to give fire to mankind.

Bunyil

A creation ancestor of the Australian Aborigines. He took charge of the Cosmos when it was still formless Chaos, and used his magical arts to divide it into heaven and earth. After that he fashioned the sun, moon, and stars and set them in their places, moulded the shape of the earth and planted it with trees and all the other growing things, and breathed life into all the creatures of the water, land, and air.

But he had not yet made anyone in his own likeness, and he was content to enjoy his handiwork until he began to feel lonely. Then he took a handful of clay and formed it into the shape of a man, using dry grass for its hair.

Bunyil's new creation pleased him so much that he made another man, and then breathed them both into life. He taught them to sing and dance so that they might join him in corroboree, and spent many years in teaching them all his magic. When they in their turn created the race of Aborigines they were able to teach the Aborigines all the wisdom of Bunyil.

Cancer

The great crab who rules the fourth House of the Zodiac. She is a survivor from the days when Hercules was performing his Twelve Labours.

The second was the killing of the monstrous nine-headed Hydra, who lived in the marshes of Lerna. Cancer was one of the Hydra's sentries, and when Hercules approached she bit him on the foot.

Hercules immediately crushed the crustacean, but she was rescued by the goddess Hera. Hercules was one of the many illegitimate sons of her husband Zeus, ar she never lost a chance to spite these products of her husband's liaisons. She placed Cancer in the heavens, where the crab survives forever as a symbol of the Great Mother.

Cancer, like all crabs, is somewhat retiring in nature. She likes to remain in concealment while she considers what is to be done, but once she has made up her mind she uses her claws to seize the object of her desire. She opens her embrace to those whom she trusts but quickly scuttles away from undesirable attentions. Neurotic, sensitive, and selfish, she can be a bad enemy but she is maternal and caring for those she loves.

Those humans born when the planet earth entires the fourth House of the Zodiac may display similar characteristics.

Capricorn

The stellar manifestation of the great god Pan. This son of Hermes was one of the few gods to be born imperfect, with the body and arms of a man but the hindquarters of a goat. His grinning face bears sharp horns and a billygoat beard.

These seeming disadvantages proved very useful in his favourite sport of chasing and seducing the nymphs, but during the war of Olympus against the Titans he was one of the gods who had to escape by changing their shapes. Pan jumped into the River Nile and changed himself into a fish below the navel and a goat from the waist upwards. When the cosmic war was over, Zeus rewarded Pan for his ingenuity by changing him into the constellation Capricorn, which is named after the two Latin words *capris* goat and *cornus* horn.

Pan used his goat legs to climb to the summit of the heavens, and his character has not changed since he capered through the forests of Arcadia. He can be a loyal friend and he has the ingenuity, industry, and creativity which enabled him to invent and play the Pan pipes, but when the mood takes him he is malicious, secretive, and selfish. It is no wonder that human beings born in the tenth House of the Zodiac, when Capricorn is in the ascendant, may share some of Pan's personality traits.

Chaos

Every race or tribe records the period of Chaos, when mystic creation spirits still brooded over a Cosmos still without shape, order, or natural laws. In some places Chaos was total darkness, because the creation spirits had not yet pricked holes in the curtain of night. In others it was a desolation of shrieking winds, with the spirits of all the creatures who were to inhabit the earth still trapped within rocks and stones. Over the Pacific Ocean, Chaos was a gloomy sea rolling eternally from one horizon to another, silent apart from the call of a lonely bird which was to carry the messages of creation.

In many places, Chaos became the site of titanic battles between the gods of creation and the evil spirits who rule the elements. The gods had to use all their magical powers to harness the winds, conquer the raging ocean, set the heavenly bodies in order around the sky, and settle the earth down into its present form. They could not create mankind until they had conquered all the forces which might destroy him, but they were always too impatient to finish their task. Many of the evil spirits are still able to break their bonds, and to continue the battle with their weapons of hurricanes, earthquakes, tidal waves and volcanic eruptions.

Cu Chulainn

The Irish folk hero, exemplar of all that is ardent, gallant, and mystic in the character of Ireland.

As a child he was named Setanta, the foster-son of four wise men who taught him wisdom, warfare, magic, and poetry. He first showed his mettle when they offered him the choice of a long life or fame, and he chose fame. They predicted he would gain it in terrible combat, and that his first and last exploits would be the killing of a dog.

The four wise men also laid certain mystic laws upon Setanta. Among other things he was never to pass a hearth without tasting the food being cooked there, but he must never eat the flesh of a dog.

Setanta made the first prophecy come true when he was only seven years old, when the great hound of Cullan the Smith attacked him while he was playing ball. Setanta stopped the hound's gaping mouth with his ball and then dashed out its brains. Cullan complained about the death of his dog but Setanta replied 'I promise to act as the watch-dog of Ulster for the rest of my life.' For this promise he was named Cu Chulainn, meaning Cullan's Hound.

After this first exploit he had to face many other ordeals, but he survived each of them by his courage, skill, and magical powers. He won all his warlike equipment by courage and guile, and he could swim like a fish, run like a deer, and leap as high as a flying bird. In courtly circles he was a pleasing companion for the sweetness of his nature and his ability to compose poems for any occasion, but on the field of combat he was a terrible enemy.

The fame promised by the wise men came to him when he was challenged by the giant warriors Thratauna, Trita, and Apta. His friends begged him not to fight them, but he was filled with the true frenzy of battle and greed for fame. He galloped forth to meet the giants in a chariot drawn by his steeds Black of Saingliu and Grey of Macha, which were born on the same day as himself.

He was a brave and terrible sight as he sped to the fray, adorned with splendid jewellery and with his long hair, tinted in many colours, streaming behind him. He chanted his war song louder than the thundering hooves and his eyes flashed fire as he fell upon the challengers.

They were no match for his berserk fury and he cut off their heads and slung them from his chariot. On the way back he captured a stag to run behind him and a flight of swans to fly overhead to signal his coming.

The people of the court feared that in his warlike frenzy he might attack them, but the Queen of Ulster contrived a way to calm him down. She led all her ladies naked to meet him, and when Cu Chulainn politely closed his eyes her warriors seized him and plunged him into icy water.

Cu Chulainn's love of fame and lust for battle led him into many adventures both honourable and disreputable. He suffered grievous wounds but never flinched from enemies, although they sometimes humiliated him. When he and his followers raided the Otherworld with the help of the sorcerer Cu Roi, but refused to share their spoils with him, Cu Roi buried Cu Chulainn up to his armpits and shaved off all his hair.

Eventually Queen Medb, the leader of Ulster's enemies, wove a great curse which paralysed all the country's warriors except Cu Chulainn. He fought off Queen Medb's forces single-handed, and she enlisted sorcerers to bring about his downfall.

They learned of the taboos which he must not break, and when he rode forth to another battle three sorceresses roasted a dog by the roadside. He had to stop and eat some of the meal, but he knew that his taste of roast dog would deplete his magical powers.

Thus it happened that in his last battle his enemies could deal him a mortal wound. He escaped from them and washed his wound in a lake, but as he did so an otter, known as a 'water dog', drank from the bloodstained water. Cu Chulainn killed the otter and then realised that the prophecy of his final exploit had been fulfilled. Determined not to show any further weakness to his enemies, he bound himself to a stone pillar so that they might kill him as he stood there.

Daedalus and Icarus

The first aviators, who showed men the way into the skies. This father-and-son team originally lived in Athens, where Daedalus was the supreme technologist of his day. His ingenuity was in great demand all over the ancient world. When Pasiphae, wife of King Minos of Crete, fell in love with a bull, he designed the labyrinth in which she concealed their dreadful offspring the Minotaur.

But Daedalus was so proud of his ingenuity that he resented the fame of any other inventor. When his nephew Talos invented the chisel and compass he lured Talos to the top of the Acropolis and pushed him off. The Athenians banished Daedalus and Icarus to Crete, where King Minos welcomed them until he learned how Daedalus had helped Pasiphae in her illicit affair.

The king imprisoned Daedalus and Icarus in the labyrinth but Pasiphae released them secretly. They had to find a way to escape from the island and the ingenious Daedalus stole feathers from eagles and made wings, which he and Icarus fastened to their shoulders with beeswax.

The wings functioned perfectly and Daedalus set course for Italy. Father and son flew steadily across the Mediterranean until Icarus became so self-confident that he departed from the flight plan and steadily gained altitude, unconscious of the fact that as he rose nearer to the sun its rays were melting the wax that secured his wings. This first example of pilot error became apparent when the wings fell off and he fell into the sea.

Daedalus, the older and more cautious aviator, landed safely in Italy. Minos pursued him there but was no match for the technologist, who contrived a cunning way to kill him.

The flight of Daedalus and Icarus is said to have inspired the saying 'There are old airmen and bold airmen, but no old bold airmen.'

Dreamtime, The

Before the Aborigines appeared in Australia, the continent was occupied by the spirit ancestors of all the people, plants, and animals living there today. Some lived alone, and others in tribal groups similar to those of the Aborigines.

During their timeless occupation of the land, these creation ancestors formed it into its present shape. Each had its own territory and left a permanent record of its activities in the features of the land. For example, the hunter Mirragan formed many of the rivers, caves, and waterholes of the Blue Mountains when he drove his spear through the mountains in pursuit of the great fish Gurrangatch.

The spirit ancestors also created the elements and the natural phenomena. The sun was created when the emu-spirit and the brolga-spirit had an argument, and the brolga threw one of the emu's eggs up into the sky. It broke against a pile of sticks

gathered by the sky-people and the egg yolk burst into flame.

The Rainbow Serpent dug out many of the rivers and waterholes as it writhed across Australia, and even nowadays it arises from the waters to arch as a rainbow across the sky. Lightning flashes are the spears of the lightning man Wala-Undayua, the Milky Way is the canoe of Nurunderi, and stones scattered down a mountainside are the bodies of locusts killed in a great battle with kangaroos.

The Aborigines were created in different ways in different parts of Australia. In one place, an old blind woman rose miraculously out of the ground accompanied by two girls and a boy. In another place, the spirit ancestor Bunyil fashioned the first men out of clay.

The Aborigines now see everything in their country as a reminder of their Dreamtime ancestors. River reeds are the spears thrown after an eloping couple; the curlew is a mother bewailing her dead son; the trunks of some trees are twisted because they turned their heads to watch the flight of the first boomerang. Everything that lives and moves, all the plants, and all the natural features were formed by the spirit ancestors in their wanderings, fights, and rituals.

Consequently, the Aborigines see their spiritual beliefs preserved in every part of the land and its waters, but their strength is eroded by the white man's destruction of their Dreamtime heritage.

El Nino

This cosmic power has no known shape or form although it has great influence over the southern Pacific. Some researchers believe that the enigmatic stone heads of Easter Island were constructed as a representation of El Nino. The brown pelican of the Peruvian coastline is both a symbol of El Nino's power and the messenger who carries advice of mankind's needs or misdeeds.

The Incas and other races who inhabited the region before the Spanish invasion knew

El Nino well, although their name for the power is either forgotten or secretly preserved. The Spanish translation El Nino, meaning The Child, possibly refers to the child-like benignity of the power in its desire to help mankind. When humans obey the fundamental laws of nature, El Nino does everything possible to assist them. When they break the laws the results may be devastating.

El Nino controls the winds, the ocean, the creatures of the depths, and the climate of lands in and around the Pacific. When all matters are in balance, seamen enjoy prosperous voyages and fishermen's nets are full. When natural laws are broken the penalties are inescapable.

Peruvian fishermen are confident that El Nino has caused temperature changes in currents along their shores, thus affecting the ocean life, as a punishment for over-fishing. Further afield, El Nino has caused the death of coral reefs because of the pollution and misuse of the shining waters of the Pacific. The use of Muraroa Atoll for atomic bomb tests has grievously affronted El Nino.

Climatic changes ascribed to El Nino have inflicted a series of droughts upon Australia, by way of revenge for environmental misuse of the continent.

The more benign aspects of the power may be seen in its assistance to the voyage of the *Poppykettle*, when a group of Peruvian gnomes crossed the Pacific to become the first gnome settlers in Australia.

Eros

The God of Bringing Together, who inspires physical attraction between men and women to ensure the continuity of life.

Regrettably the Olympians gave this important duty to the youngest and most mischievous of the gods. They armed him with a bow, and arrows tipped with lead or gold, and sent him on his eternal mission. The golden arrows are to inflict the pangs of love on suitable couples while the leaden arrows make unsuitable men and women dislike each other.

The passing centuries might have taught wisdom to Eros but he became a confidant of Venus Aphrodite, who loves to meddle in amatory affairs and delights in the seduction of men and gods. She even allows Eros to sit by her couch while she sports with such mighty lovers as Hercules.

Her aphrodisiac example soon made Eros the juvenile delinquent of Olympus, so that he uses his golden arrows mischievously instead of wisely. Often he fires them into the hearts of men and women who are quite unsuited to each other, and shoots leaden arrows at those who might be quite happy together. Even worse, he will shoot a golden arrow into the heart of a would-be lover and a leaden arrow into the object of desire, to create the agonising pangs of unrequited love.

Probably Eros has caused more mischief than any other of the gods. All too often, his malicious titter is heard above the marriage bed.

Fates, The

The controllers of our lives from whom there is no escape. They are all women: Ilithyia the Goddess of Childbirth, Nemesis the Inevitable, and the sisters Clotho, Lachesis, and Atropos who are the daughters of Night.

Ilithyia attends every childbirth and decrees how long a mother is to suffer the arrows of pain. If Ilithyia is kindly disposed towards the mother she will bring a quick deliverance.

When the child is born the three daughters of Night take charge of its destiny. Clotho at her spinning wheel spins the thread of life out of the filaments of hope and happiness, success and failure, love and despair. She chooses different quantities of each material for each thread of life, but her sister Lachesis often adds that little portion of good luck which may change a person's destiny.

Atropos stands brooding by her sisters with a pair of shears, watching the thread of life as it grows longer. Suddenly and without warning she cuts it off, whether it be that of a child or of an old and evil man.

Nemesis stands ready to punish us whenever we break the laws of life. She brings inevitable sickness to our bodies when we abuse them, and inevitable destruction to those parts of the earth which we do not cherish in accordance with the laws of nature.

We would be wise to remember that Nemesis may even intercede with Atropos. If we live in accordance with the laws of the gods, then Nemesis may persuade Atropos to allow the threads of our lives to be spun for a little longer.

Fire, The Owners of

The great gods of Olympus never intended mankind to enjoy the precious jewel of fire. They created it for their own delight, out of the burning rays of the sun and every colour of the rainbow. The gods knew that fire is too dangerous to entrust to men, whose meddling curiosity would inevitably use it for the wrong purposes.

But fire also existed in many other parts of the heavens and it was even owned or discovered by various creatures of the earth. In North America, numerous Indian tribes received fire when the tribes of heaven fought each other and their lightning spears and arrows fell down to earth. In Finland, Ukko the father of the heavens created fire when he struck his sword against his fingernail. The spark fell to earth and would have been quenched in a lake, but a trout leapt up and swallowed it. A salmon then swallowed the trout, a pike swallowed the salmon, and the folk hero Vainamoinen caught the pike. When he cut the pike open the spark leapt out and rolled over the earth, setting fire to trees and houses before Vainamoinen trapped it in a copper jar.

In some parts of the earth, fire lay slumbering within trees or within various rocks and stones. Witch doctors discovered that if they spoke the correct incantations they could release fire by rubbing pieces of wood or striking these stones together.

In other places, wise men or women obtained fire by sending messengers to the sun, to beg some of its heat and warmth. Naturally they sent birds as their messengers and many such birds still bear the marks of their hazardous journeys. Magpies, which were originally white, now have black scorch marks on their bodies. Other birds still glow with the red marks of fire, while crows and ravens were scorched quite black.

Fire-breathing dragons brought fire to many parts of the world and various types of snakes and reptiles also kept fire in their bodies. They gave it to men as a reward for helping them.

The gods and other owners of fire always warned mankind about its dangers, but men have rarely heeded warnings from the heavens. They have found many ways to steal fire from its eternal owners. The gods tremble for mankind as they look down upon the mushroom cloud and other signs that men have robbed the cosmos of even more of the power of fire.

Force

This element has a vital place in all human affairs and it has special deities of its own. In the Infernal Regions, the god Kratos possesses the Power of Force despite the attempts of his brothers and sisters Jealousy, Victory, and Violence to wrest it away from him. In the Japanese heavens, the God of Force once played an essential role. The Sun Goddess, Amaterasu, had retired into a cave in heaven and blocked the entrance with a great boulder, so that the world was plunged into darkness. The other gods consulted in great anxiety as to how they might persuade her to return, and among other tricks they collected a number of cocks to crow outside her cave. When at last she peeped out, to see what was going on, the God of Force seized her hand and pulled her out to restore warmth and light to the world.

Futuresight

A god-like talent very occasionally inherited by mortal men and women. The seventh son of a seventh son is likely to be endowed with Futuresight, but in these days of the nuclear family such people are rare.

Some members of the fairy aristocracy, especially the queen, possess Futuresight but they are unreliable prophets because they do not care to look upon evil. Elves, pixies, gnomes, leprechauns and similar creatures often claim Futuresight but they often make up fantastic stories for their own amusement. A mortal who believes them is likely to be led sadly astray.

Wizards, sorcerers, gypsies, witches, and shamans devote enormous effort to researching the science of Futuresight. Some claim to achieve it by interpreting the shapes and colours of smoke arising from a fire of feverfew, agrimony, mallows, woodbine, tansy, dog grass, and madder. These plants have to be gathered at specific phases of the moon, dried in the rafters so that they may absorb the power of all other magical incantations, and mixed together in a recipe on which no two sorcerers agree. Consequently one may doubt Futuresight predictions arising from this process.

Even the great magician Merlin, who possessed Futuresight to a remarkable degree, could not foresee that if he seduced the Lady of the Lake he would spend eternity as a prisoner locked within an oak tree.

Gemini

The collective name for the twins Castor and Pollux, occupants of the third House of the Zodiac. They were born from the eggs laid by Leda after Zeus seduced her in the guise of a swan.

Like so many of the children of Zeus they enjoyed a lawless and adventurous existence during their time on earth. They fought in the siege of Troy, sailed with Jason on the quest for the Golden Fleece, and eloped with the daughters of Leudippus.

This exploit led to swordplay with Idas and Lynceus, who had been courting the sisters until the twins took a fancy to them. Idas slew Castor, and Pollux grieved so deeply over the death of his twin that their father Zeus placed them both among the stars.

The handsome and adventurous young men perpetuate the memories of a roving carefree life by acting as the protectors of sailors and of hospitality. Their nature is energetic and volatile, vain, talkative, and curious. Naturally they impart these characteristics to some humans born between May and June, when the House of Gemini is in the ascendant.

George, Saint

The patron saint of England and of army officers. As a Roman cavalry officer he was a powerful and courageous soldier, a noble sight as he rode on his white horse at the head of the legions. When he was converted to Christianity he showed that a Christian need not necessarily be meek and mild. He was the only warrior who dared ride out to fight and kill a dragon which was tormenting the people of Cappadocia.

His example had great appeal for the knightly heroes of early England, because it showed them how to convert their lust for battle into socially acceptable forms. They knew St George would guide their weapons as they set forth to rescue damsels in distress or slay some magical monster.

St George responded to their faith in him by ensuring success for the arms of England, especially when the knights crossed the sea to fight against the pagans. His Red Cross became the Banner of England, and he aids her soldiers whenever they carry it in a noble cause.

Giants

Supermen and superwomen born out of Chaos when the Creators of the Cosmos were striving to impose order on the elements.

Giants existed in many parts of the world from Ireland to Japan. Neither mortal nor immortal, often possessed of magical powers, and with a resemblance to enormous humans, they were uncouth and awkward characters who fought violently against the gods' efforts to control them. When at last they were flung out of the various heavens they settled in various parts of the earth.

For many centuries they caused great mischief by joining in human quarrels, gobbling up flocks of sheep, drinking rivers dry, trampling crops underfoot and tearing mountains apart. The only way to kill a giant or giantess is to cut off his/her head, and so it took a long time for various knights and folk heroes to dispose of this nuisance.

Gogmagog

This arrogant giant took his name from a Biblical reference which means 'all the enemies of the earth.' Presumably he thought his strength equalled that of all other fighting men.

In ancient times he led the rapidly diminishing race of British giants. There were only twenty of them left, but they protected Albion against all invaders until the advent of Brutus the Trojan.

Brutus, who was exiled from Troy for accidentally killing his father, allied himself with another Trojan exile, Corineus. They and their men set sail for Albion to conquer it for themselves.

When Gogmagog heard that these adventurers had landed he rallied his giant

followers and they pounded across country to repel the invaders. They sighted the Trojans near Totnes, and without hesitation bellowed their thunderous warcries as they galloped to the attack.

But Corineus stepped forward to meet Gogmagog, dodged his whirling club, struck off his head and threw the great body over a cliff. The other giants immediately broke and ran, to vanish into deep caves from which they have never emerged.

Brutus soon conquered Albion and changed its name to Britain. He rewarded Corineus with a present of the western portion, which he named Cornwall in honour of the giantkiller.

Golden Age, The

The period at the beginning of the world when man and nature lived in perfect harmony. When the Titans of Olympus set the first men upon earth it provided all their needs without calling for more than a little agreeable labour. In a climate of perpetual summer there was no need for clothing or housing. Trees bore both fruit and blossom the whole year round, bees had no stings and gladly yielded their honey, cows stood still to be milked and berries flourished on every bush. Men never quarrelled because there was more than enough for all of them, there were no women to arouse jealousy and nobody envied his neighbour's possessions. Weapons were unknown, the beasts and birds of the forests had no fear of man, and the gods of Olympus never interfered with men's destiny.

The Golden Age ended when the Titans fought the gods for dominance over Olympus, and their cosmic wars destroyed the peace of the world.

Haiowatha

A hero of the Indians of North America. Like all great heroes he first displayed his prowess as a child and he quickly became the leader of his tribe. Often he vanished from them on mystic journeys to visit the shamans of the spirit land, who taught him the totems of every living creature and gave him a magic canoe to carry him between the worlds of spirits and men. All the people of the Iroquois nation revered Haiowatha except for Atotarho, a powerful shaman whose hair was a nest of rattlesnakes and whose eyes could kill with a glance.

The Iroquois nation revelled in war and its tribes often fought together. Sometimes they combined to fight their neighbours, the Algonquin, and both these great peoples spent much of their time and energy on plotting or waging war.

The wisdom that Haiowatha learned from the shamans taught him that war leads only to misery. He planned a great alliance of all the people so that they might live peacefully together, but Atotarho opposed him violently in the tribal councils. During one of their arguments, Atotarho called down a great totemic eagle to kill Haiowatha's daughter.

Even this deadly blow did not shock Haiowatha into making war, though he despaired of his own people. He used his magic canoe to go to the land of the Oneida, whose chief Dekanwada befriended him and agreed with his mission of peace. They worked together to convert all the Indian nations to their ideas and at last persuaded Atotarho that peace is better than war.

When Haiowatha was satisfied that the tribes would live peacefully together, he paddled away in his magic canoe to join his beloved daughter in the land of the spirits. He thought the people of the earth had no further need of him and so he burnt his canoe, but in the absence of the great peacemaker the Indians soon fell back into their warlike ways.

Heavens, The

The skies are occupied by so many heavens, each belonging to a different race or religion, that it is difficult to know where one ends and another begins. In 1796 the monk

Alexander of Beograd prepared a map of the heavens but it contains many cloudy areas.

The gods of each religion built a heaven when they had created the Cosmos out of Chaos, but changes in religious beliefs have necessitated a number of multi-storey heavens. Sometimes the occupants of what might be termed 'basement' heavens make very rowdy neighbours. The Christian heaven above Greece and Italy cannot escape disturbance from the gods roistering in Olympus.

Fortunately there is no end to the Cosmos or there would not be sufficient space for all the heavens which lie above the Middle East and Asia. Numerous religions have succeeded one another in these areas but there is space for Isis and Osiris to move around the heaven of ancient Egypt, for the Gods of Elam to rule above Iran and Iraq, and for the Lady of Byblos to reign above Syria and Lebanon. They exist eternally, between the heavens of even more ancient religions beneath them and that of Islam above them.

The occupations of heavenly inhabitants vary greatly from one heaven to another and there are great differences between their politics and ethics. Men of the Islamic paradise enjoy unlimited female company whereas those in Valhalla spend their nights in drinking and feasting.

The landscapes of heaven have a strong resemblance to the most attractive regions of the earth beneath them. Possibly the most beautiful is the Japanese heaven, approached by the heavenly bridge Amo-No-Hashidate. It is exactly similar to the islands of Japan before they were spoiled by industrial pollution.

Helios

The God of the Sun, who sees and knows everything but cannot keep secrets. In the cosmic wars between the gods and the Titans, the Titans drowned him in the eastern sea but Zeus revived him and gave him a golden chariot drawn by seven winged white fire-breathing horses.

Each morning the Horae, the goddesses of the seasons, harness the seven horses to the chariot of Helios and he sets out on his journey across the sky. He and his horses are so dazzling a sight that mortal eyes cannot bear to look upon them and no man has ever made out the details of their glory. Fire flames from the horses' nostrils, the chariot flashes with a million rays, and the golden helmet and breastplate of Helios glow with a heat and light such as that emanated by molten gold in the crucibles of Hephaestus. A mortal cannot even look into the eye of Helios, as he stares through the eye-slit of his helmet down upon the world.

Helios once had a mistress named Clytie, daughter of the King of Babylon. His own illicit affair did not prevent him from gossiping about the loves of the other gods, and when Venus Aphrodite was unfaithful

to her husband, Helios quickly spread the news. Venus revenged herself by inspiring Helios with a passion for Clytie's sister Leucothea.

Clytie was so jealous that she told her father, who had Leucothea buried alive. Helios tried vainly to restore her by pouring his warmth into her cold body, while Clytie destroyed herself because she had lost his love. She lay naked upon the wintry earth and refused to eat or drink, but her love for Helios was still so strong that her body took root and became a beautiful flower, the heliotrope, which still watches Helios as he makes his daily journey across the sky.

Hephaestus

The God of Metalworkers, whom the Romans called Vulcan. He was born with a massive body and arms but crippled legs, and his mother Hera was so ashamed of him that she flung him out of Olympus. He fell into the ocean, where two nymphs took care of him until he could be apprenticed to a blacksmith. He quickly learned all the arts of a metalworker and became friendly with Dionysus, the God of Wine, whose product slakes the thirst of men toiling at anvil, crucible, and furnace.

He had not forgotten his mother's cruelty and he revenged himself by making a beautiful golden throne and sending it to Olympus. Hera received it with delight, but when she sat in the throne it seized her with golden claws and would not let her go. The other gods tried to force or persuade Hephaestus to return to Olympus and set her free, but he resisted them until Dionysus got him drunk and carried him to Olympus on a mule. Even then, Hephaestus would not free Hera until the gods gave him Venus Aphrodite as his bride.

The marriage did not bring him happiness because Venus soon left him for the beds of other gods and mortals. He consoled himself by building a great workshop out of bronze and creating two girl apprentices out of gold. Their task is to support him as he stumbles around his workshop on his twisted legs.

As time went by he was reconciled with Hera and he even tried to protect her during one of her furious arguments with her husband Zeus, over his relentless pursuit of other women. But Zeus seized him by his crippled legs and flung him out of Olympus for the second time.

The old god set up the first of a number of workshops under the earth, and he is now present wherever molten metal is poured and forges resound with the clangour that is music to his ears. Attired in his leather apron, leaning upon a great staff and with the sweat glistening on his hairy chest and arms, he stands ready to give advice and help to any mortal worker in metal.

But the gods found they could not do without him in Olympus, and when he returns there on some commission the thunder of his great hammer echoes through the skies. Whenever he returns to earth, he stokes up his furnaces again and the smoke and flames pour from the chimneys which we know as volcanoes.

Izanami and Izanagi

These Japanese divinities appeared in the Seven Generations of Gods who existed while the Cosmos was still Chaos. The other gods presented the handsome young couple with the Heavenly Jewelled Spear and ordered them to create solid land. They climbed on the bridge of the rainbow, leaned over its parapet, and dipped the spearpoint into the formless mass of earth and sea. When they stirred it a little, a drop from the spearpoint created the first island, Onokoro.

The young couple built themselves a splendid palace on the island, with a great pillar standing in the garden. Like any other young couple they found each other attractive, and as they chatted together Izanami remarked that she seemed to be strangely lacking in one part of her body. Izanagi mentioned that he had excessive flesh in the same region.

These revelations prompted them to unite themselves in order to conceive the rest of the universe, and in a kind of courtship ritual they walked around the pillar in opposite directions until they met face-to-face. Izanami exclaimed coyly 'What a pleasure to meet such a handsome young man!' but Izanagi scolded her because she was a woman and should have waited for him to speak.

After this little tiff they fitted themselves together and Izanami eventually delivered her first child. It was a disappointment because it was only a leech-baby, and they rid themselves of it by setting it adrift in a boat made of reeds.

The next baby, a small island, was equally disappointing. Izanagi asked the Seven Generations of Gods why these strange children appeared and the gods explained that it was Izanami's fault for speaking first. When they repeated the courtship ritual, Izanagi spoke first, saying 'What a pleasure to meet such a beautiful maiden!'

After this, Izanami gave birth to all the islands of Japan and some of the elements, until she died after delivering the God of Fire. Izanagi continued the work of creation alone, to establish most of the Cosmos as we know it today.

Japanese women still know that, whenever any important work is to be done, it is wise to allow their husbands to speak first.

Jotnar, The

The Frost Giants: the first cosmic beings of Scandinavia and other parts of northern Europe. These monsters, born to Ymir the Ice-Father, had a particularly appalling appearance. Their hair beards, and finger-nails were icicles, their eyes glared as coldly as the full moon reflected upon ice, and whenever they spoke their mouths emitted a blizzard of ice particles.

Despite these frigid characteristics they were warm-blooded. When Odin fought the Frost Giants, one married couple survived by sailing away on a sea of giants' blood. Their escape enabled them to create a new generation of Frost Giants to inhabit the Baltic countries, where they caused great trouble until they perished in the final battle between gods and giants.

Joyboy

The West Indian character who personifies the human need to dance, sing, and jubilate. He is a relation of the Lord of the Dancers who inspires festivals in colder countries and it seems likely that he travelled to the Caribbean with an early shipment of slaves from West Africa. Joyboy smiles perpetually at all the foibles and problems of mankind and cures human troubles by tapping out an irresistible rhythm on his drum. Whoever hears the music of Joyboy is compelled to dance and sing along until he or she has shaken the black cloak of despair from the shoulders. Some jazz players claim to have captured Joyboy rhythms, but their efforts are a pale imitation of the dance frenzy which can keep humans dancing until they drop.

Judges of the Dead, The

Those who decide whether a soul shall pass into the Kingdom of the Dead or be cast into the Underworld. Egyptian priests who prepared the mummies of the dead made sure they were equipped to face this tribunal. In the mummy case they placed a passport to secure safe passage from life into death, certain charms to ward off evil spirits, and various amulets. In the tomb, they positioned scores of tiny statuettes known as Answerers.

After crossing the terrible wasteland between life and death the dead men entered the Hall of Double Justice. Forty-two Judges of the Dead awaited him, each with a sword in his hand. The new arrival had to speak to each of these in turn, to prove he had committed no sins and was worthy to enter the kingdom of Osiris. Each Judge of the Dead cross-examined the applicant about his or her behaviour on earth.

A final test, the weighing of the soul, followed this ordeal. A huge pair of scales stood in the hall, ready to weigh the soul against a feather placed on them by Maat, the Goddess of Truth and Justice. If the scales remained in perfect balance then Osiris allowed the applicant to enter the Kingdom of the Dead. If the soul was so laden with sin that it outweighed the feather of truth, then Amemait, the dreadful monster part-lion, part-hippopotamus, and part-crocodile, devoured the applicant.

Those who passed through into the Kingdom of the Dead began a life of eternal happiness, even though they had to cultivate the fields of Osiris. But if the priests had placed sufficient Answerers in the tomb they would answer the calls to labour and allow the dead to spend eternity in peaceful relaxation.

Knights

Human exemplars of the god-like virtues of faith, courage, gallantry, compassion, and aid to the weak and oppressed.

There are those who believe that knights were only smelly brutal men in rusty armour, superstitious and greedy, who lived upon the labour of the peasants and went on wars of conquest on the excuse that they were obeying their kings.

The reality was quite different. The orders and rituals of knighthood were clearly established and the great brotherhood would never have accepted such unsuitable members. A man could not even become a knight unless he was a youth of noble blood, and he had to beg an established knight to take him into service. Acceptance was by no means certain, because a knight's squire had to combine youthful beauty with the promise of superb manhood. He had to entertain the knight by singing sweetly to the lute, act as messenger between the knight and suitable ladies, serve him gracefully at dinner, and generally act as body servant, confidant, and admirer, always prepared to heap lavish praise upon his master for some deed of gallantry.

Sometimes this apprenticeship was cut short when a knight was captured in battle. It was appropriate for the squire to offer himself for ransom, and stay in captivity while the knight rode off and tried to raise the ransom.

If all went well the time would come for the squire to win his spurs. The armourers fitted him with his first armour and made his lance, sword, and poignard, while the heralds worked out an appropriate device for his shield. If the squire could afford it he bought various magic charms to protect himself against evil.

The young knight practised ardently in the tiltyard in order to grow accustomed to his armour and weapons, until it was time for his first tournament. The ladies in the audience assessed him carefully as he took his place in the lists, and tittered mockingly if his opponent unseated him with a great clangour of armour.

After the first tests of skill and courage the knight rode forth in search of noble deeds. If he was fortunate there would be a war against the pagans, but if not then he had to sally forth alone. By that time he would have fallen in love with some demure virgin, and she gave him a glove or scarf to wear on his helmet. Some older knights

wore ladies' stockings streaming from their helms, but a young knight was so pure in heart that such a sight made him blush with embarrassment.

On this first knightly journey he had no need of a squire or other retainers. His armour shone brightly without polishing and the light of beckoning glory sustained him without food or sleep. As the hooves of his charger beat along the forest paths he looked eagerly for some fitting opponent.

When he entered a village he listened eagerly for news of a dragon or wicked lord in the neighbourhood, preferably the abductor of a fair damsel. He would not be averse to tackling sorcerers, magical beasts who destroyed cattle by breathing on them, or even giants who ate the children of widows. It was, however, preferable to return home with a dragon's head slung behind him and a rescued damsel upon his saddlebow.

Any acceptable feat won him the golden spurs of true knighthood, and after that he could spend the time enjoyably in hunting, hawking, fighting in tournaments, feasting, or defending his king against enemies.

Unfortunately a young knight's purity of heart gave him many uncomfortable moments. Every knight had to have his lady and he treated her strictly in accordance with the rules. He sent troubadours to serenade her, presented her with the mailed gloves of opponents killed in the lists, and sighed beneath her castle windows on moonlit nights. But the time would come when a lady expected more ardent attentions. A knight would hardly dare to drink his wine for fear that it contained a love potion, and he might be obliged to kill a friend if the impatient lady looked kindly upon him.

It was even worse when the wife of a great lord, or even the queen herself, began to languish for the attentions of a young knight. The only remedy was another knightly journey, on the excuse that he found himself unfitted for love of women and must devote himself to the pursuit of honour. It was always a relief when the king summoned his knights for a slaughter of pagans, and they could enjoy the sport without being distracted by ladies.

The time would come, however, when a knight found his joints creaking as loudly as his armour and his head growing bald from the pressure of his helmet. There was no more need to resist the blandishments of womankind and he could settle down with his mulled wine by the hearth. He exchanged stories of dragon hunts with other superannuated knights and showed the scars won in battle with the king's enemies. They all agreed that modern squires and knights behaved disgracefully. When a lady let down a silken ladder, so that a knight might climb up into her chamber, he would actually use it. The age of knighthood was doomed when knights began to pay more attention to women than to damsels in distress.

Kupala

The Goddess of Fertility. In appearance she is tall and smiling, with eyes blue as the summer skies and hair as golden as the ripening wheat. Her strong round arms are creamy as the milk of young cows, her bosom deep with promise and her hips curved like the swell of the earth itself.

The people of ancient Russia worshipped her because her favours bring increase to all the crops and animals. If she does not receive the correct devotions then her displeasure causes barren herds and empty fields.

The correct time to worship Kupala is on Midsummer Day. Men and women should bathe naked together in the rivers, jump hand-in-hand over bonfires, and make wreaths to cast on the waters. The ceremonies include the sacrifice of a cockerel at the foot of a tree stripped of all its lower branches, and as the cockerel dies the worshippers should dance around the tree with songs of praise for Kupala. She shows her pleasure in these festivities by causing women to become fertile and bear children in the following spring.

Leir, King

The ancient king of Britain whose story is a warning to close one's ears to flattery.

During his long reign he encouraged craftsmanship and did much for the prosperity of the nation, but his daughters Goneril and Regan discovered his weakness for flattery. They praised him for his strength and wisdom and for all he had done for his kingdom, so that he gave Goneril a quarter of his kingdom for her dowry when she married Duke Maglaurus of Albany and another quarter to Regan when she married Duke Henwinus of Cornwall.

Cordelia, the youngest daughter, pitied her father in his old age and refused to profit from his vanity. She supported the old king until she married King Agapinnus of France and went to live with him.

Regan and Goneril soon seized the rest of Leir's kingdom. Their husbands left Leir with some shreds of his former glory but the

sisters stripped it away until he had only a single servant. He turned his back on his greedy daughters and went to join Cordelia, who persuaded Agapinnus to provide him with an army.

The old king displayed his former powers of leadership when he landed in Britain again and defeated the hosts of Maglaurus and Henwinus, but he lived only for another three years. He was buried near Castle Leir, now known as Leicester.

All men of power should remember the story of Leir and know that even those who seem closest may betray them.

Leo

The lion who dominates the fifth House of the Zodiac. He is one of the most powerful creatures of the Zodiac because he is related to both the sun and the moon. In one of his earliest manifestations he lived on earth as the Lion of Nemes, until Hercules killed him and made an armour out of his pelt.

In happier times, Leo was worshipped by many of the races of antiquity. He still enjoys pride of place as the archetypal symbol of courage, nobility, and enterprise. But he enjoys comfort as much as any other feline and he spends much of his time snoozing in his den. He is a magnificent creature when he is aroused, and stalks forth with his eyes blazing yellow as the sun and his mane bristling like its rays, but he does not enjoy exerting himself and he soon pads yawning back into the shade.

Despite his fangs he is a friendly and affectionate beast, a loving father of his cubs and protective husband of the lioness. He radiates confidence and assurance, but his massive strength attracts a surfeit of admiration. Sometimes this makes him vain and dictatorial and he uses his strength to command rather than to lead.

Leo reigns over the months of high summer when his cousin the sun mounts highest in the sky. Those humans born in late July or early August may find themselves under his influence.

Libra

The Golden Scales which stand in the seventh House of the Zodiac, under the control of Venus Aphrodite.

The dual personality of this goddess frequently tempts her to tip the scales in one direction or the other. Sometimes, as Venus the serene beauty, she places a finger on the scale known as Zubenelgebunubi and tips it in favour of peace and happiness. At other times she is Aphrodite, the flashing-eyed seductress who lusts after the pleasures of the flesh and cares nothing for the laws of gods or men. Then she presses down the scale known as Zubeneschalami and the balance tips towards riot and wild revelry.

The Golden Scales stand at the balance of the year, when the seasons of the northern hemisphere are about to pass from mellow autumn into the cold and storms of winter. Therefore it is understandable that those born under the influence of Libra may swing between good and bad, selfishness and unselfishness, reliability and deceit.

Loki

The God of Malicious Mischief and youngest of all the Aesir. Originally he was a simple fire demon, the son of Farbauti the originator of fire and Laufey a spirit of the trees. The young demon grew into a handsome youth, plausible and charming, and he soon wheedled his way into the beds of the goddesses of Asgard. The gods also fell victim to his charm and he even deceived the all-wise Odin, so that they made him one of the Aesir.

The dignity of this promotion gave full scope to Loki's meddlesome and mischievous nature. He borrowed the magical possessions of the gods, such as the feathered robe of Freya which enabled her to fly anywhere on earth, and got them and himself into many kinds of trouble.

Often he had to talk himself out of dangers incurred by his own mischief, as on the occasion when he cut off the hair of Thor's wife, Sif, while she was asleep. Thor lost patience with Loki and began to break all his bones, but Loki yelled desperate promises to replace the shorn tresses with golden locks which would grow like real hair.

He managed to fulfil this promise by persuading the dwarf goldsmiths to make the golden hair, and also to make two magical items for Odin so that the chief god would forgive his mischief. They were a spear which never fell short of its target and a ship which always sailed straight for its destination.

But Loki's narrow escape had not taught him wisdom and he boasted about the work of the goldsmiths to two other dwarfs, Brokk and Sindri, who were famous for their magical craftsmanship. In the ensuing argument he bet his head that Brokk and Sindri could not create such marvels.

They accepted the challenge and he soon saw that he might lose his head. He changed himself into a gadfly, to sting and torment the dwarfs and divert them from their task. They made, however, a ring which ensured perpetual wealth for its wearer, and the great hammer of Thor which would defeat all enemies.

The gods agreed that these marvels were even better than the work of the dwarf goldsmiths, and Loki once more had to use his tongue to save his life. When Brokk and Sindri demanded his head, he said they could have it but the bet did not say anything about his neck. Therefore they must not harm any part of his neck when they chopped off his head.

Baffled by this argument, Brokk could respond only by sewing Loki's lips together so that he could not deceive any more of the immortals.

Loki soon pulled out the stitches, but he had offended so many of the gods that he thought it best to leave Asgard. In his loneliness he brooded maliciously until he heard that the gods were holding a great feast. He was furious because he had not been invited, but he strolled smilingly into the banquet chamber and ignored the cold looks of the gods. With his usual charm he wheedled one after another into letting him join in.

Then, as he ate and drank, he revenged himself by insulting one Aesir after another. He had spied on their shameful behaviour and slept with most of the goddesses, so that his torrent of scandal could flow on and on. At last he boasted of his affair with Sif and Thor threatened to smash in his skull.

Loki ran out of the hall with a final fusillade of threats and abuse. He said the Aesir might revel in their present power but their time would soon come to an end.

They laughed at his threats but they came true when they hired one of the Frost Giants to rebuild Valhalla. They promised him the goddess Freya by way of payment, but when the work was done they laughed him out of Asgard. The infuriated giant began the great wars between giants and Aesir which devastated Asgard and opened the way for a new and gentler race of gods.

Love, The Goddesses of

Most races have a particular goddess who supervises the rites of love and fertility and they all seem to share the same capricious nature. They are personified by Venus Aphrodite, the love goddess of men and mortals in the time of Olympus.

Venus had an unpromising beginning, because she was created when Zeus castrated his father and the drops of blood fell into the sea. There they changed into white sea foam and gave birth to Venus.

She caused trouble from the moment she stepped through the gates of Olympus. The gods could not find words to describe the perfection of her face and form, while the goddesses were jealous of a beauty which overshadowed their own. Venus is the essence of seductive female beauty and she conquered the gods with the grace and charm of her nature and the swooning delight of her presence. As though these things were not enough she wears a magic girdle which radiates the power of seduction. Exquisitely worked and embroidered, it promises both love and its consummation.

All the gods desired her while the goddesses resented her. They first drew unfortunate mankind into their jealous quarrels when Eris, God of Discord, tossed a golden apple marked 'For the Fairest' among the guests at an Olympic wedding. Venus, Hera, and Athene each claimed it was meant for her, and Zeus settled the argument by making a mortal judge between them. He was Paris, son of King Priam of Troy, who inevitably chose Venus as the winner of the beauty contest. Hera and Athene took out their spite on him by devastating Troy and making Paris fall in battle.

The immortals had always revelled in passionate love but they had never known anything like the desire which Venus aroused in them. She soon reigned supreme as goddess and creator of love although she had many sides to her nature. She was sweet and gracious to gods and mortals who worshipped her but furious towards those who slighted her. When the girls of Amathus denied her divinity she robbed them of modesty and turned them into prostitutes.

She first married Hephaestus the lame metalworker, but she soon turned away from him and fell in love with the beautiful youth Adonis. She used her beauty relentlessly to seduce both gods and mortals, or to send them on hopeless quests after other women. Even Zeus could not resist her charms and she tantalised him into a series of adventures with mortal maidens.

Venus personifies the magical beauty of women, the comfort of their arms and the rich rewards of their bodies together with the subtleties and complexities of their minds. Men still suffer from her caprices and the torments of love which she inflicts upon them.

Mars

The God of War. Like many soldiers, Mars had a peaceable beginning to his working life and he only switched careers after he had tasted blood. Initially he was devoted to agriculture, but as one of the sons of Zeus and Hera he became involved in the squabbles of Olympus. He began to enjoy fighting for its own sake, although he was not a brilliant warrior. He often blundered into battle and was easily tricked. The goddess Athene defeated him twice, Hercules forced him to retreat from earth to Olympus, and the Giants imprisoned him in a bronze

vessel for thirteen months.

He was equally clumsy on the battlefield of love. He raped the vestal virgin Rhea Silvia, and when he entered the couch of Venus Aphrodite her husband trapped them there with an invisible net. They had to lie locked in their embrace while the other Immortals guffawed at their predicament.

On another occasion the gods tried him for murdering the son of Poseidon, but released him on his plea that he was saving his daughter from rape. One may doubt this because he is an ingenious liar. When his sons Romulus and Remus were born to Rhea Silvia he spread the story that they were not his boys at all, but the children of a servant girl who united herself with a mysterious penis which arose on the hearth of her employer.

However, the character of the boys appears to betray their parentage. They enjoyed a career of juvenile banditry before Romulus slew Remus in a quarrel over the proposed site of Rome.

The brutal and blundering figure of their father became the god of purposeless war. The Greeks despised him but the Romans made him a hero and he always supported their legions.

Roman military glory has faded into the past, but Mars still teaches warriors how to find early graves.

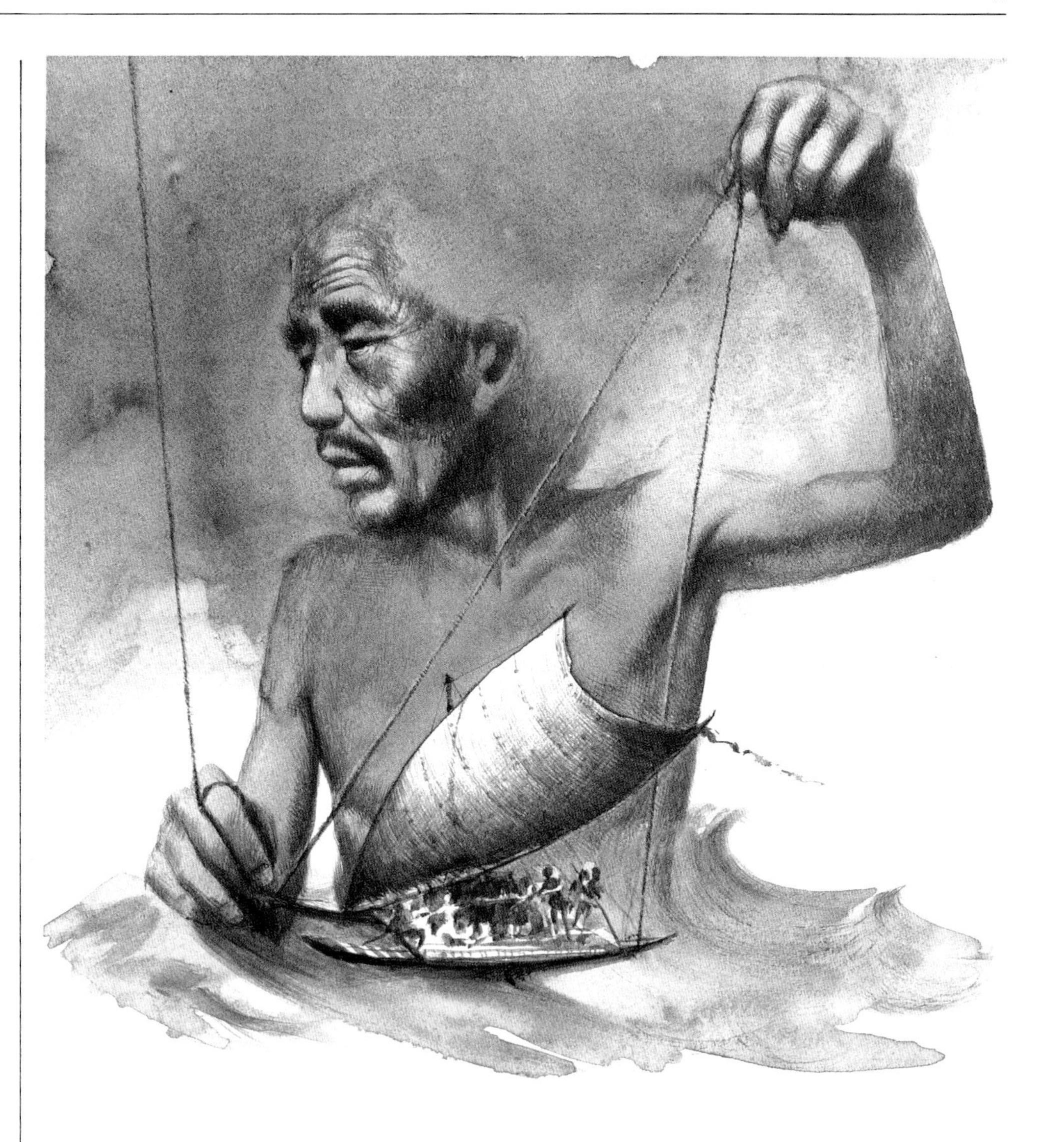

Maui

The creator of many islands and peoples of the Pacific. In the days when the world was nothing but dark ocean he was born to the woman Taranga, a daughter of Hine-nui-te-po the Goddess of the Underworld. She was a fearsome creature with hair of tangled kelp, a fish's mouth full of sharp fangs, and eyes of red fire, but Maui grew into a strong handsome young man.

He became tired of perpetual darkness and raised the heavens from the ocean, pinning them to the stars. This allowed the winds to range unchecked across the world and the sun to behave as it pleased, but Maui pursued the north, south, and east winds and trapped them in a hollow coconut. He releases them when they are needed although the west wind still eludes him.

Maui's next task was the control of the sun. It used to run quickly across the heavens on the legs of its rays, in a hurry to reach its bed beyond the horizon, so that the days were very short. Maui tamed it with a magic club from his grandmother and strong ropes from his mother. When the sun jumped up out of the east he caught some of its legs and tied them with the ropes, then beat it with the magic club until it agreed to run more slowly between one night and the next.

After that he fished the land up out of the sea. He made a fishing line, and a fish hook out of the jawbone of an old woman, but he had no canoe. His brothers refused to lend him their canoe and so he hid aboard it, baited the hook with his own blood, and drew up a huge fish. His brothers tried to steal it from him, but it writhed so wildly that it upset the canoe, drowned all the brothers but Maui, and turned into the first land.

Next, Maui decided to steal fire for use on earth. Fire lived in the Underworld in the fingers and toes of his ancestress Mafuike, who lent it to Maui's mother each morning so that she might cook their food. One morning Maui went into the Underworld and asked Mafuike for a cooking fire. She lent him one of her fingers but he pretended to drop it into a stream, and returned for more. He played this trick nineteen times until Mafuike had only one toe left. When he asked yet again for fire to cook his food she lost her temper and chased him back to earth, where she flung fire after him when he escaped. The fire lodged in a trunk of a tree, and Maui released it by rubbing the tree.

Maui created all the elements of life on earth and thought them so good that men should live forever to enjoy them. But the only way to secure eternal life was to kill his demon ancestress Hine-nui-te-po, who would die only when someone crept right through her body from the lower orifice to the mouth.

When Maui set off on this mission he met his friends the birds. They asked to go with him, and he told them they must keep quiet or the sleeping goddess would awaken and kill him. They agreed, but when Maui crept up into Hine's body they all burst out laughing. The demon goddess awoke, felt what was happening, and crushed Maui within her body.

Men, The First

Before the Titans were expelled from Olympus they made the first men in the image of the gods, and placed them upon earth. These fortunate beings lived in an atmosphere of continuous festivity, free from sickness or anxiety and without women to load them with responsibilities. They passed their days in singing, dancing, sporting, and feasting, and in admiring the beauty of nature all around them. In fact the first men enjoyed all the gifts of the gods except immortality. They appeared on the earth as handsome young men, and death took them in a sweet sleep before they were plagued with old age.

This happy breed vanished in a great deluge during the cosmic wars between Zeus and the Titans, and Prometheus later had to create mankind anew.

Merlin

The wizard whose support of King Arthur enabled Arthur to secure the crown of England. Gossip in Camelot rumoured that Merlin was the child of a nun seduced by an evil spirit. This mixed parenthood gave him magical powers but he could use them only for good causes.

A wizard is always careful not to allow a likeness to be made of him, in case an enemy uses it to rob him of his powers. Consequently there is some doubt as to the appearance of Merlin, although most reports mention his thick flowing beard, deep luminous eyes, and conventional wizard's garb of pointed cap and flowing robe embroidered with zodiacal symbols.

Merlin had especial powers over metal, water, and stone. These enabled him to plunge a sword through an anvil, make a millstone float, control the raging sea, and make the castle walls of Camelot throw down enemies who tried to scale them. He was also gifted with Futuresight, although King Arthur did not always believe his predictions.

Unfortunately Merlin's magical powers did not protect him from human weakness. He was seduced by Nimiane, the Lady of the Lake, and she wheedled him into teaching her his spells and incantations. When she grew tried of him she used one of the spells to imprison him in an oak tree.

Occasionally a wanderer in the forest is startled by the appearance of a brooding face in the bark of an ancient oak, but Merlin cannot harm him and must remain imprisoned until Nimiane relents.

Morpheus

The God of Dreams, who bestows one of the most precious of all gifts upon mankind. Whether we are waking or sleeping, Morpheus may enter our minds to weave the spells which release us from bondage to reality. He is the son of Hypnos, who brings us sleep by fanning his dark wings; the nephew of Thanatos the God of Death; and grandson of Night. The whole family is kindly disposed towards mankind, and each in his own way will bring us ease from pain, sickness, or anxiety. Regrettably, certain

wizards have discovered methods to pervert the gifts of Morpheus and Hypnos, which now in some of their forms inflict great torment on mankind.

Muses, The

The nine beautiful sisters who inspire various types of performing and creative artists. Originally they performed together in an Olympic choir and orchestra led by Calliope, but as time went by they received so many prayers from mortals for help and inspiration that they formed themselves into a kind of arts advisory panel.

Euterpe, the flute player in the Muse orchestra, now guides the fingers of those who play or compose for wind instruments. Terpsichore, the guitarist, responds to those human players of stringed instruments who implore her tuition. She also finds time to impart her heavenly grace to the feet of mortal dancers.

The sisters decided to devote special attention to actors, who play so many different parts. Thalia looks after comedians while Melpomene inspires tragedians. Polyhymnia, the lead singer of the orchestra, gives general guidance and assistance to all actors and also aids the creation of songs and hymns.

Both astronomers and astrologers may appeal to Urania, who draws aside the curtains of darkness which obscure the stars. Clio, the trumpet player, accepted the task of helping historians to record the glory and brilliance of the past.

As for Calliope, she assists all writers and elocutionists who seek to express themselves in words. However, she is only interested in serious literature and her sister Erato accepts responsibility for romantic prose and poetry.

For some reason the sisters do not interest themselves in men and women who express themselves through paint or pencil, or through materials such as wood and stone. These creative artists have to seek inspiration from the spirits of the materials with which they work.

The Muses often relax from their self-imposed duties by playing classic Olympic melodies. The singing group of five sisters, backed by a combo of flute, trumpet, and guitar, creates music fit for the gods.

Nai-No-Kami

The God of Earthquakes. He lives, of course, within the earth, and no one knows exactly when he will awaken or what will displease him. The people of Japan only know that from time to time he inflicts terrible punishment upon their islands, usually with the assistance of Kagu-Zuchi the God of Fire, Taka-Okami the God of Rain, and O-Wata-Tsu-Mi the God of the Sea. All the other gods, including those of roads, homes, gardens, and ricefields, are powerless to resist them.

There are those who believe that Nai-No-Kami is particularly infuriated by men overloading his earth with buildings of steel and concrete, instead of the traditional Japanese houses of timber and thatch.

Others fear that he may be irritated by the deep probes of oil and gas drills which invade his domain. If one of these pricks him he may respond with an earthquake more terrible than ever before.

Odin

The All-Wise, greatest of all the Aesir who rule over Asgard. In some manifestations he resembles a tall and magnificent man, similar to the great chiefs of the Vikings. Like them he has supreme skill in the arts of both war and peace: in sea-cunning, sword-terror, man-knowledge, and saga-spinning. He taught men how to make their weapons and to build the dragon-prowed ships which carried them on voyages of exploration and conquest, and how to compose the sagas which tell, in cadenced rhythms, the countless stories of gods and men.

Odin knows everything in the world because of his two ravens Huginn and Muninn, whose names mean Thought and Memory. Each morning he sends them forth to fly through the domains of the living and the dead, and each evening they return to sit on his shoulders and tell him all the secrets of men and spirits.

In Odin's eternal quest for wisdom he may ride his eight-legged horse Sleipnir across the land or sea, or change himself into any kind of creature. He may appear as a giant among the giants, a gnome among the gnomes, an elf among the elves. A man who sees a watersprite never knows whether she is a true creature of the lakes and rivers or Odin seeking to learn more of the mysteries of water.

Normally he appears to humans in the guise of a poor traveller, so that they may trust him and reveal their secrets.

Odin is married to the beautiful goddess Freya, Mother of the Earth. They have many children but they both enjoy amorous adventures with mortals or immortals.

He is perpetually conscious of his knowledge that, one day, the gods will have to fight the last great battle against the forces of evil. It is for this reason that he brings all the world's most heroic warriors to Valhalla, so that they will fight for him in the final cosmic combat.

Olympus

The sky kingdom of the gods, which took form out of Chaos and Night. Its first inhabitants, Uranus the starlit sky and Gaea the deep-breasted Goddess of Fertility, were brought together by Eros. Their descendants included Cronus, the first ruler of Olympus, and his brothers the Titans.

Zeus and his siblings eventually fought their cousins the Titans for domination of Olympus. They fought cosmic war for ten years, using all the forces of the elements as their weapons, until Zeus defeated the Titans.

The next attack came from the race of Giants, who sprang from the blood of Uranus. They strove to reach Olympus by tearing up the mountains and piling one upon another, Ossa on Pelion and Oeta on Pangaea.

But they were no match for Zeus and the other Immortals, who buried their leader Enceladus beneath the island of Sicily. The island is shaken by earthquakes whenever he turns in his grave.

After these wars the countless Immortals of Olympus often fought together but they never challenged their ruler Zeus. They are a fierce but jocund tribe who delight in duels, athletic sports and games, practical jokes upon each other or on the mortals of earth, passionate love affairs, all the creative and performing arts and the work of skilled craftsmen.

Their battles always end happily because they can never die. When arguments are settled they relax on their couches, feast on nectar and ambrosia amid the ever-changing beauty of clouds, stars, and the skies, and exchange all those cosmic jests which are a perpetual enigma to the peoples of the world.

Orpheus

Mortal musicians may call upon the Muses to help their compositions and performances, but Orpheus, son of Apollo, is even more likely to breathe a special magic into their music. He takes a special interest in those who play upon stringed instruments.

As the son of Apollo, he perhaps had an unfair advantage over all other musicians of his time. When he played upon his lyre he never lacked for an audience. The wild beasts came running out of the forests to listen to him, and when he moved away the trees would uproot themselves to follow him, yearning to hear more of the sweetness of his instrument and the beauty of his voice.

Like many musicians he was a passionate lover, but unlike some of them he was single-minded in his love. He married the nymph Eurydice, and was so devoted to her that he even followed her into the Underworld after her death from snakebite.

He charmed his way past Cerberus, the fearsome dog who guards the entrance to the Underworld, by playing to him on his lyre. Hades and Persephone, the rulers of the ghostly regions, also fell victim to his charm of manner and sweet music. They agreed to release Eurydice, but only on one condition. As he led her from the Underworld into the joy and sunlight of the world above, he must not look back at her until they had passed through the gates of Hell.

He agreed, and waited with his back turned until he heard the voice of Eurydice behind him. In ecstatic expectation he led the way through the dark caverns, but desire was so strong within him that he could not resist one glance around at his beloved. Even as he looked at her she vanished forever into the abode of the dead.

Orpheus might easily have found consolation with other women. The ladies of Thrace tried hard to tempt him, but at last became so infuriated by his devotion to a dead woman that they tore him in pieces and threw his head and lyre into the river.

Yet the spirit of Orpheus the musician still lives on, in the sweetness of the love songs he has helped mortals to compose during their centuries on this earth.

Osiris

The first apostle of non-violence. When he became Divine Ruler of Egypt he found its people were mere savages; ignorant and pagan. He could have forced them to obey his laws but he abhorred violence and he taught them kindly how to achieve happiness through settling into communities, cultivating the land, and living in accordance with his code of morale and ethics. But he was no puritan, and when they grew crops under his guidance he showed them how to make wine and beer for enjoyment as well as bread for nourishment.

He built towns and temples, sculptured the first images of the gods, and invented music for pleasure and worship. Under the

rule of Osiris and his wife Isis the nation became the greatest in the ancient world and he decided to spread its civilisation throughout the earth.

As a believer in non-violence he did not attempt to conquer by force of arms, but by the bewitching strains of his songs and music. Nation after nation surrendered to their charms and by the time he returned home he had civilised the entire world.

Isis had continued his work by teaching Egyptian women how to spin and weave and the men how to cure the sick. She invented marriage, so that men and women might share their joys and labours. Under the enlightened rule of Isis and Osiris there seemed no reason why the world should not enjoy perpetual harmony, but his treacherous brother Set brought an end to this Golden Age.

Jealous of the people's love for his brother, he led a band of conspirators who killed Osiris and threw his coffin into the Nile. It floated out to sea to be washed up on a beach in Phoenicia, where Isis found it and restored her husband to life.

Set killed him again, and this time he hacked the body into fourteen pieces and scattered them over Egypt. Isis sought patiently for the pieces, found them all except the penis which had been eaten by a crab, and invented the technique of embalming to restore Osiris a second time.

But he now chose to become the ruler of the Kingdom of the Dead, where he still looks after Egypt by ensuring the fertility of the soil and bringing down the lifegiving waters of the Nile. Jealous Set still strives against his brother by causing droughts and sandstorms.

Isis had an unhappy end. Her son Horus wanted to take revenge against Set, and when she pleaded with him not to use violence he became so angry that he cut off her head. She now helps the dead on their approach to Osiris, and a good man may be sure that this divine couple will smooth his way into eternity.

Pisces

The fish which swims through the watery regions of the twelfth House of the Zodiac. Throughout late February and March he floods the northern hemisphere with the water which ensures good crops in summer.

His origin is lost in mystery although the peoples of the world have always known of his existence. He is the ruler of seaweed, mosses, ferns, water lilies, and all other plants which grow in water, and of the sand and rocks on the fringe of the sea.

The nature of Pisces is not that of the shark or other ravagers of the ocean. Rather it is that of the whale: massive yet agile, gentle and noble, possessed of knowledge and wisdom still barely glimpsed by man. In the female form, Pisces is graceful, mysterious, and alluring as a mermaid.

As Pisces glides through the depths he knows there are no limits to wisdom and that those who seek will always find. Those who are born under his influence may share the same characteristics.

Poseidon

Supreme Lord of the Inner and Outer Seas, Overlord of Lakes and Rivers, Master of all that swims beneath or upon the surface of the waters.

With his brothers Zeus and Hades he fought mightily in the cosmic wars against the Titans. After their defeat the brothers divided the Cosmos between them, and Poseidon took command of the waters from the Titan named Oceanus who had created them.

As controller of water he became supreme arbiter of the destinies of earth, which must have water for its sustenance. But each province of earth belongs to a different god and Poseidon soon fought with them over land rights. In his arrogance he thought he should own everything, because he supplies the water which keeps it alive. When all the gods and spirits of earth and its creatures sought for the judgment of Olympus, Poseidon refused to listen to reason. He responded by flooding their territories, drying up rivers, and causing droughts which devastated the land.

All the disputes over land rights exacerbated his touchy temper and at last he retreated to his golden palace in the depths of the ocean. There he broods over his wrongs, and from time to time he has sea monsters harnessed to his chariot and gallops furiously over the oceans. As his chariot parts the waves it causes raging storms which sweep across the waters, destroying ships and lashing against the coastline, while he spears the clouds with his trident to release disastrous floods upon the land. Then he returns to his palace and sullenly forbids the water to moisten the earth, so that it dries and cracks under the sun.

Punchinello

The background of this shady character, who represents the untameable aspect of masculine personality, is betrayed by his name. He comes from Italy, where people called him Pulcinello because he uses the word *pulcino*, meaning 'chicken', as an endearment.

Short, deformed, hook-nosed, boastful, and arrogant, he has strutted through history since the early days of mankind. During his lengthy career he has been cuddled by the Queen of Sheba and taken up by St George to ride upon his charger. These and other notable people must have known his true character but possibly they saw him as the true symbol of mortal man. Like many other men he is frequently in trouble because of his arrogant stupidity but, also like other men, he squirms out of it with a blend of lies, trickery, and force.

His only true friend is his dog Toby, which is unperturbed by his knavery. His long-suffering wife, Judy, tries to reform him despite frequent beatings, and he regards their baby only as an encumbrance. He often tries to throw it away but it always bobs up again.

Greedy, drunken, lustful, and immoral, he has often been in trouble with the police and has even faced the gallows, but at the last moment he tricked Jack Ketch into releasing him. Despite his failings he is not without courage and he has fought with crocodiles, dragons, and other monsters.

Punchinello has travelled far and wide within Britain and Europe and has even visited the colonies, where his coarse humour, violent treatment of women, and contempt for authority have made him much admired.

Quetzalcoatl

The Master of Life. In the early days he reigned over a vast region of America from the deserts of Arizona to the peaks of the Andes. He was especially welcome in the desert territories because his appearance always brought rain.

Quetzalcoatl appeared to his worshippers in numerous forms. Sometimes his worshippers saw him as a handsome young man with skin the colour of wheat, magnificently attired in a cloak of feathers from the quetzal bird. Frequently he arched himself across the heavens as the Plumed Serpent. He was then an awe-inspiring sight, with the shimmering multi-coloured scales of his body blending or contrasting with the bright feathers of neck and head.

As Master of Life he brought great prosperity to his people by ensuring ample rain and continuous fertility. He was also the God of the Wind, creator of all life forms, and loving father of the entire Cosmos.

Once he had provided his earthly children with all their physical needs he taught them the arts of civilisation. He taught artists and craftsmen to create objects of use and beauty, gave humans their songs, dances, and poetry, and guided their leaders in justice and mercy.

After many centuries he revealed to his people the precious gifts which lie beneath the ground. They opened the great veins of gold and silver which run like rivers through the earth, and found the glittering jewels locked within common stones. With Quetzalcoatl's gift of fire, they turned gold and silver into every kind of ornament and artefact.

Under his benign rule the people enjoyed great wealth and happiness. They built splendid temples to show their gratitude and thousands of priests sang and danced in praise of Quetzalcoatl.

But there was one great flaw upon this golden age. Tetzcatlipoca, God of War, of the Sun, and of the Moon, was jealous of the people's love for Quetzalcoatl.

He was a personage of terrifying powers and appearance, like a man with a bear's face striped yellow and black. His temples

rose alongside those of Quetzalcoatl and his priests tore out the bleeding hearts of youths and virgins to satisfy him, but even these offerings did not placate his jealousy of Quetzalcoatl.

Tetzcatlipoca began to torment both god and man. He seduced Quetzalcoatl's nieces, so that people lost their respect for women and the law. He turned men against each other in bloody wars, and taught them to be greedy for gold and silver instead of enjoying their beauty. In a series of sorcerer's tricks he killed thousands of men and women in natural calamities.

Quetzalcoatl despaired of the future and decided to abandon his people for a time. He destroyed his great palaces, buried his treasures, and turned his servants into birds. After promising to return to his worshippers he sailed towards the rising sun, with his bird-servants flying in brilliant flocks around him.

The people mourned his departure and waited anxiously for his return. When the Spanish conquistadors appeared upon the eastern sea, the people thought that Quetzalcoatl had returned and welcomed them with great joy. The emperor gave them a cloak of quetzal feathers, thinking that the god would wish to resume his robe of power.

But Tetzcatlipoca had played yet another trick upon the suffering people. The Spaniards soon showed themselves to be fierce and greedy invaders, who destroyed the great empire founded by Quetzalcoatl.

Ra

The great god of Egypt, lord of the sun and the sky. He lived for countless millennia in a lotus growing in the depths of the ocean until he ascended in his full splendour.

Neither gods nor men existed until Ra created them. He created Shu and Tefnut, ancestors of all the gods, out of his own body, and created mortal men and women out of his tears. Consequently they have known little but sorrow.

But gods and mortals lived happily enough together until Ra began to grow old. Men and gods then plotted against each other for supremacy and the universe was wracked with such quarrels that Ra grew weary of the world and left it for the sky. He stepped into a heavenly boat and began an eternal voyage around the Cosmos.

For twelve hours each day he sails across the heavens from east to west, with his great eye still watching and helping the affairs of men. Occasionally the great serpent Apep, which lives in the Nile, attempts to swallow his boat and when this happens the eye of Ra is hidden and the noise of their combat clamours across the sky.

After dark, his boat takes him for twelve hours through the Underworld. He brings a little light and warmth to those condemned to reside there although he has to fight off many monstrous enemies. Fortunately he

always defeats them and emerges triumphantly to sail across the daylight skies.

In the past he only left his boat when one of the Pharaohs married a new wife. He would then get her with child so that the men of the dynasty of Pharaoh would be sons of Ra. Nowadays he still sails over Egypt but there is no need for his marital services.

Sagittarius

The great centaur, half-horse and half-man, who rules the ninth House of the Zodiac.

Most centaurs are drunken lustful creatures who revel in mischief. One of their few exceptions was Cheiron. As a boy-colt Apollo and Artemis instructed him in music, medicine, archery, gymnastics, and other useful arts and sciences, and endowed him with their own gifts of prophecy. When he grew into horse-manhood he combined the wisdom, grace, and agility of gods and horses, so that the parents of young gods valued him as a teacher of their offspring.

He moved in aristocratic circles and became a good friend of Hercules, but by a sad irony he was wounded by one of the poisoned arrows which Hercules shot at the Erymanthian boar. Cheiron, an immortal like all centaurs, feared the poisoned wound would torment him for the rest of eternity, but Zeus rewarded him for his services to the gods by changing him into the constellation Sagittarius the Archer.

Cheiron is now free to gallop joyously over the celestial pastures with his bow and arrows. Unlike Eros, another well-known bowman of the pantheon, he never shoots his arrows maliciously.

He rules over the period when the old year is dying and the world may look forward to renewal. Those humans born when Sagittarius is in the ascendant may be as wise, bold, farseeing and inspirational as Cheiron the teacher, but sometimes they partake of the less attractive qualities of the centaur breed and become coarse, fierce, lustful, and greedy.

Scorpio

The power and guardian of the eighth House of the Zodiac, descended from Selket the Scorpion-goddess of Egypt. She is the goddess both of fertility and of the after-life and she guards one of the four gates to the Underworld. Like the insect which is her symbol she will not harm those who leave her alone but she inflicts agonising punishments upon meddlers.

Scorpio is perhaps the most powerful and mysterious of all the cosmic beings of the Zodiac. She has power to destroy or enlighten, create or eliminate. The venom of her sting may be as deadly as a serpent's, or as pure and lifegiving as the essences which flow between man and woman. It is no wonder that, in men and women born under the sign of Scorpio, these powerful forces may release themselves as creativity and loyalty or as egotism and the desire to overpower the weak.

Shaman

A powerful sorcerer of the races which live in the northern quarters of the globe. A true shaman is born, not made, and he or she inherits magical powers while still in the womb. The surest sign of a shaman is when a child is born with a full set of teeth and a commanding power of the tongue spoken by its parents. Naturally such powerful shamans are rare. It is more usual for a shaman to serve a long apprenticeship to those who gain their powers from the long line stretching back to the beginning of time.

A would-be shaman spends the early years of apprenticeship in gathering the herbs, seeds, leaves and other items required in sorcery, memorising ritual songs, and learning the first steps of the Sun Dance and similar ceremonies. As he grows older he may assist in such work as the carving and painting of totem poles.

His true apprenticeship begins at puberty, when his teachers equip him with the necessary charms and send him on a solitary journey which may last for many years. He soon finds companionship among the birds, the animals of the plains and forest, and the fish of the rivers. He takes some time to learn their languages but eventually he can talk with them and learn their secrets.

Also he learns the Inwardness of rocks, trees, lakes, mountains and other natural features. Their spirits speak to him and reveal their unchanging knowledge. The rays of the sun and the voices of the wind also converse with him.

A shaman's solitary journey, and the knowledge which he gains, will vary greatly from one part of the world to another. A shaman of Greenland or of Siberia will learn different things from those of a shaman of Canada or Finland, although the basic tenets of sorcery are much the same.

When the apprentice shaman returns to his tribe he still has to learn many things from his elders. They teach him those secrets of the human heart which are sweeter than the first blossoms of spring and more terrible than the blizzards of winter.

Eventually, when the years have changed his hair to snow and wrinkled his face like the bark of a pine tree, he is a fully-fledged shaman. He is able to bring rain when it is needed and to wheedle the seeds of grain into sprouting. Without his sacred songs the fruit and berries would not ripen, the animals which feed and clothe the tribe would not increase, and there would be no fish in the rivers.

His education in sorcery gives him the power to appear and to disappear, to fly

through the air to consult with spirits, and to give especial power to the weapons of hunters and warriors. He looks into the smoke and flames of his sacred fire and warns the people of catastrophes which the elements plot against them.

The shaman knows that there is a time for all things on this earth, and that humans may be happy only when they live in harmony with the great rhythms of the Cosmos.

Tangaloa

The creator of some of the islands of the western Pacific. In the beginning, Tangaloa was the only being apart from his messenger, the bird Tuli. There was no form to the world except for a huge ocean which Tangaloa watched from the sky. Tuli flew endlessly over this ocean but at last he grew tired and begged for somewhere to rest, and Tangaloa threw down the rocks which became the islands of Fiji, Tonga, and Samoa.

Tuli then complained that the islands gave him no shade from the sun. Tangaloa gave him a vine to plant, and as it grew it sprouted men and women instead of leaves. These people settled on the islands and became the races of the western Pacific.

Taurus

The great bull which rules the second House of the Zodiac, where he roams the lush pastures of late spring. He is a massive beast with great forequarters and a proud head bearing a massive crescent of horns, his black pelt shining with the reflection of the stars and his bold eye bright as the full moon.

Taurus is closely related to many of the great bulls of antiquity, including those who were worshipped by the Egyptians. He does not, however, care to be reminded about his disreputable cousin the Minotaur, the son of an illicit union between a bull and a woman.

There is no more gallant sight than Taurus throughout the pastures of heaven. As he stands proudly surveying his domain, or trots lightly through the emerald grass with his great horns poised for combat, he is the personification of strength and vitality. Like any other bull he is pragmatic and stubborn, loyal and determined, and extremely protective of the cows and calves in his herd. Humans born between April and May are likely to display similar qualities.

Thor

The God of War and Thunder. A huge warrior with a dense red beard and terrifying blue eyes, clad in the classic Viking garb of winged helmet, breastplate, tunic, and leg-cloths secured with crossed garters. His favourite weapon is a huge hammer.

Despite his prowess in the elimination of giants and monsters he is an honourable warrior and gentle lover, although other women often tempt him to leave the arms of his wife Sif. His hammer is also a symbol of marital ardour.

He has the true warrior's courage and nobility, but as so often happens these are balanced by a certain simplicity which allows him to be tricked or deceived. He accepts men at their face value and they often betray him.

The sorcerer Utgardaloki once humbled Thor's martial pride by challenging him and his retinue to a series of contests. Thor's companion Loki had to complete with the sorcerer's servant, Logi, in an eating contest; another of Thor's men, who could run as fast as the lightning, had to race with a giant named Hugi; while Thor himself had to lift a cat from the ground, drain a horn of mead, and wrestle with an old woman.

Thor was confident of victory, but when Loki began eating against Logi the latter consumed the entire meal before Loki could start, and then polished off his boots and the eating trough. Thor's runner could not catch up with Hugi, and Thor could not lift the cat, drink up the mead, or defeat the old woman.

The sorcerer then told Thor that there are forces even greater than his mighty power. Logi was Fire, Hugi was Thought, the cat was part of the coils of the serpent Midgard which holds the earth together, the horn contained the sea and the old woman was Old Age.

Thor's struggle to lift the cat sends earthquakes rumbling through the world, while his gulping at the horn of mead causes the tides to rise and fall. Fire eats faster than any man, no warrior can conquer Old Age, and the speed of Thought is faster than any runner known to god or man.

Titans

The first race of heavenly beings: the six sons and six daughters born to Gaea the deep-breasted earth and Uranus the starlit sky who was both her husband and her son.

The twelve Titans, who were like enormous human beings of great physical splendour, created most of the universe and its beings including the first men. Their own children became the gods of Olympus.

The reign of the Titans ended when Zeus, the son of Cronos, led a family revolt against his father and uncles. In the subsequent cosmic war the gods buried many of the Titans beneath the earth, punished Atlas by making him bear the heavens on his shoulders throughout eternity, and allowed only a few of the Titans to remain in Olympus.

Tristram

This knightly hero may be seen as an eternal symbol of lovers' misunderstandings.

Tristram, a nephew of King Mark of Cornwall, fought gallantly for his uncle in a great battle between Cornwall and Ireland. At first it seemed that Ireland would win because of their secret weapon, the giant Morholt. He fought with a poisoned spear and laid the hosts of Cornwall around him like harvested corn.

Tristram received terrible wounds from the poisoned spear but cut off the giant's head. King Mark's sorcerers had no medicine to heal the wounds and he was near to death until an Irish lady, Iseult, cared for him so tenderly that he recovered.

When he returned to the court of King Mark he could speak of nothing but the grace, charm, and beauty of the Lady Iseult. His vivid descriptions made King Mark fall in love with her and he sent Tristram to ask her to be Queen of Cornwall.

Tristram could not bear to think of Iseult as the bedmate of the king, but his knightly fealty made him carry out this long-distance wooing. However, the words in his mouth turned into burning declarations of his own love for Iseult. They could not marry for fear of offending the king and so they began a passionate affair which lasted until King Mark arrived to seek his bride for himself. He found Tristram playing love songs to Iseult on his harp, and attacked the young knight with such fury that Tristram fled to Brittany.

He served the King of Brittany as a noble warrior but still yearned for Iseult, until he decided, quite wrongly, that she must have forgotten him. He succumbed to the blandishments of another Iseult, She of the White Hands, but when they were wed he could not bring himself to consummate the marriage. His love for Iseult of Ireland was

still so great that no other woman could replace her.

He sought forgetfulness in war, until he was carried home bleeding from many wounds. Even in this extremity he would not allow Iseult of the White Hands to attend him, and begged faintly that she should send for Iseult of Ireland.

Understandably, she refused, and Tristram died of his wounds and of the anguish in his heart.

Tu-of-the-Angry-Face

An ancestor of the Maoris: one of the seven sons of the Sky Father and Earth Mother. For countless centuries these two kept their sons wrapped in their warm embrace until the brothers had created the entire universe, but even then they refused to let them go. Eventually Tu-of-the-Angry-Face, who was the only brother with human form, grew tired of struggling to escape and shouted 'Let us kill our parents!'

But Tane, father of the forests, suggested it was better to pull their parents apart so that the world would have the sky above and the earth below. They all argued furiously about the best thing to do until Tane forced the sky and earth apart and the universe tumbled into its present form.

But Tawhiri, father of storms and winds, was still angry with his brothers. He lashed the world with storms which tore up the forests of Tane and disturbed the domain of Tangaroa, father of fishes and reptiles. Many reptiles fled from the sea into the forest.

Tangaroa quarrelled with Tane for allowing the reptiles into the forest, and Tane gained revenge by showing Tu-of-the-Angry-Face how to make canoes, spears, nets and fish hooks from the forest plants, so that he might catch the fishes of Tangaroa.

As time went by all the brothers quarrelled with each other but Tu-of-the-Angry-Face outwitted them all. He made traps for the creatures of the forest and sails to capture the wind. He ate the children of Rongo, the father of cultivated foods, and pulled up the children of Haumia the father of wild plants.

Tu's children became masters of the land and sea, but he taught them to worship Mother Earth, who produces their food, and Father Sky, whose tears of sorrow at separation from his wife still fall as rain upon the ground.

Underworld

The dreaded region ruled by Hades, wearer of the Helmet of Darkness and owner of all the wealth under the ground.

Hermes, the messenger of the gods, and God of Cunning, Luck, and Theft, escorts the spirits of the dead to the Underworld. They enter it by crossing the River Acheron, but if their relations have not given them a coin to pay the ferryman they must wander forever on its gloomy shores.

Several ordeals await them as they grope their way through the dark caverns beyond the river. They must drink from the River Lethe, whose waters make them forget their lives on earth, and then face the three-headed dog Cerberus whose mouth dribbles black venom. If they do not have cakes of barley and honey to feed him they will spend eternity at his mercy.

Then they have to pass by the three terrible judges of the dead, who decide their eternal fates. Those who have committed unnatural crimes will be tormented forever by the Erinnys, the winged daughters of Night whose hair is hissing serpents. The other sinners are flung into the rivers of woe, wailing, and flame. The ghosts of those who were neither good nor bad are sent to wander eternally on the bleak plains where the only flowers are the black lilies of asphodel. The only spirits released by Hades are those of virtuous men and women, who go to the Elysian Fields and spend eternity in a perpetual joyous summer.

Virgo

The queen of the sixth House of the Zodiac has an unhappy history. In mortal life she was a daughter of King Icarius of Attica, whose shepherds killed him when he made them drunk. His virgin daughter Erigone set out to find him with her dog Maera, which discovered the hidden grave. In their sorrow, Erigone hanged herself from a tree and Maera drowned himself.

This tragedy aroused the pity of Zeus and he placed the trio among the stars. Maera became the Lesser Dog Star and Erigone became Virgo.

She hanged herself when the fruits and grains of summer were ripening for harvest, and so Virgo has forever symbolised the ripeness of womanhood which has not yet surrendered itself.

As befits her royal birth she is a maiden of regal appearance: tall, slender, calm, yet curved and tender with the promise of riches yet to be bestowed. But like any mortal girl her moods change rapidly and she may be helpful and dependable or flighty, untidy, and dreamy. A human born under the influence of Virgo may well have a personality which shows such quickly varying moods.

Woman, The First

After Zeus conquered Olympus from the Titans, he ordered Prometheus and Epimetheus to re-populate the ravaged earth with men and beasts. Prometheus fashioned a splendid new race of men, but he envied the strength and cunning which Epimetheus gave to the beasts. He determined to give men a unique power, and stole fire for them from Olympus.

Zeus, infuriated by the theft, inflicted a terrible punishment on Prometheus and ordered the gods to decide upon one for mortal men. Together they worked out a subtle but eternal revenge. They moulded the figure of a beautiful maiden out of clay, gave her all the qualities of an irresistible goddess, and named her Pandora or The All-Gifted One. As a parting gift they presented her with a sealed golden urn of exquisite design, but warned her she must never look inside.

Pandora was the first woman to appear among men, who felt strange new emotions as they gazed upon her beauty and felt the magnetism of her sweet voice and limpid eyes. But she chose to marry Epimetheus, who had gone to live among the mortals.

Their life together would have been happy but for many arguments about the golden urn. Epimetheus warned her she must obey the gods, but they had created her as a complete woman and knew she would eventually have her own way.

At last she prised open the lid of the urn and there was an angry buzzing as though from a swarm of bees. Invisible wings brushed her cheeks, but when she looked into the urn it was empty except for Hope crouching at the bottom.

The first woman had released lust, greed, pride, avarice, jealousy, and all the other sins upon mankind. The gods had been revenged, but Hope remains to compensate us for the evil that men do.

Wotan

The God of Battle, Master of Fury, and Leader of the Wild Hunt. In Britain he is known as Grim, and in other parts of northern Europe as Woden or Wodan. Possibly he is one of the many manifestations of the great god Odin although he is very unlike Odin in character and appearance. Where Odin is wise and intelligent, interested in all things including war, Wotan is interested only in battle and blood sports.

Wotan is unconcerned with the rightness of any cause. He is a macho personality who

makes a fetish of physical strength and the cunning of hand and eye. When rumours of war spread around his territory he is the first to sharpen his sword and roar boastfully at his followers, urging them to mount their steeds and follow him in the first great onslaught on the enemy. Any enemy and any war will do.

Galloping ahead of his troops he throws himself upon the opposition in a blood fury which carves a way through their host, but he has an unfair advantage in that he is immortal and can receive the most bloody wounds without permanent harm.

When peace returns he is grumpy and restless until the hunting season opens. Then he mounts his steed in pursuit of stags, roaring through the forests with his companions yelling behind him. Even if the stag takes refuge in the skies they will follow him through the dark clouds to his death.

Wotan is always first in at the kill and with a bellow of triumph he waves his bloody spear to show that, once again, he has proved his manhood.

This brutal and swaggering god has an important influence on men. He urges them into countless bloody adventures and prompts them into destructive mischief. In another manifestation he is a fertility god, representing the ruthless drive to implant his seed and create more men and gods to revel in military glory.

Xolotl

The God of Ball Play. He was originally worshipped by the Aztecs but his power is universal and he plays a substantial part in ensuring victory for his favoured side or player in any game which uses a ball. Sometimes he helps by endowing a player with unusual expertise, but if a game is going badly for his favourites he may resort to tripping or otherwise fouling the opposition.

Xolotl has a great affection for twins and he acts as their protector in the game of life. Also, his sporting nature gives him great sympathy for crippled or deformed people. By helping them he tries to even the score against them.

Yggdrasil

The Tree of the World. A great ash tree on the summit of the world, with one root extending into Asgard, another into the land of the Frost Giants, and the third into the Kingdom of the Dead. These roots draw water from the Well of Fate, the Spring of Wisdom, and the Source of all Rivers. Three sisters, the Norns whose names are Fate, Being, and Necessity, tend to the tree and supply all its needs for earth and water.

The branches of Yggdrasil encompass the universe and drop the dews of fate and wisdom upon mankind. The tree will stand sturdily during the final cosmic wars triggered by the wickedness of men, when they and the gods will perish in fearful combat and the earth will be devastated. But when the wars are over the gentle gods Lif and Lifdrasir will emerge from the branches of Yggdrasil to create a new and better world.

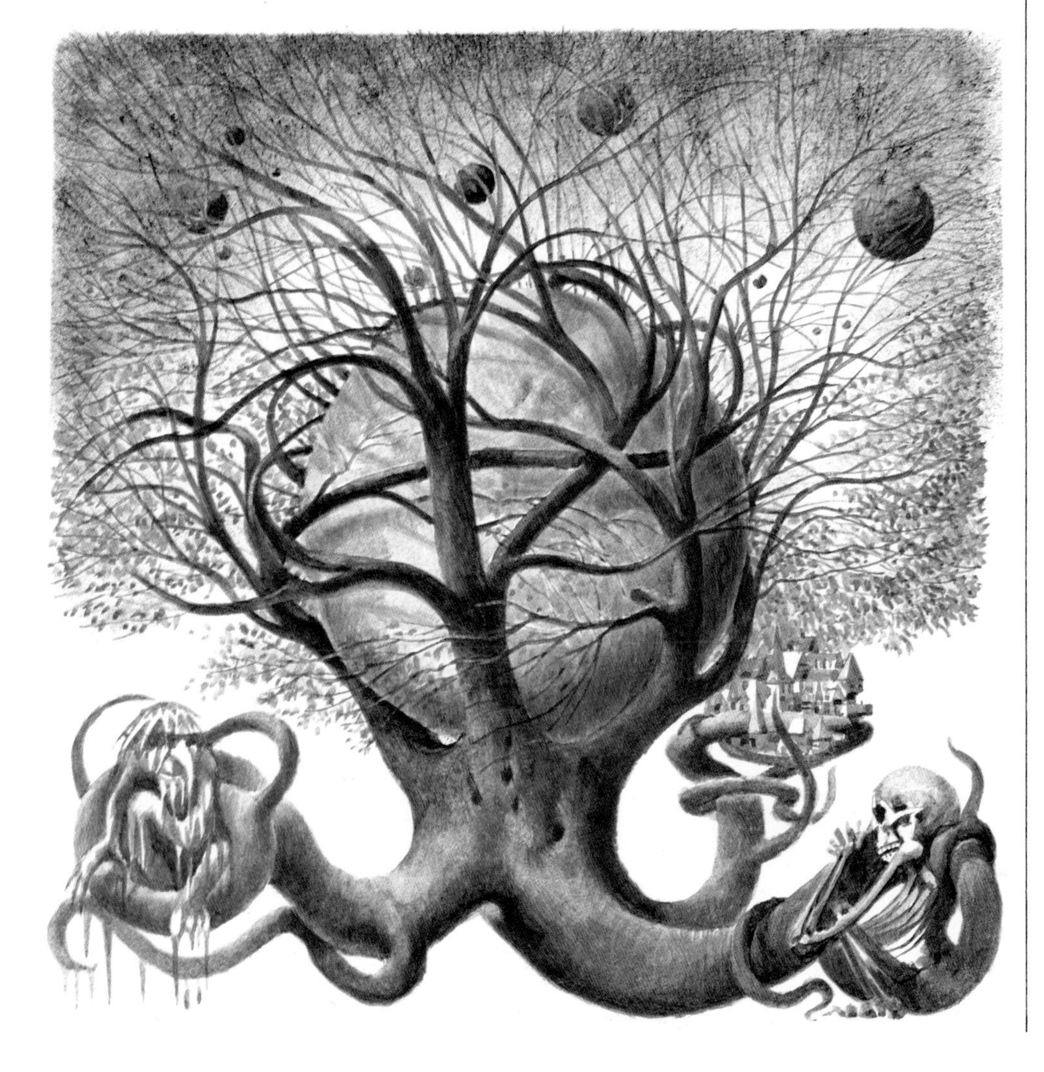

Zeus

Sovereign Lord of Olympus. A god with many fine qualities, counterbalanced by his unforgiving nature and unquenchable lust for women. In his manifestation as a mature man he radiates wisdom and compassion but the mere sight of a seductive figure is enough to make him shatter all his own laws.

After a difficult youth he gained supremacy over Olympus by courage and guile, to establish himself as the supreme arbiter over gods and men. He is the protector of all laws and morals, mortal or divine, and the source of all good or evil. He cares for the poor and weak, for prisoners and fugitives, and for the hearths and homes of families. Parliaments and similar assemblies are assured of his benign interest and he helps to secure the bonds of friendship and marriage.

He never refuses genuine supplicants for his aid but he inflicts terrible punishments on those who offend him. When Prometheus stole fire from Olympus, Zeus had him secured to a rock for 30,000 years and sent an eagle to feed on his liver every day.

Unfortunately he has lost much well-merited respect because of his total amorality over women. Even the wives of his dearest friends are not safe from his goatish lust. In his passion for conquest he stops at nothing and if his arts of seduction fail he turns to trickery, deceit, or rape.

Zeus has been married a number of times but he has never hesitated to abandon one wife and take another, or to pursue a dewy virgin while he was still fresh from the bridal bed. Most of the goddesses succumbed to his overpowering masculinity, but when Demeter refused him he changed himself into a bull and raped her. The nymph Asteria escaped him only by changing herself into a quail and flying away. Taygete, daughter of Atlas, was saved at the last moment when Artemis changed her into a deer so that she could run faster than Zeus.

Eventually he was forced into a lasting marriage with Hera, Queen of the Sky, who resisted him until he turned himself into a cuckoo and pretended to be frozen with the cold. She took him into her bed to warm him, but even when she found a man instead of a cuckoo in her arms she refused to surrender until he promised marriage. He soon found that her physical beauty was not matched by her character and she proved a jealous and vindictive wife.

Zeus has a particular fancy for nymphs

and uses many tricks to seduce them—and to fight off their angry male relations. Mortal women, whether married or unmarried, are never safe from him. No matter how their guardians try to protect them he always finds a way into their beds. Acrisius locked his daughter Danae in a tower of bronze, but Zeus poured himself through a crack in the form of a shower of gold. Leda, the beautiful wife of Tyndareus, was bathing in a pool when a beautiful swan floated towards her, and when she caressed the bird it changed into the ardent god. He eloped with Europa by changing himself into a splendid but gentle bull, which so attracted the girl that she climbed on its back and wreathed its horns with flowers. All at once the bull sprang into the sea and carried the girl to Crete, where it changed into Zeus and mounted her beneath a plane tree.

In these and countless other ways the ruler of Olympus possessed innumerable women, who gave birth to a great number of mortal or immortal children. The trouble they caused Zeus over the centuries must sometimes have made him wonder whether the brief ecstasy of seduction is worth the prolonged payment.

Zodiac, The Houses of the

Planet Earth voyages upon an eternal rhythmic cycle ordained when the first creators fashioned the Cosmos out of Chaos. It moves and revolves within the vast complexity of the other heavenly bodies, of which some still lie beyond our knowledge and consciousness. As the entire Cosmos journeys on its way through time, space, and destiny, so Planet Earth travels on its ordained passage through the twelve Houses of the Zodiac.

As the planet enters the sphere of influence of each House, its vibrant powers irradiate everything that grows or moves upon the voyaging globe. At the same time, other stars and planets exert their mystic influence, depending upon the position of the earth as it travels within each House. Each heavenly body has a specific power which may strengthen or distort that of the beings of the Zodiac.

During each annual cycle, Planet Earth moves first through the House of Aries, who causes plants and animals to respond to the invigoration of spring. Next it enters the region of Taurus, whose virility flows into man and every other animal as they busy themselves with procreation.

Then, as the planet passes through the invisible walls between the Houses of Gemini and Cancer, and into the House of Leo, we flourish in the summer months which urge the spirits of plants and animals towards maturity. The cool eyes of Virgo survey us as we move out of summer into autumn, and then into the Houses of Libra and Scorpio who supervise the gradual death of the year.

Sagittarius the Archer fires the first arrows of winter as the planet travels towards the House of the Goat, Capricorn, who poises on the summit of the year. Next come the regions of Aquarius the Water Carrier and Pisces the Fish. They are cold and wet, and the creatures of earth retreat into shelter as the two beings pour down the water which ensures the renewal of life.

Then the cycle begins again, and the inhabitants of earth know that their fortunes will once more follow the cosmic laws. There may be some confusion in obeying them, because they were first ordained for the northern hemisphere, but the characters of all mortals are fashioned by the Zodiacal beings who control their destinies.

CHAPTER TWO

THINGS OF THE GROUND AND UNDERGROUND

THINGS OF THE GROUND AND UNDERGROUND

Once upon a time, the invisible world which surrounds us was very much closer than it is today. In the days when church bells were the loudest sound of the English countryside, a wanderer through the meadows in the fecund stillness of a summer twilight was conscious of a magic which cannot exist in such contrivances as video games. The spirits of the earth and trees all hovered on the verge of revelation, and spoke messages now inaudible to minds cluttered with the debris of technology. There could be no doubt that fairies and pixies, gnomes and goblins, lived in the flowering hedgerows; that a ramshackle cottage was the home of a witch and that bodies peeped through the knothole of a hollow tree. Everyone knew it, as certainly as he knew that hell lay beneath the graveyard and heaven above the summer skies.

And so it is in every other part of the world. Forests, jungles, mountains, deserts, and prairies all have a mysterious population which lives in a dimension slightly different from that of humans and other animals. Sometimes they break through the barriers of consciousness and reveal themselves to humans, with good or evil results. Witches and warlocks can summons them to appear, or advise humans on the correct spells, offerings, and behaviour to control or placate them. They are an important influence on human affairs because they help people who please them or torment those who break their implacable rules.

There is a modern theory that myths and legends were invented only to explain natural phenomena. The absurdity of this belief is demonstrated by the huge amount of information available on the beings who co-exist with us above the ground or live under our feet. It is impossible to believe that anyone could have invented such complex stories simply to explain such mundane matters as thunder and lightning, storms and earthquakes. The fact is that our ancestors, whose minds were much less confused than ours, were able to see, hear, and record all the mysteries of a world invisible to modern eyes.

This portion of the book describes a number of its inhabitants, so that we may know and recognise them and perhaps learn how to see them for ourselves.

Abatwa

The tiniest creatures in human form, who live in the anthills of southern Africa. Sightings are rare because the Abatwa are the shyest and most elusive of all creatures in human form. When they do reveal themselves, it is only to children under four years old, wizards, or pregnant women. A woman in the seventh month of pregnancy who sees an Abatwa male knows that she will give birth to a boy.

The Abatwa are perfect miniatures of African tribespeople and they maintain a clan and family structure similar to that of the tribes, but they are not a warlike race and they never seek dominance over the ants with which they share their quarters. They live by foraging for food among the roots of grasses and other plants.

Adekagagwaa

The great spirit, a relation of the Earth Mother, who spends a part of each year with the tribes of the North American forests and gives them the warmth, beauty, and fertility of the summer months. The bounty of Adekagagwaa makes the tribespeople fat and contented and ensures them ample stores of pemmican for the winter, together with the furs and skins which will keep them warm.

When the forest blazes with the brilliance of autumn it is the signal for Adekagagwaa to return to his home in the south, but before he departs he promises the Earth Mother to return again in the following year. He leaves a portion of his spirit asleep in the earth as a symbol of this promise.

As soon as Adekagagwaa leaves the forests, Hino the Thunderer roars through the sky with his flaming bow and arrows, heralding the winter storms. Ga-Oh the wind giant releases the bear of the north wind and the moose of the east wind, and Gohone, the old man who is the spirit of winter, stirs in the lair where he has slept from spring to autumn. Soon he emerges and prowls through the forests, striking the trees with his club to bring down their leaves.

So the months pass until Adekagagwaa fulfils his promise and returns from the south. His sleeping spirit awakes and melts the snow from the land, new leaves and grass appear, hibernating animals leave their dens, and the tribes look forward to another season of richness as Adekagagwaa supplies all their needs.

Amazons

A nation of militant women who live near the southern borders of Turkey. Some ancient histories claim that each Amazon woman has her right breast amputated, so that she may draw her bow more easily, but this is a fallacy. Their name derives from the Greek word *mazos*, meaning 'breast', with the prefix 'a' denoting an amplitude. Amazon women are tall, lithe, and full-breasted, their limbs powerful from constant exercise, their features stern and noble and their gaze sharp and challenging. They know themselves superior to men, whom they use only as sex objects. Each year, a selected group of Amazon virgins visits a neighbouring tribe, the Gargareans, in order to conceive children. They return any boys to the fathers and bring up the girls in their own occupations of agriculture, hunting, and war.

A regiment of Amazons on the move is an awe-inspiring sight. The archer companies are naked but for brief tunics and armed with bows and arrows. The others wear tight trousers, tunics, and caps, and carry spears or axes. Amazon fighting tactics comprise a sudden rush by archers, who release a blizzard of deadly arrows upon the enemy to soften them up for the stabbing and hacking assault by axe-women and spear-women.

Amazon society is a matriachy ruled by a queen, who is elected at regular intervals out of the fiercest and strongest of the regimental officers. The Amazon capital, Themiscyra, is a small but noble city where the queen lives in an elegant palace of classical design, but she makes frequent expeditions around her country to inspect the forts, agricultural villages, and training

camps. Amazon women spend a portion of each year in looking after their farms and the remainder in various necessary crafts, military training, and manoeuvres.

The Amazons once terrorised much of Asia Minor and even raided as far as the islands of Samothrace and Lesbos. Nowadays they rarely leave their own territory except for the annual fertility visits to the Gargareans, and they are left in peace because their neighbours dare not challenge these redoubtable women.

Annwn

The Underworld of the Celts and Gaels, ruled over by King Arawn. Some parts of Annwn are similar to the most beautiful countryside of Britain, with verdant forests and undulating pastureland gay with primroses and daffodils. Other regions are dark, ominous, and wild. It may be likened to a combined heaven and hell, except that Annwn does not feature the dreadful punishments usually reserved for sinners. They suffer only by having to spend eternity among the silent dead, who wander the darker regions of Annwn in endless contemplation of their sins. Those who have merited a pleasant afterlife spend it in a kind of perpetual party. They join King Annwn in his hunting of the deer, refresh themselves from fountains which flow with wine, and eat from a magic cauldron always brimming with savoury stew.

The existence of this cauldron tempted many heroes of the past, including King Arthur, to lead expeditions into Annwn. If any of them could have seized the cauldron and brought it back with them to the Upperworld, it would have assumed magically curative properties. Any sick or injured person lowered into it would have been immediately restored to health, and might have expected to live considerably longer than his contemporaries.

King Arawn always gave gracious welcome to the invaders of Annwn, who lost all their fears and antagonism when he invited them to join the hunt and the subsequent festivities. But whenever they thought they might seize an opportunity to smuggle the cauldron out of Annwn it was surrounded by the hosts of the dead, and despite all their efforts they had to return disappointed to the Upperworld.

Arachne

The Spider Queen. Originally she was a Lydian maiden who was noted for the speed with which she spun sheep's wool into thread and then wove the thread into brilliant tapestries.

Arachne became so proud of her skill that she challenged the goddess Athene, who wove the garments of the gods, to a weaving contest. Athene smiled at this impertinent challenge, and was so sure she could outclass

any mortal maiden that she offered Arachne the chance to withdraw.

But Arachne refused, and the girl and goddess set to work with distaff, shuttle, and loom. Their fingers moved like lightning as they spun their threads and then wove them into tapestries. Arachne finished first and offered her tapestry to Athene for inspection.

Athene pored over the beautiful tapestry, her anger growing as she failed to find a single imperfection. She could not even find a knot where Arachne had broken and tied a thread. Suddenly she realised that she, a goddess, had been beaten by a mere mortal. In her angry humiliation she changed Arachne into the first spider and condemned her to spin and weave eternally with thread drawn from her own body.

The Spider Queen still weaves her beautiful webs for the admiration of mankind, and her family is known as the Arachnidae.

Artemis

Also known as Diana: the goddess with enormous influence over all things that grow in or on the ground, and over the fertility of all creatures and animals including man.

Artemis is one of the daughters of Zeus and twin sister of Apollo the Healer. Immediately she was born she asked Zeus for hunter's garments and the weapons of the chase. He gave her a golden bow and a quiverful of arrows, which she used to deadly effect on early adventures with her brother. After that she retreated to the rugged wilderness of Arcadia and devoted herself to hunting and to supervising the produce of nature.

For company in her wild life she assembled a band of twenty nymphs, whose principal task is the care of her pack of savage hounds. Despite her obsession with fertility and fecundity, her love of nature and every kind of sport and exercise, she has no time for the opposite sex. She is not only a fierce protector of her own virginity but she also insists on chastity among her retainers. When one of them, Callisto, allowed herself to be seduced by Zeus, Artemis would not listen to her excuses. Zeus tried to protect her from the wrath of Artemis by changing her into a she-bear, but the huntress tracked her down and slew her with an arrow.

Actaeon, another mighty hunter, one day chanced upon Artemis and her nymphs as they bathed naked in a forest pool. The exquisite beauty of the goddess attended by her gambolling nymphs forced him to stop and stare, but when Artemis became conscious of his lecherous gaze she instantly changed him into a stag and set his own dogs to tear him to pieces.

Artemis personifies both the beauty and bounty of nature and its ruthlessness towards those who break its laws. She takes good care of farmers who recognise her powers, and offer her the first fruits of every harvest, but her wrath is terrible when this courtesy is neglected. When Oeneus omitted the offering she sent a gigantic boar to ravage his fields and destroy his family. She punished Admetus for similar neglect by filling his bridal chamber with poisonous snakes.

Men who see the glory of Artemis as she races ahead of her nymphs, her pack of hounds yelping around her as she notches an arrow to her bow to bring down a splendid stag, should look quickly away in case she punishes them for the desire they cannot hide. Her grace and beauty symbolise the mysterious spirit of women which men must forever pursue in vain.

Barbegazi

Gnome-like people of the mountainous regions spreading from France into Switzerland. The name is probably a corruption of *barbes glacées*, meaning 'frozen beards'. Contrary to the usual rule, the barbegazi hibernate during the warmer months and emerge only after the first heavy snowfalls of winter. Consequently they are rarely seen when the temperature rises above zero. They never venture below the tree-line and the few specimens who have been trapped by mountaineers, and taken down to the alpine villages, survived only for a few hours.

Barbegazi bear some resemblance to the gnomes of other regions, except for their large feet and the fact that their hair and

beards resemble thick growths of icicles. When these icicles melt—as in the case of the captured specimens—they reveal normal hair underneath. They use their large feet as a kind of combined ski and snowshoe. They enable barbegazi to run at remarkable speed over snowfields or to ski down almost vertical slopes. They are also useful for digging. A barbegazi can conceal himself in thick snow in a few seconds, or dig himself out no matter how deeply he may be buried.

Both sexes wear garments of white fur resembling modern jump-suits, so that it is difficult to distinguish between males and females at a distance. Their speech has been likened to the whistling of marmots, the small mammals of the Swiss Alps, but they can communicate over long distances by a kind of eerie hooting which may be mistaken for the winds among the crags or the sound of an Alpine horn.

Barbegazi habitats are networks of caves and tunnels excavated close to the summits of high peaks, entered by tiny openings shielded by curtains of icicles.

The attitude of barbegazi towards humans is still uncertain. Some mountaineers believe that St Bernard dogs take much of the credit for the helpful activities of barbegazi. Others say that barbegazi whistle or hoot to warn of an imminent avalanche, although they themselves enjoy avalanches and ride them down the mountainsides.

Much of the bargegazi lifestyle remains a mystery to humans because they usually appear only when blizzards and freezing temperatures force mountaineers down from the higher altitudes.

Basilisk

The basilisk or cockatrice is a horrid monster which emerges when a cock's egg is stolen and hatched by a snake or serpent. The basilisk, about the size of a cat, has some resemblance to both a rooster and a snake, but it is far more terrifying than any other known reptile.

The basilisk's weapons are its eyes and its teeth. Even the most pure-hearted knight cannot conquer a basilisk, because he would perish at a glance from those fearsome eyes. A basilisk glare causes plants to wither, trees to die, and birds to fall from the air. The only plant able to withstand the searing stare of a basilisk is the rue (*Ruta graveolens*) or 'herb of grace' which is of course extremely useful in witchcraft.

Basilisks would undoubtedly lay the whole world waste if it were not for their two enemies: the cock and the weasel. Any home may protect itself against basilisks by keeping a rooster, because a basilisk dies at the sound of a cock's crow.

Weasels are immune from basilisk stares and they attack the creatures without mercy. Basilisks fight back with their razor-sharp teeth, but weasels know that rue leaves will cure basilisk wounds and they have no fear of the monster. A weasel always wins the contest.

Plotinus of Antioch, who was blind from birth, is said to have befriended a basilisk in the Nubian desert and to have hooded its eyes so that it might be tamed. But when he led it to the city it died at the sound of a cock's crow.

Beanstalks

Much horticultural research has been devoted to attempts to discover the exact strain of beanseed planted by Jack the Giant Killer and his mother. Researchers believe it was a cross between the common broad bean (*Vicia faba*) and the French or climbing bean (*Phaseolus vulgaris*), combining the strength and structure of one with the upward-reaching tendencies of the other. So far, all attempts to reproduce the bean, classified as *P. gigantis*, have failed. The co-operation of white witches has been ineffectual, and black witches refuse to assist. They claim that an ancient hex forbids them to interfere in the affairs of giants. Researchers now believe that a fertiliser of the type described by H. G. Wells, in *The Food of the Gods*, may have been used to grow the original beanstalk.

Airline companies have shown some antagonism towards the experiments, but military finance may be available with the idea of growing a beanstalk cordon around large cities to fend off air attack. The problem is that a proliferation of cloud-climbing beanstalks could create many difficulties. The ripening of the beans and bursting of the pods would shower surrounding communities with beanseeds of unknown size and weight. The growth of huge quantities of beanflowers will fill the atmosphere with pollen, and inflict great suffering on hay fever patients. Cascades of dry leaves will add to pollution problems. Beanstalks of the supposed height and strength are likely to affect the weather, by attracting electric storms and causing undue precipitation.

Researchers also have discussed the possibility that a new beanstalk would attract another giant down to earth. Jack cut down the beanstalk in the days before suburban sprawl, but the destruction of a giant by similar methods nowadays would cause immense amounts of bad publicity, claims for compensation, conservation rallies, and so on.

The feeling is that any further experiments should be carried out inside a specially constructed beanstalk tower, reaching no higher than Cloud Cuckoo Land, so that any adverse effects may be limited before they grow out of control.

Bendith Y Mamau

A particularly unpleasant clan of Welsh fairies, possibly the result of interbreeding between fairies and goblins. Unlike true fairies, who are noted for their good looks, the Bendith Y Mamau are stunted and ugly little creatures. They have little to do with mortals except for stealing their children, possibly out of envy for their beauty. Again they differ from true fairies, who only steal newborn children, because they may take a child who can walk and talk and substitute one of their own ugly children, known as Crimbils. A parent who can pay for the necessary spells may regain a stolen child through the intercession of a witch. When the Bendith Y Mamau return a stolen child to its home, it remembers nothing of its experiences except for a vague recollection of sweet music.

Bhogavati

A great underground city located somewhere beneath the continent of Asia, possibly under the Himalayas. It is the capital city and principal home of the Nagas, or snake-spirits, who are half-human and half-snake. This might seem to be an unattractive combination but the Nagas are in fact an extremely handsome race. The Naga maidens are so wise and beautiful that a mortal male may count himself fortunate if he manages to persuade one to marry him.

Most Nagas are benevolent towards humans but some are violently antagonistic. The demon Naga-Sanniya, who causes nightmares about snakes, may be a relation of the Naga clan. Nagas who take an interest in humans may help them to find buried treasure, win prizes in lotteries, or enjoy similar windfalls.

Bhogavati has never been seen by human eyes but it is known to be a noble and beautiful city of great white edifices carved out of the rock. Its streets are paved with mosaics of emeralds, rubies, sapphires, diamonds, and other jewels, rescued from the Ocean of Milk during the great battles between gods and demons at the beginning of time.

Brownies

Scotland is unique in many ways, and one of these is the possession of brownies. These earth spirits enjoy a reputation for being cheerful and helpful little creatures. They are devoid of mischief and prefer to live in harmony with mortals.

If it were not for their cheerful nature they might not be very attractive. They are small and hairy, with flat faces and pinhole nostrils, but their happy smiles and extrovert character create an instant feeling of goodwill.

Mortals with similarly cheerful and innocent natures will often see brownies, but the unfortunate fact is that very few mortals, except for children, possess brownie characteristics. This accounts for the fact that most brownie sightings are reported by children, and for the general adult disbelief in brownies.

Brownies enjoy playing with children, telling them stories, and helping them to make such artefacts as wildflower posies and daisy chains. They vanish at the approach of a disbelieving adult, but this does not inhibit them from helping adults in countless minor ways. One of these is that of guiding cows home to the farmyard at milking time and ushering hens to their roosts in the evenings. Brownies dislike any expression of gratitude for such assistance, however, and will never accept gifts left out for them.

The presence of a few brownies is a sure protection against goblins. The brownies correct any goblin mischief so quickly that mortals are not even aware of a goblin presence.

Brownies prefer their homeland, but a good many have accompanied Scottish families in their migration to various parts of the world. Consequently, it is possible for a cheerful and innocent mind to become brownie-conscious almost anywhere.

Boggarts

These household spirits appear to have some relationship to both bogies and brownies, although they are much more malicious than bogies and they are certainly not as helpful as brownies.

Their appearance betrays the bogey-brownie relationship. They are gnomish little creatures dressed in tattered dusty clothing, dark and hairy, with meddling fingers and clumsy feet.

The presence of a boggart around a home or farmstead is betrayed by an unusual number of minor mishaps and persistent noises after dark. They tip over milk jugs, break the cords of window sashes, put hens off laying, frighten cats, cause dogs to bark senselessly, slam doors, leave taps running, block gutters, blow out candles, and awaken sleeping babies by tweaking their noses.

The problem with boggarts is that no one has yet learnt how to appease them or get

BOGGARTS
GREMLINS
BOGIES
LEPRECHAUNS
TROLLS
BROWNIES
HOBGOBLINS
GOBLINS
PIXIES
ELVES
FAIRIES
GNOMES

rid of them. Householders afflicted by a boggart infestation sometimes have no choice but to move to a new home. The move should be made very quickly, however, and with little previous discussion, or the boggarts are certain to hear about it and ride along in the moving van.

Bogies, Bogey-Men, Bogles, Bogey-Beasts

These generic terms cover a very wide range of mischievous but fairly harmless spirits of the ground and underground. They like to live in darkness or semi-darkness and so may take up residence in cupboards, cellars, barns, lofts, hollow trees, abandoned mine workings, hillside caves and crevices, and similar retreats. Bogies are particularly fond of places where humans have stored items for which they have no further use but cannot bring themselves to discard. An attic full of dusty old furniture, luggage, and similar clutter will invariably harbour a number of bogies. Whenever the house is quiet they may be heard moving around with attempted stealth, but they tend to clumsiness and betray themselves with bumps, scuffles, and creaks. Junk shops, ramshackle barns with recesses crammed with mouldering hay and worn-out machinery, abandoned hen-houses and toolsheds, the offices of old-fashioned lawyers filled with stacks of yellowing papers, and all other places redolent of abandoned human efforts are popular with bogey-men. They are quite likely to sneak into modern houses, however, and occupy cluttered closets and cupboards which offer plenty of concealment. They try to lie silently in such retreats but now and again a clumsy movement will cause muffled creaks and thumps.

Bogies amuse themselves with minor mischief which shows very little in the way of creative tampering. They pull the bedclothes off sleepers on a cold night, and create vague uneasiness by hovering behind one's back in an empty house. They are very interested in human activities and like to spy on and listen to them.

Bogey-men are vague and amorphous in appearance, with some resemblance to a large puff of dust. A sure test for bogey occupation is to look quickly through a knothole in a wooden partition. If there is a bogey on the other side you will catch the dull gleam of his eye before he has time to dodge away.

Black Annis

The rolling moors and hillsides of the Scottish Highlands harbour this witchlike creature. She has been seen in many parts of Scotland from Ben Lomond to the Pentland Firth, and so it appears she has no settled home. Probably this is because any report of her appearance causes mothers to keep their children indoors and even the bravest Highlander to walk in company, thus robbing her of her prey and forcing her to move on again.

Terrified gillies returning from the moors have described Black Annis as a hideous hag, easily distinguishable from any other old woman by her blue skin and her single piercing eye. They have only glimpsed her in the distance, because anyone who approaches closely enough to see Black Annis clearly will not escape from her clutches. The manner in which she deals with her victims, and whether she eats them raw or cooked, is therefore unknown.

Usually the reports of her presence say she is sitting on a pile of bones outside a cave, but when a party assembles to hunt her out of the district she has always moved on. Only the pile of bones remains, and when the party inspects these relics they see that Black Annis often has to content herself with a diet of sheep or deer when humans are not available.

Black Dog

Pedestrians of Celtic or Gaelic descent should never venture along lonely roads without a companion. A walkmate will not necessarily ward off the black dog, which is sometimes visible to one of a pair but not the other, but he or she may bestow some measure of protection. The ideal companion is a descendant of Ean MacEndroe of Loch Ewe. In the year of Culloden, MacEndroe rescued a fairy entangled in a bramble bush and she gave to him and all his descendants, even to the seventh son of a seventh son, perpetual immunity from the power of the black dog.

Black dog sightings were once restricted to Scotland and Ireland, but widespread emigration from those nations has attracted the black dog to many parts of the world. Descriptions are vague because those who see the dog are seized by such a chill despondency and despair, generally progressing to a decline of all their vital faculties, that they have little interest in defining the experience.

Some say the creature is no larger than a Labrador: others that it is as big as a calf or 'as stout as a kelpie.' All agree that it moves in utter silence, without the panting and claw-clicking which accompanies most canine progression. If the person whom it follows utters some nervous comment, the dog takes no notice.

Members of Clan MacLartin have particular reason to fear the black dog. Its appearance foretells death on a dunghill. The last member of the clan to see the black dog was Lord Jamie MacLartin in 1715. A few days after it followed him, English dragoons hanged Lord Jamie at Arbroath and threw his body on a dunghill.

Bokwus

The fearsome spirit of the great forests of north-western America. Bokwus is seldom if ever seen distinctly by humans, but the Indian hunters of that region are always very conscious of his presence when they venture into the forests of spruce, larch, and fir, where the dense boughs filter the sunlight dimly through to the forest floor. There, when all is silent except for the breathing of the wind through the topmost branches, the evil aquiline face of Bokwus scrolled with totemic warpaint may be glimpsed as he peeps quickly around the great trunk of a tree. At other times he may be seen flitting through the close-ranked trees on the banks of a roaring creek or river, and it is here that he is most dangerous. He depends on the sound of rushing water, and a fisherman's absorption in gaining a good catch of trout or salmon, to cover his approach as he creeps closer and closer until he can push the fisherman off a slippery rock. He has a special affinity for the spirits of the drowned, and as soon as the soul leaves a dead body tumbling through the cascades he secures it and escorts it to his forest

home. No living person has ever discovered what happens to it there.

Cats

Most cats associated with magic and mystery are descendants of the ancient Egyptian cat (*Felis lybica*) which was imported to Europe by the Romans and crossbred with the European wildcat or Cat o' the Woods (*Felis silvestris*). Egyptian cats were particularly jovial felines, associated with Bast the fertility goddess who has a cat's head. Bast gave mankind the great gifts of happiness and the warmth of the sun.

Egyptians paid tribute to her by worshipping cats, who responded with great cheerfulness and generally wore broad smiles. Whenever a cat died, he or she was buried with much ceremony in the huge cat cemetery at Bubastis.

The cats brought to Europe did not receive the same kind of reverence and they soon became independent and introverted. When they mated with Cats o' the Woods, their descendants inherited the mystic lore of the dark forests of Europe, so different from the sunny spaces of Egypt. As time passed by, so cats became increasingly aware of matters not generally revealed to humans and for this reason they were befriended by witches, warlocks, and wizards. Feline agility and sense of balance enable them to ride on witches' broomsticks and to dance in mystic rituals.

Some notable cats, including the tabby known as Grimalkin, developed magical powers of their own and used them to hypnotise humans into doing their bidding. Fortunately for humans, however, the majority of cats are too indolent to develop their inherited powers to their full potential. On the whole they are content to receive human worship, even in its modern attenuated form, just as they did in ancient Egypt. A contented cat is likely to attract good fortune to its hosts, but will never join in the orgies and water festivals with which Bast and her attendant cats were honoured in ancient Egypt.

Centaurs

The wild and beautiful race of Centaurs inhabits the mountain regions of Arcadia and Thessaly, in Greece. Nothing could be more striking than the sight of a troop of Centaurs galloping across a mountain slope, with the heads and trunks of splendid human males like figureheads upon the bodies of potent stallions.

Their nobility of appearance is belied by their character, which may be blamed upon their ancestry. Ixion, a noted rascal, was the father of one branch of the tribe, and Chronus of the other. However, the descendants of Chronus and his wife Philyra, a beautiful sea nymph, are of a very different nature from those of Ixion.

Zeus invited Ixion into Olympus in order to purify him of his sins, but Ixion repaid this hospitality by an attempt to seduce the goddess Hera. She escaped him by changing herself into a cloud, and Ixion had to satisfy himself with Nephele. The first of the Centaurs sprang from this union.

The Centaurs quickly showed that they combine the strength of stallions with the greed, lust, and arrogance of human males. They love to drink wine almost as much as they delight in running down a nubile female, and they glory in a drunken brawl. They showed all these qualities when they gatecrashed the wedding of Ixion's human son, Peirithous, to Deidameia. The Centaurs got drunk on the wedding wine and made such blatant attempts to rape the bride that Theseus and Peirithous had to fight them off.

The Centaurs give allegiance only to Eros, God of Love, and Dionysus the God of Wine. A cavalcade of Centaurs out on a spree, with Eros whipping them on and Dionysus lolling drunkenly in his chariot, makes every wise householder lock up his wife and daughters and barricade his wine cellar.

The descendants of Chronus remain aloof from such revels. Chronus and Philyra begat Cheiron, a learned Centaur who brought up and educated a number of Greek heroes. His offspring pursue a sober and studious way of life, in great contrast to the drunken brawling and womanising of the other branch of the family.

Chenoo

The great stone giants who live in the territory of the Iroquois tribes of North America. These enormous clumsy creatures never managed to learn the use of such weapons as the bow and arrows, knife, or spear. In the frequent battles among themselves, which make the hills resound with thunderous noise, they uproot trees to use as clubs and fling great boulders at each other.

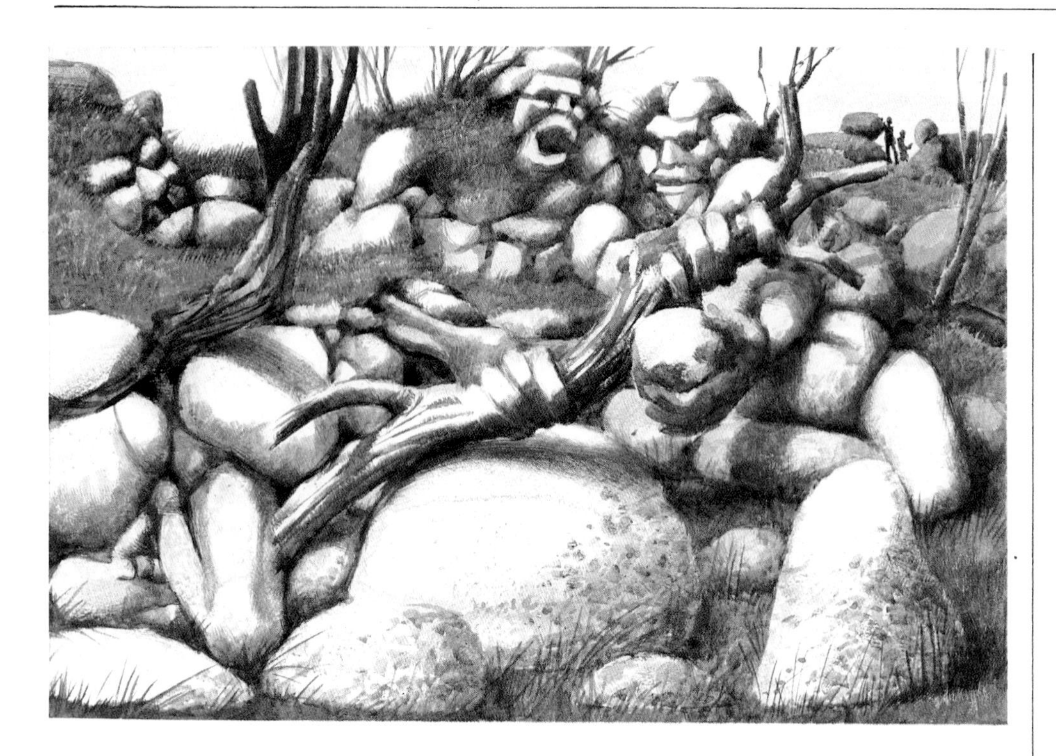

Normally a chenoo is harmless to humans and in fact the chenoos are a little afraid of the tribesmen. When a human approaches their territory, the chenoos are likely to camouflage themselves by such total immobility that they blend into the rock formations. A witch doctor or shaman may be able to pick out a chenoo from its surroundings, however, and if he knows the proper spells he can force it to obey him.

Cluricauns

Cellar spirits who resemble mini-innkeepers in their garb of breeches, stockings, silver-buckled shoes, white shirts and aprons, and red caps. They live in the wine cellars of inns and houses. A cluricaun gives no trouble in a well-run establishment and simply takes his share of whatever food and drink are available. But, in bad hotels or inns, he gobbles up the provisions and swallows the drink in such quantities that he soon puts the landlord out of business. In a private home owned by a man too fond of wine, the cluricaun is likely to imitate the householder and consume excessive quantities of the finest vintages, so that the winelover scratches his head in puzzlement at the number of empty bottles.

The worst problem with a cluricaun is that he may become a nasty type of drunk. In such instances the house is never free from the sound of breaking bottles, drunken shouts and songs, and the general tumult as the cluricaun blunders around the cellar. There is no way to control a cluricaun and the only solution is for the homeowner to abjure strong liquors and cut off the cluricaun's source of supply. After a period of abstinence the cluricaun will soon seek more hospitable quarters.

Da Duku

This large lizard of the Andaman Islands (*Varinadae salvator* or Indian monitor lizard) was once the only inhabitant of the islands until the appearance of the civet cat. Da Duku found the civet cat so attractive that he married her. Their offspring, who could swim and climb as nimbly as the lizard, and were as skilled in hunting as the cat, developed into the human population of the islands. They pay tribute to their lizard ancestor by tattooing themselves, in an attempt to reproduce the beautiful and elaborate patterns of his skin.

Dama Dagenda

The jungle spirits of Papua New Guinea. They resent human intrusion into their jungle habitat and inflict painful sores and ulcers upon invaders. They understand the languages of all the human tribes who live in their region but ignore any pleas for safe conduct through the jungle. The only way to escape attack by the dama dagenda is to ask a witch doctor to teach you a language which they do not understand. You must then sing or talk loudly to yourself in this language as you progress through the jungle. The dama dagenda waste time in trying to work out what you are saying, and by the time they have decided that you are tricking them you should be beyond their reach.

Dogs

Most members of the canine family are such hearty extroverts that they are not favoured for thaumaturgy or the Black Arts, although there have been some notable exceptions. The bull terrier Articroak, who lived with the notorious witch Ailinn of Penzance, often appeared in the form of a seal and stole some of the catch of local fishermen. His guilt was proven when, in canine form, he showed a liking for cooked mackerel.

The Greeks and Romans did not even consider dogs to be worthy of sacrifice. Some backwards tribes of Asia Minor employed dogs as scapegoats, to be loaded with the community's sins at the turn of the year and driven into the wilderness, but dogs are not generally favoured for this purpose because they are liable to find their way home again and return the sins to their owners.

Most famous of underground dogs is Cerberus, the three-headed dog who guards the entrance to Hell. He has to be placated with gifts of honey and barley cakes before he admits dead souls to their eternal home. But even Cerberus has his softer side, as Orpheus demonstrated when he charmed his way into the underworld by playing to Cerberus on his lyre.

Of all the canine family, the various breeds of hound are most useful as instruments of revenge or retribution. (Although the Hound of the Baskervilles is a purely fictional creature.) The Hounds of Heaven pursue sinners in order to drag them back to repentance, and if sinners escape the heavenly pack the Hounds of Hell take up the scent and never leave it until they have dragged a sinner screaming down to the underworld.

It is easy to distinguish between the two packs. The Hounds of Heaven have a bell-like cry which resounds through a sinner's soul, whereas the Hounds of Hell, with their fiery eyes and appalling fangs, may be heard yelping savagely in the distance but their cry fades into silence as they come closer to a victim.

In Sumatra the Rajah Guru, messenger of the gods, owns two hounds named Sordaudu and Auto Porburu. When it is time for a person to die the Rajah sends the two hounds to warn him and then to escort his soul to judgment.

The fairies of the Scottish Highlands own an enormous hound named Cusith. He is said to be as large as a bullock, dark green in colour, with feet as big as a mortal's and a long tail braided like a woman's plaits. Whenever his baying resounds over the moors the farmers lock up their women, because it is the mission of Cusith to round up human women and drive them to a fairy mound so that they may supply milk for fairy children.

Dwarfs

A race of small men and women sometimes confused with gnomes. There should be no difficulty in distinguishing between the two races because gnomes are perfectly formed while dwarfs have twisted bodies, big heads and gnarled faces.

Dwarfs normally live underground but emerge from time to time to celebrate various festivities such as weddings and anniversaries. They are wary of mankind but when the weather is inclement they may occupy men's homes in order to enjoy their festivities in comfort. In such instances the householder and his family are always welcome to join in, but if they reject the invitation the dwarfs will inevitably bring ill fortune on the dwelling and its occupants.

Dwarfs are particularly skilful miners, metallurgists, and metalworkers, with magical powers which enable them to find the richest veins of precious metals and work them into every kind of weapon or artefact. One well-known example of dwarf craftsmanship is the Ring of Odin, made for the wife of Thor, which bestows perpetual wealth upon its wearer. The dwarfs also work in base metals and they have made numerous magic swords and spears, possibly including Excalibur.

Miners sometimes meet dwarfs when they break through into one of their underground workshops, or into a seam which a gang of dwarf miners is exploiting. If the human miners exchange the proper courtesies the little men with their picks and hammers do not resent these accidental meetings. They may even help the miners to a rich discovery.

Dwarfs have a strong ability to foretell the future (Futuresight) although they never employ this for commercial purposes and rarely if ever use it for the benefit of mankind. They do not have any written language and pass on their craft knowledge through apprentice dwarfs, who may have to spend centuries in learning the magical properties locked into the hearts of base or precious minerals.

Doppelganger

The shadow-self which accompanies each of us wherever he or she may go. Unlike an ordinary shadow, which is cast by the sun or any other light, a doppelganger is invisible to human eyes except those of its owner and is not reflected in a mirror or similar surfaces.

A doppelganger always stands exactly behind its owner, and always moves so swiftly that, no matter how quickly you turn your head, it always dodges out of sight. There is no particular reason why it should be so shy,

since it always imitates your movements precisely, echoes your voice so promptly that its tones fade into your own, and assumes your facial expressions. Researchers can only theorise that if you were able to see and hear yourself imitated so exactly you might be overwhelmed by shame, and a normal doppelganger does not like to embarrass its owner.

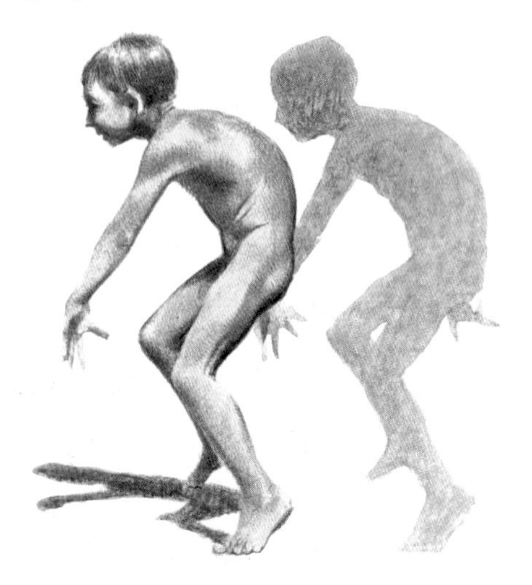

A doppelganger's function is to provide sympathetic company. One never need to feel truly alone, because a doppelganger is always prepared to listen carefully, to answer questions by imprinting the replies within one's mind, and, by a kind of physical osmosis, to guide one's actions. For example, a doppelganger often moves quickly enough to prevent one from taking a dangerous step out into moving traffic.

Dogs and cats have an instinctive ability to see doppelgangers. When a cat suddenly looks wide-eyed over your shoulder, it has seen your doppelganger. When a dog runs barking after you, it has been perturbed by the sight of your shadow-self imitating every step. Old people are often conscious of their doppelgangers and may be heard conversing with them.

The only danger from doppelgangers is when one of them is affected by malice or mischief. Then, it may decide to act of its own accord. Sometimes this is of minor consequence, since the doppelganger will simply make itself visible for a little while, and cause your friends to swear they saw you in places where you were not physically present. But a malicious doppelganger may commit crimes of which you will be accused, or, even worse, assume a personality different from your own. In such cases you will never know a moment's peace. Your doppelganger will constantly urge you to do, think, and say things foreign to your true nature, put words into your mouth, affect your hearing, and spur you into dangerous activities. A person with an unruly doppelganger is greatly to be pitied.

Echo

A nymph of the Oread family, who inhabit mountain caves and grottoes. The great god Zeus, who enjoys nothing better than the seduction of a comely nymph, persuaded her to act as his co-conspirator in this pastime. His wife Hera became suspicious of his frequent absences from Olympus, but whenever she descended to earth in the hope of trapping Zeus in the arms of a nymph she was distracted by Echo. Following the instructions of Zeus, Echo would sing, gossip, and chatter loudly, until Hera could hardly remember why she had come down to earth.

But Hera eventually understood the reason for Echo's behaviour, and she condemned the nymph to perpetual silence except for repeating the last word she had heard. While Echo was suffering this punishment she met the beautiful youth Narcissus and they fell in love at first sight, but poor Echo could not respond to his ardent declarations of love except by imitating the last word of each sentence. Narcissus thought she mocked him and went angrily away.

Echo returned to one of the mountain caverns where her family lives, and nursed her grief until she died of a broken heart. Her bones turned to mountain stone but her love for Narcissus was so great that her voice lives on, still hoping to be able to reply to him.

One may still hear her hopeful cry among the mountains, but it can do no more than repeat the last word uttered in the locality.

Elder Trees, Old Lady of the

Elder trees (*Sambucus niger*) of which different varieties flourish throughout the northern hemisphere, have vigorous magical powers. The flowers, berries, and even the wood itself may be used as the basis for a number of unguents and potions in both black and white magic. The stake which must be driven through a vampire's heart to put an end to his or her depredations, should ideally be made from the trunk of an elder sapling. Possibly the tree's magical powers derive from the fact that Judas Iscariot hanged himself from an elder tree, but they are certainly perpetuated by the Old Lady of the Elder Trees whose spirit lives within each and every one of the elder family. She comes from Denmark, the original home of elder trees, and soon spread to many parts of the world. In Germany, her presence is recognised by the custom of doffing one's hat in the presence of an elder tree.

She is rarely seen by humans except in spring, when a grove of elders is smothered with its crests of white flowerlets, or in autumn when the ripe black berries hang heavily from the boughs. Those who have seen her, usually in the light of a rich harvest moon, describe her as a hobbling little creature dressed in a gown as black as elderberries, with a cap and shawl as white and lacey as the flowers. She supports herself with a gnarled stave cut from an elder branch.

It is particularly unlucky to use the wood of an elder tree for any purpose other than magic wands or similar artefacts. A baby placed in a cradle made from elder wood will never thrive; household furniture made from the timber will soon warp and collapse; and a house with roof beams of elder timber will never know good fortune.

But if anyone is obliged to use elder wood, for lack of any other material, there is a way to neutralise the Old Lady's spells. When cutting wood from the tree, one should say 'Old Lady of the Elder Trees, please give me some of your wood, and when I grow into a tree you may have some of mine.'

Elves

Spirits of the wild woodland, who live mainly in northern Europe. Elves are miniature reproductions of mankind, but a good deal handsomer and better made. A female elf is so extremely beautiful that a human male who glimpses her will spend the rest of his life seeking hopelessly for a maiden of equal beauty.

Elf society is organised on traditional lines. They have an Elf King, whom they serve faithfully, and hereditary officials and aristocrats, but the character of each elfin community differs between one country and another. The elves of Germany are sometimes helpful to humans but occasionally malicious, so that the Germans treat them very cautiously. The elves of England are full of benevolence and kindness and they like nothing better than the doing of good deeds for friendly humans.

Elves possess great wisdom, and the power of seeing into the future, but they are far from solemn in nature. They revel in festive occasions and enjoy dancing all night until the first cockcrow heralds the sun, when they vanish instantly and leave nothing but their footprints in the dew-wet grass.

Men should never venture close to elves dancing in the moonlight. A mortal man who sees the supreme beauty of elf maidens dancing will be so bewitched that he must join in their circle. When they vanish at cockcrow he will disappear with them.

Fairies

Also known as the Little People, the Green Men, the Good Folk, the Lordly Ones, and by many other synonyms and euphemisms. An international community of immortal beings who originated in Italy, where they were known as Fatae. When Roman civilisation spread through other countries the Fatae went along with the Roman emigrants and settled throughout the same territories. In France, the name Fatae was corrupted to *fée*. When the Romans invaded Britain the *fées* accompanied them and were known by that name for some centuries until it was Anglicised as 'fays', which the countryfolk eventually changed into 'fairies'.

Fairies never managed to settle in Greece because the nymphs and dryads soon drove them out, but they spread eastwards, from Roman settlements in the Middle East, into many parts of Asia. During the last four centuries they have accompanied emigrants from Europe to North America, Australia,

and other parts of the New World. In Britain and Ireland they live everywhere except in the counties of Cornwall, Devon, and Somerset. They settled there soon after the Roman occupation but soon clashed with the original inhabitants, the pixies. During the reign of King Arthur the pixies fought the fairies in a great battle and drove them east of the River Pedder.

The function of the original fairies, the Fatae, was to appear in a household soon after a birth and bestow various gifts upon the newborn child. If the baby's relations treated them with extreme tact and sensitivity they donated such gifts as beauty, tranquillity, and loving kindness. But if any of the Fatae took offence at her reception she would balance these benefits by some taboo or embargo which affected the child for the rest of its life. In extreme cases, an offended Fatae might afflict adult members of the family with baldness, deafness, rheumatism, or other physical problems.

Fairies throughout the centuries have continued this original function, but they have also expanded their activities very widely into other types of meddling in human affairs.

A fairy, whether male or female, usually assumes the form of a perfect miniature human. Those who have seen them say they are 'As high as a small man's knee' or 'About as high as a dog's head.' They may, however, increase or decrease this size at will, to shrink to the size of an acorn or grow to the stature of a human adult.

Contrary to popular belief, fairies do not possess the power of invisibility. Birds, horses, dogs, cattle, and all other animals except humans see them clearly. But humans see fairies only between two blinks of an eye, so that one may catch only fleeting glimpses of the fairy folk.

There are, however, some exceptions to this general rule. One is when the fairies themselves use their magical power (known as 'glamour') to enable a mortal to see a fairy troop or individual. Another occurs during certain seasons or phases of the moon—for example a full moon on Midsummer Eve. On such occasions a mortal may see fairy dances or other celebrations, but if he watches too closely they may punish him with moon-sickness. A third exception is caused by the use of a self-bored stone, i.e. a stone in which a hole has been made by tumbling in the waters of a brook. (Self-bored stones found on sea beaches are not suitable.) If a mortal holds such a stone to his eye and looks through the hole he will see fairies distinctly.

There are two distinct species of the fairy family: the Troop Fairy and the Solitary Fairy. The former live in troops or *fatara* whereas the latter always live alone. Troop Fairies wear a green livery, sometimes embellished with a red cap ornamented with a white feather, while Solitary Fairies dress entirely in red.

Troop Fairies live inside hollow hills or in the great mounds of earth, known as barrows or tumuli, which prehistoric tribes erected either as forts or as monuments to dead chieftains. Mortals are strongly advised to avoid these after dark, especially during a full moon.

The notion that there is a separate habitat known as Fairyland is erroneous. Fairies co-exist with us in our own world, which is fairyland enough for all who have eyes to see its magical beauty.

Troop Fairies who joined human migrations to the New World commonly choose natural features with some resemblance to the tumuli or barrows as their residence. As in Europe, they tend to retreat within them during the cold winter months and emerge again during spring. Fairy signs are often sighted in the New World. The Aborigines of Australia say that the swirls of dust seen along bush tracks are infallible indications of a fairy army on the march.

Fairy society is organised along much the same lines as that of mortals but may be generally described as matriarchal. Each community of Troop Fairies is ruled by a Fairy Queen. There is also a king, although he might be more truly described as a consort because he does not have the same powers as a queen. The entire fairy race is governed by Queen Titania and Prince Oberon, whose court is located somewhere near Stratford-on-Avon in England, but they rule with a very light hand and leave most of the work to the queens of the various troops. Titania is a strictly moral person but Oberon is an ardent lover who spreads his favours widely among fairy and mortal maidens.

There is an annual international conference of queens but it is not a very serious function. The delegates spend much of the time in gossiping, singing, and telling new stories about the foolishness of mortals.

Fairy queens and their attendants are very fashion-conscious and they dress in elaborate costumes of fabrics woven from the finest spider-silk and spangled with dewdrop sequins. A peculiarity of these garments is that, whenever a queen appears to a mortal, they cannot be touched or even felt by human hands.

Each community of Troop Fairies has a number of craftsmen, who make all the artefacts required and sell them at the regular fairy markets. Solitary Fairies attend these markets to sell material such as the spider-silk which they have collected, or the shoes and other items they make in their lonely haunts. The currency used in the markets is fairy gold, which vanishes if it is touched by human hands.

The queens maintain strict discipline in their troops and have supreme powers of enchantment. Whenever a queen has occasion to punish a rebellious fairy she sends him or her into exile, with orders not to return until some specific task has been performed. The queens are capricious ladies and so these tasks may either be beneficial to mankind or quite mischievous in purpose. She may tell a fairy to ensure that a farmer's cows always render creamy milk, or to stop the church bells ringing on a Sunday morning.

Occasionally a fairy cannot perform a task, either because he or she takes pity on a mortal or is insufficiently versed in enchantment. In such instances a male usually chooses to become a Solitary Fairy. A female finds a different way out of the predicament.

She places herself in the path of some unfortunate mortal male and causes him to see her in full human form. A man will fall instantly in love with a fairy maiden and so he takes her home to be his bride.

Such marriages always end tragically. A fairy bride is a hopeless housekeeper and an overly fastidious lover. She yearns for the carefree life of her troop and she is terrified by the need to attend church with her husband, because fairies cannot be Christians and they pay homage only to the Old Religion. As soon as a child is born she runs away with it before it can be baptised and returns to her fairy home. The queen forgives her because marriage to a mortal male has been punishment enough, and the child is reared as a fairy.

Fairies are often regarded as flimsy and insubstantial creatures, but in fact the males are heroic warriors who guard the habitats against invasion by goblins, pixies, and similar creatures of the ground and underground. A battalion of fairy soldiers armed with swords and spears is a match for any number of goblins.

Most fairies are vegetarians, who enjoy a wide and varied diet. They eat honey, cheese, the eggs of many types of birds, berries, fruit, grain, and all types of garden produce. They are particularly fond of cake. They do not like milk, which they find too thick for their taste, and generally drink dew or spring water. Occasionally they distil a kind of nectar from blossoms, but on the whole they find that the fact of being a fairy is intoxicating enough.

The problem is that they are too impatient to be gardeners or agriculturists. Their need to gather food, now that so much of the wild country has been tamed, brings them into frequent conflict with farmers, beekeepers, gardeners, orchardists, and other mortal toilers. But fairy morality is generally that of 'One good (or bad) turn deserves another.' If a mortal allows them a small portion of his crop they do everything they can to help him. They guide the bees to pollinate fruit blossoms, frighten the caterpillars away from cabbage leaves, and help seedlings find their way to the surface. But if a mortal resents the payment of tribute to the fairies they will torment him unmercifully.

Fairies are not good cooks and so they like to make off with some of a housewife's baking. The best way to prevent them from taking too much is to mark most of the bread and cakes with a cross.

Unfortunately the goodwill of fairies may be just as embarrassing as their malice. There is a well-documented case of a fairy troop which decided to help a friendly farmer by bringing in his wheat harvest. He was astonished to find that his entire harvest had been reaped and stored overnight, but on subsequent nights the fairies also reaped the harvest of all his neighbours and stored it in his barns. He had great difficulty in talking himself out of this demonstration of fairy generosity.

Fairy attitudes towards humans range from dangerous mischief to an earnest desire to help and please. The latter quality is shown when fairies reveal themselves as mini-females with gossamer wings, carrying magic wands, simply to conform with human beliefs. In fact, they do not need to fly, because fairies have the power of vertical and horizontal levitation, and they do not need wands. Fairy magic, properly called 'glamour' after the old Scottish word *glamerye*, operates through a kind of thought power which mortals cannot understand.

Fairy malice usually arises out of lack of understanding. They are so graceful, sensitive, and tactful that they cannot comprehend the clumsiness and stupidity of human beings. All other animals are careful not to trouble fairies but a mortal may go blundering through a fairy market without even seeing it, or tramp noisily over a hill containing a community of Troop Fairies. The fairies feel that men should have enough sensitivity to know when they are offending in such ways and punish them accordingly. Punishments may range from the infliction of bad dreams to severe curses which prevent a man from tasting his food, or to subtle tricks such as that of Fairy Gold.

This is a confidence trick in which a man becomes convinced, with fairy encouragement, that he knows the location of buried treasure. He follows a trail through the forest until he sees the gold gleaming in the moonlight, and shovels it into a sack with gleeful certainty that he is rich. But as he carries the sack home it becomes lighter and lighter, and when he opens it again it contains nothing but dead leaves.

Fairies have a gossipy interest in human love affairs and are sometimes tempted to intervene. If they approve they do all they can to help the happy couple, but if they feel a mortal lad and lass to be unsuited to each other they may attempt to break up the courtship. They become extremely angry with faithless lovers and commonly punish the males with baldness and females with toothlessness.

Fairy curiosity often leads to misunderstandings. They like to inspect human artefacts very carefully, and may take some possession away to be discussed by the rest of the troop. Normally they return it, but not necessarily to the place where they found it. A human searching for some misplaced item should never allow himself such remarks as 'Them dratted fairies have been and made off with my pitchfork!' or they are certain to be offended.

The most serious anti-human activity practised by fairies is that of stealing beautiful babies and putting changelings in their cradles. The reason for these thefts is still unknown. It may be that the fairies cannot resist the beauty of the babies and want them for their own. One theory is that they need humans, who will be brought up under a perpetual enchantment, to help them with such heavy labour as grinding wheat for flour and baking the bread. Another is that they have to give hostages to the devil so that he will not interfere with them.

Fairies like to join in mortal festivities and assume human form for this purpose. Their vanity is such that they usually appear as handsome blond youths, or beautiful blonde girls, to take part in the revels, but they sometimes betray themselves by some unfamiliarity with human customs. A mortal

who notices this would be wise not to mention it. Fairy sensitivity would inevitably prompt a revenge for the insult, whereas a tactful mortal who ignores some clumsiness is likely to be rewarded.

Fairies have no difficulty in communicating with mortals. They speak their own language, which sounds like a mixture between the twittering of blackbirds, the prattle of a stream, and the murmur of a breeze through the forest, but they also speak and understand the language of a host country together with the language previously spoken in that region, such as Latin, Celtic, Gaelic, Teutonic, Pictic, or old Scots.

There is a fallacious belief in 'good fairies' and 'bad fairies'. In fact, fairies are neither good nor bad. Like humans they vary in mood and temperament but on the whole they are genial, festive creatures who desire only to be left in peace to pursue the lifestyle they have fashioned over many centuries, and the functions appointed to them since the foundation of the Cosmos. They only reveal their more sinister aspects when they are affronted by the brutality and stupidity of human beings.

Fauns

The spirits of agricultural fertility, probably related to the deity Faunus. They are sometimes confused with Pan and even with the satyrs, because sighting reports mention them as having the characteristics of both men and beasts. It seems probable, however, that fauns are much prettier and more graceful creatures than the shaggy satyrs or Pan with his goatish extremities. A faun is more likely to have the legs, tail, and ears of a deer with the body and face of a handsome youth: smooth-skinned on the torso and arms and smooth-haired on the legs.

Their ancestor Faunus is credited with the invention of the shawm, a kind of flute, and the fauns are expert with this instrument. Nymphs have no fear of fauns, who are gentle harmless creatures, and a band of nymphs and fauns dancing together to the music of shawms is a pretty sight. Unfortunately the music often attracts a troop of satyrs, who come galloping up to seize the nymphs while the fauns scatter into the forest.

Farmers and winegrowers like to have a resident faun on their properties. He is no menace to their womenfolk, makes an interesting conversation piece, and is a beneficial influence on the fertility of grain and grapes. There is a danger, however, that the enchanting notes of a faun's shawm will tempt an agriculturist's daughters out to dance naked in the moonlight.

Fomorians

In Scotland a race of giants; in Ireland a race of evil demons. In both countries they were the original occupants of the land, who had to be subdued by any invaders.

The Partholons, who were the first to invade Ireland, fought many bloody battles against the Fomorians but could not defeat them, and eventually died in a kind of biological warfare when the Fomorians afflicted them all with plague. They were followed by the Nemeds, who lost their very first battle against the demons. The Fomorians enslaved them and forced them to pay an annual tribute of cattle and children.

Successive waves of invaders included the Fir Bolga, who managed to subdue the Fomorians and live peacefully with them on the island. When the Tuatha conquered the Fir Bolga, they dealt more subtly with the Fomorians. They made friends with them and even married some of the demons, but when the Fomorians allowed themselves to relax the Tuatha set upon them and slaughtered the entire community.

The Fomorians of Scotland were a less warlike race than those of Ireland. Despite their giant stature they offered little resistance to invasion and gradually allowed themselves to be absorbed by their conquerors, which may be the reason for the size and strength of many Scotsmen of the present day.

Gin Seng

The Man-Plant whose root often displays the physical characteristics of a human male. It has two legs, a strong body, rudimentary arms, and an appendage resembling the male sexual organ. The head consists of the stalk and leaves which appear above the ground.

The aristocracy of the Middle Kingdom, who were ardent lovers, were the first to discover that a drug prepared from the Man-Plant enabled them to satisfy an endless series of concubines. The value of each plant depended upon the size of its penile lookalike. A Man-Plant which was particularly well-endowed, with a rooty phallus almost as long as its legs, sold for its own weight in gold to the doctors who prepared the drug. The skill and knowledge required for preparation of the aphrodisiac meant that it could be afforded only by emperors, mandarins, war lords and wealthy merchants.

Originally the most powerful Man-Plants grew wild in Manchuria, but the demand was so heavy that the plant became an endangered species. The imperial court at Peking, perturbed by the prospect of waning virility, forbade the harvesting of Man-Plants until they could be artificially cultivated. Korea, the Land of the Morning Calm, adopted Man-Plant cultivation as an industry and the phallic powder is now freely available, at a price appropriate to those males who believe that the Man-Plant's rooty rigidity will have beneficial effects upon their amorous abilities.

Gnomes

The international family of gnomes dates back to the era when the form of the globe consolidated out of Chaos, and the forces responsible for precious and base metals and precious stones implanted them beneath the surface of the earth. Unlike men, gnomes learn from the past and they also have the ability to predict and learn from the future. Their name derives from the Greek word *gignosko*, meaning 'to learn, understand', and the principal gnome characteristic is an acute understanding of every aspect of the Cosmos.

Gnomes are about twelve centimetres tall and formed in proportion. They resemble the original people of their host country, so that a Beijing gnome is Chinese in appearance, a Hairy Peruvian gnome resembles a native of Peru, and so on. Apart from their small size, a notable difference between gnomes and humans is their expression of ageless good humour. They lack the human facility for worrying, practise therapeutic festivity, and consequently live for several hundred years.

Gnome character is helpful and benign. *Gignosko* provides them with insight into the spirits of all animate and inanimate creatures and objects, so that they find it easy to influence and co-operate with trees, tools, animals, plants, and every other creation of the Cosmos and its inhabitants.

Their diet is largely vegetarian, basically cereals and root vegetables, although they consume great quantities of chutney and sausages during their festivities. They brew excellent ale but use it in moderation except in some festivals. Gnomes pioneered many crafts, such as weaving and woodworking, but they have not felt disposed to explore more complex technologies. They live in simple comfort and avoid the problems of industrialisation.

Their original duty was that of supervising and surveying the mineral treasures of the earth. Each group of family looked after a lode of copper, a vein of gold, a pipe of diamonds, a seam of coal, or some similar resource implanted underground. Each gnome colony lived underground, close to their particular area of responsibility. To facilitate their work they developed the ability to move or 'swim' through the earth.

Their helpful nature inspired them to assist men in discovering natural treasures, in such ways as guiding the feet of prospectors and influencing the science of geology, even though *gignosko* warned them that men would use these treasures for evil as well as good. But even their gift of prediction, or 'future mining', could not foresee the unending extent of human avarice and its consequences.

As men delved deeper into the earth countless gnomes found themselves displaced. Clumsy miners wrecked entire colonies and the roar of explosions made life unbearable. Some gnomes turned against the miners, and began a kind of guerrilla warfare by pulling away pitprops, diverting underground streams into adits, and other contrivances. But the majority decided to emigrate to the surface and begin a new existence in the light of day.

The first surface gnomes (unkindly known as 'superficial gnomes' by their underground brethren) emerged into the forests of Britain and Europe at about the time of King Arthur. They found the dimness of the huge forests compatible with their underground nature, and established colonies in the root systems of great trees.

As time passed, their benign character tempted them to aid in human affairs. The little milkmaid weary of her task would find all the milk pails filled before she rose in the morning, the sleeping shepherd awoke to find his flock had been rounded up for him, and many a poor tailor or shoemaker prospered when gnome families worked night shifts in their workshops.

Humans often glimpsed the gnomes but never succeeded in capturing one. *Gignosko* always keeps gnomes a step ahead of humans and the most cunning of gnome traps never tempted a victim. Eventually humans simply accepted their presence and knew that gnomes would not harm them.

Gnome lifestyles changed yet again when humans felled the forests just as they had looted the earth. Gnomes had to retreat further and further away from the homes of men, and they are now seen only in the few

remaining forests of Britain and Europe. In other parts of the world, gnomes have adapted themselves in various ways. Some still try to assist humans by imparting some of their own gift of understanding. A few have turned mischievous, like their cousins the gremlins, and they torment humans with minor but irritating activities. Other gnome families, like the Leprignomes of Ireland and the Hairy Peruvians of South Australia, have travelled as far as Australia in search of a new life.

Goblins

Gnomes, pixies, gremlins, elves, and leprechauns hate to be confused with goblins. Fairies become extremely angry when goblins are portrayed as their companions. They are all spirits of the earth but they have no more than a slight family connection with goblins.

Goblins originated in France, which they entered through a cleft in the Pyrenees. Once they had a foothold they spread rapidly over Europe and they entered Britain as stowaways aboard the first dragon-ship of the Vikings. In Britain the Druids called them 'Robin Goblin', later abbreviated to 'hobgoblin'.

Like other earth spirits they have human form, but no human ever wore expressions of such malicious mischief and depraved cunning. A goblin smile curdles the blood; a goblin laugh causes milk to sour and fruit to fall from the trees. Even a witch will not allow a goblin at her fireside. She has no fear of it but it is always such a meddling nuisance.

Fortunately, a goblin's capacity for mischief is limited. Unlike their distant cousins the gremlins they cannot be bothered to learn about tools and machinery. Their only real abilities are luck-spoiling, and weaving nightmares to be inserted into the ear of a sleeper. They do like, however, to torment humans in such ways as tipping over pails of milk, hiding hen's eggs, blowing soot down chimneys, puffing out candles in haunted houses, and altering signposts.

Goblins have some facility with design, but it is limited to gargoyles and depictions of serpents, dragons, and basilisks. They can communicate with flies, wasps, mosquitoes, and hornets, and their favourite summer pastime is to direct these insects towards warm-blooded creatures such as humans and horses and watch the results.

They pester horses in the stable or the field, and a sure sign of goblin presence is the sound of a horse blowing or stamping in an effort to get rid of them, or rolling in the sand to scratch them off his back.

Goblins have no homes. They infest mossy clefts in rocks and the surface roots of ancient trees but they are too capricious to settle down for long. The squeals and titters of a goblin gang as they plot some fresh mischief should serve as a warning to any human to keep well clear of them.

Gorgons

Researchers in gorgonology are uncertain as to how many of these creatures existed—or may still exist. Some say there was only one gorgon. Others name at least three of them: Medusa the Queen; Stheno the Mighty; and Euryale the Far-Springer. There is equal disagreement as to whether they are creatures of earth, of the underground, or even of the air. Gorgons do have wings but no one has ever seen a gorgon in flight, and so the wings may be merely decorative or rudimentary appendages.

The basic problem in gorgonology is that anyone who looks into a gorgon's eyes is instantly turned into stone. There is a strong possibility that some of the innumerable stone figures of men and women excavated in countries of the Mediterranean region, and commonly regarded as statues, are in fact the calcified remains of gorgon-watchers.

It appears, however, that a gorgon has the body of a human female, with a large head having a round face, flat nose, large protruding teeth, and a lolling tongue. These characteristics may not be very different from some other types of monsters (or even some humans) but the infallible sign of a gorgon is that her hair consists of a tangled mass of snakes.

A peculiarity of the three gorgon sisters is that Medusa was mortal whereas Stheno and Euryale are immortal. Medusa was killed by Perseus, who decided that a gorgon's head would make an unusual wedding present for King Polydectes.

Perseus found that the only reliable guides to a gorgon habitat were the Graeae, three old women who had only one eye and one tooth between them. The Graeae normally refused to betray the gorgons, but Perseus solved this problem by stealing their tooth and eye and refusing to return them until the old women revealed the secret.

Armed with a magic sickle, he evaded the calcifying glance of the gorgons by polishing his shield to mirror brightness and using it as a kind of periscope. In this way he was able to approach Medusa and cut off her head with one blow. No doubt he would have fallen victim to her sisters, but as she died the winged horse Pegasus sprang from her blood and he was able to mount this steed and escape.

But when Perseus took Medusa's head to

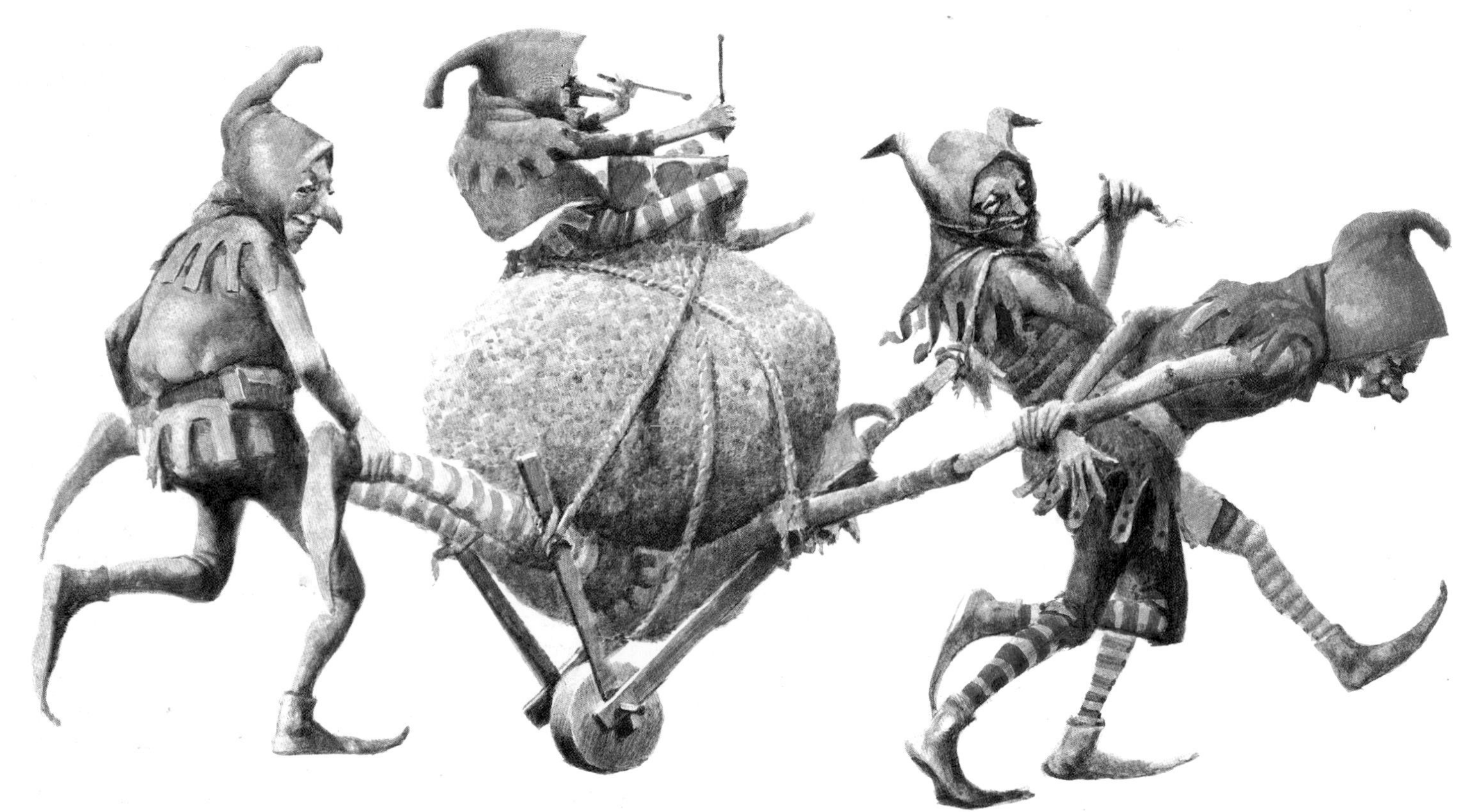

Polydectes he found that the king was persecuting his mother. Instead of presenting the head to the king he held it up so that Polydectes looked into its eyes, and even in death the power of a gorgon is so great that Polydectes turned to stone. Perseus later disposed of the head by presenting it to Athene.

Gorgonologists say that a serpentine lock of gorgon hair is an infallible protection against the evil eye, but gorgon hair is now virtually impossible to obtain because the whereabouts of Stheno and Euryale is unknown.

Grain Gods and Guardians

The donors and protectors of the cereal crops which nourish mankind. Different regions have different types of gods and guardians. Some actually created the various cereals, some protect them against evil spirits which would wither the standing grain, while another variety destroys insects and animals which would plunder a farmer's crops.

The goddess Demeter gave the first seeds of wheat to mankind and taught Triptolemus how to cultivate the soil and make bread from the grain. He acted as her missionary and spread the art of wheatgrowing around the countries of the Mediterranean, assisted by such deities as Adoni, who actually lived within each grain of wheat growing in Phoenicia; Ceres, who changes the wheat from green to gold; and Flora who protects it against crop diseases.

Even as the green tide of wheat began to creep across Europe and Asia, the gods of other countries created different types of grain. In North America the Master of the Winds gave corn to his son Iosheka, who taught the Huron and Iroquois tribes the art of growing the golden cobs. In Asia, various gods bestowed the gift of rice upon their worshippers. Inari, the Japanese god of rice, still nurtures and protects the crops. He is a benign old gentleman, smiling and calm, whose throne is a sack of rice. He is attended by two foxes who carry his instructions to the farmers. A farmer who sees a fox slinking through his rice paddy should never chase it away, because it may be one of Inari's messengers inspecting the progress of the crop.

Several gods influence the grain harvests of China. Prince Liu, their leader, is general overseer of millet, rice, wheat, barley, sorghum, and corn. Hu Shen protects the crops against hail and General Pa Sha fights off the hordes of locusts which attack green grain. Other gods play their parts during the seasons of ploughing, sowing, and harvesting, while the Princess Tien Hou ensures an ample supply of rain.

European farmers depend upon a number of beings for the welfare of their cereal crops. In northern Europe, invisible packs of wheat-dogs or rye-dogs guard the grainfields and chase away evil spirits. These guardians are so lightfooted they can run across the top of standing grain, but their presence is betrayed when great ripples pass over a field of wheat. Some people think this effect is caused by the wind but the real reason is a pack of sentinel dogs chasing evil spirits away from the grain.

Poleviks and poludnitsa keep a close eye on the enormous grainfields of Russia. Poleviks are creatures of semi-human appearance, with hair and beards as green as young wheat, while poludnitsa are handsome young women with hair as golden as wheat straw. Both these personalities will punish intruders onto a farmer's property, and even deal harshly with lazy farmers who do not give proper attention to their crops.

In England, where wheat is known as corn, each farm has an individual Corn Spirit. She appears when the first green shoots probe through the soil and thereafter lives with the ripening grain, encouraging its growth and helping to ripen the kernels. At harvest time, when the harvesters cut the golden corn and stack it into sheaves, she retreats from one patch to another until at last there is only enough corn standing to make one final sheaf. The harvesters approach it with reverence, because the sickle which cuts the last sheaf may also kill the Corn Spirit, but when the last crisp stalks have fallen the harvesters fashion them into a Corn Dolly and keep it until the following year. In due course the Corn Spirit emerges from the Corn Dolly and starts her work again.

Green Man, The

A malign spirit of the English countryside. There seems some doubt as to whether he appears in the form of a naked man with green flesh or whether he is composed of timber, with tree trunks for legs and body and leafy branches for arms. Some people claim to have heard him blundering through the woods with a sound like leaves rustling and branches breaking, but others dismiss this story and say that the sounds were no more than a storm blowing through the treetops. It is perhaps more likely that the Green Man flits among dense timber, camouflaged by his colour, and seizes his chance to fall upon woodcutters or gamekeepers. Fortunately he is a fairly timid creature, and although he may be distinctly sensed in any deep woodland he never pounces unless he is certain he will not be seen.

Possibly he is related to the Apple Tree Man, although this creature has a very different character. He lives in one of the trees of an apple orchard and supervises the blossoming and ripening of the fruit. A treasure lies beneath any tree in which the Apple Tree Man takes up his abode, and occasionally a foolish orchardist roots out all his trees in search of it. But by the time he reaches the tree in which the Apple Tree Man was living the orchard spirit has taken fright and departed for another orchard, taking his treasure with him.

Gremlins

Mischievous minor spirits of tools and machinery, distantly related to both gnomes and goblins. Like gnomes, they were once helpful to mankind. They could make tools work faster and better, guide the hands of craftsmen and inspire new inventions. American gremlins helped Benjamin Franklin with his electrical experiments and a Scottish gremlin, Hector o' the Clyde, drew James Watts's attention to steam power by bouncing the lid of a boiling kettle up and down.

If humans had understood the importance of gremlin power in technological development then history might be different. Regrettably, most engineers and mechanics lacked insight into gremlinology and so they claimed credit for all new inventions without giving credit to the gremlins.

This insult soured gremlin attitudes towards mankind. Instead of helping, they now use their knowledge of the 'thingness' of tools and machinery to make life difficult for humans. They insert gremlin effect, known to technicians as GE, into all man-made tools and machinery.

In its simplest form, GE manifests itself in the sudden diversion of a hammer towards your thumb when you are driving a nail. Home handymen, who lack the confidence which weakens the powers of GE, are especially open to gremlin effect. When they attempt to saw through a plank, they find that GE has placed an intractable knot in the path of the saw. When they paint a ceiling, GE makes paint run down their arms.

Each household has an hereditary gremlin, which entered it as an occupant of a sewing-machine or some other household item. The gremlin holds down the lever of pop-up toasters so that toast burns instead of ejecting, chokes the fuel pipes of lawn-mowers, lets the air out of a car tyre when you are late for work, alters the hot and cold mixture when you are taking a shower, and inflicts similar minor torments on humans.

The first person to identify GE was Pilot Officer Prune of the Royal Air Force. During the second World War, he realised that the inevitable breakdown of machinery when it was most urgently required could not be blamed only on aircraft mechanics. On further investigation, he discovered that the main characteristic of GE is its action upon some very minor component. Skilful manifestation of GE ensures that a mechanic will take an engine to pieces before discovering that a fault could have been corrected by tightening a screw.

Hell

The interior of the globe is compartmentalised into a number of regions of eternal punishment, each belonging to an existing or now obsolete religion. (The fact that a religion has fallen out of fashion does not, of course, eliminate the places of eternal punishment for those who sinned against that religion.)

Each separate hell has a certain similarity to all the others. The principal differences between them are the types of punishment. Some hells have areas of ice as well as of fire (Frigido and Inferno) while others have regions of eternal darkness in which moaning sinners wander but never make contact with each other. The Underworld of Greece, ruled by Hades and Persephone, has a river of fire but it also has a dreary grey expanse in which wandering sinners must forever meditate upon their crimes.

The officiating demons within each hell wear different types of uniforms, carry a variety of instruments of torture, and appear in innumerable fearsome aspects, but on the whole they all have a strong family resemblance.

Variations between hells include the routes by which sinners enter them and the judges who assess their sins. The approach to some hells is simple and efficient. Most modern religions have streamlined the process so that a man's or woman's sins are computerised throughout a lifetime, and if a sinner exceeds a specific allowance then he or she will find himself abruptly translated from life into eternal torment with little chance of parole. Other methods, past and present, are a good deal more complex.

In China, two Soul Messengers come to fetch the soul of a dead person, but they first have to present their credentials to the Door Gods who ensure that their owner's time has come. The sinner then has to undergo interrogation by the God of Walls and Ditches, who may treat him quite kindly or administer a good beating. This ordeal is followed by appearances before a series of judges, each of whom executes a particular punishment before passing the sinner on to the next judge. If one judge ordains that a sinner should be torn to pieces by monsters, then the body is restored to its complete form before proceeding on to the next ordeal. There is some hope in sight, however, because the final judge will restore the sinner to earth in some form appropriate to his past crimes: perhaps as a worm, an ant, a dog, or even some more complex creature.

Some hells are much simpler than others. That of Fiji is occupied only by Rati-Mbati-Ndua, who deals expeditiously with sinners by crunching them up with his sharp single tooth. Other hells, such as that of New Zealand, are populated by a great hierarchy of demons and monsters who not only deal with dead sinners but also meddle with the

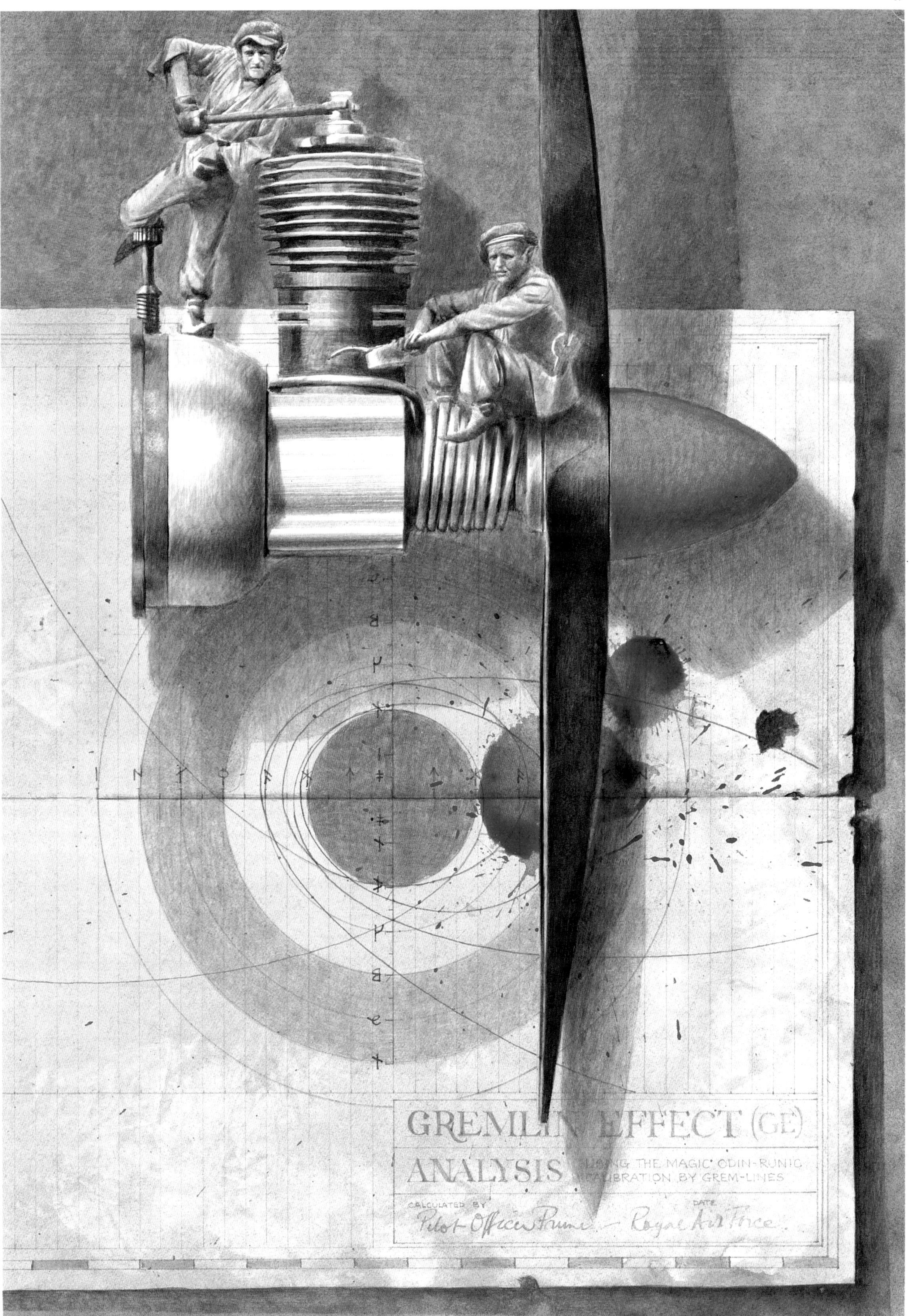
GREMLIN EFFECT (GE)
ANALYSIS
THE MAGIC ODIN-RUNIC
BY GREM-LINES
CALCULATED BY
DATE
Pilot Officer Prune — Royal Air Force

affairs of the living. The perpetual mystery is that sin still exists even though it is rewarded by such miserable destinies.

House Gods and House Spirits

Every edifice built by man has its own god or spirit, who takes up residence as soon as the building is completed and lives there as long as it is occupied by mankind. Occasionally such spirits remain in an empty or ruined building, and in such cases they become so lonely that they may cast a spell upon some passer-by and force him to live with them. The unhappy men and women who find shelter in derelict buildings are usually under the spell of house gods who no longer enjoy the warmth of family life, and have attracted equally lonely or abandoned people to live with them.

House gods very quickly take on the character of the family with whom they live. If the family is happy and prosperous, and pay due respect to their god of hearth and home, then the house god will be contented to do all he can to help them. If a family is lazy and quarrelsome then a house god adds to their misfortunes in such ways as weaving cobwebs in corners, leading insects into pantries, or boring holes in the roof.

People in modern society do not pay enough homage to house gods and consequently suffer many domestic misfortunes. The Romans always kept an altar close to the front door and decorated it with offerings of flowers, so that the resident house god would welcome them back into their homes and impart peace and tranquillity. In Russia, the house god Domovoi who lives under the doorstep, and his wife Domovikha who lives in the cellar, take a keen interest in their family's well-being. They appreciate occasional mentions of their names and respond by bringing happiness to a home. In Japan, a whole group of house gods looks after each family. There are gods of the kitchen, of the front door, of pots and pans, of the bathroom and toilet. A few grains of rice and a few drops of wine, sprinkled through the house on festival days, keep the gods contented and bring prosperity to the home.

The people of some countries perform elaborate rituals to their house gods, but these beings really ask very little of their hosts beyond recognition of their presence. Some small offering such as a vase of flowers kept in a special place, and dedicated to the spirit of the home, will keep a house god happy and ensure family contentment.

Jigoku

The underground hell of Japan, comprising eight regions of increasingly fierce fire and eight of ice and snow. It is the home of demons known as Oni, who have red and green bodies and horse heads. The Onis ride forth in chariots of fire in search of sinners, whom they carry back to Jigoku for judgment. Emma Hoo, the king of Jigoku, judges the male sinners while his sister judges the females. Each sinner has to stand before a mirror which reflects all his or her sins, and Emma Hoo or his sister decide upon the region of Jigoku which will receive the sinner for all eternity. The hellish couple are not totally devoid of mercy, however, and if they hear sufficient prayers from the living for the soul of a sinner they may lessen the punishment or arrange for rebirth and a chance to reform.

Kabigat

When the Philippine Islands were created at the beginning of the world they were completely flat. A great flood swept over them and washed away all the inhabitants except for the brother and sister Wigan and Bugan. These two saw that they had to re-populate the earth and their first son was Kabigat.

Kabigat felt the islands were unsatisfactory places to live on in their flat and featureless form and he set to work to make them more interesting. He dug out valleys and heaped the earth into mountains, thus creating the present geography of the Philippine Islands.

Kilyakai

These forest demons of Papua New Guinea bear some resemblance to the human tribespeople of the western highlands of that country, except that they are very small and as wizened as very old men. It is possible they are babies who have grown old without reaching adult stature, because the kilyakai reinforce their numbers by stealing babies and endowing them with demonic personalities.

The kilyakai also steal pigs, and cause various types of mischief including sickness. The debilitating and often deadly disease of malaria, which is endemic in Papua New Guinea, is caused by the kilyakai firing poisoned arrows at people walking through the jungle.

Kisin

The god of earthquakes who lives beneath the ground in southern Mexico and other parts of Central America. Like other gods and spirits of the earthquake he makes his presence known by roaring beneath the earth and shaking it violently, but unlike most of the others he also reigns over a specific portion of the underworld in which dead souls must reside before passing on to final judgment. From time to time, the number of dead souls in Kisin's kingdom accumulates to such a number that they try to overcome him and escape back to the freedom of upper earth. Kisin's battles with the army of the dead, who always lose such conflicts, are one of the reasons for earthquakes. When he has won a battle, and chased all the dead into another region of the underworld, his kingdom is quiet again except for his occasional warning roars at another accumulation of dead souls.

Knockers or Knackers

These helpful underground spirits first made themselves known at the time of the Phoenicians, who sailed from the eastern Mediterranean to Cornwall to barter their manufactured goods for tin, silver, copper, and lead. Before the arrival of the Phoenicians the Cornish miners had not had to delve very deeply into the ground before they found sufficient minerals for their own use, but the trade boom brought an escalation in demand and the miners had to dig deep shafts into the bowels of the earth.

Soon they heard mysterious knockings, which they thought to be the sound of tools from other miners working nearby. But experience taught them that the knocks either warned of impending disaster, in the form of a collapsing adit or drive, or were signals which led them to a rich vein of ore.

The miners quickly developed the science of knockology, and skilled knockologists could easily decipher the knocker's code which guided them in various directions or warned them to take care.

When the Cornish miners emigrated to various parts of the world they soon discovered that the knockers exist elsewhere, although they sometimes have slightly different names. In Australia, where the Cornish worked in the copper mines of South Australia, the knockers are known as knackers.

No one has ever caught more than a fleeting glimpse of a knocker. Occasionally a trickle of pebbles from an interstice in the rock will show where a knocker has quickly dodged out of sight, or a miner may see a pattern of tiny footsteps, which disappear even as he studies them, in the mud at the bottom of a shaft. A knocker is, however, believed to have some resemblance to a gnome.

Kobolds

Every household should have a kobold, who proves to be a most useful and faithful servant. These little men, with their wrinkled faces betraying extreme old age, work tirelessly for the home which shelters them. They carry water, milk the cows, collect the eggs, groom the horses, chop wood, and sweep the yard. Kobolds enjoy the chores of everyday living, and with a little practice they will work indoors as efficiently as in the garden or farmyard.

They ask little in return for their labours. The scraps from the dinner table make a good meal for a kobold, but if the housewife forgets to feed him he will take instant revenge. She will break dishes, burn her fingers, or trip over the mat, and the kobold's malicious chuckle will remind her that she has forgotten to feed him.

Leprechauns

Fairy cobblers who make shoes for fairies. The name may derive either from the Gaelic *luacharma'n*, meaning 'pigmy', or *leith brogan*, meaning 'maker of one shoe'. The latter interpretation seems the most likely because a leprechaun is never seen with more than one shoe in his possession. He hides the other one in case he has to escape quickly when a mortal sights him.

Leprechauns usually hibernate underground during the winter and emerge in summer, when the distant rhythmic tapping of their hammers may be heard floating over moors and meadows in a dreamy afternoon. Unlike other fairies a leprechaun may be seen quite easily by mortals. Those who have seen one describe him as a merry little fellow dressed in green, with a red cap, leather apron, and buckled shoes.

Leprechauns know the location of hidden treasure and are eagerly sought-after for that reason. A leprechaun may, however, be caught, but never held. As soon as a human tries to interrogate a trapped leprechaun he flings the contents of his snuffbox in the questioner's face, and when the human recovers from a bout of sneezing he finds that the leprechaun has disappeared.

Leshy

One of the multitude of wood spirits which inhabit forests in every part of the world. Some are malign, some merely mischievous, but their presence can always be felt. As one ventures deeper into a forest, with the thick canopy of branches filtering the sun into a green twilight and the tree trunks seeming to move in to prevent escape, the sense of being observed and followed grows increasingly strong. You may then be certain that a wood spirit is on your trail, but it is useless to swing round in the hope of glimpsing a pursuer. A wood spirit always moves faster than you can and dodges behind a tree trunk.

The leshy, who lives in the dark pine forests of the Baltic countries, resents invaders of his eerie fastness and punishes travellers by leading them astray. In the winter he moves behind them to brush their footprints out of the snow, so that they cannot retrace their steps. At other times of the year a leshy causes such bewilderment of the senses that every tree trunk looks alike, so that a wanderer strays deeper and deeper into the forest.

Foresters claim that the leshy is a skinny little creature with a blue skin and green hair and eyes. They say it is easy to break his spell by putting your shoes on the wrong feet and turning your clothes back to front. This procedure confuses the leshy, who cannot tell which way his victim is going, and you soon find your way out of the forest.

Malekin

An unusual example of a child taken by fairies reappearing in human form. Some centuries ago, the people of Dagworthy Castle in England heard the voice of a little girl speaking to them. She said her name was Malekin and that she had been taken from her cradle as a baby. At that time she had lived with the fairies for seven years, but she claimed that fairies always release human children when they reach the age of fourteen.

Malekin eventually revealed herself to one of the castle servants, who saw her as a pretty little girl dressed in white. She asked for human food to be left out for her, because that would help her restoration to human form. The servants provided her with regular meals, which always disappeared, but after a while they heard no more from her and she left their offerings untouched.

The end of her story is unknown. Possibly the fairies discovered she had been talking to humans and prevented her from doing so. But, if Malekin told the truth, it leaves one unanswered question. What happens to all the other children released after fourteen years captivity by the fairies?

Mandrake

A plant much valued by sorcecers because it shrieks when pulled out of the ground. Also known as the mandragora. Widely distributed throughout the Mediterranean regions, North Africa, and Asia, it is a low-growing but gaudy and even flamboyant plant, with purplish bell-shaped flowers and fleshy orange berries. Drugs made from its root include poisons, love potions, and narcotics. Cleopatra, Queen of Egypt, enjoyed 'highs' from drinking a potion of mandragora.

Commercial cultivation of mandrake plants is not recommended because of the appalling supersonic shrieks they emit when pulled out of the ground. These are so piercing that they may cause hysteria or even madness in mandrake collectors. It is possible, however, for an experienced sorcerer, who knows the correct phases of the moon for mandrake-lifting and the appropriate incantations to utter while he eases the plant out of the earth, to collect mandrakes without psychic harm.

Like the Gin Seng or Man-Plant, the mandrake's root often has a close resemblance to the lower portions of a male body including the legs and sexual organs. For this reason it is valued as a source of powerful love potions.

Manes

The ghosts of the dead who live in the bowels of the earth, and may emerge through any deep shaft, cave, or chasm. Normally they are shy and harmless, although they have sometimes been known to lead speleologists astray. In Latin, *manes* means 'the good people' because each family has its own assemblage of ancestral ghosts.

There is no reason to suppose that one's ancestral ghosts are likely to cause any harm but it is wise to propitiate them in the correct manner. Between 13 to 21 February each year, one should place offerings of food, wine, and flowers in broken pots in the middle of a road. At midnight on 9, 11, and 13 May the father of each family should get out of bed, fill his mouth with dried beans, and then slowly spit them out with the words 'With these beans I ransom me and mine. Ancestral ghosts, begone!'

Manticore

This monster of the Asian forests, especially those of India, Malaysia, and Indonesia, is the most dangerous predator of the tropical regions. It has the body of a lion and a head with some resemblance to that of a human male, except that the awful gaping mouth is filled with three rows of razor-sharp teeth. The tail is as scaly as a snake and tipped with a ball of poison darts, possibly envenomed with the juice of the upas tree.

The manticore stalks humans through the forest and creeps near enough to fire a volley of poison darts at a victim. Death is immediate and the manticore then uses its terrible teeth to crunch up every fragment of its meal. Skull, bones, clothing, and even such items as gourds carried by women when going for water, all vanish down the manticore's voracious gullet. The total disappearance of a human from a forest village is proof positive of the presence of a manticore.

Mimis

The rock spirits who live in the hills of Arnhem Land in northern Australia. They make their homes in the crevices of rocks and consequently are extremely thin and attenuated creatures. Mimis emerge from their hiding-places only to seek their food, which usually consists of yams and other roots, but if a man passes by they may decide to eat him instead. They have to keep a careful watch on the weather, because a strong wind might blow them away, or even break their necks, if they emerged when it was blowing.

Minotaur

This unhappy monster, with the body of a man and the head and horns of a bull, was the result of a broken promise and unnatural desire.

His story began when Minos of Crete sought the throne of that kingdom. To impress the Cretans, Minos told them that the gods would answer any prayer he addressed to them, and challenged the Cretans to put him to the test. The Cretans told him to ask Poseidon, Lord of the Ocean, to send him a bull out of the sea, and followed him to the seashore to watch him make this seemingly absurd request. Minos prayed fervently for it to be granted, and promised that if the bull appeared then he would sacrifice it to the glory of Poseidon.

To the awe and astonishment of the Cretans, the waters parted and a magnificent white bull swam ashore. They promptly elected Minos as their king, but he could not bring himself to sacrifice the splendid white bull from the sea. He added it to his own herd, and sacrificed an ordinary bull to Poseidon.

The Ocean God was so infuriated by this broken promise that he caused Pasiphae, the wife of Minos, to fall in love with the bull. She lavished caresses and embraces upon the animal, but it showed no interest in her desire until she persuaded the inventor Daedalus to build her an artificial cow, so that she might crouch within it to be served by the bull.

In due course she gave birth to a monster with a calf's head and a man's body, which quickly developed into a full-grown male with the head of a great fighting bull. The crescent of its sharp horns was wider than a man could span with outstretched arms.

The Cretans named it Minotaur, the bull-son of Minos, and the king might have accepted this curse of Poseidon if the Minotaur had not developed a taste for human flesh. Minos dared not destroy it lest he offend Poseidon yet again, and so he ordered Daedalus to create a special prison

for the monster. Daedalus created the Labyrinth, a maze of chambers and passages built partly above and partly beneath the ground, from which the Minotaur could never find a way out.

At about the time when the Minotaur was born, the king's son Androgeus journeyed to Athens to compete in the Olympic Games. Androgeus was a great athlete, and he won so many of the events that the Athenians barred him from further contests by cutting his throat. Minos responded by attacking the Athenians and laying siege to the city. The siege dragged on until the Athenians begged a truce, but Minos granted it only on condition that, in every ninth year, the Athenians should send seven youths and seven maidens to be devoured by the Minotaur.

In the ninth and eighteenth year after the siege was lifted, the Athenians selected seven handsome youths nd seven beautiful maidens and escort hem to the waterfront in a great wailing p ocession of mourners. The sacrifices boarded a ship with black sails and voyaged to Crete, where the henchmen of King Minos took them one by one to the Labyrinth. Each terrified youngster groped through the gloomy passages until he or she heard the bull-like snuffle of the Minotaur scenting its prey, and then met a dreadful fate.

In the twenty-seventh year, Theseus the son of King Aegeus of Athens offered to take the place of one of the victims and try to kill the Minotaur. He promised his father that, if he succeeded, he would change the ship's black sails from white ones on the homeward voyage.

Theseus did not know how he would kill the Minotaur and also find his way out of the Labyrinth, but one part of this problem was solved when Ariadne, daughter of Minos, fell in love with Theseus at first sight. When the guards drove him into the Labyrinth she contrived to slip a ball of thread into his hand.

Theseus paid out the thread as he moved boldly into the Labyrinth, listening for the approach of the Minotaur. He walked through the confusing maze of passages until he heard the pad of its human feet and then the bull-like bellow as it charged upon the Athenian.

But instead of a juicy youth or maiden the Minotaur encountered an agile warrior who dodged its charge, caught one of its horns and forced it to the ground. Those outside the Labyrinth heard the snarls and roars of fearsome combat as Theseus wrenched the Minotaur's head around by its horns, until he broke its neck with a ghastly snap.

Theseus found his way back into the open with the help of Ariadne's thread. The young Athenians rejoiced at the victory of their young prince, and the story ended happily for them but not for Ariadne and Aegeus. Theseus proved himself a singularly ungrateful lover. He enjoyed Ariadne's favours until the ship reached the island of Naxos on the homeward journey, but when Ariadne fell asleep on the beach he quickly set sail again and left her there.

And, in the triumph of his victory, he forgot his promise to his father. Aegeus had watched every day from the clifftop for the ship's return, and when it hove in sight with the black sails still spread he flung himself down into the sea now known as the Aegean.

Mopaditis

The spirits of the dead who haunt some parts of northern Australia. Usually, mopaditis assemble in groups and keep each other company, but it may happen that one of them becomes separated from the others. The lonely mopaditi has a great yearning for company and will attempt to steal the spirit of a living person as a friend.

An Aborigine who travels alone through the bush will soon become aware of the presence of a lonely mopaditi. When all the birds fell silent in the noonday heat, and there is nothing to see but the motionless trees surrounding him in every direction, the traveller senses an invisible presence stalking him. His skin crawls and his hair stands on end, but he attempts to scare off the mopaditi by singing and shouting loudly. If he is carrying a firestick he lights a torch of bark and waves it around his head, hoping the smoke and flame will protect him. If such measures fail he tries to hide himself until he feels the mopaditi has lost sight of him.

But a lonely mopaditi is so hungry for company that, when the traveller at last staggers into camp, it may be that his spirit remains in the bush. Medicine men strive to recall it to the exhausted body but rarely succeed, and the tribe soon has to sing the death-chant over another victim of the mopaditis.

Nagumwasuck

A fairy tribe attached to the Passamaquoddy Indians of the USA. Unlike European fairies they are very ugly, and no doubt it is for this reason that they are extremely self-conscious and always try to dodge out of human sight. They have a friendly interest in the fortunes of the tribe, however, and try to help them by creating good luck in hunting, fishing, and other activities.

The Passamaquoddy people were strongly conscious of the Naguwasuck presence until comparatively recent years, but the Indians now feel that most of the fairies may have deserted them. It seems likely that a good many of the Nagumwasuck paddled themselves away in a stone canoe.

Narcissus

A handsome but conceited young man who fell in love with the mountain-nymph Echo. He thought that she spurned his love because she could not reply to his wooing, but only repeated his words back to him.

The gods punished him for his lack of understanding by ordaining that he should fall in love with his own image. Narcissus evaded this fate until the day when he bent to drink from a forest pool and saw his reflection smiling back at him. He thought it so beautiful that he immediately fell in love with his mirror image, and ignored his friends' urging to abandon this phantasy lover. He remained by the pool, languishing hopelessly for his own reflection, until he perished from hunger and exposure. When his friends returned to search for him they found an exquisite flower blooming in the spot where he had knelt by the pool, and they named it narcissus in memory of his ill-fated love.

Nymphs

The large family of beautiful maidens who inhabit all larger plants and natural features of the earth. Different branches of the family have different names. The Dryads are the nymphs of forests and trees, the Napaeae of glens and groves, and the Oreades and mountains and grottoes. Another section of the family is connected with water and is dealt with separately in this volume.

The nymphs do not perform any particular function apart from enhancing the beauty of nature. Any aspect of the environment is improved by the sight of a slim naked maiden posing amidst the rocks and trees, although the nymphs are very shy of mortals and rarely allow themselves to be seen. A dryad, for example, is likely to transform herself instantly into a slender sapling if there is any likelihood of a mortal male glimpsing her nudity.

Normally the nymphs have sweet delicate voices, so that their singing or conversation may be confused with the breeze through the trees or the ripple of a stream over stones. They do, however, shriek loudly when being pursued by satyrs and they may even sing rather indelicate songs during festivities arranged by Pan or other forest deities. They dance with exquisite grace, and the rare records of nymph-sightings try ineffectually to describe the enchanting beauty of a party of nymphs dancing the welcome to spring.

The problem with nymphs is that they have so much time on their hands that they have frequently been the cause of trouble among gods or mortals, either through girlish mischief or because of their innumerable love affairs.

Some members of the family have gone very much to the bad, although this may be ascribed to temptation from gods such as Dionysus who taught them to drink wine and join in drunken revels. Innocent and virginal nymphs are always at the mercy of such lustful gods as Zeus, who sometimes go to great lengths to trick them into surrender.

Ohdows

Underground tribal people who live underground in North America. The American Indians have never seen them because they never leave their subterranean homes and so there is no clear record of their appearance. They are believed, however, to be a race of small well-formed people with features similar to those of the Indians.

The ohdows have certain magical powers which they use for the benefit of mankind and other animals of the earth. In what might be described as the lower basement of the underworld there are gigantic earth spirits which are anxious to rise to the surface and revel in the sunlight, but if they ever achieved this ambition they might devastate the earth and destroy all its creatures. The ohdows use their magical powers to control these spirits and keep them in their place, but from time to time the earth spirits rebel against their imprisonment with angry rumblings and beat furiously against the walls of the deep caverns. So far the ohdows have always been able to subdue them, so that they sink back into the darkness and allow the earth to rest in peace again.

Pan

The wild free spirit of the hills. Sometimes mistaken for a satyr because he also has the legs and horns of a goat, probably because his mother Penelope was raped by the god Hermes in the form of a billy goat. His face, however, is that of an intelligent young man, while a satyr's face has some resemblance to a monkey's. And, unlike satyrs, he is not totally mischievous. He takes a special interest in the well-being of shepherds and their flocks.

Pan loves the timbered mountainsides and spends much of his time skipping nimbly through the trees, his hooves clicking on the rocks as he looks eagerly for a dryad or some other nymph who may have strayed from the companions. Once he has spotted her she has little chance of escape.

If he sights a band of unwary travellers he may amuse himself by waiting in ambush until he can rush out to frighten them. The sudden apparition of a being who is half-man and half-goat is astonishing enough, but he also has the power to inflict the emotion known, naturally, as panic, so that they run shrieking among the trees.

Such mischievous activities, and his ardour for the naked nymphs, would make him very much like the satyrs if it were not for his feeling of responsibility for shepherds. He bestows fertility on their flocks of sheep or goats, helps hunters to track the wild beasts which prey on them, and causes rich pastures to flourish on the high hillsides. His gifts to shepherds include the syrinx or pan pipes, with which they beguile the lonely hours by playing woodland melodies.

Like the shepherds, Pan enjoys sleeping in the midday heat. He is normally friendly to mankind but he is very surly if a clumsy wanderer wakes him from this sleep, and may punish the transgressor by inflicting strange dreams and visions upon him and his family.

Probably it was Pan's interest in sexual sports and fertility which inspired the story that he fathered Priapus, born to Venus Aphrodite. Priapus was born with enormous genitals and a permanent erection, so that Venus abandoned him and he was fostered by shepherds. He acted as the god of bee-keepers, agriculturists, and fishermen until he was tempted into the drunken entourage of Dionysus, whose activities gave him full scope for his unusual endowments.

Pixies, Piskies

A race of beings who inhabit the far western counties of England, especially Cornwall. Their origin is unknown. Some theorists believe they came to Cornwall with the Phoenicians, and spread as far east as Devon and Somerset. Others claim that the pixies were the earliest inhabitants of England. When the fairies arrived in England, at the time of the Roman conquest, the pixies at first welcomed them but then, fearing a takeover, waged war against them until the fairies retreated out of the three counties.

Pixies are usually no larger than a human hand but they can increase or decrease their stature at will. They have red hair, turned-up noses, malicious smiles, and squinting green eyes. (Note that a full-grown redheaded male with squinting green eyes, who passes himself off as a human, is indubitably a pixie.) Their costume, for both males and females, is a closefitting suit of bright green which acts as camouflage in the lush pastures of the west of England.

Pixies are malicious tricksters. Their favourite trick is to lead mortals astray, but a traveller through pixie country may easily foil them by wearing his coat inside-out. In some cases the pixies may confuse a mortal so thoroughly that he or she never recovers, and wanders aimlessly over the countryside singing or talking in mysterious languages. This condition is known as 'pixie led.'

Farmers usually keep on good terms with pixies in their district by leaving buckets of water outside at night, for pixie mothers to wash their babies in; leaving milk on the kitchen table for them to drink; and keeping the hearth swept clean for pixies to dance on at midnight.

Puck, Pooka

A rural sprite of the southern counties of England. In appearance he is a somewhat pixie-like creature, similarly dressed in a closefitting suit of green, but unlike the pixies he is friendly with fairies. He frequently plays his flute, made from a willow twig, to accompany their moonlight dances.

In some of his qualities he resembles Pan. He is generally beneficial to all plants and creatures of the fields and forests but, unlike Pan, he takes no interest in sheep, goats, and other domesticated animals. He prefers squirrels, rabbits, foxes, and other untamed creatures of the wild woodland.

Puck loves to play tricks on humans, such as pulling the stool away just as a milkmaid sits down to her task. Like the pixies, he leads people astray when they wander off the beaten track. Generally his tricks are fairly harmless, but he can become very stern in revenge of maidens scorned by their lovers. Young men who betray country maidens may find themselves afflicted by such unpleasant consequences as a lethargy of the vital organs.

Ratwife

Rats are possessed of such cunning and cruelty, nefarious industry and gang instinct, that they are historically supposed to be related to the human race. Humans, like rats, are fond of music, while rats, like humans, believe in magic spells, charms, and talismans.

The brown rat (*Rattus norvegicus*) which stowed away aboard Viking longships during the eighth century A.D., and set forth to conquer the world, is the fiercest yet most gullible of the race of rats. In its home country, Norway, it is controlled by Ratwives.

A Ratwife's training begins at about the age of puberty. It comprises the playing of mystic rat-tunes on a three-note pipe; detection of rat colonies; physical exercises; and small boat handling. A novice Ratwife, or Ratmaiden, spends some time as apprentice to an accomplished Ratwife before setting up in business for herself.

When a rat-plagued community calls upon the services of a Ratwife she first negotiates her fee, which is paid in advance. She then locates the nest of the local chief rat, stands nearby, and plays a selection of traditional rat tunes on her pipe. Attempts by ordinary musicians to imitate these tunes have always proved fruitless.

The chief rat soon responds to the mystic music, and sits at the Ratwife's feet until the rest of the colony has assembled behind him. The Ratwife then demonstrates her need for physical fitness as she leads the rats away, playing continuously on her pipe, until she reaches the sea or any large body of water where she has beached her boat. Most Norwegians communities are within reasonable distance of lakes or fiords, but even so the Ratwife may have to march over moors and mountains with a host of rats running and leaping behind her, until she reaches her boat. Then, with scarcely a break in the eerie music, she sculls one-handed away from shore, showing great dexterity in the use of one hand to finger her pipes while she rows with the other.

The rats plunge into the water and swim after her. The weakest soon drown and one by one the rest of the tribe disappears, until none but the chief rat follows the Ratwife in her boat. At last he can swim no longer and sinks beneath the surface, just as the last note of the Ratwife's pipe floats across the lonely waters.

Red Cap

This evil goblin lives in one or another of the ruined castles and watchtowers along the border between Scotland and England. He shifts his residence fairly often to avoid the attentions of exorcists, witchfinders, and other authorities. A wanderer along the lonely border tracks might be tempted to explore one of the brooding old piles of stone, but he would be wise to keep well away in case it should be a temporary residence of Red Cap.

He is easily distinguished, even from a distance, because of his large fiery red eyes and red cap. As he comes closer, moving with remarkable speed despite the fact that he wears iron boots, he is seen to be a short, stocky old man with long grey hair and eagle's claws instead of hands.

Red Cap seeks human prey in order to renew the colour of his cap, which he dips in the blood of his victims. He can overcome even the strongest human unless the intended victim remembers to quote a few words out of the Bible before Red Cap's talons sink into him. At the sound of the holy words the goblin instantly disappears.

Reynard the Fox

The most cunning member of his race, who lived in the days when King Noble the Lion ruled over the world of four-legged animals.

King Noble, a wise and kindly monarch, once decreed a great court of justice so that all the animals might present any complaints against one another. Reynard knew that many animals would complain about him and said he was too sick to appear.

One animal after another told the king that Reynard had done him some harm, and Noble at last sent Bruin the Bear to drag Reynard before the court. Reynard did not resist, but said that Bruin must first have a feast of honey. He led the bear to a hollow log where bees had made a hive and split it open with a wedge and mallet. When Bruin pushed his nose into the split to eat the honey, Reynard knocked out the wedge and the bear was trapped.

King Noble then sent Tybert the Cat to summons Reynard to court, but Reynard promised Tybert a good feed of mice. He led Tybert to a nearby farm, where the cat was caught in a fox trap set for Reynard. He managed to escape, but only after the farmer had given him a good beating.

Grymbart the Badger, who was Reynard's best friend, then volunteered to fetch the fox to court. He persuaded Reynard to go with him by playing on the fox's vanity, and saying he could talk his way out of any trouble.

But the evidence against Reynard was overwhelming and Noble sentenced him to be hanged. Tybert gleefully prepared the gallows, but Reynard begged the king for postponement of execution while he confessed all his sins. Noble agreed, and Reynard reeled off a long story which made each of his misdeeds sound like the fault of another animal. Finally he said that Bruin, Tybert, and Crymbart had conspired to kill the king, and said he knew the location of a treasure they had assembled to pay their followers.

King Noble was convinced that Reynard had been unjustly accused, and released him on condition that the fox should lead the king to the treasure.

Reynard managed to escape this commitment by pleading that he had promised to go on a pilgrimage to Rome, but he soon returned to his wicked old ways. Noble summonsed him to justice yet again, and appointed Isegrim the Wolf as his prosecutor. But Reynard argued his way out of every accusation, until Isegrim lost patience and challenged him to a tournament.

The animals thought that Isegrim's greater strength was certain to defeat Reynard, and when the fox turned up for the tournament they roared with laughter at his appearance. He had had his body shaved except for his bushy tail and his naked skin was glistening with oil. When the tourney began, he used his tail to flip dust into the wolf's eyes and Isegrim could not get hold of his slippery body.

Nevertheless he fought savagely to conquer Reynard and at last pinned him to the dust. He was about to tear out Reynard's throat when the fox began to flatter him about his strength, wisdom, and endurance. Isegrim paused to listen and Reynard sprang free again, to continue the fight until Isegrim was exhausted.

King Noble gave a great feast to celebrate Reynard's victory and invited the fox to be his counsellor. But Reynard did not care to live under the eye of the king and excused himself with the plea that he was unworthy of the honour. He loped away from the court and soon resumed his old way of life.

Every modern fox is proud of Reynard, the ancestral fox who proved that a quick wit and a ready tongue will find a way out of any predicament.

Robin Goodfellow

A rare example of a child born to a fairy father and mortal mother and brought up in the world of humans. Usually, fairy males are not much interested in human girls, whom they find to be clumsy and coarse, but the fairy king Oberon fell in love with a country maiden in the time of Richard the Lion-Hearted. Robin Goodfellow was born of their union.

Instead of whisking the child away to be brought up in a fairy community, Oberon left Robin to his mother but gave him the power to change his shape whenever he needed to assist or punish mortals.

Robin grew into a handsome man and those to whom he has revealed himself describe him as a fine example of a mediaeval Englishman, with a smiling weatherbeaten face and a sturdy body clad in jerkin and hose. There is, however, an air about him which is very different from that of a rough-and-ready countryman of 800 years ago. He has a slant to his eye and a quirk to his lip which hint of some special knowledge, and a bearing of springy independence which befits one who combines the power of both mortal and fairy.

Robin is an irresistible lover, especially since he is always willing to help kitchen-maids and dairymaids in their arduous work. Countless descendants of Robin Goodfellow live in the English countryside today and a multitude of Englishmen have at least a trace of his fairy blood.

He is a good-humoured personality and rarely changes his shape unless he feels impelled to punish some oppressor of the common folk. One of his favourite tricks is to change himself into a replica of a rich man's favourite horse, so that he may toss the rider into a deep cold stream.

Robin is not often seen nowadays. As the concrete tide floods over the sweet English countryside he retreats further into the remaining forests or to the tops of the highest hills. On a sleepy summer afternoon a wanderer may glimpse him reclining there like the spirit of ancient England, with a wry smile on his lips as he remembers all that Englishmen have exchanged for the trumpery gifts of modern magicians.

Salamander

The alchemist's lizard. Has a strong resemblance to the small black and yellow lizards which inhabit damp and mossy places in Britain and Europe, but unlike common lizards it is able to live in the heart of the hottest fire.

Salamanders useful to alchemists are likely to be found on the slopes of volcanoes, especially when an eruption sends cascades of red-hot lava pouring down the rocky sides. The easiest way to catch salamanders is to wear a suit and boots of salamander skins, because these are resistant to the fiercest heat and enable a collector to walk unharmed on the burning lava. It is, however, unfortunately a 'chicken and egg' situation for an alchemist, who can rarely catch enough salamanders to provide him with this protective clothing.

Alchemists use salamanders as a part of the lengthy and complex process of turning lead into gold. The salamander acts as a kind of temperature-gauge. When the fire is hot enough to begin the conversion process a salamander will leap into it and frolic among the blazing coals.

Sometimes, when a fire is hot enough, a salamander will actually appear amidst the flames. It is possible, therefore, that the world's population of salamanders actually consists of those who have escaped from alchemists' laboratories.

Satan

Also known as Lucifer, Beelzebub, Lord of the Flies, the Great Goat, Overlord of Hell, and by numerous names which it would be unlucky to reproduce in print. He is one of the few beings who walks both underground and above ground. Those who are justifiably terrified of his powers depict him as a repulsive creature of goat-like aspect, but this is probably incorrect. As Lucifer the Bringer of Light he was a strong and handsome angel before he was dismissed from heaven for the sin of pride, and obliged to seize domination over hell. It seems likely that he retains his original saturnine good looks and that the hooves, tail, and horns with which he is credited are nothing but superstitious inventions. Those to whom he has appeared during recent years, to make extremely tempting offers for their souls, describe him as having the appearance of a well-dressed businessman. He has large dark eyes, a swarthy complexion, a neatly trimmed black moustache and beard, and shapely well-manicured hands. The only unusual features are his sharply pointed ears and his need for a good deodorant to mask the faint but unmistakeable odour of corruption.

He carries a briefcase made from an attractively smooth leather, which seems to vary in colour from the pinkish tones of Nordic skin to the deep ebony of an equatorial male. Its zipper of pure gold opens silently when he extracts the soul-transfer documents for signature, and in a deep seductive voice he promises every kind of earthly power and delight in exchange for one's soul. He is in fact a supreme salesman and it is very difficult to resist his apparently easy terms.

He has always kept up with fashion throughout the ages. In the time of the early Christians he wore sandals, a linen tunic, and a cloak of purple samite. In mediaeval days he wore a tight-fitting jerkin and hose of scarlet velvet, with a cap and hood of the same material and a flowing cape of midnight gaberdine. Nowadays he attires himself in an exquisitely tailored suit of plum-coloured Italian silk, with Gucci loafers on his slender feet.

As a businessman he is never short of capital to back up his seemingly extravagant promises. He administers an international consortium in which the arms and drug industries occupy only two of many departments.

Those who have enjoyed a friendly

business discussion and a few drinks with Satan, in the most expensive suite of a fashionable city hotel, always find it difficult to believe he will really demand their souls. When at last they are led through the Gates of Hell they still think their old business friend will see reason and—perhaps after a few jovial threats and warnings—release them to enjoy eternity in the style to which they have become accustomed to earth.

But then they are dragged before Satan in his true manifestation as the King of Hell, and they discover that he is very different from their suave old friend.

Satyrs

Untamed creatures of the wilderness, half-man and half-beast. A satyr has the body, arms, and sexual organs of a man smothered with coarse hairs, the legs, hooves, and tail of a goat, and a monkey-like face with goat's ears.

Satyrs have the nature usually ascribed to a bully: cruel, greedy, lazy, lustful, and malicious. They perpetuate their race by raping nymphs (except for water nymphs, because they are afraid of water). They indulge in drunken orgies, frighten sheep and cattle, and delight in terrifying lonely travellers by pouncing upon them with shrieks of satyric laughter. A couple of satyrs can be a great nuisance to a shepherd, especially if he has offended them by warning the nymphs that there are satyrs in the vicinity. They will hide among the trees and rush out to scatter his flock as he moves it from one pasture to another.

Perhaps the only redeeming feature of satyrs is their love of music and dancing. They have a special dance, the sikinnis, which they perform with great agility to the strains of a syrinx orchestra made up of fellow-satyrs.

A number of satyrs accompany Dionysus on his perpetual mission of spreading the double-edged delights of wine among mankind. Their drunken mischief has done a lot of harm to the cause of serious winebibbers and humans are often blamed for the vandalism perpetrated by satyrs.

Scapegoats

Should any community be labouring under an excessive load of sin there is an easy way to solve the problem.

On New Year's Eve the elders of the community should select a large mature goat (preferably a billy goat because most sins are masculine in origin) and lead it to the outskirts of the town or village.

The community must then gather around the goat and curse it severely as the cause of all their sins, but it should not be beaten (or at least not too heavily) or it may not be able to carry the load of sin away with it.

The chief priest must then pronounce the final curses which transfer all the communal sins onto the goat. After that, the community should drive it into the wilderness with a shower of sticks and stones, and forbid it to return.

The people may then begin the New Year with a clean conscience, and the comforting knowledge that if they are tempted into further sins they will always be able to find another scapegoat.

Sphinx

There are several species of this dominantly female creature. The Grecian species has the face and breasts of a woman, the body of a lion, and the wings of an eagle. The Egyptian, or Andro-Sphinx, is similar to the Grecian except that she has no wings, while an Egyptian sub-species, the Crio-Sphinx, has the head of a ram or a falcon.

Persia, Assyria, and Phoenicia harbour sphinxes of both sexes. The males have beards and long curly hair. The sphinx of ancient Rome was female and probably of Egyptian origin, because she wore an asp, the serpent of the Nile, around her forehead.

Middle Eastern sphinxes are renowned for their wisdom, perhaps because they rarely reveal their knowledge and appear to be content to bask in the reverence of their worshippers. The Grecian species betray a totally different personality. They are voluble, aggressive, itinerant, and predatory, and have a relish for human flesh. Normally they walk around the countryside on their lion feet, but there are sphinx flight-paths between various Greek islands. A marked characteristic of Grecian sphinxes is the feline, or female, practice of talking to and teasing their victims before devouring them. They are, however, what are known as 'sore losers', and if a victim escapes a Grecian sphinx she may fly into a self-destructive fury.

The best-known of the Grecian sphinxes is the one which the goddess Hera commissioned to punish the people of Thebes for their drunkenness, after Dionysus taught them to make wine. In typical sphinx style she was not content simply to crunch up some unwary Theban, but diverted herself by asking him a riddle (known, of course, as the Riddle of the Sphinx) with the promise of freedom if he could answer it.

Nobody solved this riddle until Oedipus of Corinth approached Thebes during his self-imposed exile. The sphinx pounced out of ambush, licked her lips at the sight of the handsome young man, and after a little preliminary banter purred out her usual riddle: 'What is it that walks on four legs in the morning, two legs at noon, and three legs in the evening?'

Oedipus answered 'Why, a man, of course. He crawls on hands and knees as a baby, walks on two legs as an adult, and supports himself on a stick in the evening of his days.'

The sphinx was so furious at her defeat that she flung herself into the sea, but it may be said that she won after all. The governor of Thebes was so pleased by the disappearance of the sphinx that he married Oedipus to the widowed queen, Jocasta, and made him king of Thebes. But it transpired that Jocasta was the mother of Oedipus and

the Fates inflicted terrible punishments upon them for this crime.

Talking Trees

Trees possessed of the power of speech are found in many parts of the world. Sometimes the tree addresses a person in need of assistance, but occasionally it is a spirit inhabiting a tree who pronounces a spell or imparts some useful information.

Trees have a great deal of time for thinking and observing and a philosophical acceptance of their fate, which is to be made use of by the creatures of the world from woodcutters to woodpeckers. In accordance with this philosophy their conversation is generally of an advisory and helpful character, such as that of the Bemberg Oak. This noble tree, now several centuries old, answers lovers' questions as to the faithfulness of their partners.

A huge elm in Sherwood Forest, which stood for countless generations until it perished of Dutch Elm Disease, was much consulted by hunters who sought their prey in the forest. Its answers were, however, often enigmatic, in some such terms as 'When the wind shakes my branches from the west, the deer will put thy arrows to the test. When east winds scatter leaves about thy feet, then look to furry rabbits for thy meat.'

On the island of Tonga in the Pacific, the islanders recall that one of their ancestors, Longapoa, was once saved from starvation by a friendly tree. During a canoe voyage he was wrecked on an island which offered him nothing to eat, but when a puko tree heard him bewailing his fate it advised him to break off one of its branches and bake it in an earth oven. When Longaroa opened the oven he found the branch had turned into a savoury feast of pork and yams.

The trees of Ireland are especially voluble, and some give information to those who seek treasure hidden by leprechauns. There is no record, however, of the discovery of leprechaun treasure and so the trees may only be showing a good-natured willingness to help.

Those who have talked to trees find it difficult to describe the sound of arboreal voices. They say it is like a combination of sighing, murmuring, and groaning. Large trees have deep thick voices, whereas smaller and slimmer trees whisper so quietly as to be almost inaudible.

Whenever a tree speaks clearly, especially if it is in the voice of a young woman, the questioner should suspect that it is not the tree talking but some spirit inhabiting the trunk. In such cases, any guidance received should be accepted with reservations. Some tree spirits are harmless and helpful but others are malicious.

Travellers' Friends

Whenever a mortal ventures far from home he should seek the protection of one of the travellers' friends such as the gods of the road. In Egypt, one may travel with the aid of Min, God of the Eastern Deserts and Lord of Foreign Lands. Min's perpetual erection shows that his principal duty is that of assisting fertility and procreation, but he never ignores the prayers of a traveller who is about to set forth with his camels and donkeys. An amulet purchased from the priests of Min will ward off the devils of desert and mountains, and help one to find the way by the stars.

Japanese gods of the road, including Yachimata-nito, have a double function. They not only protect travellers from brigands and keep them on the right track, but also protect communities against any evil which might be introduced by wayfarers. Like Min, the Japanese gods of travel are sexually potent. They are symbolised by stone phalluses, somewhat similar to the stone milestones of western countries.

Christians who have to set out on a journey should seek the patronage of Christophorous of Syria. Christophorous was originally a giant who wanted to serve a master without fear. He worked for the King of Canaan until he found that the king feared the devil, and transferred to the devil's service until he realised that the devil is afraid of the Cross. A hermit converted him to Christianity, and he decided to serve mankind by helping wayfarers to cross a dangerous river at a place where there was neither bridge nor ferry.

Whenever a traveller happened along, the giant hoisted him and his baggage onto his broad shoulders and plunged into the raging torrent. He revelled in each battle with the waters and carried even the bulkiest traveller across without difficulty, but one day he found himself staggering under the weight of a little boy. The rocks rolled beneath his feet and the current was so fierce that Christophorous and his burden were almost swept away, but he battled through to safety and gasped, 'If I had carried the whole world it could not have weighed more than thee!'

The little boy replied 'Marvel not, for

thou hast indeed carried the whole world and Him who made it!'

Christophorous is now regarded as the patron saint of ferrymen and travellers, and those planning a journey should regard St Christopher's Day, 25 July, as the most auspicious day to set out from home.

Tree Geese

There is considerable disagreement as to whether these creatures are fish, fowl, or vegetables, but modern opinion is that they should be placed in the latter category.

Unlike true geese, they originate as the fruits of a tree which grows near the water's edge in such wild areas of the world as the Shetland Isles, south-west Tasmania, parts of New Zealand and northern Norway. The goose tree bears fruits about the size of an ostrich egg, and like other fruit they are green and bitter when immature. It is impossible to collect ripe goose tree fruit because it remains immature in the presence of humans, and ripens very suddenly during the hours of darkness. At the moment of ripeness it falls into the water and immediately breaks open to release tree-geese chicks, which grow quickly into adulthood and fly away. Observers claim that they have a particularly beautiful colouration of subtle pinks and greens.

Tree geese have been sold as food but they are not generally popular because there is so much disagreement as to the method of preparation. Some cooks say they should be boiled like vegetables, others that they should be roasted like fowl or fried like fish.

Trolls

The giants of the Scandinavian wilderness, who live in the forests, mountains, and moorlands. Some never emerge from caverns deep underground and are believed to be Lords of the Goblins. Occasionally a lonely wanderer may hear their subterranean growls and grumbles as they direct their mischievous subjects on one mission or another.

Trolls appear most frequently during the

'light nights' of the northern summer, when the sun rests only a little way below the horizon and the whole land reposes in a mysterious silent twilight. The birds do not sing, the breezes do not blow, and even the rivers and cascades seem to run more quietly. It is then, when it is still light enough to see but all honest folk are asleep, that the trolls appear and wander over the countryside. Those who have glimpsed them say they are vast amorphous creatures without distinct bodies, limbs, or heads, but somehow seeming to have all these attributes as they drift aimlessly through the silence. There is a theory that they are in perpetual mourning for their distant ancestors, the great giants who held sway over Scandinavia before the appearance of the gods.

Trolls are occasionally antagonistic towards mankind and may snap the neck of any human whom they encounter during their wanderings. At other times they may kidnap sleeping children, but nobody knows why. They have an unfortunate effect on domestic animals. When a troll is in the neighbourhood the cows and reindeer fail to give milk, the hens do not lay, horses are reluctant to work and even the dogs and cats go into hiding.

It is said that a human who sees a troll will never be the same again. For this reason, men and women are reluctant to go outside their homes during those brooding mystic hours of the northern summer nights and they make sure their children are safely tucked up in bed. Some trolls are very curious and they may peep wistfully through windows or even stretch attenuated arms into houses to finger human possessions. The best safeguard is to close all doors and windows firmly, draw the curtains, and sleep soundly until the first rays of the sun send trolls back into their hiding places. They dare not linger until the sun rises because sunlight turns trolls into stone.

Uldra

The Little People of Lapland in the far north of Sweden. They live underground but often come up to the surface, especially in winter

when their task is to feed sleeping bears and other hibernating animals.

The Lapps are a migratory people, who wander over the vast snowfields in search of the moss which feeds their herds of reindeer. Sometimes, when they pitch their tents of reindeer hide, they hear the Uldra moving about underground and take this as a warning that they must move on, because they are blocking the Little People's access to the surface. If the campers fail to move, the Uldra may punish them either by poisoning the reindeer or by stealing a baby and putting an Uldra baby in its cradle.

Uldra babies have long sharp teeth and faces covered with black hair, and opinions differ as to how an Uldra mother may be persuaded to take her baby back and restore the human child. Some Lapps say the best technique is to beat the baby with a burning tree branch, until its screaming grows so loud that the Uldra mother rushes up to rescue her child. Others believe it is best to treat the little Uldra so kindly that its mother will be grateful and restore the human baby to the cradle.

Unicorn

A particularly beautiful creature once widespread throughout the northern hemisphere. Known under different names in different countries, but now popularly known by its Latin appellation deriving from *unus* = one, *cornus* = horn. The *Unicornus sinoensis* roamed the forests of China, Japan, and Indonesia; the *Unicornis carcadan* was found throughout Arabia, India, North Africa, and much of the Middle East; the *Unicornis europa* lived in most European countries; and the *Unicornis alba* was native to the British Isles.

Generally the unicorn was a solitary creature. Unlike other hooved animals it did not pasture in herds but walked alone, and after the male and female unicorn had come together for mating the male would resume its solitary habit. A unicorn colt, which was born without a horn, stayed with its mother until the horn had grown to full length and then went off on its own.

The different varieties of unicorn had specific variations in appearance, but all had the head and body of a horse, the legs of an antelope, the tail of a horse or a lion, and the beard of a goat. The dominant distinguishing feature was the long, sharp, twisted horn growing from the middle of the forehead.

This horn was a fearsome weapon, especially since the unicorn was a very fierce and aggressive animal which could run faster than any other creature of the plains and forests. Adult unicorns protected their territory with single-minded fury. Even an elephant would steer clear of a unicorn. Lions, being carnivores, often lived amicably in unicorn territory since the two animals did not threaten each other's food supplies, and a lion never attacked a unicorn for fear of its great horn.

Unfortunately for unicorns, men discovered that their horns were absolute proof against poison. If poisoned wine was poured into a drinking-cup fashioned from unicorn horn (or unihorn) the poison became innocuous. Plates and serving instruments made from unihorn rendered poisoned food quite harmless to the consumer. The rulers of the ancient world, who lived under constant threat of poisoning by their subjects or relations, paid great sums for unihorn and hunters risked their lives to supply them.

Unicorns moved so fast and were so intelligent that it was impossible to kill them with a bow or spear or to lure them into traps, and so the hunters developed a dangerous technique. When a hunter saw a unicorn he stood in front of a tree, and when the unicorn charged him he dodged quickly aside. The tremendous force of a unicorn's charge drove its horn deep into the tree, and held it fast so that it might be killed.

Many hunters misjudged the speed of a charging unicorn and were transfixed to trees, but profits from unicorn-hunting were so high that the dangerous practice continued until one of the hunters happened to take his virgin daughter on a hunting expedition. To his astonishment a unicorn trotted out of the forest and approached her with such affection that she was able to hold its head in her lap. It lay there unresisting while the hunter sawed off its precious horn.

After that, virgins were in great demand as unicorn lures. Unicorns seemed to feel that the loss of a horn was a small price to pay for virginal embraces. The inevitable result was that when the virgins released them again they had no weapon against predators, and the entire unicorn family eventually became extinct.

Upas Tree

In the Javanese tongue of Indonesia the word *upas* means 'poison'. The upas or poison tree, botanically known as the anchar (*Antiaris toxicaria*) is a noble member of the fig family, with a straight trunk rising twenty to thirty metres before the first great boughs stretch out their leafy arms. The stately beauty of the great tree is, however, belied by its evil reputation. Early visitors to the Sunda Islands reported that the upas tree was so poisonous that it breathed forth its malignancy over a broad circuit all around its roots—some said for as much as thirty kilometres. No bird could fly within this toxic sphere of influence and no other animal, including man, could approach on the ground without suffering instant death. Unfortunately the poison was odourless and gave no other warning of its presence, so that a man's first clue to the presence of a upas tree was the discovery of skeletons scattered over the ground. By that time it was too late, and the blood roared in his ears as increasing breathlessness heralded his doom.

Luckily the evil powers of the upas tree began a slow decline during the sixteenth century. By the time the Dutch colonised the Sunda Islands the Javanese could already walk right up to a upas or anchar tree. The only remnant of its previous potency was the poisonous quality of the sap, which the islanders used to envenom their weapons. Like the airborne upas poison, the sap causes a victim's heart to beat so fast that he cannot breathe.

Ure

The totemic leader of a group of Aborigines of northern Australia. In the Dreamtime their tribal territory was under the ground. They lived there very comfortably, because their subterranean home provided most of their needs and was lit by a light which never went out.

No animals lived there, but Ure went up to the surface every day and caught plenty of fish, birds, reptiles, and other food. One day he emerged earlier than usual, just as the sun was rising. He had never seen the sun rise before and he was so surprised by this strange sight that he mistook the sun for a kangaroo. He hunted it unsuccessfully throughout the day, until it escaped beyond the western horizon and he found himself in unaccustomed darkness. He could not find the way back to his underground territory, and he was very frightened until the sun rose again. After that he decided that the alternation of light and darkness was more interesting than the perpetual light of underground, and he persuaded the tribe to move up to the surface where they lived ever since.

Wandjinas

A large population of these beings has lived in northern Australia since the Dreamtime. Before the coming of white men the wandjinas frequently appeared to the Aborigines, who preserved their likenesses in innumerable rock paintings.

A notable feature of the wandjinas is the 'space helmet' type of headdress, which gave rise to the modern belief that wandjinas arrived in Australia from outer space, lived there for a while, and then returned to the planet whence they came. It is said that the meteorite craters of the region were made by the impact of their space ships.

But the fact is that the wandjinas are weather spirits who control the climate, the fertility, and the general well-being of their territory. They live within the mountains and emerge when it is time to change the seasons from wet to dry or vice versa. They have eyes, but no mouths, and this phenomenon has given rise to the 'space helmet' theory. But if the wandjinas had mouths they would open them and release all the weather which is stored within their bodies, thus causing perpetual rain and cyclones instead of the rhythmic pattern of the seasons.

Wandjinas are human in form but about three times larger than an adult human male. Their colouration ranges from black to red or yellow, their large eyes have heavy eyelashes, and they wear various types of headdresses apart from the 'space helmets'.

Wendigo

Every man who ventures alone into the wilderness should fear the spirit of the lonely places, known as Wendigo in northern Canada and by different names in other parts of the world.

The cunning of Wendigo is that it knows how to keep out of your sight. As you travel, it is always behind your back. No matter how quickly you may turn, it moves faster. As you tramp through bush or forest, hills or desert, with no other company but your thoughts, you become slowly aware that Wendigo follows you. You may struggle against the temptation to swing around, but at last you turn and there is nothing. But you know that Wendigo has dodged behind you again, and you move quickly to surprise it. Again nothing, except perhaps the slightest movement of a bush. A breeze, or an animal, or Wendigo? You gaze everywhere around you, but there is nothing . . . or so it seems.

Wendigo torments some men until they empty their rifles blindly into the bush, screaming defiant challenges. But when the shots and cries have died away the silence settles again. The traveller plods on, and Wendigo follows. At night, it hovers outside the circle of the campfire. At dawn, it retreats into the forest mist.

As the days pass, Wendigo speaks to the traveller in little sighing whispers: words which he is not quite able to distinguish. Sometimes they sound like the voice of a friend, so that he shouts an amazed reply. Vainly he assures himself it is only the wind. He may even glimpse Wendigo, as a shadow moving between the trees or grass bending beneath invisible feet.

At last the traveller runs before Wendigo, casting aside weapons, provisions, and all other gear that hampers his flight. Sobbing desperately he runs until the end of his strength, and falls exhausted and alone.

The deep wilderness silence settles around the body, although the treetops sway as though a wind had passed through them. Wendigo has gone, but will always return.

Will O' The Wisp

The vague dancing lights which one may see in the darkness over boggy ground, especially on the English moorlands, are displayed by a notable sinner named Will the Smith.

Blacksmiths are usually hearty and honest craftsmen, but Will fell among evil companions as soon as he finished his apprenticeship. He was a plausible rogue, and although he broke every law of God and man he always managed to talk himself out of trouble. Even when an outraged husband despatched Will from this earth, the blacksmith managed to wheedle St Peter into giving him another chance. St Peter returned Will to earth to try again, but on this second time around he did not mend his wicked ways. When his new life ended he could not talk his way into either heaven or hell.

But the devil took pity on him, and gave him some burning coals from hellfire to keep him warm as he wandered through eternal darkness. Those coals may still be seen glowing in the distance as Will drifts perpetually between heaven and hell.

Yakkus

The demons of disease which infest the Indian sub-continent. Each yakku is the demon of one of the innumerable ailments which afflict mankind.

Yakkus generally reside in places dark and inhospitable to man, such as bat-haunted caves, deep crevices in the rock, hollow trees, overgrown gardens and abandoned buildings. They leave them only to mingle with the people in crowded streets and bazaars, and remain invisible until they choose to manifest themselves.

A yakku can assume the form of any animal, including man. The yakku of a particular disease may choose to appear as a pariah dog, vulture, jackal, beggar, or any other two-legged or four-legged animal. Sometimes it may even take the form of a beautiful and seductive woman.

Each yakku has an appointed time of day or night for preying on mankind. When this time arrives the demon emerges from its hiding place and assumes the form it has chosen for that day. With this apparently harmless appearance it awaits the approach of a victim. The man, woman, or child who comes close to a yakku may glance casually at what seems to be a chicken pecking in the dust, but all at once this seemingly ordinary creature changes back into a yakku. Such an appalling apparition, whether in the pale light of dawn or dusk or the full glare of noon, gives the victim such a shock that he cannot resist the yakku's special type of disease.

The yakkus are, however, all henchmen of the great sickness demon Maha-Kola-Sanni-Yaksaya, who has promised the gods to spare mankind from disease if he and his followers receive proper sacrifices to feed on. The family of a sufferer has only to offer such sacrifices and the yakku who inflicted the illness will restore him to health.

Yakkus should not be confused with yakshas and yakshis, the earth spirits who are usually friendly to humans although the females (yakshis) may sometimes steal and eat little children.

Yeti

Otherwise known as the Abominable Snowman. Probably related to Bigfoot, although the two creatures inhabit very different parts of the world. Bigfoot's habitat is the wilderness of North America, while the Yeti is restricted to the uplands and mountains of Nepal and Tibet.

Both creatures appear only in the winter months. They have a particular dislike for bears, which hibernate during winter, and they walk with some difficulty except in deep snow. They emerge from their dens in autumn, but do not move far away from them until the ground is covered with snow.

The Rufous Yeti, which lives in the higher mountains of Nepal where the snow lies all year round, is an exception to this rule. Apparently it does not hibernate and is active all year round. Claims to have seen Bigfoot during the summer months are always proved to have been the sighting of an unusually large bear.

The tracks of both Bigfoot and Yeti have some resemblance to a bear's hind feet, being long and heavily padded, but the difference is that Bigfoot and Yeti walk with long two-footed strides and their tracks show four humanoid toes on each foot. The depth to which the tracks are pressed into the snow shows that the creatures are of substantial size and weight.

Both Bigfoot and Yeti appear to be harmless to humans, although a sudden confrontation with either creature might cause it to lash out in alarm.

The people of Bigfoot and Yeti habitats claim to have heard the creatures grunting and snuffling outside their tents during the long winter nights, but they never venture out in pursuit.

Their superstitious fear of the creatures has given rise to such unjustified names as the Abominable Snowman, although conservationists are certain that Bigfoot and Yeti are merely the harmless survivors of an endangered species.

Zaltys

A snake of the eastern Baltic countries, non-venomous and non-aggressive. In fact, the presence of a zaltys around a farmstead is generally fortunate, and if it can be tempted into the house by such gifts as saucers of milk then the prosperity of the family and the fertility of the crops and animals are assured. The zaltys is appointed, however, by the gods to keep a careful eye on the morality of mankind, and if the farmer and his family misbehave themselves then the zaltys is likely to glide silently away. All the good things that the family has enjoyed will then disappear with the zaltys.

CHAPTER THREE

THINGS OF WONDERLAND

THINGS OF WONDERLAND

Wonderlands have existed ever since Chaos cohered into the Cosmos. They are the places where wondrous things may happen, not necessarily pleasant because a Wonderland is simply a 'country full of surprises'. They have always lain just on the other side of the ranges, or across the turbulent seas, or even beyond the stars. As soon as men began to travel beyond their own villages they brought back tales of all kinds of Wonderlands: of people, places, and creatures so amazing they could hardly be credited by stay-at-homes. How could a man who had never seen anything larger than an ox believe stories of whales and elephants?

But, as time went by, such tales of Wonderlands were proven to be true. When, then, should one not believe in Wonderlands not recorded on our maps? There is a far greater world around us than may be recorded by solemn cartographers, because it exists in dimensions they cannot delineate. Wonderlands lie beyond the horizons of land and sea but not beyond those of the imagination, and one may set off for them without the slightest difficulty. They have the great advantage that one may visit them at will, by taking ship with Sindbad or going on trek with Allan Quatermain, and return with a fresh new perspective upon a world whose wonders have become too familiar to our eyes.

We need Wonderlands because they provide escape routes out of an existence besieged by folly and disaster. They provide the Treasure Islands on which we discover riches beyond the reach of credit cards: King Solomons Mines which supply the uncut diamonds of imagination. Some Wonderlands may impart the agreeable thrill of horror, and others a glimpse into a world where all our problems have been solved. They may make us feel better or worse about the way we live, but at least they help us to feel different. They all teach us that there is more in life than our eyes can see.

The keys to Wonderland (like the golden key which allowed Alice into the garden of the King and Queen of Hearts) is always ready to our hands. Alice had to make herself smaller before she could walk through into Wonderland, and no doubt we should follow her example.

Aeaea or Aiaia

A small island in the Aegean Sea, very prettily situated but shunned by the people of other islands because it is infested by lions pounce upon unwary wolves and the survive by preying upon each other. The lions pounced upon unwary wolves and the wolfpacks corner solitary lions.

The only building on the island is the ruin of the magnificent palace built by Queen Circe of Sarmatia, after she poisoned her husband and exiled herself to the island. Circe was a powerful sorceress who despised men, although she often made use of them in obscene orgies and rituals. After she settled on the island she used to welcome wandering seafarers and treat them to a banquet, but as they roistered happily in the company of their beautiful hostess she slipped a potion in their wine which changed them into animals. Naturally the lions and wolves ate most of the other animals and became the dominant species on the island.

All went well for Circe until the great hero Odysseus of Ithaca landed on Aeaea on his way home from the Trojan Wars. She welcomed him and his crew in her usual manner, but his suspicions were aroused by the unusual number of feral animals roaming the island. Hermes, the helpful messenger of the gods, had given Odysseus a supply of the herb moly, which renders humans immune to enchantment, and before he sat down to the banquet he swallowed a dose of this potent drug.

Very soon his seamen began to snort and snuffle like pigs, their noses turned into snouts, their ears grew longer, their hands and feet turned into pigs' feet, and before the banquet was over they had turned into a herd of swine. Odysseus met Circe's puzzled glances when he alone retained his human form, and as the pigs rooted and snuffled through the remains of the banquet he drew his dagger and advanced upon the sorceress.

Odysseus quickly persuaded Circe to change the pigs back into seamen, but he found that he was not immune to her sorcery after all. She caused him to forget about his wife Penelope for a year and a day, and instead of continuing his voyage he stayed on Aeaea to enjoy Circe's favours. He pleased her so greatly that when his memory returned she directed him on the best way to sail home to Ithaca.

But Circe's period of dalliance did not

change her wicked ways. She continued to work her spells on seafarers until her relations became ashamed of her and she was murdered by her son-in-law.

Apes, City of

The slavegirl Scheherezade, whose remarkable knowledge of the Oriental world is collected in the Book of Hazar Afsana, recorded that the City of the Apes is pleasantly situated between the sea and the forest on the western shore of the Arabian Sea. The inhabitants live in elegant highrise buildings overlooking the sea and the busy port enjoys a lucrative trade in coconuts. A notable feature of the city is the enormous number of small boats comfortably fitted with every convenience, drawn up along the ocean beaches or anchored just offshore.

The city's economy depends upon the hordes of vicious apes which inhabit the inland forests, and the citizens live in a strange symbiosis with these creatures.

At sunset each evening the people troop down to the beaches and take their boats out to sea, where they enjoy a peaceful night while the apes swarm into the city in search of booty and prey. They break into the buildings and seize whatever they desire, and kill and eat any citizen foolish enough to miss his place in the maritime exodus.

At dawn, the apes retreat to the forests and the people land again. They first clear up the chaos caused by the apes and then prepare great baskets of stones. Armed with these, they venture into the forest in order to bombard the apes. As soon as the apes hear the people coming they scamper up coconut palms, and when the first stone is thrown they respond by flinging coconuts at their attackers. The battle continues until all the stones have been thrown, when the people fill their baskets with the coconuts flung by the apes and carry this harvest back to the city. Several times a year, the collection of coconuts grows so large that they can load ships with them to trade with other cities. This trade brings so much prosperity to the City of the Apes that its people regard the marauding apes as benefactors and vigorously oppose any suggestions for the extermination of the species.

Apes, Mountain of

In the days of the mighty Caliph Haroun Al-Rashid an ambitious young merchant named Sindbad lived in Baghdad. Trading in the bazaars did not offer enough opportunity for his ambition and he decided that fortune lay in overseas commerce. Having saved 300 gold dirhems he bought a quantity of merchandise and took it aboard a dhow sailing out of Al-Basrah, to trade with the mysterious lands surrounding the Arabian Sea.

On his first two voyages he had startling adventures but laid the foundations of his fortune, and decided to risk a third voyage. On this venture, all went prosperously until the crew and passengers of the dhow saw a great rocky island looming upon the horizon. A strong wind and tide drove the dhow steadily towards the craggy shores, and the captain suddenly cried 'O know, ye people, whom God may preserve, that the wind hath driven us, by evil fortune, towards the Mountain of the Apes, from which none ever escape.'

The crew saved the dhow from running on the rocky shore by dropping the anchor, and Sindbad felt there was some chance of escape. But then he saw a horde of ape-like creatures bounding down the mountainside, and a few minutes later they swam to the ship and swarmed aboard. The apes were of hideous appearance, having yellow eyes, black faces, and manes like lions. First they gnawed through all the ropes of the dhow, so that it could not put to sea again, then seized Sindbad and the others and dragged them all ashore.

The marooned voyagers wandered hopelessly around the island, whose shores were strewn with the timbers of wrecked ships, until they came to a fortress with tightly closed doors and windows. The ashes of cooking fires and a quantity of charred human bones littered the ground outside the fortress, and great cooking pots gave an ominous hint of the fate in store for Sindbad and his companions.

But they were so weary that they could only lie down and sleep until sunset, when a fearsome monster emerged from the fortress. He was as tall as a palm tree and as black as coal. His eyes blazed like two fires, he had tusks like a boar, a mouth like a well, lips like a camel's hanging down to his chest, ears reaching to his shoulders, and nails like a lion's claws.

The monster seized, roasted, and devoured one of the sailors, and on each following evening he made his supper from another of the voyagers. At last Sindbad told the survivors that there was only one way to escape their horrid destiny. They made rafts from the wreckage along the shore, then found a way into the fortress and put out the monster's eyes as he was sleeping.

But the monster had a mate, and as he staggered to his feet he bellowed for help. She guided him in pursuit of Sindbad and his friends as they ran for their rafts and paddled frantically away from the island, and helped him to bombard the escapees with huge boulders. The monsters sank one raft after another, but Sindbad and two companions managed to paddle out of range.

After many hardships they landed on what seemed to be a pleasant island, only to find that it was the home of a gigantic snake. This reptile ate Sindbad's friends but he was lucky enough to be rescued by a ship passing the island.

Atlantis

When the great gods divided the Cosmos between them, Poseidon the Lord of the Ocean took possession of a chain of islands stretching from Spain to Central America. The largest of these islands was as big as the whole of Asia Minor.

When Poseidon inspected his new domain he found the islands to be more beautiful than anywhere else in the world. Every leaf on every tree glistened as brilliantly as an emerald, and the rolling pasturelands were as sleek and green as the waves of a summer sea. The flowers were so richly scented that they made the warm air as intoxicating as wine. Great herds of tame cattle grazed the pastures, the water in the streams was as clear as crystal and as fragrant as clover, while the hillsides shone with veins of white, black, and red marble and with deposits of every kind of precious metal.

The great god discovered that the people of the islands were singularly handsome and intelligent, but so newly created that they had no leaders or social organisation. They had not even given a name to their island home.

As Poseidon explored the land he came to a high hill rising from the very centre of the largest island, and he climbed through its flowering forests until, close to the summit, he found the abode of the most beautiful woman he had ever seen. She told him her name was Cleito. The dazzling glance of her sea-blue eyes, and the sumptuous beauty of her face and form, aroused such lust in the potent deity that he conquered her without delay. She responded ardently to his power and splendour and in due course bore him ten fine sons. They named the firstborn Atlas, and Poseidon named the islands and the surrounding ocean in honour of his son. They became Atlantis while the ocean is the Atlantic.

Poseidon is the most violent and jealous of the gods, distrustful of all mortals including Cleito, and so he isolated her upon her hill by digging three great moats around it. Each was about a kilometre wide, and separated from the others by a circle of land of the same width. Thus the Hill of Cleito was surrounded by great concentric circles of land and water.

When Poseidon's ten sons grew to maturity he made them all into kings, each with responsibility for one-tenth of Atlantis. Under his orders they formed themselves into a council, led by Atlas, to rule the nation for the benefit of all its people.

The Atlanteans were so vigorous and intelligent, so adept at developing their arts and technology and so industrious in exploiting the resources of the islands, that they soon established the world's first and finest civilisation. With Poseidon's permission, and under the guidance of the ten kings, they built a magnificent city upon the circles of earth surrounding the Hill of Cleito. Atlantean architects used the red, black, and white marble of their country to design buildings of dazzling splendour, with the three colours artfully blended or contrasted to attract and please the eye. On the Hill of Cleito they built her a great palace, and this together with the palaces of the ten kings and the temples to Poseidon all blazed with inlays of gold and precious stones. The principal temple to Poseidon was the wonder of all the world. The pinnacled roof was so high that clouds drifted around its spires, and it contained an enormous image of Poseidon riding in his chariot attended by sea nymphs and dolphins.

The unique beauty of the city, on its circles of land linked by great bridges across the circles of water, was further enhanced by brilliant gardens, groves of flowering trees, and innumerable sparkling fountains. Great universities, observatories, libraries, laboratories, and academies for people of all ages showed that Atlantis was the well-spring of human arts and sciences.

Portions of the city were devoted to commerce and industry, because the Atlanteans used the discoveries of their scientists and technologists as the basis of a flourishing trade with other nations. They dug a great canal from the city to the sea, so that ships could sail right up to the water-circles and pass from one to another by tunnels dug through the land-circles.

Visitors to the city wrote enthusiatically of its beautiful women and handsome men; of the freedom they enjoyed under the laws of the ten kings; of the skilled craftsmen who wrought in base and precious metals, and of the fresh sea breezes which cleared the smoke of their foundries from the air; of the busy markets where countryfolk sold the rich and colourful produce of their farms; and of the frequent festivals which brought throngs of Atlanteans singing and dancing into the streets.

The greatest of these festivals was staged once every five years, when the ten kings assembled in Poseidon's temple for their quinquennial parliament. While they deliberated, stockmen drove a number of splendid bulls in from the outlying ranches and corralled them within the temple grounds. Great crowds assembled to admire these monstrous animals with their sleek hides and sword-like crescent horns, while warriors and noblemen prepared for the bull-hunt. When the parliament was over, the bulls were released and the hunters chased them barehanded through the temple grounds, dodging their charges as they attempted to seize one and throw it to the ground. At last a group of hunters would manage to corner a bull and wrestle it to the ground, and the animal was then sacrificed to the glory of Poseidon. The other bulls were taken back

to their ranches and the festival concluded with a great public banquet.

The scientists and technocrats of Atlantis were not jealous of their skills and learning. They acted as industrial missionaries who spread their knowledge all over the known world. They taught the Egyptians and the Mayans how to build pyramids and the Greeks how to construct Atlantes, the sculptured figures of males which support the architraves of temples and other buildings. They spread their knowledge of metallurgy, astronomy, medicine, magnetism, and many other arts and sciences, wherever the ships of Atlantis could sail. They invented reading and writing, mathematics, agriculture, architecture, and all the concepts of human civilisation. It was rumoured also that Atlantean scientists expected to discover the mystic force which powers the Cosmos, and that when they had harnessed this force there would be no limit to human achievements.

For many centuries, Atlantis was the centre of the world. The peace and security of the nation were protected by a great army and navy, too strong to be challenged by any other country, and the Atlanteans enjoyed long contented lives of achievement and prosperity.

But, about 1200 centuries ago, the Parliament of the Ten Kings began to alter its attitude towards the outside world. In one of the quinquennial parliaments, the kings decided that it was not enough for the Atlanteans to spread their civilisation far and wide. Those who benefited from the Atlantean technocracy should also become its subjects and pay tribute to their imperial masters.

Thus the Atlanteans embarked upon the conquest of the world. Their ships took

expeditionary forces to Central and South America, where they overwhelmed the Incas, Aztecs, and Mayas and sent rich booty back to Atlantis. Another force conquered the whole of North Africa, and regrouped in Egypt so that they might invade Greece and then sweep eastwards through the kingdoms of Asia.

In about 9500 BC, a great Atlantean invasion fleet sailed into the bay of Athens, where a vastly outnumbered force of Athenians waited to resist them. When the two armies clashed the arrows flew in such clouds that they darkened the sky, the hooves of the chariot horses were like thunder upon Olympus, the brazen armour of the Atlanteans dazzled the eye and their spearheads seemed as multitudinous as wheat growing in a field. But the Athenians fought desperately in defence of their city-state and at last the massed battalions of Atlantis faltered, fell back, and turned in headlong retreat towards their ships.

The Atlantean fleet was about to set sail when the whole sky turned the colour of dry blood, and a mass of black clouds swept across it with such a dreadful sound as had never been heard before. The seas rose in gigantic waves which swallowed the entire fleet, while the whole world reverberated with earthquakes and the ocean roared and rushed from one sea to another like water swilling around in an immense bowl.

For days on end it seemed the whole Cosmos would fly apart. The skies deluged the earth with water, the mountains shuddered and cracked apart, the oceans were a torment of monstrous waves. When at last the seas became calm again a few battered ships crept into port. They brought the news that Atlantis had disappeared, and that the Atlantic Ocean rolled over the place where this magnificent empire once flourished in all its glory.

Ever since those days, historians have debated the reason why Atlantis was obliterated. Some say that Poseidon was angered by the Athenian victory, and punished his people with total destruction. Others say that an Atlantean scientist had discovered the forbidden secrets of the Cosmos, and released the forces which may eventually destroy the whole of mankind.

Avalon

The abode of heroes, more correctly written as Ynys yr Afallon which in the Welsh language means 'Isle of Apples'. The island lies in the centre of a great lake whose still waters gleam like blue steel, and are surrounded by dark forests. A hero slain in battle must find his painful way through these forests until he reaches the shores of the lake, where a boat draped in black cloth awaits him with a mysterious woman sitting silently at the helm.

The boat glides across to the island without causing a ripple on the still waters, and as it approaches Avalon the hero's gaping wounds become whole again. With all his manly vigour restored to him he steps onto the beautiful island, where the sun always shines and rough weather is unknown. Orchards of apple trees laden with glowing fruit rise up from the water's edge, and as he walks amongst them the grass is like a soft green lawn beneath his feet.

Towards the centre of the island there are green silent forests with flowery glades, filled with such peace as men will never know on earth. When the dead hero wanders contentedly through this forest he slowly becomes aware of the other inhabitants of the island. They are heroes like himself, who have perished in the defence of the right against the powers of darkness, together with a race of beautiful women who are the keepers of that magic which inspires mankind with charity, courage, kindliness, and pure-hearted love.

In the depths of the forest there is a small church built by Joseph of Arimathea, and it is there that the hero finds the supreme joy of worshipping the Creator who gave him, during life, the strength to combat evil and defy the oppressor.

Balnibarbi

An island to the east of Japan, visited by Lemuel Gulliver on 16 February 1708. Balnibarbi was then subject to the monarch of the flying island Laputa, and shortly before Gulliver's visit it was administered by the Lord Munodi, to whom Gulliver had letters of introduction. Munodi had, however, recently been relieved of his duties because of 'lack of understanding'.

Gulliver found a remarkable contrast between the lifestyles of Munodi and the other inhabitants of the island. Munodi had a splendid palace in the capital city, Lagado, and a fine country estate. All the other Balnibarbians lived in oddly proportioned houses of which many were almost ruinous and the best were sadly neglected. Munodi was a reasonable and cultured man, whereas most other Balnibarbians had a ragged and dishevelled appearance, a fixed stare, and a way of hurrying wildly through the streets. When Munodi took Gulliver to his country estate, Gulliver noticed that the farms along the way had excellent soil but that it was merely being churned up by the farm labourers, and he could see no likelihood of crops resulting from their aimless toil. Everyone seemed busy and preoccupied but looked haggard and miserable.

At Munodi's estate, everything was neatly arranged and the farmlands were prosperous. The gardens of Munodi's country home were elegant and beautiful and the house was in perfect repair.

Gulliver complimented Munodi on these matters but the nobleman only sighed, and remarked that the Balnibarbians ridiculed him for setting such a poor example to the rest of the kingdom. After supper that night, he said with a very melancholy air that he would soon have to pull down his house, and the houses of his tenant farmers, and rebuild them in the new fashion. Also, the farmers would have to uproot their crops and cultivate their fields in a different way.

He told Gulliver that, about forty years earlier, a group of Balnibarbians had spent five months on the flying island of Laputa. This brief acquaintance with the scientific theoreticians of the flying island had given them only a little learning but a vast number of new ideas, so that they decided to reform the entire economy of Balnibarbi. The king, who was always in favour of new ideas, gave them a royal warrant to establish an Academy of Projectors, i.e. of men who invent and promote new projects, schemes, theories, and ideas.

This new breed of intellectuals proclaimed that Balnibarbi was about to enter a golden age. They said their new techniques would enable one man to do the work of ten, great buildings to be erected in a week out of materials that would last forever, and farmers to reap rich harvests whenever they wished.

The Balnibarbians accepted this new doctrine with great enthusiasm. Academies of Projectors sprang up in every city, and the Professors of Projection devised new rules and methods for agriculture and building, together with new instruments and tools for every kind of art, craft, trade, and profession. The Balnibarbians abandoned all their old working methods in favour of the new ones, but they soon discovered they were only theories which had not been practised. Nevertheless the people believed the claims of the intellectuals and tried to make their theories work, until the whole countryside had been laid waste, the buildings were falling down, and the citizens were ragged and starving.

As one example of the projectors' theories, Munodi showed Gulliver a ruined building on a nearby mountainside. He said he had once had a fine watermill on his estate, big enough to grind the grain from most of the farms, but the projectors assured him that instead of using the river to operate the mill, as had been done from time immemorial, it would be better to pump the water up to the top of the mountain and let it run down again. Munodi accepted the idea because the Balnibarians were beginning to regard him as old fashioned and opposed to progress, and employed 100 men for two years to dig a canal along the ridge of the mountain and pump water up to it. When the scheme did not work properly the projectionists blamed him for its failure.

Gulliver was greatly interested in any new theory and so he visited the Academy of Projectors in Lagado, an assembly of large buildings containing about 500 rooms. Each contained one or more projectors working on a new scheme to improve the lot of mankind.

In the first room he found a man working on a project to extract sunbeams from cucumbers and preserve them in hermetically sealed containers, so that they might be released during inclement summers. He had been working on the scheme for eight years and felt sure that in another eight years he would have trapped sufficient sunbeams to supply the governor's garden.

In other rooms, Gulliver met projectors engaged on such schemes as turning ice into gunpowder, teaching blind apprentices to mix colours for artists by feel and smell, and training spiders to spin strong and richly-coloured silks by feeding them a diet of coloured flies, gum, and oil. An agricultural projector was developing a scheme for ploughing farmland by the use of hogs, thus saving the farmer the cost of ploughs, horses, and labour. He would only have to bury acorns, chestnuts, dates, and other food favoured by hogs in the field to be ploughed, and then set a herd of 600 hogs to work in it. The hogs would root up the ground in search of the buried food and also fertilise it with their dung. Experiments so far had been unsuccessful but the projector was working on improvements.

Another projector had observed that bees and spiders always build their homes by starting at the top and working downwards, and had concluded that this must be the most natural and efficient way of building. He had designed a way for human habitations to be built from the roof downwards.

One of the most noted projectors was known as the Universal Artist. In his laboratory, fifty assistants were hard at work on such projects as softening marble for use as pillows, and condensing air into a dry tangible substance. The Universal Artist was himself working on two important projects. One was to prevent the growth of wool on lambs, so that Balnibarbians might have a breed of naked sheep and be saved the trouble of shearing them. The other was to sow land with chaff instead of seed. He showed, by various experiments Gulliver could not understand, that chaff contains the true seminal virtue of growing plants.

In another room, Gulliver inspected a book-writing machine. This consisted of a large wooden frame filled with wooden cubes strung upon wires. A piece of paper was pasted on each side of each cube, and on these papers were written all the words of the Balnibarbian language. To work the machine, forty of the projector's pupils turned handles on the sides of the frame, so that all the cubes turned and presented the words on their upper surfaces. Thirty-six of the pupils then read off the lines of words, and when they found any which made up a sentence they repeated it to the other four pupils, who acted as scribes.

This process was repeated again and again in various combinations and permutations, and the projector had already assembled a number of volumes full of the broken sentences read off the frame. He intended to piece them into consecutive texts and the result would be a complete library of arts and sciences. The work would be greatly expedited if only the public would contribute towards the construction of 500 book-writing machines.

In the School of Languages, three professors were consulting on methods to improve the language of Balnibarbi. One scheme was to delete all words except nouns, which would suffice to nominate all things imaginable. Another, which was greatly favoured, was to do away with talking altogether. This plan would extend human life, because conversation corrodes the lungs and leads to an early death. There would be no problems of communication, because men would simply carry with them such things as it was necessary for them to discourse on. Gulliver noticed a number of wise men carrying such bundles of things on their backs. When two of them met they opened their bundles and held conversations for an hour or so by showing the things to each other. Inside a building, rooms were stocked with all manner of things so that people might converse by pointing them out to each other. The projectors claimed that the idea might lead to a universal language between civilised nations, but it found no favour with the women and ordinary people of Balnibarbi.

In the School of Mathematics, students learned mathematical propositions by writing them on thin wafers with cephalic ink, and then swallowing them on an empty stomach. After that they had to live for three days on bread and water, so that the cephalic ink might rise to the brain and infuse it with the mathematical knowledge. So far the scheme had not been successful because the wafers tasted so foul that the students often spat them out, or if they did swallow them they insisted on living on other foods than bread and water.

Gulliver was intrigued by some of the techniques projected in the School of Politics. One was that when a politician argued vehemently in favour of some proposal, he should be obliged to vote against it. The Professor of Politics said that this idea would infallibly result in the good of the public.

He also proposed that when two political parties could not agree the authorities should choose 100 members of each party, saw open their skulls, and effect a brain exchange by transplanting half of each politician's brain into the skull of an opponent and vice versa. This would enable the two half-brains, fitted within one skull, to debate the matter at issue and come to an understanding. The professor did not foresee any problems of tissue rejection because he said there is a negligible difference between the brains of politicians.

Two of the professors had developed an effective new system for raising taxes. One was a tax upon vices and follies, with each person to be judged by a jury of his or her neighbours. Another was a tax on beauty for women and wit, valour, and politeness of men, with each person assessing the amount of these qualities in himself or herself and being taxed accordingly.

Gulliver enjoyed some lengthy discussions on politics with the various professors, but on the whole he found Balnibarbi an uncomfortable place of residence and he was glad to leave it for the island of Glubbdubdrib.

Blefuscu

An island lying south of Australia, and separated from the island of Lilliput by a channel 727 metres wide. Blefuscu is about the same size as Lilliput and the people, flora and fauna, lifestyles, and buildings are very similar, although the languages are totally different. There is a considerable trade between the two islands and a long-established tradition that young Lilliputians and Blefuscudians of good family should spend some time travelling in each other's island, by way of seeing the world.

Despite these neighbourly connections, the Emperors of Blefuscu have caused considerable resentment by intervening in the conflicts between the Big-Endians and Little-Endians of Lilliput. This conflict began in about 1600 AD, when the people of both islands customarily ate their eggs by breaking them open at the big end. A Crown Prince of Lilliput happened to cut his finger when following this tradition, however, whereupon the emperor ordained that Lilliputians must henceforward open their eggs at the little end.

This edict caused a division of Lilliputians into Big-Endians, who insisted on following ancient custom, and Little-Endians who obeyed the new law. The Emperor of Blefuscu encouraged the Big-Endians to revolt against their rulers and gave sanctuary to Lilliputian refugees, while the clergymen and statesmen of both countries quarrelled bitterly over the words of the prophet Lustrog. He wrote in the Brundrecal (the Lilliputian-Blefuscidian Bible) that 'All true believers shall break their eggs at the convenient end.'

About 11,000 Lilliputians suffered martyrdom in the cause of the Big-Endians, who were forbidden to publish books or articles on their belief or to hold any government employment. Thousands more escaped to Blefuscu, where the people sympathised with their plight and assisted their plans to restore the old beliefs in Lilliput.

The most grievous consequence of the controversy was a series of bitter wars by land and sea. When Gulliver arrived in Lilliput the most recent war had been raging for some time and the Lilliputians had lost 30,000 men, forty battleships, and many smaller craft. The Blefuscidians had assembled a great invasion fleet and Lilliput lived in fear of a Big-Endian victory.

Gulliver helped them by wading and swimming across the channel between the islands, capturing the Blefuscidian fleet, and towing it back to Lilliput. But it seems likely that the subsequent peace conference resulted in no more than a pause in hostilities, and that the Big-Endians and Little-Endians each remain convinced of the rightness of their cause.

Brobdingnag

A substantial kingdom inhabited by giants. It is located in the northern Pacific Ocean, and connected to the North American mainland by an isthmus of huge mountains capped by active volcanoes. The coastline consists almost entirely of towering cliffs and jagged rocks and the country has no seaports. Attempts to enter Brobdingnag by air are inadvisable because of the proliferation of enormous eagles, each large enough to lift a European-sized cottage in its talons, to say nothing of other birdlife of comparable size.

Brobdingnag is an autocracy which has been ruled by the same royal family since the seventeenth century, or even earlier. Before that time the country was wracked by civil strife between the king, the people, and the nobility, until one of the kings (possibly Barangatch I) instituted a new legal code and created a militia of 208,000 infantry and cavalry to keep the nation in order. This powerful force, in which each horseman mounted on his charger is thirty metres high, discourages any thought of intervention by foreign powers even though the royal family abhors the invention of firearms and refuses to introduce them into the nation.

The kings of Brobdingnag reject any alliances or contacts with other countries. King Barangatch III gave it as his opinion, after discussions with Dr Lemuel Gulliver, that the human race outside Brobdingnag is 'the most pernicious race of little odious vermin that Nature ever suffered to crawl upon the surface of the earth.'

Gulliver landed in Brobdingnag, after the ship in which he served as surgeon had been blown off her course by persistent storms. The ship anchored off the coast and Gulliver went ashore with some of the crew to find water, but was marooned when a huge Brobdingnagian appeared and frightened the other men away.

Gulliver left a comprehensive description of the country and he appears to have been the last visitor from the outside world. He found the Brondingnagians, despite their gigantic size, to be a rather simple and contented people, without much interest in the subtleties and mysteries of politics. King Barangatch told him that 'Whoever could make two ears of corn, or two blades of grass, to grow upon a spot of ground where only one grew before, would deserve better of mankind, and do more essential service to his country, than the whole race of politicians put together.'

No law in Brobdingnag must exceed in words the number of letters in their alphabet, which contains only twenty-two characters. Gulliver found that most laws contain even fewer than twenty-two words, and their clarity and brevity mean that everyone can understand them. There is little need for lawyers, and in fact the profession of law is fraught with danger. Even the writing of a commentary on any law is punishable by decapitation.

The Brobdingnagians invented printing at about the same time as the Chinese, but publish comparatively few books. The king himself has only about a thousand volumes in his library. Gulliver was allowed to read them, which he did by having each book propped against the wall and using a machine constructed for him by the queen's carpenter. This was a kind of ladder about eight metres high, with each step sixteen metres long. When it was placed against a book, Gulliver walked along the top step to read the first line of the text and then descended the steps to read each of the subsequent lines. He climbed the ladder again to read the facing page, and used both hands to turn over the pages, which were as thick and stiff as pasteboard.

In one of these books he learned that, in ancient times, the Brobdingnagians were even larger than when he visited them. Huge bones and skulls had been unearthed in various parts of the kingdom, and some people thought that the Brobdingnagians were very puny folk compared with those of the past.

Gulliver found that their authors wrote very smoothly and clearly, because they do not use unnecessary words. They devote themselves to practical matters such as the improvement of agriculture and other useful arts and have no liking for abstractions. The king believed that common sense, reason,

FLANFLASNIC
AD 1703 BROBDINGNAG
LORBRULGRUD
ONE GLONGLUNG = 87 KM

justice and lenience are the only qualities required for the government of a country.

When Gulliver landed in Brobdingnag he was terrified by the difference in size between him and the inhabitants. He hid from them in a wheatfield where the stalks were thirteen metres high, and narrowly escaped death when farm labourers began to harvest the field with enormous sickles. One of them picked him up and took him to the farmhouse, where the farmer placed him on the table and fed him with morsels from the family dinner. The farmer and his family were fascinated by the miniature man found on their property, and when he became a little used to the Brobdingnagians he thought they were a comely people, although he was deafened by the thunder of their voices and their skins seemed repulsively rough and coarse. When the farmer's wife suckled her baby he was disgusted by the sight of her monstrous breast. It protruded for two metres and had a nipple half the size of his head, and was so covered with great spots, pimples, and freckles that he felt nothing could be more nauseating.

He slept in the kitchen under a handkerchief, which was as large and coarse as a ship's sail. During the night he was attacked by rats as large as mastiffs, and had to kill one with his sword.

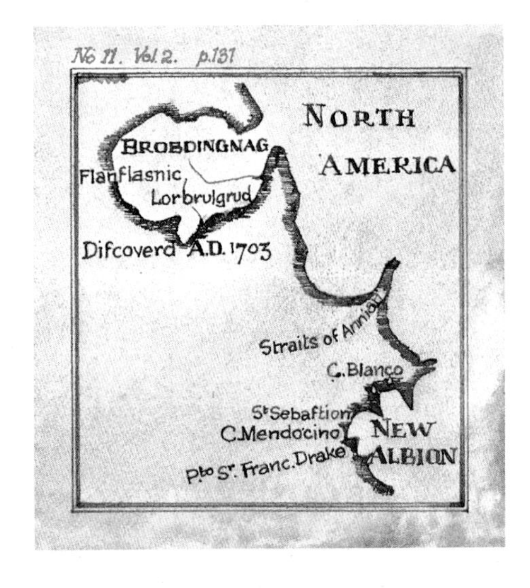

The farmer's daughter, a girl of nine years old who was only twelve metres high and was regarded as small for her age, took charge of Gulliver and looked after him very well. She taught him the language of Brobdingnag, made him new clothes from fine linen which to Gulliver seemed as harsh as sackcloth, and gave him the name of Grildrig which means 'manikin'. Gulliver called her Glumdalclitch, meaning 'little nurse'.

He was just becoming accustomed to the strangeness of living with people whose ankles were as high as his head when a friend of the farmer suggested that he should display Gulliver in public for an entrance fee. The crowds of giants who flocked to see the manikin made this a fearful and exhausting experience for Gulliver, but the venture was so successful that the farmer decided to take him on a tour of the kingdom. He rode in a padded box secured to Glumdalclitch's belt as she rode pillion behind her father. Horse travel in this manner was very uncomfortable for Gulliver because the horse travelled about thirteen metres at every step, and trotted so high that the motion was like that of a ship in a violent storm.

The farmer displayed Gulliver in many towns and villages before they reached the capital, Lorbrulgrud, which means 'Pride of the Universe'. The ardours of travel and public performances, when huge faces stared at him and the voices roared like thunder above his head, exhausted Gulliver so completely that the farmer thought he would die and made him work even harder, so that the farmer might make as much out of a good thing as possible.

But Gulliver was saved by a command from the royal court that he should be taken there for the diversion of the queen and her ladies. They were so taken by him that they bought him from the farmer for 1000 pieces of gold, and he began a new and more comfortable existence.

When the king first saw Gulliver he thought the manikin was an ingenious clockwork toy, because the Brobdingnagians are very skilled in making such items. But he soon became friendly with Gulliver and often debated the differences between their two countries.

The queen retained Glumdalclitch as Gulliver's nurse and guardian and ordered a special box for his bedchamber. It was about five metres square and four high and fitted with windows, doors, and closets.

Skilled craftsmen made Gulliver-size furniture out of a substance like ivory, and padded the walls of the box so that Gulliver would not be injured when it was carried about. The queen also ordered that he should be fitted out with new clothes made from the finest of Brobdingnagian silk. He found this was not much thicker than an English blanket and he soon became used to its weight.

The queen and the princesses became so fond of Gulliver's company that they made him their constant pet. He enjoyed their company except at mealtimes. When the queen put a morsel of bread into her gaping mouth it was as large as two English loaves, and she crunched up lark's wings nine times as large as a turkey's. She drank out of a huge golden cup, swallowing more than a hogshead at a draught.

Gulliver's greatest problem was the queen's favourite dwarf, who was only ten metres high. He was jealous of Gulliver and played many tricks on him. Once he tried to drown Gulliver in a bowl of cream, and on another occasion he stuck Gulliver's legs into a marrow bone.

During the hot summer, Gulliver was greatly plagued by flies as big as sparrows. He was disgusted by having to see every detail of a fly in such enormous magnification, but at least he was able to fight them off with his knife and was not in such danger as when he was attacked by a flight of wasps. Each wasp was as big as a partridge, with a sting four centimetres long, and they droned like bagpipes as they stole Gulliver's breakfast and swarmed around his head. In a battle with these monsters he killed four with his sword before the others flew away.

The queen provided a coach for Glumdalclitch to take Gulliver on trips around Lobrulgrud, which is the largest of the fifty-one cities and more than ninety walled towns of Brobdingnag. It is three *glonglungs* long and two-and-a-half wide (a *glonglung* equals about eighty-seven kilometres) and contains more than 80,000 houses. The chief buildings include the principal temple of the Brobdingnagian religion, but it disappointed Gulliver because it was only 1,000 metres high. It was, however, splendidly built from stone blocks fourteen metres square, with walls more than thirty metres thick.

Great crowds jostled to see Gulliver whenever Glumdalclitch carried him around the city, and he found this a repugnant experience because of their overwhelming stench and their enormous skin blemishes. Also he could see the lice on their clothes, so large that he could distinguish the limbs and snouts of these parasites.

He was equally repelled by the queen's Maids of Honour when Glumdalclitch took him to visit them in their chamber. Because of his miniature size they did not hesitate to change their clothing in his presence and the immensity of their nudity filled him with horror and disgust. Their skins seemed coarse and uneven, an occasional mole looked as big as a dinner plate, and their body hairs were as thick as packthreads. The prettiest of them, a frolicsome girl of sixteen, set Gulliver astride one of her nipples and played various other tricks with him.

Gulliver spent nearly two years in Brobdingnag and had many other experiences and adventures, including the time when the queen's pet monkey carried him away and he was rescued with great difficulty. Eventually he was taken on a Royal Progress through the country, which ended at the seaside palace near Flanflasnic. Glumdalclitch fell sick and could not look after Gulliver, but she entrusted his box to one of the court pages and told him to take Gulliver for an airing on the seashore. The page set the box down and wandered off among the rocks, and a little later one of the great eagles of the country snatched up the box and carried it away. After flying for some distance it was attacked by other eagles and dropped the box in the sea, where it drifted for several hours until a passing English merchantman plucked it out of the water.

Gulliver found it was very difficult to accustom himself to people of his own size, especially since he had become used to shouting loudly in order to make himself heard. The ship and everyone aboard her seemed absurdly small, and even when he reached home again his wife and daughter seemed like pygmies. After a little while he became used to them again, but they found it very difficult to believe in his stories about the country of giants.

Camelot

The castle-city of Camelot, capital of Britain and headquarters of Arthur the warrior-king, was built by a fairy king and fairy queens. Harps in hand, they created the city to the sound of music and their harps may still be heard sometimes between the shadows of one day and the next.

The city stands on a forest-girt hill arising out of a great plain. It is a short distance from the highway and river leading to the Isle of Shalott. The riverbanks are lined with willows and aspens that toss and quiver in the breeze, and on each side the fields of rye and barley stretch away to the horizon.

The traveller to Camelot sees the spires and turrets, towers and battlements, rooftops and gonfalons of the city like a misty mirage between the green haze of the forest and the arching sky. At dusk of evening and in morning mists the castle-city fades and hovers as though to deceive the eye: at night the towering silhouette glimmers with lantern-gleams through windows and arrow-slits; in the great golden light of noon the terraced buildings shimmer in the heat and the huge gate gleams golden in the sun. When storms blunder across the plain the city vanishes within a thunder cloud or hides behind grey curtains of rain. In autumn it stands above a golden ring of fading forest: in winter the white towers and snow-clad roofs can hardly be seen against the silvered plain. These endless changes, flowing one into another, make some wanderers fear that Camelot is an enchanter's city, and turn aside.

Traffic is busy on the highway and the river. Deep-laden barges ply between Camelot and the Isle of Shalott, and occasionally the Lady of Shalott skims anonymously among them in her silken-sailed shallop. Usually she stays in her four-towered castle, working at her loom while watching the highway traffic reflected in a mirror.

Red-cloaked market girls, village churls, shepherd lads, long-haired pageboys in crimson livery, fat churchmen on ambling mules, high-loaded haywains and strings of packhorses move along the highway. Men and women sow and reap and harvest in the fields, working from sunrise to moonrise, but with their labours lightened by the songs which float from the Lady of Shalott's castle.

Whenever a trumpet sounds from the turrets of Camelot, the people on the highway hasten to move aside. The silver notes herald a cavalcade of knights who canter down the winding road between the trees, riding from

Camelot onto the broad highway.

All in the blue unclouded weather, the knights make a gallant sight as they ride two by two, the heralds and standard-bearers trotting proudly between each troop with brilliant banners floating proudly high. The common folk doff their caps as the knights ride by: black-visaged Modred scowling at the throng; broad-browed Lancelot and Galahad smiling graciously at the maidens; Merlin the magician riding a little apart from the others, with his black robes and star-bedizened cap seeming to shimmer strangely in the sunlight.

The knights may be riding forth on another foray against the enemies of Britain, or perhaps on another attempt to rescue the Holy Grail. They are led by mighty Arthur himself, and the common folk hardly dare to meet his eagle glance or even to look at the caparisoned white stallion, led by a handsome squire, which carries Arthur's armour and his great sword Excalibur.

When a traveller climbs the steep road to Camelot he hears such strange music that he thinks the fairies may still be at their work of building the city. It grows louder as he steps through the gate into the first great courtyard, where he meets a guardian who makes the boldest pause. The Lady of the Lake stands there, her arms outstretched, one hand holding a sword and the other an ancient censer. Her dress ripples like water from her sides, a trickle of droplets falls from wither hand, and her grey eyes are fixed on such eternity as to make an evildoer's heart turn in his breast.

Each side of the gateway is carved with emblems and devices symbolising Arthur's wars, so cunningly wrought that the dragon-boughts and elvish emblemings appear to move, seethe, twine, and curl.

Once past the gateway the visitor finds a city of stately palaces, rich in emblems and the work of ancient kings. Merlin, at Arthur's bidding, used his arts to give a spiralling beauty to the many-towered city, and the eye is drawn continuously upwards to the peaks of spires and turrets.

Sixteen hundred knights and barons have their quarters in Camelot, all so jealous of their precedence that one Christmas feast became a battle over who should sit nearest the head of the table. Arthur had the Round Table built so that all the turbulent knights might sit around it in equality.

Within the city, the visitor finds that the strange music he heard is the busy sound of Camelot itself. The voices of those treading the steep streets and passageways mingle with minstrel songs and the notes of lute and zither floating from casements. A melodious clangour rises from the streets of the armourers and swordsmiths, who forge and fashion armour for horses and men and send great sprays of sparks cascading from their dark workshops as they sharpen battle-axes and two-handed swords. Fletchers make arrows for hunting or for war, farriers pound glowing horseshoes on their anvils, leather workers stitch at richly coloured saddles and harness. The deep chanting of monks rises above the battlements, where pacing sentinels watch the cavalcade of knights riding into the distance.

The centre of Camelot is the Great Hall of King Arthur, surrounded by kitchens and sleeping quarters and standing next to the tourney ground. The long vaulted hall stands so high that its ceiling is lost in smoky shadows. An oak tree smoulders on the huge hearth, to warm the knights feasting on barley bread, beef, and ale. Along each wall there is a triple row of shields carved out of the stone, each with a knight's name underneath. A shield remains blank until its owner

I MINERÆ
II METALLA
III MINERALIA
IV SALIA
V DECOMPOSIT
VI TERRÆ
VII DESTI

has done one noble deed, when Arthur has the knight's arms carved upon it. If he performs more noble deeds, then Arthur has the arms coloured and blazoned. The shield of Gawain is rich and bright, but that of Modred is as blank as death.

Arthur carries out all his kingly business within the hall, and from time to time commands a tourney to be held. The prizes are no more than a lady's veil or glove, but the knights prepare as ardently as if they were to do battle with the Saracens. Within the tourney ground, the knights ride at each other on their great warhorses with lances strong as ship's beakheads. Arthur will sometimes enter the lists, but he does not wield Excalibur because this would give him an unfair advantage.

At the end of the day, when wounds have been bound up, the knights celebrate loud and long within the Great Hall. Stories of warfare, mystic encounters, and vows to recapture the Holy Grail rise to the high arches of the hall.

Among the knights, Merlin sits brooding over past and future, foreseeing the day when Arthur will be carried to the Isle of Avalon and Camelot will fade into the mists of evening.

Celestial City

This serenely beautiful and exquisitely landscaped city is the longed-for destination of everyone who journeys through our mortal world, where so many travellers stray down the byways of evil and temptation that they never see the towers of the city gleaming upon the horizon.

The weary traveller who carries his burden through all the temptations and difficulties of the world, avoiding those allurements which make so many fall by the wayside, at last sees the Celestial City shining in the distance as brilliantly as the sunrise. He hastens his steps towards it but then finds he has to cross one final obstacle. This is the River of Death, whose inky waters surround the glorious city. There is no bridge across the waters and every traveller has to summon up the courage to find his own way across.

When the traveller reaches the banks of the dark river, the people of the Celestial City assemble on the other side and encourage him to make the crossing. He gazes across at the throng of citizens in their immaculate robes, their faces reflecting the joy which they have found, and as they beckon him and call his name he sees a group of celestial trumpeters assembling at the landing place.

At last he drops the heavy burden he has carried through the world and plunges into the river. As the black water rises above his head he tastes its dreadful bitterness, but if he swallows it quickly this bitterness becomes sweet. Some travellers find the crossing very difficult and have to struggle through deep pools, while others discover that they soon reach the other side.

As each traveller steps onto the shore of the Celestial City, the trumpeters sound a triumphant peal of welcome and all the citizens greet him with joyful songs. They clothe him in majesty and crown him with a garland of gold, so that he is properly attired to enter the gate above which is written 'Blessed are they that do His commandments, that they may have right to the Tree of Life; and may enter in through the Gates into the City.'

The city is built of pearls and precious stones and paved with gold, and stands amidst beautiful gardens, orchards, and vineyards. For the traveller who has crossed the River of Death this wondrous city will be home for all eternity.

Centre Earth

To enter the world within the earth, one must travel first to Iceland and the crater of the extinct volcano Sneffels Yokul. There, at noon on 26 June each year, the tip of the shadow of Mount Scartaris points the way to a terrifying abyss or 'chimney', 853·44 metres deep. It was discovered in about 1550 by Arne Saknussemm, and rediscovered in 1863 by Professor Otto Lidenbrock of Hamburg. With his nephew Axel and the Icelandic hunter Hans Bjelke he climbed down the chimney and embarked upon the fearsome journey into Centre Earth.

They took forty days to grope their way through the passages and caverns, but they started by erroneously following the eastern instead of the western fork of a tunnel at the bottom of the chimney. Any modern expedition (which must be well equipped and provisioned) should proceed directly along the western fork. Eventually, at a distance of at least 1400 kilometres from Iceland, this leads into a gigantic cavern 141.625 kilometres below Scotland. A sea, now known as the Lidenbrock Sea, covers much of the floor of this cavern.

It is illuminated by a strange clear white light, probably emanating from the electrical and magnetic properties of the inner globe. This light produces remarkable effects on the huge shifting clouds of vapour which arise from the sea, and obscure the granite roof of the cavern. But there is no warmth in it and its general effect is melancholy and dispiriting.

The Lidenbrock Sea appears unutterably wild and lonely as it stretches away to the misty horizon. The deeply indented shores are rimmed with beaches of fine golden sand, strewn with prehistoric seashells, and the waves break on these beaches with that sonorous murmur peculiar to huge enclosed spaces. From the beaches, a line of huge cliffs curves upwards to incredible heights and forms rugged capes and promontories. The water is cold, though not too cold for swimming, and in its further depths is full of huge beds of kelp with thick fleshy

streamers at least 1,000 metres long. This strange subterranean ocean stretches southwards to a point somewhere below Italy.

Around the northern shores of the Lidenbrock Sea, the vegetation of Centre Earth comprises forests of enormous mushrooms, up to thirteen metres high, and primitive plants such as tree ferns which grow to enormous heights. Further south, the forests resemble those of millions of years ago and are floored with thick moss and many flowers, but the lack of sunlight means that all the plants and trees are brownish and faded and the flowers seem to be made of paper.

Great quantities of surturbrand (fossilised wood) lie around the seashores. Some of this is only partially fossilised, and was used by Lidenbrock's party for building a raft.

Centre Earth offers little to eke out an expedition's provisions, except for the eyeless but edible fish to be caught in the Lidenbrock Sea. The bones of countless prehistoric animals lie in the forests, and Professor Lidenbrock even found the skull of a man of the Quaternary Period. Many huge creatures still survive. Lidenbrock's party saw a sea battle between a plesiosaurus and an ichthyosaurus, and, on the southern shores, they saw herds of mastodons browsing in the forest. They also glimpsed a creature, at least four metres high, which they believed to be a giant human being.

The navigational hazards of the Lidenbrock Sea include geysers, waterspouts, stretches of boiling water, electrical storms, and fierce gales. At the southern end, the waters of the sea pour out through a tunnel blasted by Lidenbrock's party, who used this method of finding a way out of Centre Earth. However the cataract which burst through this tunnel carried them into the bowels of the volcano Stromboli, and they were blasted up to the surface on their raft of surturbrand. Obviously such an escape route is fraught with hazards, and any modern expedition would be better advised to find its way back to the chimney leading up into Sneffels Yokul.

Cockayne

Some historians believe that this happy city was located on the present site of London. Others claim it stood in France, and that archaeologists have discovered fragments of Cockayne below the streets of Paris. The French connection seems very possible because Cockayne was famed, among other things, for the excellence of its food.

The Cockaigneans (or, as some say, Cockneys) enjoyed an existence of total contentment despite their perpetual idleness. They never needed to work because they were served twenty-four hours a day, by nymphs in the daytime and gnomes after sunset. Since they were supplied with everything they could possibly need they had no politics, no army, no ambitions, and in fact none of the qualities which lead to human discontent. They did not have to suffer old age, because a Cockaignean who reached the age of fifty immediately reverted to the age of ten. Men and women enjoyed an endless series of reincarnations, which perpetuated the most vigorous years of human life.

A river of excellent wine flowed through the city and never ran dry. The streets were paved with bread and pastries, roast geese and fowls wandered about the city inviting people to eat them, and the skies did not rain water but grilled larks braised in butter. Each tree bore many different kinds of fresh fruit, always ripe for plucking the whole year round. The flower blossoms consisted of chocolates and other confectionery. The houses were made of cake, while the royal palace and public buildings were constructed of spun barleysugar, icing sugar, peppermint rock, and other hard candies, which presented a magnificent sight when they glistened in the sunshine. All these foodstuffs automatically renewed themselves whenever a person helped himself. The shops were stocked with every requirement of the citizens, who might help themselves without thought of payment.

Inevitably this happy city attracted innumerable visitors, whom the jovial Cockaigneans welcomed so long as they came only for holidays. But as time went by the Cockaigneans were outnumbered by outsiders, who settled in the city and destroyed its ecological balance. Eventually the inhabitants were forced to use commonplace materials to renew their buildings. The river of wine ran dry, the nymphs and gnomes had to work too hard and all ran away, and the Cockaigneans interbred with the newcomers and lost all their endowments of immortality and contentment.

Delectable Mountains

A mountain range standing between the Plain of Ease and the River of Death which surrounds the Celestial City. The mountains are one of the final obstacles to be crossed by a traveller making his toilsome way through the world, en route to the Celestial City.

The mountain range can be misleading because it has so many attractive aspects that travellers may ignore the hidden dangers. Well-tended woodlands cover the lower slopes, interspersed by fruitful orchards and vineyards. Above the tree line there are pastures of sweet grass grazed by flocks of sheep, which are tended by the shepherds Knowledge, Sincere, Experience, and Watchful.

A traveller crossing the ranges is well advised to make friends with these shepherds, who are helpful guides to the ranges. They will take the time to introduce such local personalities as Goodly-Man, who lives on Mount Innocent. Two vandals named Prejudice and Ill-Will find his piety so annoying that they continuously fling dirt at him, but it never sticks to his spotless robes. On nearby Mount Charity, the resident gives clothing to poor people out of an inexhaustible supply.

Travellers who are determined to reach the Celestial City will always find a way through the ranges, but doubters and misbelievers will take false steps on Mount Error and plunge into the dreadful abyss below the mountain. Hypocrites always stray off the difficult path through the ranges and wander into a canyon leading direct to hell. Mount Caution displays the sad sight of a number of blind sinners groping among dismal tombs. They are those who wandered off the path of righteousness which leads across the Plain of Ease and fell into the hands of Giant Despair, who put out their eyes.

Any traveller with the strength and will to carry his burden through the Delectable Mountains will avoid all such dangers and difficulties, and eventually see the jewelled spires of the Celestial City shining beyond the River of Death.

Delightful Haven

Some old seafarers reckon that Delightful Haven is located in the West Indies, where the rum is cheap and the island girls are kind. Others believe it is a snug little seaport in the Western Isles, where the fishing fleet returns at evening and the fishermen can walk home to cottages where buxom wives await them with a good supper and a tot of whisky. The crewmen of clipper ships, battling their way around Cape Horn against the icy winds and towering seas, believed that Delightful Haven is very much like the London Docks. They said that when a tall ship sailed into Delightful Haven the shipping master was waiting to pay off the crew with bags of gold, while all the pubs outside the dock gates were ready to welcome the seafarers with roaring fires, a sizzling platter of ham and eggs, and the strongest ale that was ever brewed in Kent. Once the pub doors closed behind a weary seafarer he would never again have to turn out for a watch on deck.

Another breed of seamen pictured Delightful Haven as one of the islands they had seen in eastern seas, lying like enormous garlands upon the jade-green sea. When their battered old ship at last came to an anchorage they would lower a boat and row to the golden beach, where laughing island maidens waited to slip necklaces of flowers and seashells over their heads and lead them to the feast prepared under the palm trees.

Wherever Delightful Haven may be situated, it is certain that no ship which puts in there is ever rigged to go to sea again. She lies there with countless companions, ranging from Spanish galleons to rusty old tramp

steamers, gently dreaming of past voyages. Across the calm waters of the haven they hear the seamen singing as they enjoy their long shore leave.

El Dorado

An abbreviation of the Spanish words *El hombre Dorado*, meaning 'The Golden Man'. He is the chief of a tribe who live in a city on an island in the middle of a lake, somewhere deep in the interior of South America. Each morning, the priests coat his naked body with resin and then blow gold dust all over the sticky surface, so that he may walk among his subjects like a glistening golden statue. Each evening, he washes the gold dust off in the lake. This practice has continued for so many centuries that the lake floor carries a great deposit of gold dust, and this sunken treasure is made even richer by the annual worship of the king. On a certain day each year, the tribe performs this ceremony by casting golden trinkets into the lake. It is estimated that many millions of gold pieces have now accumulated beneath its waters.

The Spaniards first heard the story of El Dorado early in the sixteenth century, and they found no reason to disbelieve the tale. Their conquests in Central and South America had brought them so much gold and silver that Spain became the richest country in Europe and its rulers dreamed of world domination. The Spanish conquistadors had looted palaces and temples crammed with golden images, ornaments, and ingots. They had conquered and enslaved nations whose people wore golden ornaments as casually as other races would wear strings of beads, ate from golden platters, and fashioned innumerable golden images of their gods. Before the voyages of Christopher Columbus, no European could have dreamed that such quantities of gold existed. The story of El Dorado seemed like a logical extension of their discoveries.

Gold and silver acted on the Spaniards like habit-forming drugs. The more they had, the more they needed and desired. When the years went by, and they found it more and more difficult to satiate their frenzy for gold, they began the search for El Dorado. They were quite certain that somewhere beyond the deadly jungles and fearsome mountains they would find the lake paved with gold dust and golden trinkets, and the gold mines which supplied the subjects of El Dorado with inexhaustible wealth.

One expedition after another set out in search of the lake. They slaughtered, tortured, and enslaved the tribes whom they encountered during their quest, but many of the invaders also died. As they blundered through the jungles and mountains they were struck down by poisoned darts or venomous serpents. They drowned in the deep rivers, perished from disease, exhaustion, or starvation, or died from Indian spears or arrows. Some expeditions did find more gold, but none of them discovered El Dorado. One sent 110 kilograms of golden ornaments and images back to base with an escort of twenty-eight men, but only one of them staggered into camp. All the others were dead in the jungle.

The story of El Dorado spread through Europe, so that many other adventurers joined the quest. Sir Walter Raleigh of England believed so strongly in the story that he persuaded King James I to release him from the Tower of London, so that he might seek the Golden Man. When he returned empty-handed, King James lopped off his head.

The flow of gold and silver into the coffers of Spain from the gold mines of the New World seemed like tantalising proof of El Dorado, and men continued to seek him even after this torrent faded to a trickle and then died away. Throughout the centuries, daring men have found backers for new expeditions and plunged hopefully into the jungle, only to return—if they did return—richer only in experience.

The story of El Dorado, the Golden Man, has now come to symbolise a treasure beyond achievement, but for all we know the priests of the lake may still anoint their chief with gold dust each morning, and the people worship him with a cascade of golden trinkets every year.

Elephant Graveyards

In the days when all animals were still wild and free, these graveyards existed in various parts of the world including India, Africa, Burma, Assam, and Thailand. Their locations, in deep valleys high in the mountains, were known only to the elders of each elephant tribe. When a senior elephant knew it was time for him or her to seek the graveyard, there was a solemn farewell ceremony attended by the whole community.

The departing elephant, laden with the weight of great curving tusks that almost touched the ground, then plodded off into the jungle which had been home for up to sixty years. Slowly but purposefully, the great wrinkled form ambled along the secret route which led to the foothills of the mountains and then upwards to the secret valley.

At last the elephant eased through the craggy entrance, only wide enough to admit one at a time, and entered the valley. There he selected a spot amid the myriad skeletons half-hidden by tall grass and flowers, and with serene dignity laid down to die.

The needs and greeds of mankind have imposed changes upon this ancient elephant deathstyle. In Asia, most elephants have been enslaved by men and they usually die in harness. In Africa, where the elephant graveyard lies somewhere near the Katanga Plateau, few elephants now escape the bullets of tribesmen greedy for their flesh or hunters eager for their ivory. Only a very few survive long enough to set out on the final journey, and even they are likely to meet a different fate en route.

Men have sought the graveyards for many centuries, hoping for the fortunes in ivory which lie among the massive skeletons. Some hunters have tried to follow elephants on their last journey but without success. An elephant is wise enough to know that some secrets must remain hidden from men, and he would sooner die outside the graveyard than lead an intruder to the bones of his ancestors.

Fiddler's Green

Old seamen are such notorious yarn spinners that it is difficult to know which of their stories to believe about Fiddler's Green. Some say that an old salt who is tired of seagoing should walk inland with an oar over his shoulder. When he comes to a pretty little village deep in the country, and the people ask him what he is carrying, he will know he has found Fiddler's Green. The people give him a seat in the sun outside the village inn, with a glass of grog that refills itself every time he drains the last drop and a pipe forever smoking with fragrant tobacco. From then onwards he has nothing to do but enjoy his glass and pipe, and watch the maidens dancing to the music of a fiddler on the village green.

Other old sailors say that Fiddler's Green lies at the back of the trade winds in the South Atlantic. It is a stretch of water forever calm, and green as the eyes of a mermaid, where the spirits of old ships and seamen find eternal anchorage. As the sun goes down, the strains of a fiddle float across the waters and the seamen dance hornpipes upon the tranquil sea.

There are other stories about Fiddler's Green but they are too fantastic to be believed.

Fountain of Youth

Juan Ponce de Leon, who was one of the hidalgoes who sailed on the second voyage of Christopher Columbus, was the first European to hear about the Fountain of Youth. When he was governor of the island of Puerto Rico, the Borinqueno Indians told him about an island named Bimini which lies somewhere beyond the setting sun. On this island there is a spring of crystalline water with magical properties. Any sick or wounded person who bathes in its waters is restored to immediate health and vigour, and the effect upon an aged person is even more remarkable. His wrinkled skin becomes smooth, his white hair is restored to the glossy brilliance of youth, his stiff and aching limbs become supple, and his entire mind and body recapture the eager potency of his younger days.

Ponce de Leon was then an elderly man, wearied by a life of adventure and afflicted by tropical diseases. He was so eager for the Fountain of Youth that he petitioned King Ferdinand of Spain for authority to discover and settle the island of Bimini, and when the royal charter arrived he set out in search of the island.

In April 1513, on the day known to Spaniards as *Pascua Florida* or Feast of the Flowers, he sighted a low-lying country across the western horizon and gave it the name of Florida. He explored this new land but could not find the Fountain of Youth and set out again in search of Bimini.

He discovered and explored several new islands, seeking eagerly for the wonderful spring which would not only restore his youth but also heal his companions, who were dying one after another of the yellow fever. He abandoned his search only when he was wounded in a skirmish with Indians and his men took him to Cuba. There he died of his wounds, still longing for the miraculous waters which would make him young and whole again.

Many another man has exhausted himself in seeking for the Fountain of Youth in Florida and the West Indies. One of them even gave the hopeful name of Bimini to an island of that region. Perhaps the waters of the fountain still flow on some island which lies beyond the setting sun, but perhaps it is in another part of the world.

Glubbdubdrib

One of a group of islands lying east of Japan and including Balnibari, Luggnagg, etc. Dr Lemuel Gulliver made a side-trip to Glubbdubdrib in 1708, when he was waiting for a ship to Luggnagg. It is a small island, only about a third of the size of the Isle of Wight, but prosperous and fertile.

The island is inhabited by a small tribe who are hospitable to strangers but do not allow them to stay permanently in Glubbdubdrib. They are governed by a ruling family whose eldest son succeeds to the title of Prince on the death of his father. The people of Glubbdubdrib marry only among themselves, which possibly intensifies the peculiar qualities of the island.

The prince lives in a noble palace set in a large estate, surrounded by a stone wall about seven metres high. He raises livestock and grows farm and garden produce, with the help of the same kind of labour which he and his family employ as domestic servants. By his skill in necromancy he can summons up assistance from the dead, and use any dead person as a servant for twenty-four hours. This process is, however, governed by strict rules. At the end of twenty-four hours each dead person must be returned to rest, and cannot be employed again for three months except under extraordinary circumstances. Naturally this regulation does not pose any labour problem because there is an inexhaustible supply of the dead.

Gulliver entered the palace between two rows of guards, who had expressions which made his flesh creep with inexpressible horror. He felt the same way about all the palace servants, until the prince sensed his

feelings and caused all the guards and servants to disappear while Gulliver recounted his adventures. A new set of ghosts served dinner that evening, by which time Gulliver had managed to subdue his terror although he begged the prince for permission to sleep in a house outside the estate.

Gulliver spent ten days on the island and gradually became accustomed to the presence of the dead, especially when the prince graciously enabled him to call up any spirits he chose out of the past. Gulliver enjoyed informative conversations with such people as Julius Caesar, Brutus, Hannibal, Alexander the Great, and Socrates. He also arranged for the Senate of ancient Rome to be summonsed up into one large chamber and a modern English parliament in another, so that he might compare the two. He thought that the former resembled an assembly of heroes and demi-gods, and the latter a crowd of pedlars, pickpockets, highwaymen and bullies.

After interviewing a great many people from all historical periods he concluded that those who achieve high office have always owed their success to lies, corruption, infamy, and betrayal of their supporters, and on the whole he found himself glad to leave the island of sorcerers.

Houyhnhnms, Island of

(Pronounced *Whin-nums*). In 1710, Lemuel Gulliver was appointed master of the ship *Adventure*, a stout merchant vessel. He set sail from Portsmouth on 7 September 1710, under orders to trade and explore in the South Seas. Unfortunately a number of his men died of tropical fever and he was obliged to ship replacements, who turned out to be pirates and seized his ship.

On 9 May 1711 they sighted an island which Gulliver, in a map drawn some years later, showed to be west of Madsuyker (Maatsuycker?) Island and south of Nuyt's Land. This would place the island somewhere south of Australia, and when Gulliver left the Houyhnhnms he first landed in the south-east of that continent. He admits, however, to be confined to his cabin for so long that he was uncertain of the *Adventure*'s position when the pirates sighted the island.

Despite his protestations they marooned him on the island, possessed of nothing but his best suit, his sword, and whatever he could carry in his pockets. He felt more cheerful when he saw signs of civilisation in the form of large fields of oats and pasture, and he soon found a track marked by horse's hooves and what appeared to be human feet. The island had a pleasant rolling aspect with plenty of trees, and somewhere in the distance there was a range of rugged forest-clad hills. Birds of various species strange to Gulliver flitted among the trees, but he saw no other beings until he sighted several creatures sitting in a field or perched on tree branches.

He observed them cautiously, and noticed they had some resemblance to naked humans. Sometimes they stood or walked upright but they also moved crouchingly, as though walking on four feet instead of two. When the females did this their breasts hung down and almost touched the ground. The creatures had light brown skins and thick hair on their heads, of brown, yellow, black, or red. The males had beards like goats, a long ridge of hair down their backs, thick hair on the fronts of their legs and feet, and a profusion of anal hair which Gulliver opined was to protect their bare bottoms when they sat on the ground. The bodies of the female had only a light down apart from this anal hair. Both sexes had strong claws on their hands and feet, which enabled them to climb trees as nimbly as squirrels, and they ran and leapt with great agility.

Gulliver felt instant contempt and aversion for these creatures, and continued along the track in hope of finding some human habitation. But he had not gone far before one of the creatures came towards him along the track, screwed up its ugly face in puzzlement, and lifted up its fore paw as though to touch or strike Gulliver. He drove it away with a blow from the flat of his sword, but it roared so loud that a herd of forty or more came flocking from the next field, howling and making odious faces. Gulliver put his back against a tree and waved his sword at them to keep them off, but several leapt up into the tree and discharged their excrements on his head.

Suddenly they all ran away, and Gulliver realised that they had done so because of the appearance of a noble grey stallion. This grey horse observed Gulliver with great wonderment, but when he tried to pat the stallion it disdainfully raised its left forefoot to remove his hand. Soon a brown bay horse appeared, and the two horses greeted each other very formally with a touch of their right forefeet and what seemed to Gulliver to be a lengthy conversation.

They walked up and down for a while, glancing frequently at Gulliver while they discussed him in a language which he thought sounded like German. After that they inspected him closely, touching his clothes and person with their fore-hooves and acting in such an intelligent and judicious manner that he thought they must be sorcerers. He said 'Gentlemen, if you be conjurers, as I have cause to believe, you can understand my language, therefore I make bold to let your Worships know that I am a poor distressed Englishman, driven by his misfortunes upon your coast; and I entreat one of you to let me ride upon his back, as if he were a real horse, to some house or village . . . In return for which favour I will give you this knife and bracelet.'

He took these articles from his pocket and offered them, but the horses only continued their inspection and conversation. He heard them say the word *Yahoo* several times and after a little while he repeated it loudly, then imitated the neighing of a horse. They looked at him in surprise and the grey repeated the word *Yahoo* as though trying to teach him the right accent. The bay then tried him with a second word, *Houyhnhnm*, and when he managed to imitate this they seemed amazed by his ability.

The grey and bay horses then took formal leave of each other, once more striking their fore-hooves together, and the grey horse nudged Gulliver to walk ahead of him. Whenever Gulliver slowed down it cried out 'Hhuun! Hhuun!' which apparently means 'Go ahead!'

The grey horse took Gulliver to a long low building of timber, thatched with straw and with a smooth clay floor, and with a manger running along one side of the largest room. The grey stallion neighed authoritatively to several equine occupants, and Gulliver was encouraged by the thought that the island must be the home of a very civilised race since they trained and housed their horses so excellently.

But the grey soon led him to a kind of stable, where he saw several of the human-like creatures tied up and feeding on roots and raw flesh. The stallion ordered a sorrel nag, who was one of its servants, to bring the largest creature out into the yard, where the grey and the sorrel compared it with Gulliver and frequently said 'Yahoo.'

Gulliver was horrified to realise that the Yahoo was in fact a human figure apart from such differences as its hairiness, the claw-like nails on hands and feet, and its flat hideous face. The horses could not understand Gulliver's clothing but they obviously thought he was a Yahoo, and the sorrel nag offered him Yahoo food such as a root and a piece of donkey meat. When Gulliver rejected these the sorrel tried him with horse's food: a wisp of hay and a fetlock full of oats. The nag held these items between hoof and pastern, and Gulliver later found that the horses could use their forelegs in this way to perform quite complicated tasks.

Eventually they managed to feed Gulliver by giving him milk to drink, and oats from which he made oatcakes. He lived on this basic diet while he stayed on the island and found it to be natural and healthy.

The grey stallion decided that Gulliver must be a Yahoo, but one of a superior kind. He set himself and his family to teach Gulliver the language of the Houyhnhnms, which in their language means a horse and signifies Perfection of Nature, and Gulliver soon came to understand that the island was ruled by horses who regard Yahoos as a very inferior race.

The more that Gulliver saw of the Yahoos, who resembled him in so many ways, the more he admired the nobility of the horses and the orderliness of their society. He found the Yahoos to be degraded and cowardly creatures, strong and hardy but also insolent, abject, and cruel: cunning, malicious, treacherous, and revengeful. They have a stink something between that of a weasel and a fox, and despite their sharp claws their principal means of self-protection is to leap up into trees and void a horrid excrement on the pursuer. Their perverse and restive nature makes them almost untrainable except for the roughest type of work.

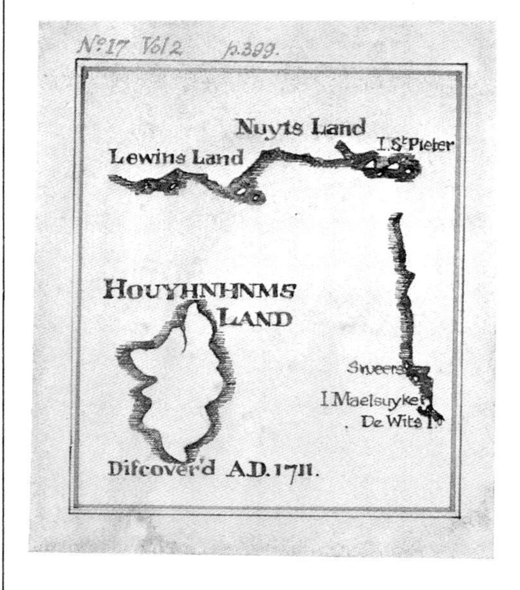

Yahoo dens are individual holes dug out with their claws, and they live on roots, herbs, carrion, weasels, and wild rats. Occasionally they unearth a rare kind of intoxicating root, which they suck greedily until its juices cause them to howl and grin, chatter and reel, and then fall asleep in the mud.

Yahoos scamper around the countryside in herds of forty or more, and these herds often fight each other for possession of a dead cow or donkey or other carrion. If five Yahoos discover as much food as would supply fifty of them, they cannot gorge themselves peacefully but instantly set to fighting over who should have the most. They are violently fond of certain shining stones dug out of the ground, fight immense battles over them, and hide heaps of them in their dens.

Gulliver was so repelled by the Yahoos,

and by the reflections of his own species which he saw in them, that he spent all his time with the Houyhnhnms. The grey stallion continued to befriend him even after he had seen Gulliver's nakedness, which confirmed his opinion that Gulliver was simply a different type of Yahoo.

The stallion did not change this opinion when Gulliver became sufficiently fluent in the Houyhnhnm language to give a lengthy account of European civilisation, including its defects such as wars, crimes, corruption, pollution, poverty, inhumanity, and selfishness. The horse simply remarked that the Yahoos of the island were bad enough, but they could not help their bestiality because that was their nature. The Yahoos of Europe, however, must be even more despicable because they were intelligent enough to know better.

The grey horse found it hard to believe that, in Europe, the Yahoos are the masters and the Houyhnhnms are the servants. He pointed out that Yahoos are obviously the inferior race because they lack the grace and beauty of Houyhnhnms. They do not even have enough hair to protect themselves against the cold, they cannot run as fast as Houyhnhnms, and they feed on such disgusting matter as dead flesh instead of healthy plant food. On the whole the stallion believed that Gulliver was making up his stories, although he found it difficult to say so because the language of the noble Houyhnhnms does not contain any words signifying a lie or a falsehood.

Gulliver lived comfortably among the Houyhnhnms and found that they have developed a technology sufficient for all their needs. They are so adept with their forelegs that they can hold even the smallest objects between the pastern and the hoof, and have thus become skilful in all the crafts which they require. They build their homes from the trunks of a very straight tree, which falls when it is forty years old. The Houyhnhnms trim and sharpen the trunks with stone tools, place them in the ground, and weave oaten straw between them to keep out the wind. The roofs are thatched with oaten straw. They make pottery vessels and bake them in the sun, to contain the milk which forms part of their diet, and weave the straw mats used in their houses. They sow and harvest their crops, and use the Yahoos for rough work such as pulling sleds laden with the crop.

The Houyhnhnms often wonder whether they would not be better off without the Yahoos, which are thieving and destructive creatures, and the grey stallion even said that Gulliver was more useless than most Yahoos. He could not feed himself without lifting his forefeet to his mouth, he never used his forefeet for walking, his eyes were so placed that he could only see directly ahead and not to the sides, he had no claws, and he was altogether a softer and less hardy creature than the genuine Yahoos. The only point of advantage that the stallion could discern was Gulliver's comparative shapeliness and cleanliness.

Despite such comments, Gulliver gradually settled down to a life of contentment among the Houyhnhnms. This noble race of horses has a simple but satisfying lifestyle devoid of the destructive passions of other communities. They do not suffer from any diseases except for old age, and in case of accidents they have herbal ointments and medicines to heal the traumas. When a Houyhnhnm knows it is time to *Lhnuwnh* (retire to his first mother) he makes a circuit of all the other horses in a carriage drawn by Yahoos, so that he may bid a gracious farewell to all his friends.

Their principal relaxations consist of running races, conversation, and poetry sessions. (They do not have any written language, but the history of the Houyhnhnms is passed on verbally from one generation to another.) Gulliver felt that Houyhnhnm poetry was inimitable in the justness of their similes and the minuteness and exactness of description. Their poems usually deal with such matters as friendship and benevolence, or praise of the champions in racing and other sports.

The Houyhnhnm language does not contain words to describe anything unpleasant and they can do so only by adding the suffix 'Yahoo' to an ordinary word. For example *Ynholmhnmrohlnw* means 'house', but to describe a poorly built house a Houyhnhnm says *Ynholmhnmrohlnw Yahoo*.

Houyhnhnm philosophy is based upon pure reason, unsmirched by passion or selfishness. They regard friendship and benevolence as the noblest virtues, and believe that strangers should be treated in exactly the same way as family or friends. Marriages are arranged on a basis of reason, with strength in the male matched to comeliness in the female and couples matched so that there will not be a disagreeable mixture of colours in the breed. Parents of noble descent (the grey, black, and bay horses) are allowed to have two children, while those of the servant class (white, sorrel, and iron-grey) are permitted to have three. This system of voluntary birth control is practised to prevent overcrowding of the island.

Houyhnhnms raise and educate their young in accordance with very strict rules. The young horses are not allowed oats or milk, except on certain days, until they are eighteen years old, and must graze for two hours in the morning and two in the evening. They are taught temperance, industry, exercise, and cleanliness, with a great emphasis on proper exercise. The young Houyhnhnms develop strength, speed, and hardiness by running races up and down steep hills, or over hard stony ground, and when they are sweating from exertion they must leap into a pond or river. Four times a year the youth of various districts assemble for sporting festivals in which they compete in running, jumping, and other contests. The victor is rewarded with a song composed in his or her praise, and there is a public banquet of hay, oats, and milk delivered by a herd of Yahoos, who are then driven away so that they may not disturb the sporting event with their habitual noise and vandalism.

Houyhnhnm society is administered by a Representative Council of the whole nation, which meets in the spring of every fourth year and debates for five or six days. The assembly discusses such matters as the availability of oats, hay, cows, and Yahoos, and if any district should be short of any of these requirements the others make up the deficiency.

This assembly also arranges the composition of families. If any parents have two male children, the assembly organises the exchange of one of these with parents who have two females. If a young Houyhnhnm dies in an accident, the parents are granted permission to have another child. If the mother is too old for breeding, the assembly decides on what family in their district shall breed another to replace the loss.

Each of the four-yearly assemblies spends a certain amount of time on discussion of the Yahoo problem. Some of the Houyhnhnms were in favour of exterminating the Yahoos and raising donkeys instead, because the latter are altogether more useful and docile.

Gulliver associated himself with the Houyhnhnms so completely that he even began to trot like a horse. The grey stallion had ordered a little house to be built for him, and he lived in it very comfortably with furniture he made for himself. He made new clothes from rabbit skins, and when his shoes wore out he repaired them with Yahoo skin. He lived healthily and happily on his diet of oatcakes and milk, occasionally varied with honey, rabbit stew, and wild herbs, and was contented in the belief that he would spend the rest of his life with the Houyhnhnms. When he once caught sight of his reflection in a pool, and perceived his likeness to the Yahoos, he was appalled by the realisation that he still resembled that detestable breed.

His idyllic existence ended when the Houyhnhnms began to rebuke the grey stallion for keeping Gulliver as a friend. They felt that Gulliver, having more intelligence than the other Yahoos, might lead them away into the mountains and then organise them into raids on the cows kept on Houyhnhnm farms. The Representative Council had decided that Gulliver should be sent back whence he came, and the grey stallion's friends continually urged him to put this decision into action.

When Gulliver heard this judgment he fainted with grief, but then accepted his fate. With the help of the sorrel nag he built a canoe to sail away from the island. The last words he heard in the Houyhnhnm language were those of the sorrel nag, who cried out *Hnuy illa maiah Yahoo* ('Take care of thyself, gentle Yahoo') as he sailed away.

After less than two days at sea he reached the south-east point of New Holland (Western Australia) and landed there on 17 February 1715, but the Aborigines drove him away. Only a day or so later he was fortunate enough to encounter a Portuguese ship, and although the crew laughed heartily at his manner of speech—which naturally resembled the neighing of a horse—they gave him safe passage back to Europe.

Hyperborea

A demi-paradise situated beyond the home of the North Wind. Hyperborea was originally the home of the Gorgons and shunned by all mankind, until Perseus rid the country of these pests by slaying Medusa, so that her sisters fled elsewhere. After that the island was settled by a race favoured by Apollo. His benign influence gives them a disease-free lifetime of 1,000 years apiece.

In recognition of this favour, the Hyperboreans send a yearly tribute to the home of Apollo at Delos in the Isles of Greece. Originally these annual gifts were carried by two maidens escorted by five men, but after several of these parties failed to return the Hyperboreans began their present practice of wrapping the gifts in wheat-straw and arranging for them to be passed from hand to hand across the intervening countries.

Visitors to Hyperborea must approach by sea, but this is possible only during the six months of perpetual summer sunshine. The subsequent six months comprise a winter of continuous darkness, when the Hyperboreans hibernate in comfortable caves. A winter approach to the island is fatal, because the sea approach is guarded by high cliffs in the form of giant women who come to life during the months of darkness and destroy any intruder.

The rugged Hyperborean coastline also includes the Leaping Rock. If any Hyperborean wearies of the prospect of living for 1,000 years, he or she bids farewell to all the others and leaps into the sea.

The Hyperboreans do, however, enjoy every inducement to live out their ten centuries. Sorrow is unknown in the country and, apart from sowing and harvesting crops which always give bountiful returns, the people spend their lives in feasting, festivities, and enjoying the unique beauty of Hyperborea.

The island has a remarkable plant life, of a colour and splendour found nowhere else in the world, and interesting forests where the tree-trunks grow in the shapes of men and other animals. Unicorns abound in the forests, a multitude of birds add living colour to the land, a huge cloud of brilliant butterflies hovers overhead, and the rivers swarm with fish and the two-headed frogs relished by Hyperborean gourmets.

Each year, the Hyperboreans enjoy six months of outdoor activity in perfect weather, followed by six months of restful sleep. It seems unlikely that many of them should decide to take the final step off Leaping Rock.

Hy Brasil

An island in the Atlantic Ocean, probably in the same latitude as the Azores, although it has been seen as far north as the latitude of southern Ireland. In ancient times the island enjoyed a thriving trade in the dye-woods, such as logwood, used to colour the fabrics of the Phoenicians, Romans, and Egyptians. Continuous contact with seafarers corrupted the morals of the islands, who were a lecherous and libidinous lot until the arrival of a number of missionary saints. The islanders were deeply impressed by the seamanship of these saints, who sailed across the ocean in boats made of stone or even floated on millstones across the waves, and quickly abandoned their wicked ways. Successive generations of the people of Hy Brasil became so pure of heart that the island itself partook of this purity and dissolved its gross earthly connections. Nowadays, Hy Brasil may be seen only by those who are free from worldly desires. Even they are likely to glimpse it only as an exquisitely ethereal apparition, shimmering above the horizon at sunset.

Island of the Mighty

Home of the Three Mothers, the Goddesses of Plenty, and also of the giant Bendeigeifran who was so huge that he could wade across the Irish Sea. His sister Branwen was one of the Three Mothers. When the King of Ireland wooed and married her, the giant gave him a magic cauldron as a wedding present.

Unfortunately the marriage was far from happy because the King of Ireland conceived himself to be insulted by one of Branwen's half-brothers, and treated her very cruelly. When the men of the Island of the Mighty heard about this disgraceful treatment they vowed to revenge Branwen, and set out in a great fleet led by Bendeigeifran wading across the Irish Sea.

In a gigantic battle the invaders killed all the Irish except for five pregnant women hiding in a cave. It was a triumphant victory, because the King of Ireland had used the magic cauldron to restore all his dead and wounded to life and strength. The invaders had to slaughter them all over and over again.

Only seven of the invaders survived the battle and even the giant Bendeigeifran was mortally wounded. Before he died, he commanded the others to cut off his head and take it back for burial in the Island of the Mighty, where it still pervades the island with magical protection against all its foes.

Island of Despair

Named on 30 September 1659 by Robinson Kreutznaer, a Yorkshire-born merchant venturer of Anglo-German parentage, also known as Bob, Robin, or Robinson Crusoe. The island lies off the north-east coast of South America, to the south-west of Trinidad and about 140 kilometres from the delta of the Orinoco River on the coast of Venezuela. On a clear day the coast of South America may be glimpsed from the highest point of the island.

A double range of hills runs from north to south of the island, with a broad fertile valley between them. The western side of the island rises fairly steeply from the coastline, which is deeply indented with coves and inlets and has a number of small bays. The eastern side is less rugged, but a broad reef and numerous shoals and sandbanks lie offshore.

On the south-west tip of the island there is a sand spit once used by mainland Indians for cannibal feasts, presumably of a ritual nature because they brought the victims all the way across from the mainland. Upwards of twenty victims were consumed at each feast and their skulls and bones may still be found buried in the sand.

Small boat sailing around the island may

be difficult and dangerous. Strong tide rips, especially around the south-east point, cause a confused choppy sea. Another strong current runs around the north of the island. In certain conditions of wind and tide these currents conflict with the outflow of the Orinoco and create very hazardous conditions, but a skilful boat handler will find that the small bays and inlets offer plenty of shelter.

The climate is pleasant from November to May, but the island lies in the path of hurricanes and from June to late October it is subject to prolonged downpours, occasional earthquakes, and cyclonic storms. During this rainy season there is a strong likelihood of contracting a kind of malarial fever.

The heavy rainfall encourages profuse vegetation over the greater part of the island. There are large trees of many species, including cedars and Brazilian ironwood. In the valley between the ranges there are broad meadow-like areas together with flourishing patches of wild citrus trees, grapevines, tobacco plants, sugarcane, and other useful species. Strangely, the coconut palm does not grow on the island.

The mammalian life consists principally of large flocks of wild goats, which are easily domesticated. There are also wild cats, hares, and foxes, but no feral animals dangerous to man and apparently no venomous reptiles.

A great variety of birdlife, including many species unknown elsewhere, populates the forests and the seashores. One type of large seabird, resembling a goose, makes good eating. Parrots and wild pigeons abound in the forest and penguins are seen on some of the rocky points—an unusual occurrence in this tropical region. Seals frolic off the reefs and turtles lay their eggs in the beaches, especially on the eastern side.

The hills are of interest because they contain numerous caves, including a deep cavern approached by a long low tunnel. This cavern is floored with loose gravel and its walls and roof are veined with mineral deposits which sparkle most attractively in the light of torches.

Entrance to some of the caves is now virtually impossible because Crusoe protected the entrances by stockades of tree trunks implanted in the soil. These took root and have now created impenetrable clumps of vegetation.

The island could now be of interest to skindivers because the wrecks of two seventeenth century merchant ships lie close inshore. Otherwise it is too far off the tourist track to attract visitors. It cannot sustain an economically viable community because of its small size and distance from possible markets, and so it remains uninhabited.

Robinson Crusoe lived on the island for twenty-eight years, as the sole survivor from a shipwreck caused by one of the hurricanes. With great ingenuity, and the use of numerous tools, weapons, and other artefacts sal-

vaged from the two wrecks mentioned above, he managed to survive at a little better than subsistence level and even to protect himself against cannibals and marooned seafarers. He was, however, obviously glad to leave the Island of Despair, and did not hesitate to take sides in a conflict with the mutinous crew of an English ship in order to do so.

Joyous Garde

A castle to the south-west of Camelot, possibly built as one of a chain of fortresses to protect England against invasion by pixie-led Cornishmen. Originally it was known as Douleureuse Garde, meaning 'Sorrowful Guard', and it was a dark and gloomy pile of weatherworn stone occupied by knights who had fallen into evil ways.

When Sir Lancelot asked King Arthur for some task to prove his knighthood, Arthur told him he might have the castle if he could seize it from its wicked owners. Lancelot, then eighteen, accepted this challenge and attacked the castle single-handed. He drove out the evil knights, renamed the castle as Joyous Garde, and began a programme of renovation and reconstruction which converted the building into one of the most spectacular castles of the western world.

He had the gloomy outer walls covered with plaster and the plaster gilded with gold leaf, so that the shining radiance of Joyous Garde could be seen for many miles. The ominous watchtowers and battlements were ornamented with fantastic decorations and connected by graceful flying bridges, while the dark inner chambers were enlivened by brilliant tapestries, painted ceilings, and gilded furniture.

Lancelot made the castle fit for a queen, but his unhappy love affair with Guinevere prevented him from marrying a suitable maiden and enjoying a normal family life. The beautiful castle eventually suffered badly when Lancelot took Guinevere there and her husband, Arthur, attacked Joyous Garde in a prolonged seige. Nothing now remains except for some heather-clad ruins, covering the vault in which the body of Lancelot reposes.

King Solomon's Mines

These rich deposits lie in the Suliman Range to the north-west of the Mashukulumbwe country, in what was once known as Kukuana-land. This lay approximately on the borders of the nations now known as Angola, Zaire, and Zambia. The Kukuanas, a tribe of Zulu

stock, were a particularly fine type of people but their king's resolve to keep them independent resulted in the destruction of their social structure during the political and military upheavals in central Africa. The tribe has been absorbed by others and no longer exists as a separate organisation.

Dom Jose da Silvestra, a Portuguese adventurer and slavetrader working inland from Mozambique, discovered the Suliman Range in 1590. He was the first European to see the treasure chamber, deep in the mountains, containing an immense store of uncut diamonds which had been mined for King Solomon. For some reason these diamonds had been left in the chamber and forgotten by the outside world, possibly because of the death of the king and the collapse of his great empire.

Dom Jose died of cold and hunger before he could exploit his discovery, but he drew a sketch map of the mountains in his own blood on a piece of cloth and left a garbled account of the location written in the same way. A slave managed to reach Dom Jose's family with these documents, and his descendants made many unsuccessful attempts to rediscover the mines. Sometime in the 1870s, a Portuguese gentleman dying of thirst, hunger, and fever in the Manica country, near Sitanda's Kraal, gave the map to the noted elephant hunter Allan Quatermain.

In the early 1880s, Quatermain saw a man named Neville fitting out an expedition at Bamangwato in the Transvaal. Local gossip reported that Neville was going in search of King Solomon's Mines, but Quatermain regarded the story as a myth and did not even bother to talk to Neville.

In 1884, Quatermain met Sir Henry Curtis and Captain Edward Good, Royal Navy, who had come to Africa to search for Sir Henry's younger brother. Quatermain soon realised that this was the man named Neville, and he told the whole story to Sir Henry.

The Englishman commissioned Quatermain to lead an expedition to find Neville, and they set out from Durban as a well-equipped party including a fine Zulu warrior named Umbopa, who had offered his services.

After many adventures they reached the great desert stretching towards the Suliman Range, and made a terrible journey across it under the flaming sun. One morning at sunrise, just after they had been saved by death from thirst by discovering a desert pool, they saw two enormous mountains on the horizon. These were perfectly smooth and rounded, and capped with round hillocks covered with snow. Obviously they were the two mountains which Dom Jose had called Sheba's Breasts, and the explorers knew they were on the right track.

But they still had to climb the precipitous ranges connecting the two breasts, and struggle through the high snowfields beyond them. They were encouraged by discovering the deep-frozen body of Dom Jose preserved in a mountain cave, and at last came to the magnificent country of the Kukuanas on the other side of the ranges.

It lay as a great rolling expanse of green veldt, with stretches of cultivated land around villages of domed huts, in a kind of basin surrounded by the ranges. They climbed down through the foothills onto the remains of Solomon's Great Road, which led them through peaceful and beautiful woodlands seeming almost heavenly after all their tribulations.

At first the adventurers were made welcome by the Kukuanas, whom they found to be a splendid warlike race with an army of 60,000 spearmen. But when they arrived in the capital, Loo, King Twala greeted them suspiciously and the fearsome witch Gagool made prophecies of doom.

Gagool was a wizened monkey-like figure, with a bald head and a face resembling that of a sun-dried corpse except for the large dark eyes, still full of fire and intelligence, which gleamed like jewels in a charnel house. Her claim to enormous age and profession of magical powers terrified the Kukuanas and even the king dared not disobey her whims. Her prophesy that the coming of the white men would cause rivers of blood to flow put Quatermain's party in a very tricky position. They felt even uneasier when they had to witness Gagool's witch-hunt through the ranks of the army. The king's guard dragged out one warrior after another, to be speared and clubbed to death, on no more evidence than Gagool's accusations of witchcraft.

After several narrow escapes, Quatermain and his friends felt unlikely to survive for long under the appalling regime of Gagool and King Twala. They were wondering what to do when their Zulu servant, Umbopa, resolved the situation by revealing himself to the Kukuanas as Ignosi, their rightful king, and leading a rebellion against Twala. Ignosi's supporters were outnumbered but many were veteran soldiers. With the help of the white men they defeated Twala's regiments in a long and bloody battle. Sir Henry Curtis fought Twala in single combat, both men armed with battleaxes, and hacked off the king's head.

King Ignosi rewarded the white men with a promise to help them in their quest, but only Gagool knew the secret of King Solomon's Mines. Compelled to help the adventurers, she led them with many direful prophecies along Solomon's Great Road to a triangle of mountains, known as the Three Witches, where the road climbed upwards through wild moorland to the snowclad ranges. On the side of one of the mountains the road encircled a gigantic pit, about a kilometre in circumference, which Quatermain recognised as a diamond mine.

On the far side of this pit sat the three Silent Ones: three colossal statues carved from dark stone. One was of a nude female and the others of males clad in robes. The female had features of severe beauty, while one of the males had a visage of calm inhuman cruelty and the other the face of a devil. They were the three strange gods Ashtoreth, Chemosh, and Milcom, after whom Solomon had gone a-whoring before he returned to the true God.

Behind the colossi lay a sheer face of rock, pierced by a narrow tunnel into which Gagool led the adventurers. They followed the hobbling witch into a rock chamber as large as a cathedral, with ice-like pillars and columns formed by enormous stalactites. Beyond this chamber lay the Hall of Death. Chuckling hideously, Gagool led the way into another great rock chamber, where the figure of Death sat in the form of a colossal human skeleton, holding a great white spear, at the head of a massive stone table. Around

the table sat many white figures like horrid statues, as though they were guests at a feast given by Death. They were the corpses of Kukuana kings, transformed into stalagmites by the water dripping onto them from the roof, and the huge figure of Death was carved from a single stalactite. The headless body of Twala sat among them with his head on its knees, awaiting this interminable process.

At the far end of the chamber, Gagool used a hidden lever to open a great stone door, so cunningly counterbalanced that it responded even to her puny strength. The treasure of King Solomon's Mines lay upon the other side. In the dim light of Gagool's lamp the adventurers saw upwards of 400 splendid elephant tusks, the finest ivory that Quatermain had ever seen, together with about a score of chests full of ancient gold coins. Then, in three stone chests, they found Solomon's great treasure of uncut diamonds.

They carried away only as many as Quatermain crammed into his pockets, because Gagool crept out of the chamber while they were gloating over the treasure and began to close the rocky door. It squashed and killed her as they struggled to prevent it from closing, and then clamped shut to trap them in the bowels of the mountain.

When they recovered from the terror of entombment, in the utter darkness of the treasure chamber, they found a ventilation hole which led to a maze of crevices in the rock. They contrived to find their way out of the trap, and tried to find a way back into the treasure chamber. But they could not discover the door's hidden lever in the Hall of the Dead.

The adventure had a happy ending for Quatermain and his friends. The diamonds in his pockets were enough to make them all wealthy, and they found Sir Henry's brother on their way back to the coast. But when they bade farewell to King Ignosi he swore that he and his men would fight to the death to prevent their ancient lifestyle from being perverted by the invasion of white men. He said he would destroy all traces of King Solomon's Mines so that there would be nothing to attract the whites.

Probably that is what happened, and no doubt the warriors of Kukuanaland perished in one of those bloody campaigns which besmirch the history of Africa.

Kor

An enormous ruined city in the land of the Amahagger, a matriachy where women have long enjoyed equal rights with men. The Amahagger, a Hamitic Caucasoid race of a region between Somaliland and Kenya, live on a plateau amid the rugged arid mountains but enjoy a climate favourable to agriculture. The people have some racial resemblance to Somalis, being tall, slender, straight-haired, and with fine-chiselled features, but unlike the Somalis they have something in their expressions which arouses very uneasy feelings in the heart of a stranger.

Amahagger women have for many centuries possessed the kind of freedoms for which women in other societies are still struggling. The legal restrictions of marriage are unknown, and a woman declares her acceptance of a mate simply by embracing him in public. She stays with him for as long as she pleases and may, if she wishes, exchange him for another partner. Her economic security is assured by the inheritance of property in the female line. Otherwise the men and women have equal rights and responsibilities, except that women are exempt from heavy agricultural labour.

A young Englishman named Leo Vincey, and his foster-father Horace Ludwig Holly, penetrated the land of the Amahagger in 1884, on their search for the Caves of Kor which they had traced through an ancient clue. They found the ruined city of Kor, now surrounded by the fields and villages of Amahagger, to be an astounding relic of a civilisation which perished thousands of years ago. The ruined city walls, upwards of twelve metres high, enclose about thirty square kilometres of ruins smothered by an encroaching vegetation. Great weathered columns show the original sites of temples and palaces, while the ruins of countless other buildings show by their splendour and fine craftsmanship that the people of Kor must have been men and women of high intellect and achievements.

The main street, of huge paving stones, leads to the ruins of the principal temple. It comprises a series of courtyards built one inside another, and in the central courtyard there is a colossal white marble statue of a winged woman with a veiled face. The editor of one of Holly's subsequent books speculated that this might be a statue of Isis, the Egyptian Goddess of Nature, and that the inscription on its base might be similar to the declaration of Isis: 'I am whatsoever was, whatsoever is, whatsoever shall be, and the veil which is over my face no mortal hand has ever raised.'

When the explorers found the Caves of Kor, in the mountain ranges around the plateau, they discovered many relics of a barbaric ancient civilisation together with living proof of transcendental events and beings.

The priestess of this mystic region was Ayesha (pronounced Assha) an immortal woman of supreme beauty. In one of Holly's numerous descriptions of Ayesha, also known as 'She' or 'She-Who-Must-Be-Obeyed', he wrote 'Fragrant was Ayesha's breath as roses, the odour of roses clung to her lovely hair; her sweet body gleamed like some white sea-pearl; a faint but palpable radiance crowned her head; no sculptor ever fashioned such a marvel as the arm with which she held her veil about her; no stars in heaven ever shone more purely bright than did her calm, entranced eyes.'

Ayesha preserved her immortality by immersion in the Fires of Life, and Holly later thought that this name might refer to some kind of nuclear irradiation.

Leo Vincey and Ayesha recognised each other as lovers from the distant past, when Leo had been the Grecian priest Kallikrates whom Ayesha slew in a rage of jealousy. After numerous reincarnations he had been mystically guided to seek his lost love in the Caves of Kor, where she stood before the flashing rays and vapours of the Pillar of Life and proclaimed that her love for him was eternal.

When Leo was Kallikrates, Ayesha was a priestess of Isis, and her slaying of the priest had been an involuntary execution of a judgment of Isis. The two lovers believed that they might now enjoy a happier destiny, but mystic forces still operated against them and Ayesha was swept away by a cloud of flame.

Leo Vincey and Horace Holly found their way back to European civilisations after a fearsome journey in which most of their companions died from various misadventures. They tried to settle down in Holly's old house in Cumberland, but Leo soon came to believe that Ayesha had been restored to life again and they set out on another search for the immortal priestess.

Lilliput

Dr Lemuel Gulliver, who had been surgeon in the ship *Antelope*, was the first *Quinbus Flestrin* (Great Man Mountain) to visit the Empire of Lilliput. The *Antelope*, on a trading voyage from the South Seas to the East Indies in November 1699, was blown off her course by a great storm. She struck a rock on 5 November in a position which Gulliver reckoned as somewhere to the north-west of Van Diemen's Land (Tasmania), the last observation having placed them in latitude 30 degrees 2 minutes south. Gulliver and five other men managed to get away in a boat and rowed for about fifteen kilometres before it was overturned and the five men were lost. Gulliver then swam for some distance before he landed on the island of Lilliput. There are no more precise indications as to its position, but the above details would place it some distance to the south of Australia between Kangaroo Island and Tasmania.

When Gulliver was able to give the island a thorough inspection he discovered that it is 5000 *blustrugs* (17·312 kilometres) in circumference and separated from the island of Blefuscu, which is about the same size, by a shallow channel 727 metres wide. The whole country is so meticulously cultivated that it has the appearance of a great garden. Woodlands, comprising fine trees of which the tallest (those in the Royal Park) are a little more than two metres high, stand in well-tended copses of about half a *stang* (1,250 square metres) apiece, amidst fertile fields each of twelve metres square.

The population, which in 1700 was probably about one million, consists of perfectly formed miniature humans of no more than 15·240 centimetres tall. All the domestic livestock, birds, crops, and other flora and fauna are in proportion to the human population. The island has been civilised for so long that it does not appear to have any feral animals.

Excellent highways connect the various towns and cities, of which the largest is the capital, Mildendo. This city is built as an exact square, each side being 152·40 metres long, and divided into four quarters by two main streets each 1·524 metres wide. The other streets, lanes, and alleys of the city are from thirty to forty-five centimetres wide.

The main streets lead into the city through great gates in each of the city walls, which are splendid constructions seventy-five centimetres high and twenty-seven wide, so that a coach and horses may drive along the broad flat tops. Fortified towers stand at three-metre intervals.

Many fine houses, two to four storeys high, stand within the city walls and accommodate its population of half-a-million Lilliputians. The imperial palace lies in the centre of Mildendo at the intersection of the two main streets. It is enclosed by a wall almost thirteen metres square, which surrounds the magnificent courtyards, halls, apartments, guard houses, and other buildings fit for the magnificence of the emperor. The Royal Park, where the emperor and his family ride and hunt the deer, lies about 100 metres outside Mildendo.

In 1700, the Emperor of Lilliput was Golbasto Momaren Evlame Gurdilo Shefin Mully Ully Gue, Delight and Terror of the Universe, Monarch of all Monarchs, etc. etc. The emperor ruled through a council including such officials as Admiral of the Realm Skyresh Bolgam, a sour and morose individual; the *Flimnap* (Treasurer); and the *Reldresal* (Principal Secretary). There was a large public service and a substantial army and navy.

The thriving Lilliputian economy is based on legal and social systems which on the whole are enlightened and logical. Citizens who obey the law for seventy-three moons are rewarded from a special fund and given certain privileges and the title of *Snilpall* (Legal). Anyone wrongly accused of a crime is compensated by the State, and his accuser subjected to condign punishment. Commercial fraud is regarded as a greater crime than theft, because an honest man is always defenceless against a knave, and it is punishable by death. Ingratitude, and the returning of evil for good, are also capital crimes.

The Lilliputians were surprised to hear from Gulliver that the laws of Britain were enforced only by penalties, with no system of rewards. The image of Justice set up in their law courts has six eyes, two in front and two behind, with one on each side, to signify that she takes everything into account. She carries an open bag of gold in her right hand and a sheathed sword in her left to show she is more disposed to reward than to punish.

Every branch of Lilliputian education is well advanced, although Gulliver thought that their method of writing, slantwise across the page, was rather peculiar. The more enlightened citizens now tend to query the belief that the earth is flat, and that on the Day of Judgment it will be turned upside down. It is for this reason that the Lilliputians follow their ancient custom of burying their dead with their heads directly downwards, so that they will be standing on their feet on the day of resurrection.

Parents of most socio economic classes, including the aristocracy, are not allowed to educate or even to bring up their own children. The Lilliputians believe that the relationship between parents and children is purely fortuitous and emotional; that children owe no obligation to parents for bringing them into this troubled world; and that parents are the people least capable of rearing and educating their offspring. Consequently the parents are obliged to contribute appropriate portions of their income towards the upkeep of communal nurseries and boarding schools, separated for boys and girls. Experienced teachers of the appropriate sexes educate and train the young Lilliputians according to carefully graded codes of manners, learning, and moral conduct.

The children of working-class parents are released from these schools fairly young, so that they may become servants or be apprenticed to useful trades. Girls of the middle and upper classes stay at school until they reach marriageable age, by which time they are thoroughly versed in all wifely duties and capable of becoming agreeable companions for their husbands. Their brothers stay at school until an age approximating twenty years old.

Apart from a complete academic syllabus, the educational system endeavours to impart such virtues as honesty, modesty, religion, and patriotism; goodwill, justice, courage, and clemency.

The children of labourers and poor country folk are exempt from this compulsory education, and are kept at home so that they may grow up to till and cultivate the earth. The aged poor are looked after in special hospitals, because Lilliput is a welfare state in which no one has to depend upon charity.

Regrettably, it would seem that the earnest endeavour to create ideal citizens is not totally successful, because crime is not unknown. Gossip, malice, spite, and pride seem to flourish just as they do in other societies, while the members of different religious beliefs and political parties behave most cruelly and jealously towards each other. The emperor does not choose his ministers for their integrity and experience, but for their skill in dancing on a tightrope, and he rewards them not necessarily for their achievements but for their agility in leaping or creeping to his command.

When a ministerial office falls vacant, the candidates are obliged to entertain the emperor and his court by dancing and jumping on a tightrope set at a dangerous distance above the ground. Those who jump highest and dance most nimbly receive the most important appointments, but many applicants meet fatal accidents during their exertions. The emperor also orders such officials as the *Flimnap* and the *Reldresal* to perform on the tightrope at regular intervals during their terms of office, to determine whether they are still fit to serve. If one of them should fall from the rope then it is of course proof of his unfitness.

The emperor also tests his officials with another ceremony, that of the stick. He holds the stick before him and raises or lowers it so that the official has to creep beneath it or leap over it. Those who prove most adept at leaping or creeping are rewarded with strands of blue, red, or green silk, which they wear most proudly around their waists as marks of royal favour.

It is uncertain whether the descendants of Emperor Golbasto still reign over Lilliput. His realm was so wracked by internal politics, and so much threatened by Blefuscidian invasion, that his dynasty may have been toppled and replaced by another. At the time of Gulliver's visit the principal political parties were the *Tramecksans* (High Heels) and *Slamecksans* (Low Heels). The Tramecksans, who wore high heels on their shoes, were the conservative and most numerous party, but the *Slamecksans* appeared to have the support of the emperor. The imperial council and all the public servants were *Slamecksans*, but they were worried because the emperor had taken to wearing a high heel on one shoe and a low heel on the other, which gave him a hobbling gait.

Lilliput
Difcoverd
A.D. 1699
Mildendo

The Lilliputians are skilled in every kind of arts and crafts, from weaving to shipbuilding. Their country provides them with all necessary resources although, in Gulliver's time, they had not yet developed the use of firearms. It is to be hoped that this omission has not been repaired because their bloody wars with Blefuscu would be even worse with modern weapons.

The arrival of Gulliver the Great Man Mountain caused a severe strain upon national resources, and it was no doubt a relief when the Admiral of the Realm, supported by the empress, took the actions which resulted in his departure. The Admiral was very jealous of Gulliver's victory over the Blefuscidian fleet, as described earlier in this chapter, and Gulliver increased the tension by a well-meaning effort to help the empress. When a fire broke out in her palace apartments, and the Mildendo fire brigade could not deal with the conflagration, he thought of an effective expedient. He had been drinking deeply of the excellent Lilliputian wine known as *glimigrim*, which has a strongly diuretic effect, and so he straddled the empress' apartments and deluged the flames with a copious flow of urine.

Far from being grateful, the empress was most annoyed and disgusted. It was a capital offence for anyone to make water within the imperial precincts, and although the emperor said he would arrange a pardon for Gulliver the empress was not placated. She and the Admiral impeached Gulliver over this matter and also over an accusation that, after capturing the Blefuscidian fleet, he had shown treasonable sympathies towards the Blefuscidians.

Gulliver's enemies wanted to put out his eyes when he was asleep and then starve him to death. He could of course have ravaged the whole country, but the emperor had been kind to him and even given him the aristocratic title of *Nardac*. Instead of defending himself against his accusers he escaped to Blefuscu, where he soon found a full-size ship's boat washed up on the beach. With the help of the Blefuscidians he repaired and provisioned this boat and on 24 September 1701 he sailed away from the two islands.

Luggnagg

An island lying between Balnibari and Japan, visited by Lemuel Gulliver on 21 April 1708. The Luggnaggians are a courteous, generous, and proud people who are polite to strangers. At the time of his visit the island was an autocracy, with a ruler styled as His Celestial Majesty. The royal court followed several curious customs, but Gulliver found the most interesting feature of the island was the presence of the *Struldbruggs* or Immortals.

A *Struldbrugg*, whether male or female, is distinguishable at birth by a small red spot over the left eyebrow. At twelve years of age this spot turns green, at twenty-five it becomes deep blue, and after another twenty years it turns black and becomes the size of an English shilling of Gulliver's day. After the age of forty-five it remains unchanged.

When Gulliver first heard about the Immortals he was greatly interested and excited. In conversation with a Luggnaggian gentleman he expounded at great length upon the ways in which one might plan to gain the utmost from immortality. He thought that nothing could be more desirable than eternal life, which would allow its possessor to accumulate the wisdom of the ages and study the whole panorama of history as it unrolled before him.

The Luggnaggian listened with a slight smile and then remarked that Gulliver had made a fundamental error in his theorising. He had assumed that eternal life meant eternal health and strength, but this is certainly not the case for the unfortunate *Struldbruggs*. They are not exempt from the usual aging process and by the time they reach ninety years old they have lost most of the physical and mental properties which make life worth living. Devoid of teeth, hair, appetite, desire, and memory, they drag out a miserable existence that can never end. A *Struldbrugg* cannot even enjoy reading, because he forgets the beginning of a sentence by the time he reaches its end.

After a few more decades a *Struldbrugg* has lost all his closer relations and has no one left but distant descendants who have no interest in him. At the age of eighty he became a non-person in the eyes of Luggnaggian law, so that he has no property and no control over events, and he exists on a dole just sufficient to supply his minimal needs.

When Gulliver actually met some *Struldbruggs* he found them to be a mortifying sight. Apart from the usual deformities of age, he thought that they acquire an indescribable ghastliness in proportion to their antiquity. He would have liked to converse with them about the past, but *Struldbruggs* lose all their curiosity and interest in anything but the immediate present.

Fortunately, only a tiny proportion of Luggnaggians are born as *Struldbruggs*. In Gulliver's time, only about 1,100 of them bore the dreaded symbol of immortality and so the number will not have increased excessively since his visit. These miserable creatures, condemned to eternal life, serve principally to hearten the Luggnaggians against any fear of death.

Lyonnesse

An island nation once situated in the neighbourhood of the Scilly Isles, in the Atlantic Ocean off the coast of Cornwall. In the days when King Arthur ruled over England, Lyonnesse was a flourishing community which enjoyed a perfect year-round climate. The fertile orchards and farmlands gave several crops a year, the cows produced thick cream and the beehives oozed with the richness of their honey.

The men of Lyonnesse were strong, tall, and handsome: the women possessed of a serene and noble beauty. The castles of the Knights of Lyonnesse had a graceful splendour which concealed their inner strength, and even the poorest folk lived in neat cottages set amidst charming gardens.

There was considerable trade and traffic between England and Lyonnesse, especially since the island was favoured as a place of recuperation for lovelorn maidens or knights weary of long adventuring.

Some people of Lyonnesse were adept practitioners of white magic, but the black arts were unknown.

Despite the virtue and nobility of the islanders, their nation sank beneath the waves at about the time of King Arthur's death: Now, when the great Atlantic rollers sweep in from the west, the fishermen of Cornwall sometimes hear the church bells of Lyonnesse tolling mournfully beneath the waves.

Lotos Land

A mountainous island of the eastern Mediterranean, distinguished by three high mountains with snowclad peaks. The lower ranges and foothills are thickly clad with forests of pine and other indigenous trees. Streams and rivers run down through the mountain valleys and in some cases they cascade over the cliffs of the island in torrents exquisitely illumined by the setting sun.

The rocky coasts are broken by long stretches of golden beach, fronting park-like expanses of meadowland rolling up towards the foothills. Numerous sub-tropical plants, including the amaranth, moly, acanthus, asphodel, and lotos, grow thickly along the banks of the rivers and streams. When the lotos is in bloom its pollen lies like swathes of thick yellow dust over the meadowlands.

Lotos Land is blessed with a particularly pleasant climate which one commentator has described as 'always afternoon.' The warm moist air is peculiarly relaxing and seems to discourage violent exertion.

The inhabitants are members of a kind of hippie commune, mild and friendly but somewhat withdrawn and melancholy. They maintain a semi-narcotised condition by consuming the products of the lotos shrub, and offer these freely to visitors.

The lotos (*Ziziphus lotus*) is a shrub which bears fruit containing a mealy substance, that may be baked into bread or fermented into a wine. Continuous consumption induces amnesia, a conviction that human striving is pointless, extreme muscular relaxation, and a hearing defect which causes the voices of companions to sound thin and remote.

Monastery of the Mountains

When Horace Ludwig Holly and Leo Vincey set out on a search for Ayesha (see Kor) they were influenced by a dream in which Vincey saw them crossing Asia and finding a monastery on the brink of a plateau. They began their quest in 1885, and travelled for sixteen years through the most desolate regions of central Asia before they found the crescent-shaped monastery in the Cherga Mountains. The monastery, and its huge image of Buddha, were in a semi-ruinous condition and the building was occupied only by a handful of aged monks who had dedicated their lives to a search for the True Path. The monks, especially Abbot Kue-en, remembered numerous events from their previous incarnations. Kue-en himself was the reincarnation of a young monk who had lived in the Monastery of the Mountains two centuries earlier, before it was partly destroyed by a tribe of fire worshippers from a different part of the ranges.

Holly and Vincey stayed for six months in the monastery and absorbed some of the transcendental spirit of the monks. From a strange tale told to them by Kue-en they believed that Ayesha had passed that way and set out again in search of her.

After fearsome adventures they found Ayesha beyond the Court of Death and above the Lake of Fire—but she was no more than a mummified relic of her former beauty although she was still alive. The power of Leo's love, which had endured over the twenty centuries since he was the priest Kallikrates and Ayesha was a priestess of Isis, restored her to her original loveliness.

Ayesha and Leo were betrothed but she continuously postponed their marriage, and the two Englishmen passed through many more strange and mystic experiences including a great battle with the Children of Kaloon. When at last Ayesha and Leo were married, Leo died in her embrace and the spirits of the two lovers were swept into eternity on a two-winged flame. Holly, who cherished a hopeless love for Ayesha, found his painful way back to England. In about 1905 he was found dead before an ancient stone cromlech in Cumberland known as the Devil's Ring.

Old Man of the Sea's Island

When Sindbad the merchant of Baghdad made his fifth trading voyage, his ship was attacked by two gigantic birds. They bombed it with enormous boulders and one scored a direct hit. Sindbad, the sole survivor, drifted for some time on a piece of wreckage until it landed him on the shore of a pleasant island. He found good water to quench his thirst, plenty of fruit trees, and vines bearing juicy bunches of grapes.

As he explored the island he came upon an old man, apparently senile and helpless, sitting by one of the streams. Sindbad thought the old man was another shipwrecked seafarer, but when he tried to talk to him the old man answered only with signs. They seemed to mean that he wanted to be lifted up to pick some fruit from a tree, and Sindbad gladly stooped to take him on his back.

As the old man mounted him, Sindbad noticed that his legs had skin like cowhide. A moment later, the old man's skinny hands closed around Sindbad's throat in such a strangling grip that he fell unconscious to the ground.

The old man slackened his grip only enough to allow Sindbad to breathe, then kicked him savagely until he staggered to his feet. Whenever Sindbad tried to throw off the fearful burden, the claw-like hands squeezed his throat again and the horny feet kicked him painfully in the chest and belly.

The pleasant island became a place of torment for Sindbad as he staggered around it with the fearsome creature perched on his shoulders, kicking him as though he was a horse controlled by its rider. The old man never slept although he allowed Sindbad occasional periods of rest before kicking him into action again.

One day Sindbad saw a number of empty gourds that had fallen from the trees, and he squeezed grape juice into one of these to make himself a drink. The old man also insisted on drinking. This gave Sindbad the idea of filling a gourd with grape juice and leaving it in the sun to ferment into wine. When he returned a few days later it had become such strong wine that it made him forget his troubles, and he sang and capered gaily along the forest tracks.

Again, the old man insisted on tasting the drink, but the wine made him drowsy instead of happy. Slowly his grip on Sindbad slackened, until Sindbad was able to throw him off and then beat out his brains with a stone.

Soon after that he met some seamen who had landed to fill their ship's casks with water, and they were astonished to hear about his escape. They told him the island was that of the Old Man of the Sea, who had strangled many shipwrecked seafarers. Sindbad had rid the trade routes of this notorious danger to navigators and the seamen were happy to give him a passage home.

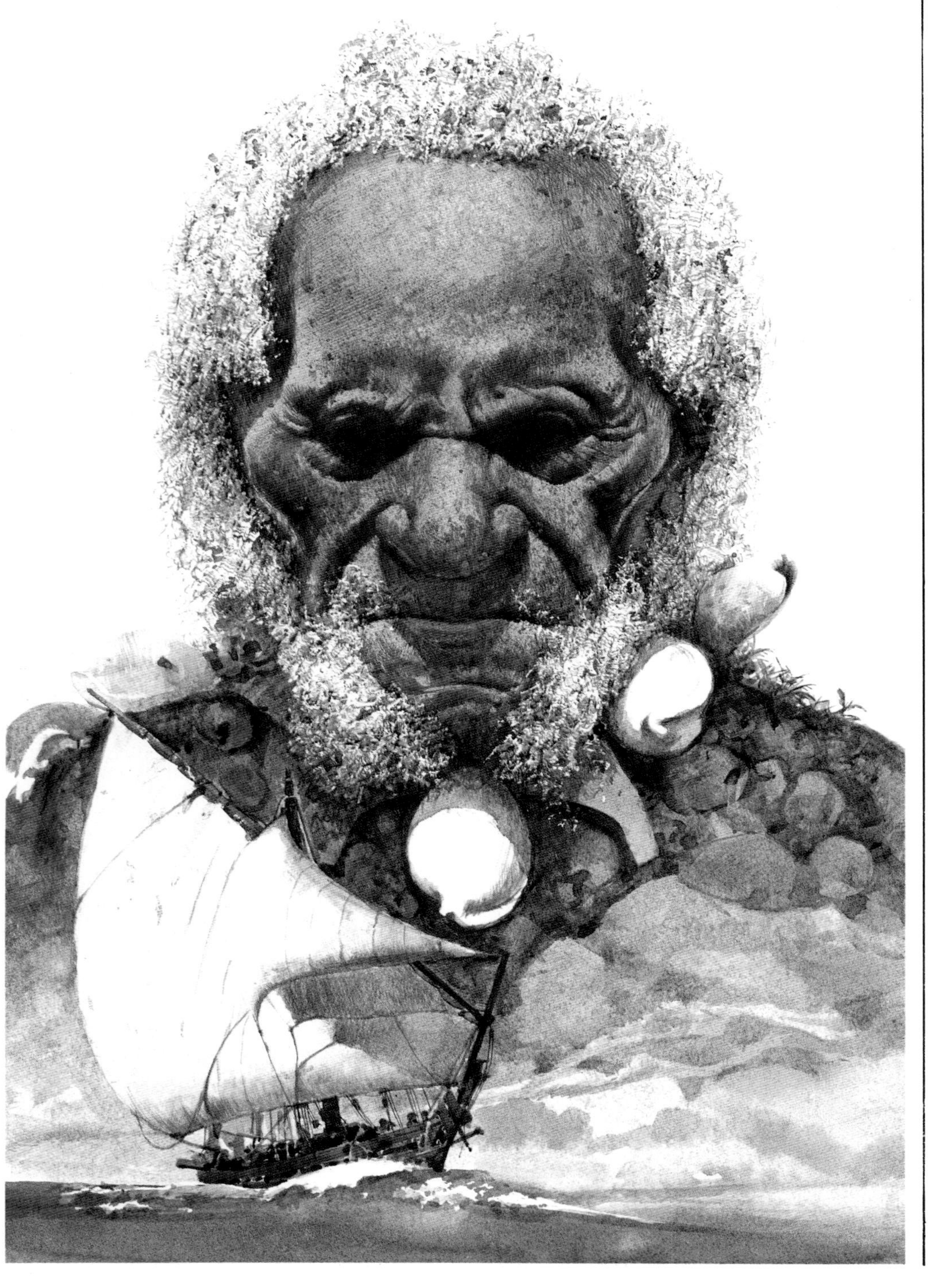

Prester John's Country

A great Christian empire which flourished during the twelfth century AD. Prester John was a man of humble origins, whom the fire of faith inspired to become a great military leader and conqueror of the pagans, but he never allowed his achievements to inflate his ego. Even when he was at the height of his powers he still used only the title 'Presbyter', meaning an elder of the church, and this became corrupted to 'Prester'.

Prester John's empire was based on Biblical teachings and there were no paupers, thieves, misers, or flatterers; no vices, lies, or arguments. He was able to take immediate action to reform any sinners, because an optical instrument in his palace grounds allowed him to keep an eye on every occurrence throughout his empire.

The empire eventually extended eastwards from the ruins of the Tower of Babel to the furthest frontiers of India, and southwards to the sources of the Nile. The kings of seventy-two nations paid tribute to Prester John, and when he held court in his great palace his personal attendants were seven kings, sixty dukes, and 365 counts. Twelve archbishops sat on his right hand and twenty bishops on his left. His chief cook was not only the king of one of the conquered countries but had also been consecrated as an abbot.

His army was organised into thirteen divisions, each of 10,000 knights and 100,000 infantry. When this great assembly marched into action, a wagon bearing a splendid cross of gold and diamonds rumbled before each division, leading them to yet another victory for the True Faith.

The army's intelligence service left a great deal to be desired, however, and after a victory over the Medes and Persians, Prester John advanced westwards with the idea of conquering Jerusalem from the infidel, but he was halted by the River Tigris. His army lacked boats to cross the river, and there were no bridges, but he was told that if he waited long enough the river would freeze over and his men could cross on the ice. He waited several years for this to happen and eventually abandoned the expedition.

The popes of the mediaeval church sent frequent messengers to Prester John, and when King John II of Portugal wanted to open trade with India in 1481 he sought the approval of the great emperor. The problem was that no one knew the exact location of his palace. Some people believed it was somewhere in central Asia while others were sure it was built in Africa. It is now conceded that the power of Prester John radiated from what is now Ethiopia, but all his mighty empire faded away after he rose to heaven in circumstances of suitable glory.

Prospero's Island

An island in the Mediterranean no great distance from Naples, originally inhabited by a number of nature spirits led by the sprite Ariel. On a date now unknown the Algerian witch Sycorax, and her grossly deformed and retarded son Caliban, were exiled to the island. Sycorax tried to convert the nature spirits into a commune of evil spirits, and when they refused she imprisoned them all, including Ariel, within the trunks of trees.

Soon after the death of Sycorax, Duke Prospero of Milan and his infant daughter Miranda landed on the island. They drifted there in a boat without sails, equipped only with some clothing and Prospero's library of books on sorcery. He had neglected the administration of Milan in order to study

this art, and his young brother Antonio, with the help of the King of Naples, deposed him and set him adrift.

Prospero quickly realised that the island was an enchanted place, because the air was full of noises, sounds, and strange music. It did provide, however, for all his simple needs, and having found a cave suitable for himself and Miranda he used his knowledge of sorcery to release Ariel and the other sprites. He found Caliban roaming in the forest, and taught this Yahoo-like creature to work as his servant.

Ariel, who had not forgotten his treatment at the hands of Sycorax, relished the opportunity to revenge himself upon Caliban with ingenious tricks and torments, but he also proved a willing servant to Prospero.

After twelve years, a ship carrying Antonio; the King of Naples; Prince Ferdinand of Naples; and other passengers passed close to the island. Prospero, with the help of Ariel and the other nature spirits, raised a great tempest which forced the ship to shelter near the island, and frightened most of her passengers into taking refuge ashore.

Prospero then used his magic arts to segregate Ferdinand from the others, whom Ariel teased and terrified by such tricks as appearing as a harpy, setting a banquet before them and then causing it to disappear, and other sorceries.

Miranda, then fourteen years old, had never seen a young man since she left Milan, and she promptly fell in love with Ferdinand. Prospero approved of the match, and all ended happily for the mortals. They sailed away and left the island to Ariel, but one would now seek him in vain. Sorceries even more wicked than those of Sycorax have now denuded the island and polluted the surrounding waters, and the nature spirits have all been frightened away by tourists.

Quivera

Francisco Vasquez de Coronado, the governor of a Mexican province in 1539, was an ardent believer in reports about cities of astounding wealth which lay beyond the deserts and mountains. In 1540 he set out to conquer the Seven Cities of Cibola, in what is now New Mexico, on the strength of a detailed description by the missionary priest Marcos de Niza. But the fabled cities turned out to be only the rock dwellings of Pueblo Indians, whose wealth consisted of blankets, pottery, and some rough silver ornaments, and so Coronado took his expedition on an exploration as far north as the Grand Canyon.

Somewhere in that region they heard another marvellous story: that of the city of Quivera in which even the roof tiles are made of gold. The storyteller gave many colourful details, including a description of the mysterious king who slumbers beneath the Tree of Bells. This beautiful tree bears golden bells instead of fruit and flowers, and the story says that all the bells will ring, and awaken the king from his long slumber, when a party of white strangers enters the city.

Coronado's previous disappointment did not prevent him from sending his tattered horsemen into Texas in search of Quivera, while he followed a clue which led him to central Kansas. But the nearest thing he found to a golden city was a village of Witchita tepees, and in 1541 he limped back to Mexico where he was prosecuted for his unauthorised explorations.

River, The

Flows through the dreamy green southern counties of the England of King Edward VII, from the heart of the earth to the insatiable sea. On one side is the River Bank, crowded with all sorts of people such as otters, dabchicks, kingfishers, moorhen, and ducks, and on the other side, beyond the water-meadows, is the dark background of the Wild Wood. Beyond that again is the Wide World, where it's all blue and dim, and one glimpses what may or may not be hills and something like the smoke of towns—or it may only be cloud drift. The people of the River Bank never venture into the Wide World.

The River runs like a sleek, sinuous, full-bodied animal on its way to the sea, chasing and chuckling, gripping things with a gurgle and leaving them with a laugh. Everything is a-shake and a-shiver—glints and gleams and sparkles, rustle and swirl, chatter and bubble.

There are backwaters off the main stream, and one of these is like a little landlocked lake. Green turf slopes down to either edge, brown snaky tree-roots gleam beneath the surface of the quiet water, while the silvery shoulder and foamy tumble of a weir, arm-in-arm with a restless dripping mill-wheel on a grey-gabled mill-house, fills the air with a soothing murmur of sound.

It was here that the Water Rat, who knows that there is nothing half so much doing in life as simply messing about in boats, brought his new friend the Mole on a picnic on a sleepy summer day in 1908.

The Mole had never seen the River before. He was entranced by all its sights and sounds, and especially by the Rat's little boat painted blue outside and white within, just the size for two animals. As they rowed downstream, the Rat told the Mole that The River was brother and sister to him, and aunts, and company, and food and drink, and (naturally) washing. What The River hasn't got is not worth having, and what it doesn't know is not worth knowing.

The Rat introduced the Mole to the other people of the River Bank, including the Otter and the Badger, and he saw Toad rowing up The River in his new sports clothes and new wager-boat: a short stout figure splashing badly and rolling a good deal.

The Mole fell so deeply in love with The River that even when he turned the boat over on his first try at rowing, and the Rat had to rescue him, it made no difference. He quite forgot his own dark and lowly little house and lived in the Rat's cosy home in the River Bank.

He loved the stories the Rat told him about adventures in and along The River; he learnt to swim and to row, and he sometimes caught the meaning of the wind's whispering among the reeds.

The Mole himself had a great many adventures, with the Rat, and the Badger, and Toad, and he saw something of the fearsome Wild Wood. When summer came again he and the Rat set off downriver in search of Otter's son Portly, who was missing from home. They began rowing in the warm darkness, and as the first light came they heard the merry bubble and joy, the thin clear happy call, of the Piper at the Gates of Dawn. The liquid run of that glad piping enraptured the Rat and broke over the Mole like a wave, so that he rowed steadily on towards the source of the music.

In a backwater of The River they landed on a little island fringed with willow and silver birch and alder, and pushed through the scented undergrowth until they stood on a little lawn of marvellous green set about with crab-apple, wild cherry, and sloe. Tremulous, awed, and fearful, they stood in the flush of dawn as it revealed the stern but kindly face and curved horns and shaggy limbs of the Piper, with Portly sleeping between his hooves.

The sun rose, the vision vanished, and the animals took Portly back to his parents. But they were strangely subdued and thoughtful as they rowed slowly back to their own home, for the music of the Piper's tune still hovered just outside their memories. The Rat thought he heard it repeated in the whispers of the reeds, and tried to hear the words, but then it died away in a murmur of *forget, forget . . .*

Rock Candy Mountain, The Great

This cheerful mountain has been sought by generations of hobos roaming the length and breadth of the United States. Each seeker for the mountain has a clear picture of it in his mind. It is capped with vanilla ice cream instead of snow, changing to strawberry flavour in the sunset glow. The streams running down its sides are foaming with bock beer, well chilled by its descent from

O THE TOWN
CANARY COTTAGE
Mole's House
OSIER BED
Rat's House
Otter's House
PAN ISLAND
HE WILD WOOD
Badger's House
TO THE WORLD
THE WEIR

higher altitudes. Cigarette trees and chewing gum bushes flourish among the verdant foliage of the woodlands, in which many trees bear crisp green dollar bills instead of leaves. Plates of sizzling ham and eggs and french fries amble among the undergrowth, which includes apple-pie plants, pickle bushes, and hamburger blossoms. The wildlife consists mainly of fried chickens and barbecued steers.

The climate is perfect for sitting in the sun and spinning tall tales of adventures on the road, undisturbed by sheriff's men, railroad police, debt collectors and mothers-in-law, who are all forbidden to approach the Great Rock Candy Mountain.

The only difficulty in discovering the mountain is that, if one is wandering through Ohio, it is in California. In Nebraska, the word is that the mountain is in Arkansas. A man could well spend his life searching for the Great Rock Candy Mountain, but when he finds it the long quest will certainly have been worthwhile.

Rollingstone the Paper City

In the 1860s, people in the United States were intrigued by a publicity campaign about a new city being developed far up the Mississippi, near the border of Wisconsin and Minnesota. Maps of Rollingstone, circulated by the promoters, showed that this new metropolis of the Middle West was laid out in a most elegant manner. It already possessed a city hall, courthouse, library, and other fine public buildings, and there were plenty of building lots for sale in the business and residential areas.

Many people, especially immigrants, hastened to pay the promoters for prime pieces of Rollingstone land and then set out to build their futures in the new city. But when they reached the site of Rollingstone they found nothing but bleak open prairie, and the few people who lived around there had never heard about the great project. They began to call it the Paper City.

The cynical promoters, having proved the adage that 'a rolling stone gathers no moss', insofar as the landbuyers were concerned, departed for parts unknown with their profits from the Paper City.

Sleepy Hollow

A community in the hills on the eastern bank of the Hudson River, in New York State. It lies three kilometres inland from the old riverport of Tarry Town and a short distance upriver from Sing Sing. The homes of the people, known in the neighbourhood as the Sleepy Hollow Boys, lie in and around a shallow valley between two high hills, with some homes prettily situated in a grove of walnut trees. A small brook glides through the valley on its way to the river. A little way from the valley, an old church stands on a knoll above a woody dell. The road leading to the church and its churchyard is overhung with great trees, which shade the road with mysterious gloom in daytime and cast a fearful darkness at night.

A drowsy, dreamy influence seems to hang over the land and to pervade the very atmosphere. Some say the place is bewitched, perhaps by the spirit of one of the old Indian chiefs. The Sleepy Hollow Boys, who are descendants of early Dutch settlers, always seem lost in reverie. They are given to all kinds of marvellous beliefs, are subject to trances and visions, and frequently see strange sights. The neighbourhood abounds with haunted places and the people like nothing better than telling and listening to ghost stories, of which their favourite is that of the Headless Hessian.

He is the ghost of a cavalryman who had his head blown off during the War of Independence, and ever since then has ridden the highways and byways around Sleepy Hollow in search of the missing head. He tethers his ghostly steed in the churchyard during the day and rides around at breakneck speed in the dark of night, pausing in his gallop only to follow some belated traveller to see whether he is carrying the head. The Headless Hessian is seen most frequently on the dark road leading to the churchyard, where he usually turns himself into a skeleton before disappearing in a clap of thunder.

A young farmer named Brom van Brunt once scared the gangling schoolmaster Ichabod Crane out of the neighbourhood by pretending to be the Headless Hessian, and flinging a pumpkin which Ichabod thought was the missing head. The practical joke had fortuitous results for Ichabod, who abandoned schoolteaching in favour of the law and later became a noted politician.

St Petersburg, Missouri

A small town on the Missouri shore of the Mississippi. The majestic river is more than a kilometre wide at this point and it carries a busy traffic of palatial sidewheelers such as the *Big Missouri*, together with huge rafts of timber drifting downstream to the St Louis lumberyards. St Petersburg is one of the many riverports along the Mississippi but it is not significant enough to be the home port of any of the sidewheelers. The only power craft permanently based on the township is the steam ferry, which plies across to the Illinois side.

The architecture of the town is comfortable but undistinguished, consisting largely of frame houses and cottages of one or two storeys such as that occupied by the orphan boy Tom Sawyer, his half-brother Sid and cousin Mary, his Aunt Polly and her slave boy Jim. There is a Presbyterian church, also built of timber and with a kind of pineboard box on top to serve as a steeple for its cracked bell; a court house; the sheriff's office and town jail; three taverns including the Temperance Tavern; the schoolhouse; and a variety of stores, offices, livery stables and warehouses. The dusty streets of the town, mostly lined with high whitewashed fences, are pleasantly shaded by locust trees that blossom in the spring. The centres of town life are the courthouse square, the town pump, where white or black boys and girls sent to fetch pails of water are always skylarking, quarrelling, fighting, trading playthings, or resting as they wait their turns at the pump.

The population, of about 1,000, is principally white because few people are wealthy enough to own slaves. It is, however, distinctly divided into professional, commercial, and working classes and a variety of drifters and ne'er-do-wells such as Injun Joe, Muff Potter, and the town drunk, Finn. Finn's son Huckleberry smokes a pipe and wears cast-off clothes, never has a hair cut, goes barefooted most of the time and has no one to force him to go to church or school. He is Tom Sawyer's best friend and the envy of all the other boys.

The Widow Douglas, fair, smart, and forty, is the leader of St Petersburg society. She lives on the summit of Cardiff Hill, in a fine mansion looked after by several slaves. On the next step down the social scale stand such people as Lawyer Thatcher, Judge Frazer, and Mayor Ward, somewhat above young Dr Robinson whose anatomical researches will lead him to a gory end. Next come Mr Sprague, the Presbyterian minister, who is supposed to be paid a dollar a day but has difficulty in collecting his stipend; Mr Dobbins, the wig-wearing schoolmaster who would prefer to be a doctor, and boards with the signpainter's family; and the sheriff, who administers prompt justice such as horsewhipping an offender in front of the court house. After them there are families like the Harpers, Fishers, Millers, Rogers, and Lawrences, whose children go to school with Tom Sawyer.

The principal geographic feature of the neighbourhood, apart from the river, is Cardiff Hill, crowned by the Douglas residence and with the Welshman and his two sons living about halfway up the slopes. In the flaming summer sunshine the hill lifts its soft green sides through a shimmering veil of heat tinted with the purple of distance. It is a hollow hill, containing the great labyrinth of McDougal's Cave. The cave is entered through a small A-shaped opening high on the hillside, barred against unwary wanderers by a massive oaken door. It is said that one might explore for days through the intricate rifts and chasms of the cave, going deeper and deeper into the earth and never finding an end. School outings, under supervision, often visit the cave, and the Widow Douglas rounds off the children's day with the rare luxury of ice cream.

About five kilometres downriver lies Jackson's Island: a long, narrow, wooded island close to the dense forests of the Illinois shore and populous with wildlife such as

squirrels, jays, catbirds, and turtles which lay their eggs in the sandbar. It is a favourite resort of Tom Sawyer, Joe Harper, and Huck Finn.

Life in St Petersburg follows a placid rhythm in which the highlights are the annual 'Examination Exercises' at the school, parades of the Cadets of Temperance, and the occasional visits of a minstrel show or travelling circus. The townsfolk fit themselves into a rustic pattern which is completed by a grave in the old churchyard, where wooden headboards lean at crazy angles and the painted names of those who rest there gradually fade out of sight and mind.

Toad Hall

The family home of the wealthy and well-respected Toad family for many generations: situated on the north bank of The River, with grounds stretching from the River Bank almost to the Wild Wood. Parts of the property, especially the banqueting hall, date back to the fourteenth century. The year in which it passed into the possession of the Toad family is now unknown. Early this century Mr Toad junior inherited Toad Hall from his father, a worthy animal who effected many improvements, including the renovation of a secret underground passage from the River Bank, where it exits into Toad Hall through a squeaky board in the butler's pantry. Mr Toad senior showed the secret passage to the Badger but asked him not to reveal it to Toad junior except in a dire emergency, saying 'He's a good boy but very light and volatile in character, and simply cannot hold his tongue.'

Toad Hall is a handsome dignified old house of mellowed red brick, with well-kept lawns and brilliant gardens stretching down to the water's edge. A small creek crossed by a wooden bridge leads off the river to the boathouse, with a sign saying 'Private. No landing here.'

Mr Toad junior, who has a tendency to hyperbole, once described Toad Hall as 'An eligible self-contained gentleman's residence, very unique . . . replete with every modern convenience. Up-to-date sanitation, five minutes from church, post office, and golf links.' This description does not, however, do full justice to the beauty and serenity of a traditional English country home and all its appurtenances. Behind the house and the stables there are hen houses and pig sties, a fishpond, a pigeon house, a dairy, and a large vegetable garden. The domestic quarters contain the kitchen and wash house, linen presses, china cupboards, butler's pantry, pantry and servants' hall. A house of this type would also have capacious wine cellars, and a brewing vat to make October ale for the indoor and outdoor servants.

This domestic economy supports a gracious lifestyle in the remainder of the house. There is a smoking room off the large entrance hall, in which Toad can entertain his friends; a Blue Boudoir used as a writing room, with notepaper embossed in blue and gold; and numerous other apartments including the billiard room which opens through French windows onto the lawn. A large conservatory is attached to the house.

The River-bankers are rather proud of Toad Hall, but it arouses venomous jealousy in the people of the Wild Wood. At one time, when Mr Toad was absent on a series of youthful adventures, the stoats, ferrets, and weasels of the Wild Wood took over Toad Hall and used it for noisy parties. They were evicted only when the Badger revealed the secret of the underground passage, so that he and Toad, the Water Rat and the Mole might attack the invaders from the rear.

Treasure Island

A narrative part-written by a Mr James Hawkins, who visited this island in his youth, and described its shape as that of 'a fat dragon standing up.' It is approximately fifteen kilometres long and eight wide, in a location which Hawkins was at pains to conceal. His narrative does, however, contain so many clues that they betray it as an island of the western Atlantic Ocean. Probably it is in the same latitude as the Bermudas, but lying closer to the east coast of the USA, rather than in the Caribbean as is sometimes supposed.

For example, he mentions that Treasure Island has a strong growth of evergreen or live oak (*Quercus virginiana*), which grows prolifically on the east coast of the USA, and he also mentions azaleas, willows, and bulrushes. These plants are all indigenous to North America rather than to the tropical islands of the Caribbean. His description of the island landscape shows that it has a sandy soil which supports forests of pine trees, and this has a strong similarity to the State of Georgia in the USA.

As far as may be determined, his party visited Treasure Island in April 1760. A letter written shortly before they left England is dated 1 March, and a Dr Livesey, who accompanied the expedition, later remarks that he was wounded at the Battle of Fontenoy. This was fought in 1745, and it would be fair to allow a fifteen-year interval between Livesey's experiences as a young army doctor and his voyage to the island, when he was a country medico but obviously a man in the prime of life. An April visit would account for the temperature variations he mentions in his part of the narrative, from midday heat to cold evening winds, which would be typical of those latitudes in that season but certainly would not apply to a tropical island.

They were obliged to sail to the nearest port to replace mutinous seamen, and their records show that they sailed directly to a port in the 'Spanish Americas'. The prevailing north to north-east winds of the western Atlantic would have been ideal to carry an undermanned ship directly southwards, either to Florida which was then a Spanish possession, or to Cuba which was ruled by Spain until early this century.

If Treasure Island does lie somewhere between Georgia and the Bermudas, then it would have been ideal for pirates to refit and careen a ship, provision her with salted goat meat from the flocks on the island, and hide accumulated treasure. By the mid-1700s, pirates had been working the Caribbean for more than a century and all its islands were so well known, and so subject to raids by the Spanish and British navies, that a refuge well to the north and off the regular trade routes would have had many advantages.

From seawards, Treasure Island presents an ominous and discouraging appearance to navigators. A heavy Atlantic surf breaks on steep beaches along the rugged coastline. The general colouring of the island is monotonous and gloomy, with much of the undulating surface covered by thick dark scrub and forest. Many tall pine trees, rising as high as sixty metres, grow singly or in shadowy clumps, with sandy stretches running palely between them.

The dominant features of the island are three strange hills, Foremast, Spyglass, and Mizenmast, along the west coast. They arise out of the woodlands like great pillars of naked rock, with Spyglass Hill about 100 metres higher than the others. It has sheer sides and a summit like the flat top of a pedestal, used by pirates as a lookout.

Foremast Hill has a two-pointed pinnacle, and a cave once used as a refuge by Ben Gunn, a pirate marooned on the island for three years.

There are three deep inlets, but the best harbour is that known as Captain Kidd's Anchorage. This lies on the south coast of the island between Haulbowline Head and the White Rock. Shipmasters should approach the anchorage to the south of Skeleton Island, which is linked to the main island by a sand spit exposed at low tide, and then alter course sharply to the north-north-west to enter the anchorage. The strong currents which sweep around the south of the island and up the west coast have scoured out a deep channel with a bottom of clean sand, and a ship may shelter there safely although it is not a healthy or appealing haven. Two stagnant streams ooze through a swampy coastline into the channel, and the air smells strongly of sodden leaves and rotting tree trunks. Thickets of live oak grow thick as thatch, their leaves a poisonous green, in the marshy tract which harbours rattlesnakes and malarial mosquitoes.

On a knoll overlooking the anchorage stands a pirate blockhouse built from unsquared pine logs, loopholed for musketry. The house is surrounded at some little distance by a stockade of logs about two metres high, and the land around this fortification has been cleared of trees and undergrowth. Attackers would have to approach across this open land and then climb the stockade in the face of the defenders' bullets. An old ship's kettle, sunk in the sand, collects water from a spring that bubbles from the top of the knoll.

J. Hawkins, son of the landlord of the Admiral Benbow Inn, made his visit to Treasure Island in curious or even dubious circumstances. A strange chain of events led to a map of the island drawn by Bill Bones, mate of a pirate ship under the notorious Captain Flint, coming into the possession of Squire Trelawney of young Hawkins' village. It showed the location of buried treasure. Trelawney and Livesey, who were somewhat eccentric English gentlemen of the old damn-your-eyes sort (one of them carried Parmesan cheese in his snuffbox instead of snuff) promptly decided to go in search of the treasure and take Hawkins along as cabin boy.

The two men moved fast but erratically. They secured an excellent ship, the 200-ton schooner *Hispaniola*, but manned her with

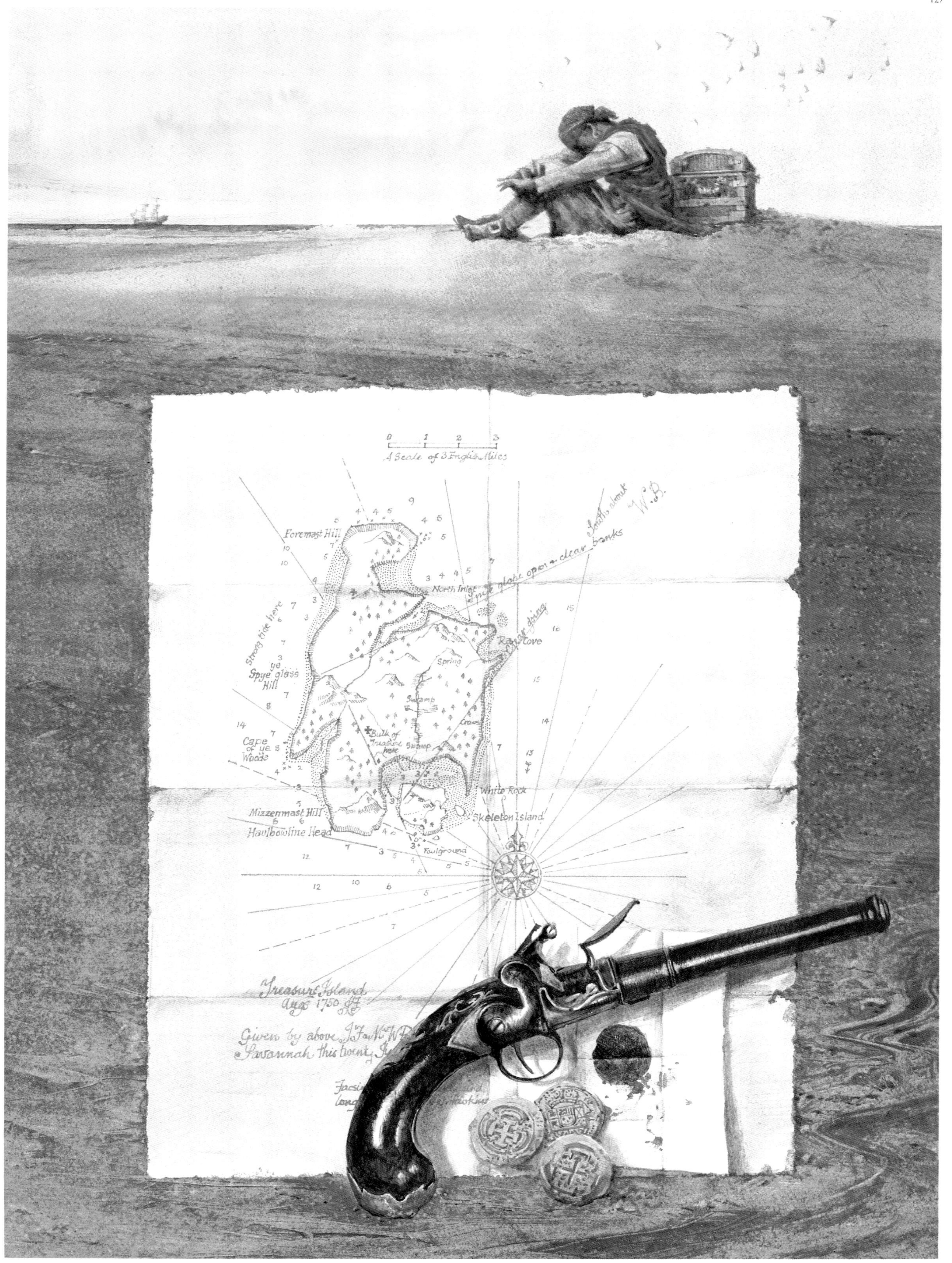

A Scale of 3 English Miles
Foremast Hill
North Inlet
Spye glass open a clear banks
South about
W.B.
Strong tide here
Spye ye glass Hill
Spring
Swamp
Bulk of treasure here
Swamp
Cape of ye Woods
White Rock
Skeleton Island
Mizzenmast Hill
Haulbowline Head
Foulground
Treasure Island
Augt 1750 J.F.
Given by above J.F. to Mr W.
Savannah this twenty

a company of rakehell seamen and ignored the warning of the shipmaster, Captain Alexander Smollett, late Royal Navy, that 'I don't like the cruise; I don't like the men; and I don't like my officer.' He referred to the mate, Mr Arrow, a drunken incompetent who soon disappeared overboard under mysterious circumstances.

As ship's cook, Trelawney and Livesey signed on the one-legged landlord of a dockside pub, known as Long John Silver but called Barbecue by the seamen. Silver claimed to have lost his leg while fighting in a king's ship but the two gentlemen did not think to query why a man who had achieved a seafarer's dream—a snug berth in a pub—should want to go to sea again. Even Silver's parrot, named Cap'n Flint after a famous pirate, which repetitively cackled 'Pieces of eight!'; and the fact that their crew used a pirate ditty as a capstan chanty, did not arouse their suspicions.

Fortunately they had a few law-abiding men among the crew, and Captain Smollett was such an excellent seaman that he found the island and conned the *Hispaniola* safely into Captain Kidd's Anchorage. Silver and his men mutinied almost as soon as the anchor dropped, and revealed themselves as ex-pirates who knew about the treasure but not where it was hidden.

The English gentlemen and their henchmen survived this problem by a combination of good luck and blundering courage, aided by the fortuitous presence of Ben Gunn who had removed the treasure from its original hiding-place and taken it to his cave.

They showed extremely poor judgment in allowing Long John Silver to change sides when he saw that he was beaten, but their discovery of a fortune in gold bullion and specie did not soften their attitude towards the three surviving mutineers. They marooned these three unfortunates on the island and ignored their pitiable pleas.

As for Silver, he remained true to type and deserted, with a small portion of the treasure, at the first port of call.

Utopia

In the days of Sir Thomas More and Francois Rabelais, who wrote books concerning Utopia in 1504 and 1535, it was believed that these authorities were describing an ideal but imaginary society. It is now obvious that, with remarkable prescience, Sir Thomas More was prophesying Australia. Despite various points of difference between the two social structures, and More's geographical errors, the similarities between Utopia and Australia are too numerous to be merely coincidental.

More gave Europeans to understand that Utopia lay off the coast of South America, to which it had once been connected. Given the rudimentary geography of that era, this is an understandable error. At least the country was placed in the correct hemisphere, and it is now generally accepted that Australia was once connected to another land mass.

Utopia was seen as an island nation with a huge inland sea. Australia does not, of course, possess such a body of water, but for many years it was believed to exist somewhere beyond the inland deserts and many explorers sought it in vain. Possibly More was under a similar misapprehension.

The portrait of Utopia as a land once barren and inhospitable, but changed into a prosperous agricultural and industrial society by the energies of its settlers and the enlightened use of science and technology, is absolutely relevant to Australia. So also is the fact that Utopians, like Australians, know nothing of their nation's history before they settled the country. The reference to Utopian criminals being kept in chains, and native-born criminals being treated worse than those from overseas, is no doubt an elliptical comment upon the early convict communities in Australia and the Australian treatment of Aborigines.

Sir Thomas portrayed Utopia as a rich agricultural nation, with government control of farm production and distribution; as a large exporter of agricultural produce, but with so much surplus production that large quantities were given to less fortunate nations; and as having such a well-developed

internal trade that no town or city ever went short of requirements. Obviously this is a precise picture of the Australian economy, which knows no poverty in the Old World sense of the word.

The capital of Utopia was described, like Canberra, as being a properly planned city totally different from the teeming rookeries of the Old World. It is true that Canberra does not have the moats, fortifications, and other defences ascribed to the Utopian capital, but it must be remembered that More was writing in an era which knew nothing of guided missiles.

The parliament of Utopia, aptly known as *Lietalk*, was situated in the capital. So is Australia's, and Australians have similar names for their national assembly. In both nations, parliamentary debates are excruciatingly long and detailed.

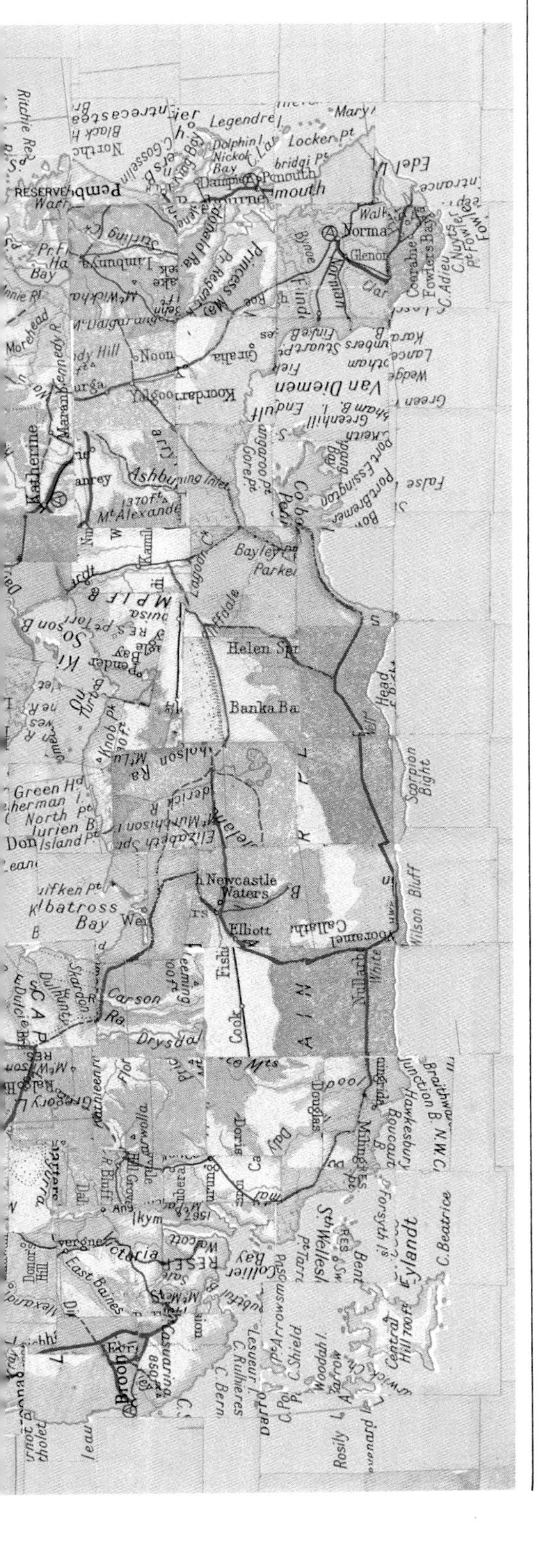

The Utopian and Australian styles of government have numerous similarities. It is true that Utopia is a republic, but so is Australia apart from some ceremonial vestiges from the past. Both nations are democracies, which elect local and national governments, and do not have aristocracies. They both enjoy religious tolerance although they have known intolerance in the past, and both have a variety of religious sects of which some are strict and others amiable. A national health service, with Utopian aspirations, also exists in Australia. Both countries enjoy good relations with their neighbours; they both welcome immigrant workers who tend to work harder than the indigenes; they have excellent armed forces raised on a volunteer basis, which see no glory in war but are nevertheless noted for their military ardour; and there is a steady outward flow of Utopians/Australians to settle in other countries, thus tending to regulate the populations.

The closest resemblances between the two countries occur in their social mores and customs. Their peoples are good-humoured, hospitable to strangers, and averse to pomp and ceremony. Both Utopians and Australians tend to break into hearty laughter at the spectacle of overdressed officials.

By Utopian custom, a betrothed couple must appear naked to each other, in the presence of a chaperon, before they marry. This wise precaution is to avoid physical dissatisfaction. In Australia, betrothed couples usually have been naked together before marriage, although they dispense with chaperons.

Both the Australians and the Utopians live in well-built individual homes and are fanatical home gardeners. Their towns are well maintained and they take great pride in their communities.

The people of both nations believe that God created them to enjoy life and so they spend as much time as possible on pleasant activities and pastimes. Both men and women go to work, but the working days are comparatively short and there are frequent holidays.

Utopians, like Australians, feel that a God-sent miracle will always save them in times of crisis: a belief strengthened by the occurrence of such miracles in the past.

Perhaps the principal difference between the two countries is that the Utopians do not drink beer. Both nations do, however, make and drink their own wine.

Utopia, as portrayed by Sir Thomas More, was favoured by a number of social benefits and customs which are still at a rudimentary stage in Australia, but there is little doubt that this favoured continent in the South Seas has a strongly Utopian flavour about its achievements and aspirations.

Valhalla

The great hall where Odin, chief of the Aesir, receives warriors slain in battle. Entry to Valhalla is reserved to the most skilled and courageous warriors, whose death in battle is sometimes arranged by Odin so that he may enjoy their company.

The enormous hall is built from shields laid upon a framework of spears, with breastplates tiling the floor. It has 540 doors, each wide enough to admit a column of marching men 800 abreast.

The floor space is occupied by countless rows of tables and benches, set about huge fires whose light is reflected by gleaming swords. Huge pigs roast over the fires and an endless supply of the warriors' tipple, beer and mead, flows from the udders of the goat Heidrunn.

Throughout the night the warriors feast on pork, beer, and mead served to them by the Valkyry. Odin sits above them and sometimes joins in the songs which resound from the rafters as the warriors bellow drunkenly and pound their tankards on the tables.

When the first light of morning casts blood-red gleams through the windows of the hall, the enormous host of warriors takes up its weapons and the hall empties as they tramp out onto the battleground.

Once outside Valhalla they quickly take sides, and then with savage cheers rush at each other with swords, spears, and axes flashing in the sunrise. All day they stab and hack at each other until the blood flows in rivers across the grey battleground, and men fall with ghastly wounds amid the heaps of corpses.

But as the sun sets so the dead rise again, and on the word of command they fall into the columns which march back into the hall. Eagerly they sniff the aroma of roasting pork as they take their places at the tables, and call for beer and mead to quench their warriors' thirsts. Another night of drinking and feasting lies ahead, with many more tales of mortal combat to be boasted across the tables.

Every day brings new warriors to Valhalla, with tales of strange new weapons and of tactics unknown to warriors who have lived there for centuries. There is always room in Valhalla for those who follow the profession of death.

Vanity

A town on the pilgrim route from the City of Destruction to Beulah Land. Satan and his horrid companions always try to divert pilgrims from the strait and narrow path which leads to Beulah Land, and they chose the town of Vanity as the site for a fair offering irresistible temptations to pilgrims. The town is controlled by such notables as Lord Hate-good, Mr Enmity, Mr Lyar, Mr Cruelty, and Mr Implacable, who welcomed Satan's business operations to Vanity and

had no objection to Vanity Fair staying open for twenty-four hours a day on every day of the year.

Vanity Fair is gaudily set out in rows and streets illumined with blood-red lights, that cast a lurid glare over the coarse and lustful faces of the stall holders. Numerous street entertainments are arranged to attract customers and these include thefts, murders, cheating, adulteries, and the bearing of false witness. These entertainments give continuous performances with no charge for admission.

The rows of stalls each sell the vanities of different countries and regions and are identified by the names of those countries. For example there is a British Row, a Roman Row, a French Row, an Italian Row, a Spanish Row, and a German Row.

Pilgrims on their way to Beulah Land are obliged to go through Vanity and to pick their way through the narrow streets crammed with fools, apes, knaves, and rogues. The pilgrims must close their ears to the wheedling of seductresses and to the hoarse yelling of merchants offering vanities at giveaway prices. The stalls are heaped with every sort of vanity including houses, lands, honours, titles, lusts, and pleasures and delights of every description. Whores, bawds, servants, lives, bodies, souls, silver, gold, pearls and precious stones are always freely available.

Even the Blessed One had to go through Vanity on His way to the Celestial City, and was met as an honoured visitor. Satan himself led Him from stall to stall, offering such vanities as the kingdoms of the world at special prices, but did not manage to persuade Him to spend even a farthing.

The people of Vanity are of a violent and capricious nature and pilgrims passing through the town should make themselves as inconspicuous as possible. Otherwise they may find themselves pilloried, or put in the stocks, on false charges of causing a disturbance, or even taken to court and subjected to the rough justice of Lord Hategood.

Vineland

(Not to be confused with Vinland, the Scandinavian name for North America.) Vineland is a Mediterranean country devoted to viticulture, possibly the original home of Dionysus (also known as Bacchus) who is the patron saint of wine salesmen and the inventor of all the arts of winemaking.

The landscape of Vineland is somewhat monotonous because the entire landscape is covered with vineyards from the coastal plains to the rolling hills of the interior. Consequently it changes colour according to the seasons: green in spring and summer, golden in autumn, and earth-coloured in winter.

Numerous small villages stand among the vineyards, each comprising a group of neat whitewashed cottages set around the winery and wine cellars. Each village is famed for its own vintage of red or white wine made from the associated vineyards, and never makes any other style of wine.

The vast majority of Vinelanders are employed on all the tasks and techniques of viticulture: pruning, ploughing, picking the grapes, carting them to the wineries in great carts towed by snow-white oxen, treading out the grapes, and so on. In the treading season, the legs of every man and woman in Vineland are stained up to the thighs with the juices of the grapes.

The nation supports various trades connected with winemaking, such as the coopers who make the casks and the blacksmiths who forge ploughshares, pruning hooks, and vintage knives, and there are the usual service industries. But all the requirements of the people are imported in exchange for their single export. Vineland wine is sought so eagerly by other countries that there are never any trade difficulties.

There are no schools, because the Vinelanders do not believe any knowledge to be valuable unless it is related to wine. All such knowledge is passed on by word of mouth and by a system of apprenticeships.

On the whole the people are temperate, despite the fact that everyone of any age is allowed to consume as much wine as he or she may desire. They believe that enjoyment of wine is dulled by excessive consumption. However, the great Festival of Dionysus, which lasts for about six weeks during the winter months, is often the occasion for disgraceful orgies.

Vineland is a kind of democracy with no clearly defined ruling body or social structure. Each village is loosely controlled by the Elders of the Vine, an assembly which meets every few weeks to discuss local affairs, but these meetings usually develop into wine-tasting sessions. Politics are virtually non-existent because each village holds all its vineyards in common and every person receives all requirements in the way of food, clothing, household goods, etc. out of a common store. Vinelanders believe that winemaking is the most important occupation of mankind; that the benign influence of wine could solve most of the world's problems; and that time spent on occupations other than winemaking is wasted.

White Cat's Castle

The aged king of a far country was unwilling to surrender his throne, but he promised it to whichever of his three sons should bring him, within a year, the smallest and prettiest dog in the world.

The youngest son, on his horse Black Diamond, sought far and wide for such a dog and eventually found himself in a strange wild land, where he was overwhelmed by a tremendous thunderstorm. But Black Diamond picked a way through the storm, to a castle where every window shone as brilliantly as the sun, and where such sweet

music was playing that it charmed the thunder into silence.

The prince pulled at a bell chain of sparkling diamonds by the castle gate, and immediately felt unseen hands urging him into the courtyard. The invisible hands took care of him and Black Diamond by leading the horse to the stables and taking the prince into the castle, where they removed his wet clothes, dressed him in gorgeous apparel, and served him a sumptuous banquet. He ate hungrily, and was about to quaff the wine in a crystal goblet when a beautiful white cat entered the chamber. Her clothing, including a silver veil streaming behind her, showed her to be a cat of high rank, and she walked with such dignity that the prince rose respectfully to greet her.

She sat on a stool of cloth of gold while he told her his story, then bade him drink up the wine in the crystal goblet. The prince obeyed, and instantly forgot all about his quest. For almost a year he stayed with the white cat in her magnificent castle and the invisible hands attended to all his needs. During the days he went riding on Black Diamond while she rode beside him on a white monkey, and in the evenings she sang to him in the sweetest voice he had ever heard.

When the year was nearly over she reminded him of his quest, and gave him an acorn to take to his father. He laughed at the idea of a dog small enough to fit into an acorn, but when he opened the acorn at his father's court the tiniest dog in the world stepped out with a silvery bark.

The king quickly thought up another quest, and sent his sons out in search of muslin so fine it would pass through the eye of a needle.

The prince rode Black Diamond back to White Cat's Castle, which seemed even more beautiful and brilliant than before. Once more he drank from the crystal goblet and spent nearly a year with her, and when it was almost time for him to go she gave him a walnut. Within the walnut was a hazel nut, and within the hazel nut was a grain of wheat, and within the grain of wheat was a grain of millet, and this contained a length of muslin so fine that it slipped easily through the eye of a needle.

The king could not deny that the prince had won both of the quests so far, but he thought up a final condition for his sons. The throne, he said, should go to the one who brought back the most beautiful bride.

Again the prince returned to White Cat's Castle, and as he rode Black Diamond towards the castle all the windows shone with the brightest light he had ever seen. Fireworks flashed and sparkled from the battlements, and the flowers around the inner courtyard all floated across to lie like a carpet beneath his feet.

As usual, the invisible hands looked after him and his horse and spread a banquet before him, and the white cat made him welcome. The prince thought she looked more beautiful and graceful than ever before, but she sighed sadly when he told her of his search for a bride. She bade him, however, to drink of the wine and once more he spent nearly a year of pleasure in her company.

When it was almost time for him to go she asked him to promise her a favour. He gladly agreed, but was horrified when she bade him to cut off her head. He protested 'Never! Never! For I love thee as deeply as any bride!'

But she insisted that he should keep his promise, and with deep sorrow he drew his sword and cut off her head. Instantly she changed into the most beautiful bride in the world, and all her invisible servants took human form.

She told the prince that an evil magician had placed her under a spell, but now the enchantment was broken and she could take her true place as queen of her country. The prince loved her so greatly that he never returned to his father's court, and they lived happily ever after as king and queen of White Cat's Castle.

Wonderland

The principal Wonderland of the British Isles, as described by a lecturer in mathematics who would surely be devoted to accuracy, is a subterranean community lying beneath the English county of Oxfordshire. It is entered through a girl-size rabbit hole under a thick hedge, but there is no guarantee of easy egress.

The rabbit hole runs like a straight tunnel for some distance before it reaches a kind of deep well, which is lined with cupboards, bookshelves, maps, pictures, and shelves holding such domestic requirements as orange marmalade. Anyone falling down the well (which is the only way to enter Wonderland) should not remove objects from these shelves.

The well is very deep, but the visitor eventually falls safely onto a heap of sticks and dry leaves at one end of a long passage. This leads into a hall about three metres high, illuminated by lamps hanging from the ceiling. There are doors all around the hall, including a very small one behind a curtain, but they are all locked. A tiny golden key, on a three-legged table fashioned from solid glass, will open this door but does not fit any of the others.

A normal mortal, even of girl-size, may open the little door but will not even be able to insert his or her head into the passageway beyond. It is not much larger than a rat-hole. A peep through the door reveals the loveliest garden imaginable, with cool fountains playing among beds of bright flowers, but the only way to enter it is by the following complex procedure. (a) Return to the glass table, on which will now be found a small bottle labelled DRINK ME, in large beautifully printed letters. The contents have a mixed flavour of cherry tart, custard, pineapple, roast turkey, toffee, and hot buttered toast, and cause the consumer to shrink to 25·400 centimetres high. (b) A person of this size will not be able to reach the key on the table, and so it is necessary to open a little glass box that will be found under the table. This has the words EAT ME written in currants embedded in its surface.

Consumption of the cake causes rapid growth to the height of the hall. This creates a problem which may be solved only if a White Rabbit drops a fan and a pair of gloves nearby. Donning one of the gloves will cause another rapid reduction in height—in fact it is almost too rapid. The glove must be removed quickly before the wearer fades away.

Miss Alice Liddell, who was nine years old when she followed the White Rabbit down the rabbit hole in 1864, fell down the well and followed the complex process aforesaid. She had just regained a height suitable for passing through the smallest door when she fell into the pool of tears she had wept in her manifestation as a junior giantess. Somehow this washed her through into one area of Wonderland, in company with a Mouse (who was greatly annoyed by her talk of dogs and cats) a Duck, a Dodo, a Lory, and Eaglet, and several other curious creatures. Alice helped them all to struggle out of the pool of salt tears, and they dried themselves by running a Caucus-race in which everyone was the winner.

But Alice offended all the creatures with persistent talk about her cat Dinah, so that they all moved off and left her. She felt very lonely and low-spirited until the reappearance of the White Rabbit, searching for the fan and gloves.

Ever since the first sighting of the White Rabbit, when Alice saw him pull a watch out from his waistcoat pocket before he popped down the rabbit hole, he had been in a state of high agitation. Apparently he was late for an appointment with the Duchess, and when he saw Alice again he mistook her for his housemaid. He told her to run home and fetch him a pair of gloves and a fan.

She found that he lived in a neat little house, easily distinguishable by the brass plate engraved with the words W. RABBIT. His servants were an Irish gardener named Pat (who was digging for apples) and a lizard named Bill.

Style
106

Alice found the fan and gloves but she could not resist drinking from another little bottle, hoping it would restore her to normal size. It did so, but she grew so rapidly that she was jammed inside W. Rabbit's house. She could not get out until Pat and the White Rabbit pelted her with a barrowload of pebbles, which changed into little cakes when they flew through the windows. When she ate some of the cakes she shrank again and was able to escape.

After an adventure with an enormous puppy she looked for something else to eat or drink that would bring her back to normal again, and during this search she came to a mushroom as high as she was. A blue caterpillar sat on top of it smoking a hookah.

The caterpillar was not in the least pleased to see her, and it engaged her in a confusing conversation before it remarked 'One side will make you grow taller, and the other side will make you grow shorter.'

Alice wondered what it meant, but as it crawled away it commented 'Of the mushroom.'

She nibbled a piece of the right-hand side, and shrank so rapidly that her chin hit her foot. She could barely manage to open her mouth, in order to swallow a morsel of the left-hand side, and when she managed to do this her neck grew so immensely long that her head shot up above the highest tree in the forest. An angry pigeon thought that Alice was a serpent trying to steal her eggs.

Her neck was so long that it became entangled in the branches of trees, but eventually she managed to restore herself to normal. After that she contrived to vary her height at will, by nibbling one side or another of the mushroom.

This ability enabled her to enter a little house in the woods, where a Frog-Footman guarded the door. Alice watched a formal exchange of courtesies between the Frog-Footman and a Fish-Footman, who brought an invitation from the Queen to the Duchess for a game of croquet, and then had a brief argument with the Frog-Footman. (She found that all the creatures of Wonderland argue continuously, usually in most confusing terms.) The Frog-Footman did not seem to care whether she went further into the house, where she found the Duchess (presumably of Wonderland) sitting on a three-legged stool in the kitchen and nursing a very noisy baby.

The cook was making soup, with so much pepper that the baby alternately sneezed and howled, while a large Cheshire Cat sat on the hearth grinning from ear to ear. To Alice's alarm, the cook began throwing everything in the kitchen at the Duchess and the baby, which screamed even more loudly although the Duchess took no notice. She simply argued with Alice on various matters, and tossed the baby roughly up and down until she threw it at Alice with the comment 'I must go and get ready to play croquet with the Queen.'

Alice was very worried about the baby, and did not know what to do with it. Luckily it changed into a pig and trotted away into the woods. The Cheshire Cat, grinning more widely than ever, now sat on a branch of one of the trees. This cat had a bewildering habit of appearing and disappearing, eventually leaving only its grin behind, but after the usual confusing Wonderland conversation it directed Alice to the houses of the Mad Hatter and the March Hare. She found the latter easily because the chimneys were shaped like ears and the roof was thatched with fur.

The March Hare and the Mad Hatter were having tea outside, crowded at one corner of the tea-table and resting their elbows on a Dormouse fast asleep between them. They cried out 'No room! No room!' as Alice approached, but she said indignantly 'There's *plenty* of room!' and sat down at the table.

She thought it was the stupidest tea-party she had ever attended, because they gave her no tea and she had to listen to a great deal of nonsense, riddles, and rudeness. She walked off into the woods, where she found a door in one of the trees. This led her back to the hall at the bottom of the well, and since she now knew how to control her size, by nibbling at pieces of the mushroom, she was able to go through the smallest door into the beautiful garden of Wonderland.

Her first encounter was with three playing-cards working as gardeners. They were painting white roses red, but they quickly threw themselves flat when the King and Queen of Hearts entered the garden, preceded by ten soldiers carrying clubs, ten courtiers ornamented with diamonds, the ten royal children all decorated with hearts, a party of guests who were mostly kings and queens, the White Rabbit talking in a hurried and nervous manner and smiling at everything that was said, and the Knave of Hearts carrying the king's crown on a velvet cushion.

The Queen of Hearts was a very angry lady, who screamed 'Off with his head!' (or 'her head' or 'their heads') if anyone offended her, but Alice easily prevented the playing-card soldiers from beheading anyone. The royal party had come into the garden to play a croquet match, which was the most curious that Alice had ever seen. The ground was all ridges and furrows, the croquet balls were live hedgehogs and the mallets were live flamingoes, and the playing-card soldiers had to double themselves over, and stand on their hands and feet, to make the arches.

Alice had great difficulty in managing her flamingo, in order to hit the hedgehog balls with its head. The soldiers and hedgehogs kept wandering all over the ground, the players all played at once without waiting for their turns, and the Queen stamped about shouting 'Off with his head!'

Alice was pleased when the Cheshire Cat's grin reappeared, and then its head, so that she had someone to talk to. The Queen wanted to have the cat's head cut off, but the executioner objected that he couldn't cut off a head which was not attached to a body.

The croquet game ended when the Queen had sentenced everyone to death, but Alice was relieved when she met a Gryphon who told her that the sentences were never carried out. He took her to meet a mournful Mock Turtle, who gave her an interesting description of his education. He had learnt Reeling and Writhing; the different branches of Arithmetic which are Ambition, Distraction, Uglification, and Derision; Mystery ancient and modern, with Seaography; and Drawling, Stretching, and Fainting in Coils. The lessons were called lessons because they lessened every day.

The Mock Turtle taught Alice the Lobster Quadrille, and various songs, before they all attended the great trial of the Knave of Hearts for stealing the tarts. All the creatures of Wonderland appeared as witnesses and even Alice had to take the stand, but she had no fear of the court because she had begun to grow larger again. As usual she found the proceedings most confusing, especially since the Queen kept insisting 'Sentence first—verdict afterwards!' and eventually sentenced Alice to be beheaded.

Alice said 'Who cares for you? You're nothing but a pack of cards!' and at this the whole pack rose up into the air and came flying down upon her. Immediately she found herself back on the grassy bank where she had been lying when she first saw the White Rabbit and followed him down the rabbit hole.

Apparently Miss Alice Liddell never attempted to return to Wonderland, although she did have some further peculiar adventures in Looking Glass Land.

Woodman's Hall

The Anglicised name for a hunting lodge known in most northern European countries, under such names as *Jaegerhalle* in Prussia and *Pavillon des chasseurs* in Normandy. The lodge is a rambling old timber building in a forest clearing, looking as though it had been added to room by room over the centuries but somehow giving an impression of snug hospitality. Little many-paned windows of thick greenish glass peep out from under the eaves, the huge door is hinged with hand-forged iron, and crooked chimneys of weathered brick sent smoke curling into the sky.

The clearing is in the midst of a great forest that has never been despoiled by man. Islands of fairly open country, studded with noble beeches, chestnuts, oaks, and elms, are set in a great dark sea of pines and firs. Not far from the house there is a fine lake of clear water, teeming with fish such as pike, carp, bass, and trout.

Every imaginable kind of European wildlife, including species like the Polish bison which are now extinct over the rest of the continent, flourishes in various parts of the forest. Capercailzies perch on the branches, huge flocks of waterbirds visit the lake or nest among the reeds, and the red deer are commonly seen among the trees. Wild boars root for acorns under the oaks, pheasants, pigeons, and partridges are as plentiful as sparrows, and there are even such predators as bears, wolves, and foxes.

Woodman's Hall is the eternal home of men who have been great hunters during their lives—but only of those who have hunted out of necessity and not out of pleasure in killing. During the days they go out to match their skills against the creatures of the wild, knowing that there are no game-keepers or sheriff's men to claim that the game belongs to some nobleman. At night they drink and feast in the snug rooms of Woodman's Hall and prepare their gear for another day in the forest.

The creatures of the lake and woods never increase or decrease in numbers, and even if one of them is caught or killed by a hunter it is still there on the following day.

Xanadu

A mountainous province of central Asia. During the thirteenth century it was a part of the enormous dominions of Kublai Khan, the Mongol emperor who was noted not only for his military prowess but also for his love of the arts, sciences, and nature.

In about 1270 AD, Kublai Khan visited Xanadu and was greatly impressed by its scenic splendour. In the green foothills of the snowclad mountains he found a deep chasm slanting down the hillsides through dense cedar forests, with the River Alph (which was sacred to the people of Xanadu) roaring through it so tumultuously that the raging waters flung rocks and boulders high in the air. The Alph then followed a winding course for about nine kilometres until it disappeared into the icy caverns beneath a glacier. The Xanudans told Kublai Khan that the caverns were measureless to man and that the Alph ran eventually into a 'sunless sea', presumably a subterranean ocean.

The roar of the river seemed to Kublai Khan like ancestral voices prophesying war, but this did not worry the great conqueror. He was so taken by the romantic grandeur of Xanadu that he ordered the building of a stately pleasure-dome close to the River Alph. It was to be a miracle of rare device, with the shadow of the sunlit pleasure-dome falling upon the raging torrent and the ice caves forming a part of the construction.

The Khan's architects were equal to the challenge and they encircled more than sixteen kilometres of the cedar forest with walls and towers. They left portions of the forest thus enclosed in their natural state, and converted the remainder into beautiful gardens of blossoming incense-scented trees, traversed by sinuous rills. The pleasure-dome itself was the focus of all this manmade beauty, amidst the rugged grandeur of Xanadu.

It is not known whether Kublai Khan spent much time in his pleasure-dome, especially since he was deeply involved in a series of unsuccessful invasion attempts

against Japan. No doubt the ruins of the dome and of the great walled garden may still be found in Xanadu, which is now part of the People's Republic of China.

Yalding Towers

A magnificent home and estate in the New Forest region of Hampshire, England, which has been the home of the Yalding family for many generations. Even the punitive taxation of modern Britain has not had much effect on the lifestyle of the Yaldings, and curious tales are told about the success of the present Lord Yalding in his numerous business ventures.

Yalding Towers was built by one of his ancestors in a florid and ornate style, which has little in common with the classic styles of English architecture. The huge building contains a domed chamber with a blue ceiling, decorated with golden stars, said to have been used by the original owner for the practice of white magic. Legends told in the neighbourhood attribute his interest in magic to a ring given to the Yaldings by a fairy. The powers of the ring include the bestowal of invisibility upon the wearer and the endowment of certain supernatural insights.

Generations of Yaldings have extended and improved the magnificent gardens, which are ornamented with many statues in the classical style and a remarkable collection of stone figures of prehistoric animals. It is said that a wearer of the fairy ring will see these figures and statues come to life.

The Yaldings refuse to discuss the legends with journalists or psychic researchers, and they have on several occasions declined to allow TV producers to make features based on the story. Whether the magic ring plays any part in their continued prosperity must be a matter for speculation, but it is interesting to note that the wearing of the ring is supposed to bring punishments as well as rewards.

Ysbaddaden's Castle

Ysbaddaden was the Chief Giant of all Britain in the time of King Arthur, and the owner of a castle in Wales. Culhwch, the Celtic hero who was a cousin of King Arthur and was reputed to be the most handsome man in Britain, was obliged to seek the hand of Ysbaddaden's daughter Olwen, because he was under a spell cast by his stepmother which prevented him from falling in love with any other woman. It was a difficult quest because he had never met Olwen and did not even know where she and her father lived.

He sought Arthur's assistance, and although the king had never heard of Ysbaddaden and Olwen he responded generously to his kinsman's request. He sent out a party of his gifted knights to find the Chief Giant's residence, but when they discovered the castle they found that, however closely they approached to the building, the great stone walls always remained just beyond their reach.

They solved this frustrating problem when they met a shepherd's wife, who told them that Olwen came to her cottage on Saturdays to wash her hair. This presented an opportunity for Culhwch to meet Olwen, who was no doubt relieved to find she was a beautiful mortal maiden. She took him into the castle and introduced him and his friends to Ysbaddaden, who responded most ungraciously by driving them away with a shower of poisoned rocks.

But Culhwch persisted in his wooing, and the Chief Giant eventually agreed that he should have Olwen in marriage if he succeeded in performing a number of impossible tasks. With the help of King Arthur, Culhwch performed all the tasks but it seems he did not trust the word of the Chief Giant. He assembled all of Ysbaddaden's enemies and returned to the castle, where they killed the giant and Culhwch lost no time in consummating his marriage to Olwen.

Zenda

A town in northern Ruritania, which was once a small kingdom between Saxony and Bohemia. Zenda has always been an important military base because it stands south of the pass between the Erz Gebirge and Riesen Gebirge ranges, and its ancient fortifications include the castles of Zenda and Festenburg.

Early this century, Ruritania was a characteristic kingdom of Mittel-Europa. A large peasant class supported an arrogant aristocracy, mainly interested in hunting and court intrigues, and a prosperous bourgeoisie. Apart from the capital, Strelsau, the country had few towns of any significance and most of the land belonged to the nobility.

Zenda assumed brief political significance during the 1890s, when there was an attempt to depose King Rudolf V of Ruritania. An Englishman, Rudolf Rassendyl, played an important part in foiling this plot although it resulted in the regency of Queen Flavia.

The Ruritanian royal family was expelled after the first World War and the nation enjoyed a brief democracy until the Nazis claimed it was a province of Saxony. It is now the Democratic Republic of Ruritania, and Zenda is a missile base and the local headquarters of the KGB.

CHAPTER FOUR

THINGS OF MAGIC, SCIENCE, AND INVENTION

THINGS OF MAGIC, SCIENCE, AND INVENTION

The difference between humans and other animals is that we spend so much time compelling inanimate objects to obey us. Other animals build homes, and a few useful artefacts such as spiderwebs, and accept the rest of the world as it is. But our brains torment us into perpetual tampering with the vital elements of the Cosmos, and into trying to understand why they obey us.

A few hundred centuries ago, the explanation was simple. When the first man blew into the first reed, and created the first note of music, he knew without doubt that the spirit of the reed was enlivened by his breath and piping up in cheerful response. And all other things possessed their own spirits, which co-operated whenever men found the right way to approach them. This is where magic comes in very handy. A person who knows the right spells and rituals can call on the gods to influence the appropriate spirits. Each god and goddess supervises a specific group of spirits, and so it is only a matter of choosing the right god, saying the right words, and making the proper offerings. The spirits of stone, metal, timber, and all other materials then work with mankind to ensure the success of a venture. Of course the humans have to do the hard work, but no project could be completed without the help of the spirits.

As the centuries passed by, magicians became technicians. They still have to know the right words and rituals to persuade materials to co-operate with them, and they certainly demand substantial offerings, but they really know very little about the spirits of their materials. Of course they have theories about atoms and molecules, but who makes the atoms and molecules behave as they do?

We may understand the effects of all natural phenomena, but we have only the vaguest notions about the causes. We don't even understand the cause of the basic miracle: thought. A modern magician may talk learnedly about such things as electrical synapses within the brain, but is speechless if one asks who invented them.

The simple answer is that the Cosmos exists in a balance between good and evil spirits, which work within us and all around us. Our magicians may influence them to some degree, and they have certainly contrived to awaken the demons which may destroy us.

In this section of the book, we examine some of the ways men work with the spirits and elements of the Cosmos.

Aesculapius

The first medical practitioner: son of the god Apollo and the nymph Coronis, who named him Asklepios. Cheiron, the learned Centaur, taught Asklepios the art of healing, but he soon outstripped his teacher and rose swiftly to eminence in the new profession. Unfortunately he was so successful in curing the ills of mankind that the great god Zeus feared he would create a new race of immortals, and killed him with a thunderbolt. He would have had to follow the path to Hades if his father Apollo had not arranged for him to be deified, so that he might carry on his work as the god of medicine.

His sons Machaon and Podalirius and daughters Hygeia and Panacea followed in their father's footsteps. The sons became army doctors and served at the siege of Troy, Hygeia was promoted to be the goddess of good health, and Panacea serves as an auxiliary goddess. The family founded the first college of medicine, the Asklepiadae, which began the tradition of teaching the art of medicine as a sacred secret.

The Greeks erected many temples to Asklepios, where sufferers went to sleep (*incubatio*) in the hope that the god would heal them. The Romans took Asklepios to Italy in the form of a snake, to rid them of a pestilence, and changed his name to Aesculapius. Ever since those days, doctors have used a snake twined round a staff as the symbol of their profession.

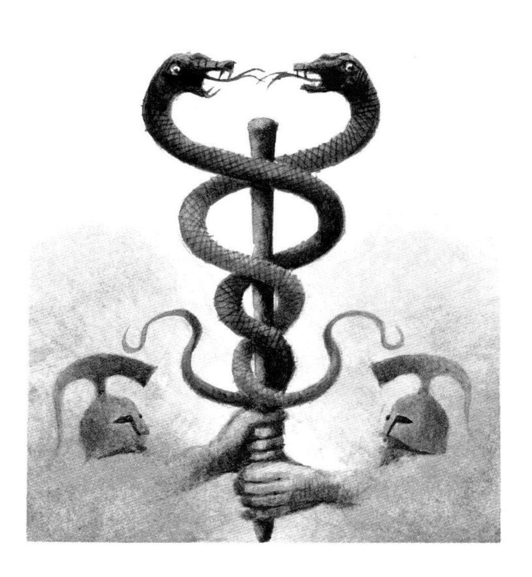

Alchemy

The science of research into the foundations of creation, so that one may compound the elixir of life (known to Chinese alchemists as *tan*); create human beings in the form of homunculi; and transform base metals into gold or silver. It is probable that alchemy was taught to mankind by the Egyptian god Thoth, the inventor of science. In another manifestation Thoth became Hermes, the ingenious Greek god of many occupations who owned such artefacts as winged sandals, a magic wand, and a sleep-inducing flute.

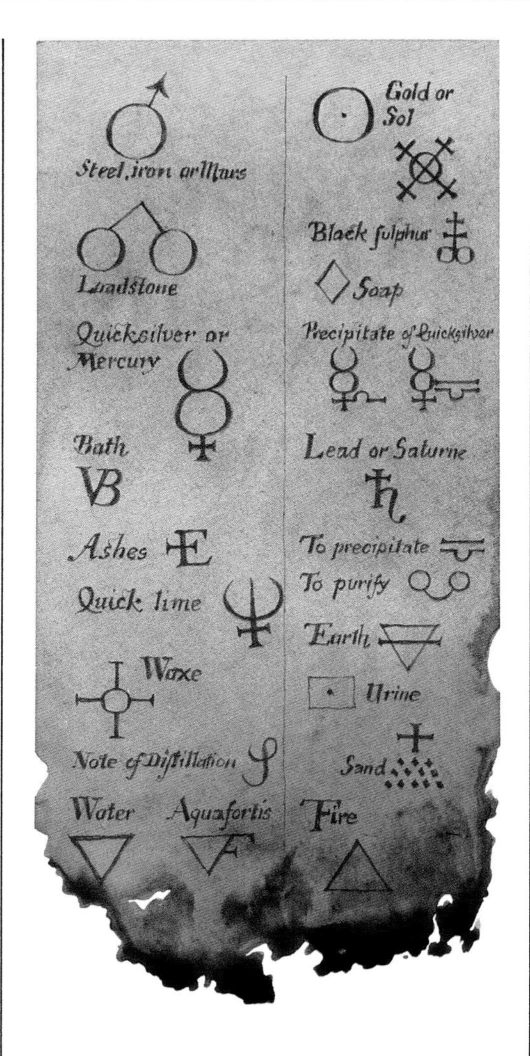

Alchemists placed the seal of Hermes on their preparations, and modern alchemists pay tribute to the god by saying that certain compounds are 'hermetically sealed'.

Alchemists believe that everything in the universe is composed of variations on one basic material, the *prima materia*. This fundamental unit is an essence of mercury, totally different from the 'quicksilver' of common usage. Alchemists create it by removing the principles of air, earth, and water from ordinary mercury. Having thus obtained a supply of *prima materia* he treats it with a philosopher's stone, which is produced by refining sulphur down to its basic principle. There are two types of philosopher's stones: white, which converts *prima materia* into silver, and yellow which changes it into gold.

Naturally the process is extremely complicated, and alchemists have to make innumerable experiments in their attempts to create *prima materia* and the philosopher's stone. One of the essentials is a fire so hot that it will attract or create salamanders, which play a vital part in the creative procedures. Consequently, the temperature in an alchemist's workshop is always stiflingly hot and the garments, beards, and hair of an alchemist and his assistants are always scorched and singed.

Chinese alchemists follow methods similar to that of the Europeans, but they believe that the proportions of the basic material (which they call *tao*) vary in different substances according to their contents of the male-female principles *yang* and *yin*.

The alchemists' search for the elixir of life, which will confer immortality, is even more difficult than creation of the philosopher's stone. The elixir must include all the four elements of fire, water, earth, and air, the three principles of animal, vegetable, and the *prima materia* or *tan*. Experiments for creation of the elixir cause an alchemist's laboratory to be appallingly dirty and cluttered as well as stiflingly hot, because he needs such an enormous variety of materials including crocodile livers, human skeletons, mandrake roots, and the gall bladders of antelopes. In fact, it is impossible to finance the search for the elixir unless he is able to convert base metals into gold.

Alectromancy

A method of divining the future by the use of a white cockerel. One should tether the cockerel to a small stake with a long cord, draw a circle in the dust around it, and write the letters of the alphabet in the dust around this circle. Next, place a grain of wheat on each letter, and address one's question to the cockerel. It will move around the circle and peck wheat from the appropriate letters to provide an answer. (As it pecks up each grain, this should be replaced so that the cockerel may indicate the same letter again if necessary.)

Before addressing one's question to the cockerel it is necessary to repeat a certain spell or formula. Any witch or warlock will provide this spell on receipt of suitable payment.

Amulet

A charm worn for protective purposes, as distinct from talismans which are worn to attract good fortune, or for specific reasons such as calming mad dogs, arresting a haemorrhage, or trapping a thief.

A general-purpose amulet will keep most kinds of evil at bay, but the purchase of such an amulet on the spur of the moment will not be efficacious. It should be 'tailored' for its wearer as precisely as a ceremonial garment. Ideally, one should consult an astrologer or soothsayer as to the best materials to be used, the phases of the moon in which the amulet should be made and paid for, and the day of the month or year on which it should first be worn. It could, for example, be useless or even dangerous to wear an amulet comprising silver and moonstones if the signs and portents indicated a golden locket, containing a text from the Bible or Koran, as the correct one for a certain personality.

Amulets may also be designed to protect one against specific health problems. An amulet containing yarrow (or made in the likeness of this herb) will protect against influenza. Lavender will protect against nervous debility, sage against indigestion, and so on. Rosemary, or its likeness, is a good all-round prophylactic and also an aid to memory, while juniper ensures good appetite and a free flow of urine.

Probably it is best not to rely upon a single amulet for protection against ills and evils, but to wear a number of different creations.

Angakuk

An Eskimo magician, either male or female, who is possessed or helped by the spirit of some other being, object, or creature. Everything has its own spirit, even ice, air, and stone.) A person wishing to become an angakuk may either participate in ceremonies designed to attract a spirit, or the spirit may possess him or her without warning. The latter phenomenon creates the most powerful angakuks.

An angakuk's principal function is to look after the well being of the tribe. If it is plagued by bad weather which prevents hunting and fishing, the angakuk performs certain ceremonies and the weather eventually improves. If the tribe runs short of the fish, seals, bears, and walruses on which it depends, then the angakuk must make a dangerous journey to the depths of the ocean to interview the sea goddess. When he returns to his igloo, which has been sealed during his absence, he emerges to pass on her advice. This will either be to move camp to better hunting grounds, or to wait until the wildlife returns to the present neighbourhood.

Anonyma

The result of a gruesome experiment in Savannah, Georgia, early last century. Dr Robert Terriman, a noted physician, had always been fascinated by the concept of restoring the dead to life, and after many years of experiment he decided to construct an artificial body which would be controlled by a living brain. He reasoned that the human body is, after all, no more than a vehicle to carry the brain around and obey its commands.

He had only the materials available in those days and so the body he constructed was a clumsy although ingenious humanoid. The motive power was supplied by Leyden jars, through which the brain would supply electrical impulses to a series of finely made cogs, pulleys, and wheels. The whole complex artefact was encased in the finest of kid leather, but resembled a human only in that it had a body and two arms and stood erect on two massive legs.

When all was ready he bribed the sheriff to provide him with the corpse of a man hanged for murder. He hurried the corpse to his laboratory at dead of night, and worked continuously until he had removed its head and connected the nerves of the spinal column to the terminals of the artificial body. To his delight the experiment worked, and he called his creation Anonyma, meaning No Name, to imply that it had no relationship to normal humanity.

Anonyma's brain, which Terriman kept alive by injections of a special fluid he had compounded, could see, hear, and speak through the usual organs of the head. In the beginning it co-operated eagerly with Terriman as he taught it how to manipulate the artificial body. But it was the brain of a coarse and brutal criminal, and it soon began to protest that existence simply as a brain, without the ability to enjoy all the sensual appetites of a carnal body, was not worth living. Terriman tried in vain to convince it of the delights of pure reason, and eventually had to control it by disconnecting various parts of the body.

The climax came when he exhibited Anonyma to a great conference of scientists. Anonyma had sullenly agreed to behave himself so that Terriman, who expected the demonstration to be the summit of his professional career, might point out all the refinements of his creation.

But when he led Anonyma onto the platform, and the audience saw the stiff awkward movements and ludicrous appearance of his creation, they exploded into laughter. Infuriated, Anonyma used his jointed metal fingers to break Terriman's neck, and then tore off his own head and hurled it at the audience.

Apples, Golden

This fruit, of pure solid gold, grows in the fabulous Garden of the Hesperides, which flourishes on the western edge of the world: beyond the Island of Hyperborea and on the border of Ocean. The garden is tended by the Hesperides, daughters of Atlas and Hesperus, and guarded by Ladon, the dragon with 100 heads.

Apart from the intrinsic and artistic value of the apples, they are of great historical importance, because Mother Earth caused them to grow as a wedding present for Hera and Zeus.

The mighty hero Hercules had to steal the apples as one of his twelve labours, and after many desperate adventures he reached the border of Ocean. There he found the giant Atlas holding up the sky. Atlas offered to fetch the apples if Hercules would hold up the sky for a while, and when Hercules agreed the giant slew Ladon, stole the apples, and returned to Hercules.

But Atlas decided he was weary of holding up the sky, and told Hercules he might as well continue with the task. Hercules pretended to agree, but said the weight of the sky was chafing his shoulders and asked Atlas to take it over for a few moments while he made a pad to protect them. As soon as Atlas took the strain, Hercules snatched the golden apples and made off with them. Later he gave the apples to Athena, who returned them to the Hesperides.

Appleseed, Johnny

An American folk hero and frontier personality who is at least partly real. He was born in Massachusetts in 1774, as John Chapman, but nobody knows anything about his life before he appeared in western Pennsylvania, then the frontier of the United States, in 1800.

John's conviction that mankind's salvation lay in his own brand of religion and the eating of apples soon attracted the nickname of 'Appleseed Johnny'. He began his missionary career by begging two barrels of rotting apples from a cider mill, and setting off down the Ohio River on a raft. At frequent intervals he extracted a number of seeds from the apple pulp and planted them in places which might attract new settlers, so that they would enjoy the benign powers of apple eating. In 1834 he settled for a while in central Ohio, but then pushed on ahead of the waves of settlement, still sowing his apple seeds, until he died at Fort Wayne, Indiana, in 1847.

Johnny Appleseed was a gentle but courageous little man who befriended the Indians and tried to reconcile them to the idea of white settlement, and established a kind of St Francis-like relationship with the wildlife of the great forests. Once, when he heard rumours of an Indian uprising, he ran 50 kilometres through the night to warn the settlers.

Many legends and traditions surround the story of Johnny Appleseed, who is now seen as the spiritual vanguard of white settlement in the Middle West.

Augurs

Originally known as *auspices*, a word deriving from *avis specio* (birdwatching) and denoting those officials who interpret the will of the gods. 'Auspices' now means the omens signalled by the gods, while augurs are those who interpret them.

To receive auspices from the gods, an augur should ascend a high hill before midnight on a cloudless night. On the top of the hill he must mark out his *templum*, or sacred circle, in the presence of a magistrate, and consecrate it with prayers to Jupiter before he sits within it and looks southwards. Every auspice seen to the left, or east, may be regarded as favourable, and those to the west as unfavourable. For example, a lightning flash to the east would be a direct indication of Jupiter's favour.

Other auspices might include thunder or falling stars, but they appear most frequently in the dawn flight of birds and must be interpreted through the birds' songs, flight paths, and other activities. The most significant birds are eagles, vultures, owls, crows, and ravens. If an augur saw several eagles flying from east to west it would be extremely auspicious, but should he observe some such occurrence as a crow attacking a pigeon, or a vulture eating the corpse of an owl, then the augur would have to interpret the auspices very carefully.

A higher degree of augury involves the examination of the entrails of a bird or animal slain in sacrifice. It is also possible to interpret many other auspices such as the appearance of the sky, the sounds and movements of animals, and the way in which a cockerel eats grain. However, the worldwide popularity of birdwatching shows that most augurs still seek auspices in the old traditional style.

Barmecide Feast

A practice invented by the noble Barmak family of Persia to test a person's poise and sense of humour. The subject should be invited to an intimate dinner at which he and his host are served only with empty plates and glasses. As one course follows another, the host will expound upon the rarity and flavours of the food being served, but should not necessarily pretend to eat the imaginary victuals or drink from the empty glasses. An individual who can endure this test with proper gravity, and with appropriate compliments to the host upon the food and wines, may be regarded as a superior person.

Belarivo

The result of a flawed voodoo spell, cast by a person (name unknown) with inadequate knowledge of this sorcery. The intention was to raise the corpse of Joachim Belarivo and use him as a zombie, to perform manual labour during the hours of darkness. The ceremony succeeded in resurrecting Belarivo, but it seems that some important component of the spell had been omitted because Belarivo refused to work and insisted on attending any neighbourhood celebrations. The sight of a resurrected corpse is not in the least attractive, and when Belarivo tried to join the dancing at a local wedding the guests stampeded in screaming confusion. Only the priest stood his ground, and with great difficulty persuaded Belarivo to return to the grave.

After that, the shuffling step of Belarivo was heard soon after the start of any kind of gathering from a birthday party to a political meeting. The people of the district commissioned the most powerful practitioners of voodoo in an attempt to control the rambling corpse, but Belarivo argued stubbornly with them, in his harsh terrible croak, that he was doing no harm and only wanted to enjoy the company of the living.

Eventually the people thought they might discourage him by staying at home, but when Belarivo began to appear at ordinary family dinners they were obliged, at great expense, to seal him into a lead coffin and bury it beneath a pile of boulders.

Bells

These instruments are extremely effective in driving away evil spirits. The impact of the clapper on the bell releases the essence, or *principia metallica*, of the metal from which the bell is made, and this is carried upon the waves of sound. Evil spirits are allergic to *principia metallica* because all the metals of the earth were originally owned by dwarfs and gnomes, against whom the spirits are powerless. Bell metal, being an alloy of copper and tin, is especially potent because these metals were once owned by the pixies of Cornwall.

Bell power is generally in proportion to the size of the instrument. The resonant far-reaching chimes of such bells as the Kaiserglocke of Cologne Cathedral, the Tsar Kolokol of Moscow, Great Tom of Lincoln, and the bourdon bell of Riverside Church in New York, send shattering vibrations through the substance of evil spirits. In human terms, these vibrations have the same effect as setting all one's teeth on edge, loosening bones in their sockets, cramping every muscle in the body, and causing a tumult of the bowels. Naturally the evil spirits put as much distance as possible between themselves and the sound of bells.

Small bells of gold and silver (for domestic use) can, however, be very efficient if one senses the presence of any evil spirit in the home. Glass bells or wind chimes, such as the strips of glass hung in a tree to tinkle when the wind blows, have no real power but often frighten the spirits, who mistake them for metal bells.

Bonfires

A vigorous fire of well-seasoned faggots is an important accessory in dispelling witches from a neighbourhood plagued by these creatures. Ideally, the fire should be built on the highest hill in the district, and carefully arranged so that the kindling will ignite immediately and set the faggots ablaze without delay. Certain nights in the year, such as Midsummer Night or Hallowe'en, are preferable for bonfire lighting. When all is ready, the entire population of a village should assemble around the tower of faggots. One of them lights the kindling, and when the flames rise high enough for each person to see his neighbour's face the villagers join hands and dance around the bonfire, chanting 'Burn, witch, burn!' until the fire dies down to ashes.

The ceremony is so effective that it is most uncommon for the cottage of a known witch to burst into flames while the villagers are dancing around the bonfire. Even if this does not happen, the cleansing power of the flames will burn away a witch's potential for evil and cause her to flee the neighbourhood.

Probably the best time for a bonfire (which of course means 'good fire' and signifies its ability to burn away evil) is after dark on May Day.

Bottle Imp, The

This being and its habitation were last heard of at Papeete, the capital of Tahiti, sometime in the 1880s. It was then in the possession of a brutal drunken ex-boatswain of a whaling vessel, who had deserted his ship in the islands.

The bottle imp lives in a round-bellied bottle with a long neck, in size about one litre. The glass of it is white like milk, with changing rainbow colours in the grain. Withinsides something obscurely moves, like a shadow and a fire.

The glass was tempered in the fires of hell and the bottle is indestructible by any force known to man. The cork can neither be drawn nor driven into the bottle. If you employ a corkscrew, it simply slides out of the cork when you try to pull it, and the cork remains as whole as ever.

If an owner of the bottle calls on the imp to appear, it will pop out and in again as swift as a lizard. But he who has called upon it will sit as though paralysed for many hours, speechless with horror.

It is not necessary for an owner of the bottle to see the imp in order to enjoy anything he might desire. He has only to ask and it is granted instantly. It is said that Napoleon Bonaparte once owned the bottle, and might have conquered the whole world if he had not sold the bottle again.

There is one drawback to ownership of the bottle. If it is still in your possession on the day of your death, you must go straight to hell. This knowledge makes every owner anxious to get rid of it before long. He knows that if the bottle imp is powerful enough to make wishes come true, it is certainly capable of sending a person to hell.

The problem is that one cannot give the bottle away. It simply returns to the owner. The only way to obtain the bottle is to buy it from one of the temporary owners, and the only way to dispose of it is to sell it for less than one paid.

When last heard of, the bottle had been sold for only two French centimes and the owner had great difficulty in selling it again. Whoever bought it, for only one centime, knew that it would be hard to find a way to sell the bottle for less than that. But the brutal old boatswain said he was destined for hell anyway, and bought the bottle for one centime so that he might booze the rest of his life away.

Nobody knows what happened to the bottle after the boatswain died, but currencies have been devalued many times since the 1880s and are still falling in value. Perhaps the long-necked bottle and its resident imp are still passing from hand to hand, bestowing dreadful powers upon the rulers of our world.

Broth of Oblivion

When the soul of a sinner is released from hell, to be reincarnated in another form such as a snake or cockroach, it must drink from the Broth of Oblivion before it leaves the precincts of hell. The broth causes a soul to forget all about its previous existence on earth, and eliminates all knowledge of human languages. The broth does not rid the soul of its human feelings, however, and in its new incarnation it must suffer for sins committed in a previous existence by knowing the degradation of its present state.

Brooms

The traditional style of broom, consisting of a bundle of willow or osier twigs bound firmly onto a strong handle, is favoured by witches for aerial transport. A witch may ride upon any object she can straddle, such as a shovel or pitchfork, but she prefers a broom because of its aerodynamic qualities and because the bundle of twigs provides a convenient co-pilot's seat for a cat or other familiar spirit.

Brooms do not possess any integrated method of propulsion. Lift-off is achieved only when a witch has anointed herself with flying ointment, and when she straddles the broom she must repeat the formula 'Go, in the devil's name, go!'

Bullets, Magic

The only type of projectile capable of bringing down a witch in flight, of wounding (but not killing) a vampire, or of killing a were-wolf. The bullets must be made of pure silver and should ideally be moulded within the confines of a churchyard.

The problem with silver bullets is that they are too soft for use in modern high-velocity firearms, or in any type of rifled weapon using metallic cartridges and

elongated bullets. The bullets must not be nickel-jacketed, in the style customary since last century, because the nickel casing would protect the victim from the silver core. It would in fact be extremely difficult to fashion a silver bullet, and to make the accompanying cartridge, for any long-barrelled weapon developed later than the 1850s. (Pistols are not recommended for hunting supernatural beings because of their short range and inaccuracy.)

The hunter should, therefore, provide himself with a smoothbore musket using a one-ounce (28·35 gram) spherical ball, the accompanying bullet mould, a quantity of pure silver (100 per cent fine) and the usual ramrod, wadding, black powder etc. The ballistic quality of silver bullets is poor, because the metal is so soft that it is distorted by the explosion of the propellant, and so the hunter should mould sufficient bullets to allow for a considerable amount of practice. The stopping power of a 28·35 gram spherical silver bullet is considerable at ranges up to 100 metres when fired from a smoothbore musket, but at longer ranges it may cause only a superficial wound and place the hunter in danger of a supernatural response.

Cat's Cradles

The string patterns created in the games known as cat's cradle are very useful in controlling the weather. At the end of a fine day, the manipulator should create a complex pattern and hold it up towards the setting sun. This will capture the sun, and force it to return on the following day to ride across cloudless skies. The procedure is most valuable in periods such as harvest time, when fine weather is essential, but should not be used too often or the sun will learn how to escape from the net.

Clay

The basic material used by some Creation Ancestors to fashion mankind and the other creatures of the earth. The usual method is for a Creation Ancestor to mould a man and woman out of any suitable deposit of clay, and then to add such ornaments as pebbles for eyes, dry grass or coconut fibre for hair, and seeds for nipples. The creator then sets the clay figures out in the sun to dry, and when they are ready he blows upon them to impart the breath of life. Naturally the creator may choose any desired colour of clay for moulding his figures, but the preferred colours for humans appear to be black, yellow, brown, white, red, and various shades of ochre.

Humans are very simple to create by comparison with all the other animals. The Creation Ancestors devote much more time to these and use considerable ingenuity in their shapes and colouration. When they are ready to be brought to life, the creators give them much more than the simple breath of life and endow them with an immense range of knowledge, instincts, and abilities, which would probably be wasted on such simple creations as males and females.

The use of pure clay for the creation of mankind explains why his soul is so earthy, and more disposed towards the grosser elements of the universe rather than the ethereal freedoms of the atmosphere.

Some creators are careless in their use of clay and the preparation of the clay figures. They mould the figures disproportionately, or leave them out to dry in all kinds of weather so that they are cracked by the sun or eroded by wind and rain. The creators are generally much less meticulous in creating men and women than they are in fashioning the other animals. Consequently, each animal resembles every other animal within its species, whereas every human is different and the clay figures range all the way from ugly to beautiful.

Corn Dollies

These intricate artefacts are woven from the dry stalks and ears of any kind of grain, but are most usually made from those of wheat. They are known as Corn Dollies or Kern Babies in most parts of England and as Maidens or Carlins in Scotland. In Europe they have a variety of names such as Corn-Mother, Corn-Maiden, Corn-Wolf, Oats-Stallion, Rye-Sow, and so on.

All of them are repositories of the spirit of the grain, which may be observed moving through or over the standing stalks when they sway and ripple in the wind. The spirit exists in every grain field, and must be placated to ensure its return each year. The last sheaf harvested from each field is made

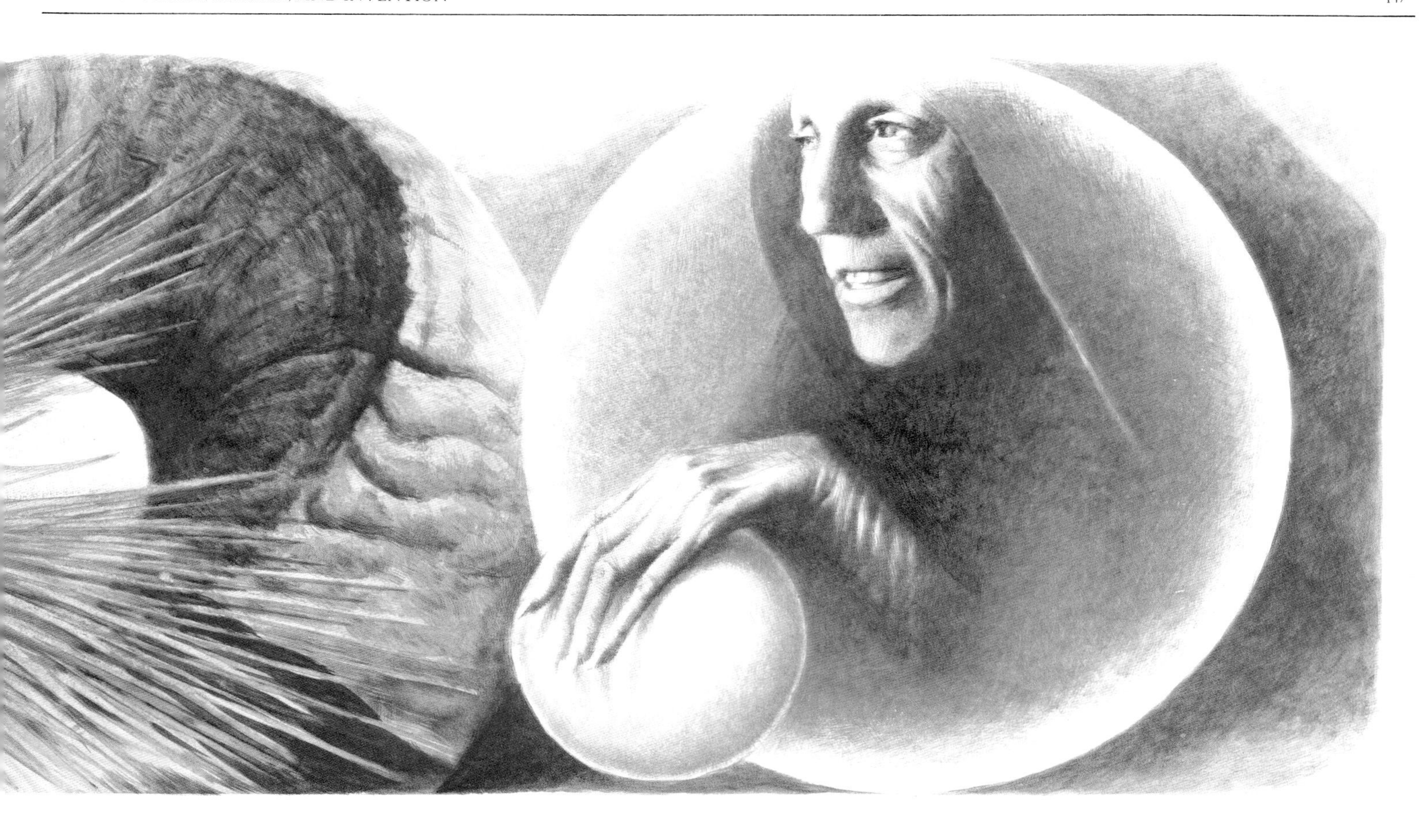

into a Corn Dolly, in which the spirit lives until the following year.

Originally a Corn Dolly was no more than a bundle of grain bent over and tied in such a way that it had a 'head' and 'body'. This would be kept in the rafters of a farmhouse kitchen from autumn until spring, when the spirit would be released into the earth at the time of sowing the new crop. But country craftsmen soon developed more elaborate ways of paying homage to the grain spirit. They wove the dry stalks and ears into elaborate representations of maidens or animals, or into complex designs such as a wreath or pyramid. The glossy gold of the crisp stalks and the shapes of the ears combine into artefacts which are aesthetically pleasing and satisfying.

The grain spirit is released into the soil by burying a Corn Dolly at the time of spring seeding, or by burning the artefact and scattering its ashes on the ground. It is unlucky to keep a Corn Dolly, even if it is a most artistic creation, any longer than the spring following the autumn in which it was made. Otherwise the grain spirit may be trapped within it and will not help the new crops to grow.

Corn Dollies are powerful symbols of fertility, and a young man courting a maiden is advised to make a special dolly for presentation at some appropriate time during courtship.

Cornucopia

A word deriving from the Latin *cornus* = horn and *copia* = plenty. Also known as 'Horn of Plenty'. The original cornucopia was one of the horns of the goat Amaltheia, which suckled the great god Zeus when he was an infant. Zeus was so grateful to Amaltheia (who apparently has some relationship to Pan) that he placed her in the heavens as the constellation Capricorn, but he took one of her horns as a present for the nymphs. Zeus spent a great deal of his time on the seduction of nymphs, and it would appear that he used the first cornucopia as a tactic in overcoming their resistance. He told them that whenever they needed anything to eat or drink, they should ask the horn and it would overflow with everything they desired. The nymphs found that this promise by Zeus (unlike some of his other promises) was amply fulfilled. Whenever the nymphs asked the cornucopia for fruit, grain, honey, wine, or any other food or drink, the horn responded so bountifully that they could feast to their hearts' content.

Crystals, Crystal Balls

The practice of crystal-gazing or crystal-scrying began among the Incas, the Apaches, and the Euahlayi Aborigines of New South Wales. Other peoples have used different substances and surfaces, ranging from water in a coconut shell to glass or metal mirrors, for the purpose of divining the future, but there can be no doubt that crystal is the most effective. It comes from the womb of Mother Earth, whose wisdom comprehends all things past, present, and future.

The word crystal derives from Greek words meaning 'clear ice', and the first essential for crystal-scrying is a symmetrical ball of ice-clear rock crystal such as that obtained from the Alps. Other types of crystal may be used but if they are veined or clouded then the future will be equally obscured. The absolute ideal is a ball of rock crystal ground into shape by Alpine gnomes, but such artefacts are virtually unobtainable nowadays. Glass balls, now commonly used by charlatans for crystal-scrying because pure crystal balls are so rare and inexpensive, are ineffective for genuine crystal-scrying.

A crystal-scryer with the true gift for divining the future, who has undertaken the prolonged course of training essential for the art and who is devoid of lust, selfishness, envy, and acquisitiveness, may read the future in a crystal ball as clearly as the ordinary person watches a television drama. He or she will see tiny figures, within the illimitable depths of the crystal's purity, enacting the events which lie beyond the doorway of the future.

This gift is rare, however, and your average crystal-scryer will see no more than colours and shifting shapes and shadows. Colours in the red and orange range of the spectrum indicate unhappiness or disaster, while the cooler shades of green and blue presage contentment. The movement of shadows within a crystal ball can hint at the destiny of subject whose future is being scryed, but require considerable skill in interpretation. Always provided that the crystal-scryer is using a ball of pure rock crystal, and not a cheap imitation, these interpretations should be taken seriously.

Dragon's Teeth

The use of dragon's teeth provides a simple method of expanding the armed forces of any country. It was first practised by Cadmus, King of Thebes.

First, prepare a piece of ground as though for sowing grain. (It is not necessary to plough it with two fire-breathing oxen with brazen hooves, as Jason was obliged to do.) Next, catch and kill any convenient dragon and draw all its teeth. Sow these in the furrows you have prepared, cover lightly, and stand well away.

The first signs of growth are spear tips sprouting through the soil. These rise quickly on the spear shafts and are followed by the crests of bronze helmets. As soon as these are clear of the ground, one may see the fierce weatherbeaten features of veteran warriors, who bellow savage war cries as soon as their lips are clear of soil. The bodies of these warriors, clad in bronze armour and armed with swords and shields as well as the spears which first appeared, then emerge rapidly from the earth and stand in ranks according to the way in which the dragon's teeth were sown.

Unfortunately these products of the earth (botanically known as *Sparti*) are such violent combatants that they will turn upon each other if no other enemy is available. When Cadmus sowed dragon's teeth, the resulting *Sparti* fought so savagely that only five of them survived. When Jason sowed the remainder of the teeth collected by Cadmus, the *Sparti* would have turned on him if he had not had the presence of mind to throw a stone at one of them. It bounced off his armour onto a neighbouring warrior, so each blamed the other for the insult. The *Sparti* quickly chose sides, and all killed each other in the subsequent affray.

The sower of dragon's teeth must therefore take the necessary precautions to control the *Sparti* as soon as they appear. Apart from this disadvantage the *Sparti* provide a quick cheap crop, and large numbers have

been produced recently in various parts of the world.

Drawings, Paintings, Portraits etc

The reproduction of a person's visage by any means, whether it is a mere pencil drawing, a full-scale portrait, or even a photograph, is most inadvisable. Some religions expressly forbid these reproductions, because he who captures a person's likeness may also enslave his soul. Most of the so-called primitive peoples of the world place an embargo on all types of illustration, except for use in sorcery or hunting magic. He who makes an image of any living creature gains power over its spirit, and may use the image or reproduction as the basis of spells and charms. Also, an artist unwittingly reveals more about a subject than the subject knows about himself, and this demonstrates the uncanniness of the whole procedure.

The extreme danger of image-making is demonstrated by the case of Dorian Gray, grandson of the Earl of Kelso and son of Lady Mary Devereux, the most beautiful girl in London, by her marriage to an army lieutenant whom Kelso contrived to murder in a duel soon after the wedding.

Dorian appears to have had the normal upbringing of a wealthy young Englishman, and in about 1870 he began the aimless existence of a man about town with a dilettante interest in 'beauty' and the arts. He appears to have been the kind of young man who would have followed Oscar Wilde's cult of 'Aestheticism': of making an art out of life. He was almost certainly bisexual, because the scandals which later surrounded his name included that of a young Guards officer who shot himself, and that of Lady Gloucester who died alone in a Mentone villa.

The principal difference between Dorian Gray and his pleasure-loving contemporaries was the possession of a singular male beauty. He was a wonderfully handsome young man, with finely curved scarlet lips, frank blue eyes, and crisp golden hair. All the candour and passionate purity of youth were in his face, and one felt he had kept himself unsullied by the world.

Basil Hallward, the noted society artist, was eager to paint his portrait, but when Dorian looked upon the finished work he displayed remarkable reactions. He actually tried to destroy the portrait, but Hallward restrained him. The young man was bitterly resentful of the fact that he would have to grow old, whereas the beauty of the portrait would remain forever youthful. He exclaimed 'Oh, if it were only the other way! If the picture could change, and I could be always what I am now!'

When Hallward sent the picture to Dorian's town house he hung it in the library, where it remained until the eruption of the first of many scandals to be associated with

Dorian Gray. The actress, Sybil Vane, to whom he was engaged, poisoned herself because he broke off the engagement with a heartless lack of emotion. Immediately after that, Dorian saw that lines of cruelty had appeared around the painted mouth of the portrait, although his own face was as smooth and youthful as it had ever been. His reaction was to remove the painting to an upper room, where none but his own eyes looked upon it until many years later.

In the meantime, his pursuit of beauty and pleasure took on sinister undertones. As the years passed by, so London society gossiped more and more about his corruption and debauchery. But even those who repeated stories about his shameful associations found it hard to believe them, because Dorian's eyes remained clear and innocent and his features as guileless as a boy's.

When Dorian was thirty-eight he met Basil Hallward again, and the artist begged him to deny the scandals circulating in society. Hallward said he found them unbelievable, but they were becoming more lurid than ever. Dorian replied 'I keep a diary of my life from day to day . . . I shall show it to you if you come with me.' He led Hallward to the dusty attic where he kept the portrait, and the artist hoped to see some written record which would prove the scandals to be fictitious. But, when Dorian drew aside the screen which concealed the portrait, the appalled artist saw a hideous painted face grinning at him. It was as though all the leprosies of sin were eating it away.

In a vehement tirade, Dorian revealed that the scandals were true, but their corruptions showed only on the face of the portrait. If his own face had shown similar marks of degradation then he would not have been able to beguile trusting young men and women into association with him, and the world would have had no doubt of his wickedness. He concluded by blaming Hallward for painting the portrait so beautifully, thus causing him to wish that the painted face, instead of his own, would reflect the changes over the years. In his passionate anger he stabbed Hallward to death, and the hands of the portrait at once became red as blood.

He blackmailed an erstwhile friend, Alan Campbell, into disposing of Hallward's corpse. Campbell did so and then committed suicide. Dorian continued his wicked ways and seemed to become even worse than before, until he fell in love with an innocent country girl and decided at last to reform. He felt such a conviction that a new life lay before him that he thought the portrait would reflect these feelings, and restore itself to its original beauty.

Full of hope, he nerved himself to look at the painting again. But when he drew the screen aside he saw that the face was even more loathesome than before, and that the red on its hands seemed as bright as blood newly spilt.

He stabbed furiously at the painting with the knife that killed Basil Hallward, believing he could kill the past and begin his new life. But passers-by heard a cry and a crash, and when Dorian's servants broke into the room they found a dead man with a knife in his heart. The corpse was so withered, wrinkled, and loathsome of visage that they recognised Dorian only by the rings that he wore.

Smiling calmly above the corpse was a splendid painting of the young Dorian Gray, in all the wonder of his youth and strength.

Drums

An essential in many types of supernatural ceremonies. Careful preparation of both the drum and the drummer (or tambour) is required to achieve maximum potency. The drum must be constructed from materials appropriate for specific rituals. For example, the drumskin should be made of fishskin or birdskin if the ritual is designed to influence creatures of water or air; of the appropriate animal hide if the intention is to control creatures which serve as food supply; and of human skin if the ritual is one concerned with the tribespeople, such as raising the dead or disspelling evil spirits from an afflicted person.

The frame and body of the drum must be fashioned to exact specifications and decorated according to tradition. If drumsticks are to be used instead of the fingers they must be carefully selected for the purpose. The thigh bones of certain types of monkey are favoured for a wide variety of rituals, whereas the shin bone of a newborn infant may be essential for others.

The tambour learns the beats and rhythms for all the ceremonies during a long apprenticeship, normally commencing at puberty and continuing for several years. Tambours are instructed by witch-doctors or wizards and may eventually become so learned and proficient that they are promoted into higher degrees of wizardry. A tambour never plays the drums for idle amusement or for simple celebrations.

The prolonged rhythmic beating of a drum will arouse even the most reluctant spirits, whether of man or beast, of water, forest, or sky. After the arousal, the continuous vibration of the drum beat has a hypnotic effect upon a captive spirit and enables an accomplished wizard to control its activities. For instance, it may be necessary to awaken the rain spirit during a period of drought and then to compel it to send down a deluge of rain. The tambour might have to beat upon a specially loud drum for many hours to awaken the spirit, which would then reply by pounding upon the thunderous drums of the sky. After that, the tambour would change his beat, to accompany the ritual dances which ensure precipitation.

When the appropriate drumming has been performed to the satisfaction of the principal witch doctor, the abrupt cessation of the drum beat releases a spirit until it is required again.

Flying Carpets

These are low-flying vehicles which accelerate from zero to superluctic speed in ·01 of a second, and carry one to three passengers instantly to any desired destination.

Flying carpets are designed and woven in India, and are available only from the manufacturer's agents in Bisnagar, capital city of the state of that name. Attempts to copy the design woven into the carpet are ineffectual, because the shapes and colours vary continuously under close examination.

In about 1000 AD the cost of a flying carpet was forty purses of gold plus twenty purses as agent's commission, but the price will certainly have escalated during the intervening ten centuries.

One of the best-known carpets was that purchased by Prince Houssain of one of the Gulf Emirates. He bought the carpet when his father said that the beautiful maiden Nouronnihar should be given in marriage to whichever of the three princes Houssain, Ali, and Ahmed, who were her cousins, brought the most remarkable object back to the Emir's court.

Ali bought an ivory tube which could see everything in the world, while Ahmed bought an apple which cured any disease. Unfortunately the Emir could not decide whether the carpet, tube, or apple was the most remarkable item, and settled the decision with an archery contest. Ali won, and married Nouronnihar. Ahmed married a fairy princess, and Houssain retired to a life of meditation. Presumably he had no further use for the flying carpet, but the present whereabouts of this vintage item of aviation science is unknown.

Flying Objects, Saucers, etc

Airborne objects of many different characteristics have been identified for at least 500 centuries and have included chariots, carpets, dragons, witches, and horses of many different breeds.

The flying island named Laputa, sighted by Lemuel Gulliver in July 1707, probably was the first of the so-called flying saucers to be described by a European. Dr Gulliver saw it in latitude 46 north and longitude 183, which is about midway between Japan and Oregon, after he had been set adrift by pirates. He landed on a small rocky island, and on the following day saw a 'vast opaque body' approaching at an altitude of about 2,500 metres. The flying speed of Laputa is unknown because Gulliver omitted this detail from his otherwise meticulous description.

The flying object (or saucer, as it would now be called) manoeuvred until it was about 100 metres above the shore of the island. Gulliver could see that its undersurface was perfectly smooth, with a mirror finish that reflected the brilliance of the sunlit sea. A crowd of people had assembled on one side, and after a little while they lowered a kind of bo'sun's chair which drew Gulliver up to join them.

Gulliver, like all other earthmen who have been taken into flying saucers, was bewildered by this experience and by the unusual inhabitants of Laputa, but after a month or so aboard the flying object (which he called a flying island) he became sufficiently versed in the language of its people to learn a great deal about Laputa.

It was exactly circular, with a diameter of 7,166 metres and a surface area of 4,046·8 hectares, which means that it was considerably larger than any of the flying saucers more recently reported. The lower surface was a huge circular plate of adamant, a rare diamond-hard mineral once so widely used that all known resources have now been exhausted. The adamantine sub structure of Laputa was 182·88 metres thick.

This immense plate supported a dome-like artificial hill, constructed from layers of rocks and minerals and covered with about 3·5 metres of fertile earth. All the moisture precipitated upon the upper surface flowed down the slopes of the dome into four large reservoirs, each of 803 metres in circumference, evenly spaced around the dome at a distance of 182·88 metres from the centre. If solar power did not condense enough water to prevent these reservoirs from overflowing, the island could be raised above the clouds to prevent the accumulation of moisture.

This description reveals two interesting points about the protype flying saucer. One, that it was self-sufficient, because its crew (or inhabitants) could raise foodstuffs on the earth covering the dome and draw fresh water for all purposes from the four reservoirs. Two, that its saucer shape must be likened to a saucer upside down, with its curve, or dome, upwards.

In the centre of the dome a deep shaft, about 45 metres in diameter, led down to the instrument-chamber and engine-room of the flying object. This area was known as the *Flandona Gagnole*, or Astronomer's Cave. It was situated 91·44 metres within the adamantine sub structure, and brilliantly lit by twenty lamps whose light was reflected by the mirror surface of the adamant. Part of it served as a storeroom for a great quantity of sextants, quadrants, astrolabes, telescopes, and other instruments of navigation and calculation, while the remainder was occupied by propulsion machinery.

This comprised a 10·972 metre cylinder of 10·160 centimetre adamantine plate, mounted on eight columns of adamant 5·486 metres high. Grooves 30·480 centimetres deep ran along each of the internal surfaces of the cylinder. These supported an axle running through a huge loadstone, or magnet, in the shape of a weaver's shuttle: 5·486 metres long and 2·743 metres at its widest point. The magnet was so delicately poised on the axle that it could be adjusted by the lightest touch.

Duty astronomers caused the island to descend by turning the magnet's attracting end towards the earth, so that Laputa was drawn downwards; and to rise by turning down the repelling end. Laputa would also move laterally or obliquely by various adjustments to the loadstone.

The flying object's range was limited, however, by its position relevant to Balnibari, the terrestrial island over which it hovered for most of the time, because the magnet was linked with the magnetic radiations of that island. Consequently the flying range was restricted to 28·985 kilometres from Balnibari and to an altitude of 6,436 metres. Laputa would hover motionless when the loadstone was placed parallel to the plane of the horizon.

Laputa was controlled by the Emperor of Balnibari, whose scientists had designed the flying object. The emperor and all his court lived aboard Laputa because the flying saucer gave him total control of his subjects. If any community showed signs of rebellion the emperor brought them to heel by stationing Laputa overhead, thus depriving them of sun and rain, or by having them bombarded with great rocks. As a last resort, Laputa could be lowered onto a rebellious town to

crush all its buildings. The emperor always advised the townsfolk that Laputa would descend very slowly, because his love for his people made him give them plenty of time for escape, but the slow descent was really to protect the sub surface of the flying saucer. The scientists had warned the emperor that a sledgehammer type of attack would crack the adamant and affect Laputa's aerodynamics.

Gulliver found that the emperor and his scientists, generally called astronomers, were dedicated to the abstract sciences, mathematics, and musical theory. They all wore a kind of uniform, of robes embroidered with astronomical symbols and musical instruments. Their minds were so engrossed in scientific speculation that they carried their heads to one side, with one eye turned inwards and the other turned upwards. They were so introspective that each astronomer was accompanied by a *climentole*, or flapper, who carried a bladder, containing a few dried peas, on a short stick. The *climentole*'s duty was to flap his master lightly on the ear or mouth with this bladder, to recall the wandering mind from its intense speculations and remind it to answer questions or attend to the affairs of everyday life.

The astronomers were all adept with scientific instruments, but slow and clumsy in every other way. Their introspective researches made them fearful of all kinds of cosmic disasters, and they were forever warning the people that one or another of these was about to occur. Their wives, however, were beautiful and vivacious. They took advantage of their husbands' absorption in scientific affairs to carry on a busy love-life with the non-intellectual members of the Laputan population.

The ultimate fate of Laputa is now unknown. It is possible that the scientists contrived a propulsion method which released the flying island from its bonds to Balnibari, and enabled Laputa to proceed on extraterrestrial exploration.

There does not appear to be any relationship between Laputa and the present generation of flying saucers, except insofar as the Balnibarian scientists paved the way. It is, however, interesting to speculate on the scientific conspiracy which has obscured the source of modern flying saucers. For at least a century, scientists have claimed that the planets Jupiter and Saturn cannot sustain any form of life. They say that these bodies consist of rocky metallic cores covered with ice, or even with a mushy mass of ice crystals and gases, at temperatures as low as minus 150 degrees Centigrade. According to these wily scientists, the atmospheres of Jupiter and Saturn consist of lethal gases such as ammonia and methane. They claim that the existence of sentient beings is impossible under these conditions, and scoff at the notion of Jupiter and Saturn sending out interstellar missions.

This scientific conspiracy is exploded by the innumerable reports received, especially from rural districts of the USA, of spacecraft with crews who mention specifically (in good English) that they have flown here from Jupiter or Saturn. These visitors have no difficulty in breathing our atmosphere, and so it is obvious that the atmosphere of Jupiter and Saturn is the same as that of earth. Some scoffers call these visitors 'little green men', but that is mere colour prejudice. It seems likely that the people of outer space have refined the principles discovered by the scientists of Balnibari, and that they build saucer-shaped flying objects somewhat similar to that visited by Lemuel Gulliver.

Flying Ointment

The propellant for airborne witches. Most witches compound their own flying ointment, and use the formula they have found to suit them best, but the essential basic ingredients are bat's blood, baby's fat, hemlock, and mandrake. Individual witches may use any additives, such as deadly nightshade, which they believe to increase flying speed or increase broomstick range. English witches often like to use a little of the wax from candles that have been used to celebrate a black mass. In southern Europe, the fat of a scapegoat is highly regarded as an additive.

The flying ointment is applied to the armpits and inner thighs immediately before lift-off, and is activated by the usual formula 'Go, in the devil's name, go!'

Frankenstein

Victor Frankenstein was born in Geneva in about 1790, son of a wealthy merchant and politician. Friendship with a fellow-student, Henri Clerval, led him into the study of natural forces, especially electricity and the sources of life. When he went to Ingoldstadt University he continued these studies and determined to 'pioneer a new way, explore unknown powers, and unfold the deepest mysteries of creation'. He decided to bring life out of death by using the bodies of the dead to create a magnificent superhuman being, about 2·4 metres tall and broad in proportion.

After careful selection of the necessary components he assembled this creature and, by methods still unrevealed, brought it to life. But he was horrified by the result. In the report of his experiment he wrote, 'His limbs were in proportion, and I had selected his features as beautiful. Beautiful! Great God! His yellow skin barely covered the work of muscles and arteries beneath; his hair was of a lustrous black, and flowing; his teeth of a pearly whiteness; but these luxuriances only formed a more horrid contrast with his watery eyes, that seemed almost of the same as the dun-white sockets in which they were set, his shrivelled complexion and straight black lips.'

Frankenstein was so appalled that he ran out of his laboratory, and when he plucked up courage to return he found that his creation had gone. He was glad to be rid of it, and tried to wipe the whole disaster from his mind. But some time later he received the dreadful news that his young brother William had been strangled, and that the boy's nursemaid, Justine Moritz, was accused of the crime. Frankenstein felt uneasily that his monster was to blame, and when Justine was executed for murder he was tormented by remorse.

About a year later, the monster suddenly confronted Frankenstein on the slopes of Mont Blanc. It told a pathetic story of how, after Frankenstein had run away, it had tried to attach itself to humans. Everyone had driven it away with horror and disgust. Even when it saved a little girl from drowning, her father had shot it in the shoulder. By ill fortune it encountered William, and strangled the little boy in a clumsy attempt to embrace him.

The monster blamed Frankenstein bitterly for creating it in the first place, and then condemning it to a life of solitude. It demanded the creation of a mate to ease its loneliness, and promised to take such a mate to the jungles of South America and vanish from human ken.

Conscience-stricken, Frankenstein agreed. He and Clerval went to England to create the monster's companion, but he found the work so repugnant he could not continue. The monster tracked Frankenstein to England and appeared in the laboratory, to beg for his creator's sympathy and the continuation of the work. When Frankenstein still refused, it said 'I go, but remember I shall be with you on your wedding night!'

Frankenstein and Clerval fled to Ireland, but the monster followed and killed Clerval. Some time later, Frankenstein married his childhood sweetheart, and the monster fulfilled its threat by strangling her on the wedding night.

Frankenstein then tried to escape by endless travelling, but wherever he went the monster followed. At last Frankenstein joined a ship bound for the Arctic, feeling that the monster could not possibly follow him there. The ship was trapped in the ice, and Frankenstein's life of torment and remorse ended with death in the Arctic loneliness.

The monster had discovered where he had gone, and came plodding over the ice shortly after the death of Frankenstein. It mourned over its creator's corpse, told the surviving crew members that it had only wanted Frankenstein's affection, and then leapt from the ship with a vow to destroy itself.

Garlic

The bulbous perennial plant (*Allium setivum*) which sprang up on the spot where Satan first placed his left foot on the earth, probably in south-west Siberia. Its cousin the onion (*Allium cepa*) sprang up in the imprint of Satan's right foot.

This infernal ancestry has not affected the value of garlic to mortals. The plant is an important protection against a variety of supernatural beings, especially vampires. Anyone plagued by any species of night-walkers is advised to weave wreaths or bouquets out of the dried bulbs and stalks of garlic, and hang them above his door and bed. The potent plant will discourage any unwelcome visitors during the hours of darkness.

Glamour, Glamarye, Glamalye

The inborn characteristic of the fairy race, and the principal distinguishing feature between fairies and mortals.

Fairy glamour, wrongly called magic, exists on three levels. Primarily it is the quality which enables fairies to live in the same world as mortals but on a different dimension, so that they remain invisible unless they choose to reveal themselves. If they do, then glamour is the radiant attraction which makes a fairy totally irresistible to mortals of either sex and any age. The stoniest heart melts at the apparition of a fairy. And, even though a mortal may not wish to obey a fairy's bidding, the power of glamour compels him to do so, and even to feel an unreasonable satisfaction in obedience.

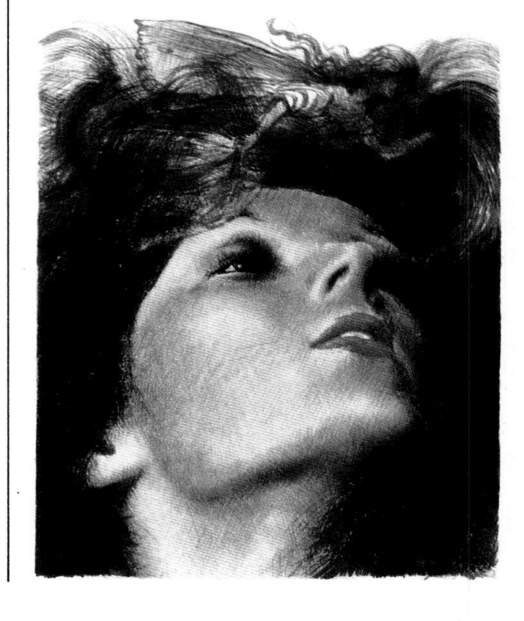

A mortal under the influence of glamour may be detected by a certain dazed expression about the eyes and a foolishly complacent smile.

Finally, glamour is the power wielded in various degrees by individuals within the fairy hierarchy, raised to its highest potency in the kings and queens. Glamour gives all fairies the ability to change their size and shape, to cast simple spells and cause annoying bewitchments, but only the senior and superior fairies are capable of using glamour with maximum force. In this highest degree it will defeat the wickedest witch, alter the character of an adult mortal for good or ill, and even enforce changes in the weather. Also, of course, it is used to endow newborn mortal infants with luck and happiness or to load them with a burden of ill fortune. Fortunately, the possessors of this awesome energy source normally wield it fairly responsibly.

Hammer of Thor

Thor, the God of Thunder, is a mighty warrior with flashing blue eyes and a bristling red beard. He loves to match himself against giants and monsters, and when he prepares himself for battle he is filled with such berserker fury that the sound of his anger reverberates through the heavens. But he is at heart a genial, honest, and straightforward personality, devoted to his family and a strict upholder of community morals.

His weapon is the great stone hammer Mjolnir, which means 'The Destroyer'. It is so powerful that he must hold it with a pair of iron gloves made for him by the dwarfs, and so heavy that he cannot lift it until he has donned the Belt-of-Strength. This girdle, which doubles the strength of his limbs, is also a product of the dwarf workshop.

Thor's fighting technique is to fling Mjolnir at an enemy. The hammer flies through the dark sky like a lightning bolt, strikes its victim with thunderous impact, and then returns in boomerang style to the iron gloves of Thor. Mjolnir never misses its mark.

But a peculiarity of the enormous hammer is that Thor can cause it to shrink to any size he desires. This is very useful when he wants to deceive an enemy, by concealing Mjolnir until some opportune moment to strike with terrible force, but it is also important for another of the hammer's functions.

Thor is the patron saint of weddings and contracts, and when two people enter into a contract—including a marriage contract—he gladly lends them Mjolnir so that they may swear upon the mystic hammer. Naturally the breaking of such a solemn vow would have unpleasant consequences.

Homunculus

A tiny artificial man produced by alchemy. Theophrastus Bombast von Hohenheim Paracelsus (1490–1541), the great German physician and alchemist, probably was the first alchemist to create a homunculus. Paracelsus demonstrated that the *limus terrae*, from which the body of man is created, is really an extract of all things already in existence. Therefore he reasoned that it should be possible to create new life by discovering the constituents of this extract.

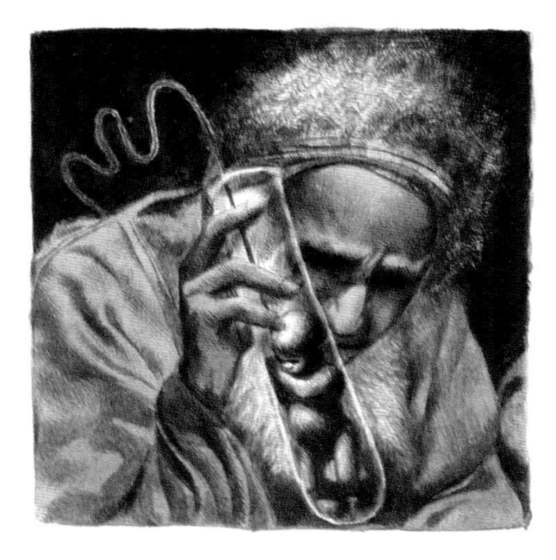

In his experiments he placed human semen, various herbs, and certain other compounds in a sealed vial, which was then incubated for forty days in a vat of horse manure. When he opened the vial he found a tiny creature he described as a homunculus, which may be freely translated as 'little man'.

Paracelsus kept the homunculus alive by feeding it human blood, but the experiment was abruptly terminated by the death of the alchemist in mysterious circumstances. Unfortunately he was a very arrogant personality, who had even assumed the name Paracelsus to show that he was greater than the great philosopher Celsus (circa 178 AD) and he made many enemies. These said that Paracelsus died of alcoholism, but his defenders claim that other alchemists, jealous of his wisdom, had him thrown down a flight of steps. Presumably the homunculus also perished, and no researchers have been able to rediscover the secret of Paracelsus' compound.

Horse, The Enchanted

This artefact was constructed by an anonymous Indian. Nothing is known of his background and he came to an unhappy end.

He appeared, apparently out of nowhere, at the court of the Shah of Persia, when the citizens of Baghdad were celebrating the New Year festival of Nevrouz. The shah had just inspected an exhibition of Persian craftsmanship when the Indian led a horse towards the imperial entourage.

The Persians are good judges of horse-flesh, and the assembly admired the proud and splendid steed with its ornate harness and saddlery. On closer examination they discovered that it was not a real horse, but so cunningly fashioned that it appeared to be alive. The shah was not however, impressed by the Indian's claim for a prize, and said that any skilled craftsman could make such an equine look-a-like.

The Indian protested that not even the Persians could make an enchanted horse, especially one that could fly. He proved his point by mounting the horse, turning a small peg in its neck, and flying it for 10 kilometres in a quarter of an hour.

The shah was so impressed that he offered to buy the horse, and the Indian said he would trade it for the shah's daughter. The shah was disposed to agree, not only to secure the horse for himself but also to prevent any other monarch from obtaining this prestigious artefact. But his son, Prince Firouz Shah, protested angrily, and after some discussion the shah told Firouz to try the horse for himself and see whether that would change his mind.

Firouz mounted the horse, turned the peg, and instantly soared away. As he vanished from sight the Indian was greatly alarmed, because Firouz had taken off without a flight plan or any operating instructions. He begged the shah not to be angry with him if Firouz came to any harm, but the shah, somewhat unfairly, had the Indian imprisoned and swore he should be executed if Firouz did not return within three months.

Firouz knew both terror and exaltation as the enchanted horse carried him so high that the mountains of his country seemed no more than a confused mass far below. When he thought he had tested the horse sufficiently he tried to turn back to Baghdad, by pulling the horse's head round with the bridle and then by reversing the direction of the peg. But the horse only flew higher and faster, and Firouz could not control it until he found another peg, almost hidden under the right ear of the horse.

He turned the peg carefully, and the flying horse began a long glide path which continued for several hours. Eventually the horse landed gently on the roof of a magnificent palace, which Firouz explored until he found a bedchamber occupied by the Princess of Bengal and her ladies.

Luckily the princess received her midnight visitor with regal aplomb. She ordered her servants to care for Prince Firouz, and on the following day he not only told her his strange story but asked for her hand in marriage. She said she must have time to think, and asked him to stay in Bengal to acquaint himself with her country.

After two months she agreed to fly back with him to Persia, and mounted behind him on the enchanted horse. Firouz now had no difficulty in operating the controls, and in a mere 150 minutes he landed the horse at a country house outside Baghdad.

He left the princess there while he went into the city to confront his father, who was delighted to see Firouz again and immediately

assented to the marriage. The shah also ordered the release of the Indian, and told him to take himself and the horse away from Persia.

But the Indian was full of resentment for the shah's high-handed treatment. When he went to collect his horse, he told the princess that Firouz had sent him to carry her back to Baghdad. Eager to see her lover again, she mounted behind him and he turned the take-off peg. In a few moments, she realised that he was not flying the horse to Baghdad but in the opposite direction.

She could do nothing but cling to the Indian as the horse flew steadily over mountains and deserts, until at last he landed in a forest of the kingdom of Kashmir. He told the princess to wait for him while he went to buy food, and on his return he told her it was time for her to surrender to his desires. She shrieked so loudly that she was heard by the Sultan of Kashmir, who was hunting in the woods nearby.

The sultan quickly led his party to her assistance, and took her and the horse to his palace. None of his people could work out the secret of the enchanted steed, the princess could not tell them, and the lecherous Indian was so angered by his second failure to obtain a princess that he remained silent. The sultan had him thrown in a dungeon and the horse placed in the royal treasury.

On the following day, the sultan told the princess that, instead of sending her back to Persia or Bengal, he had decided to marry her. This chauvinistic proposal did not please the princess at all and she promptly feigned madness.

But the sultan was so ardent for her marital embraces that he sent all his physicians to treat her, and when she fought them off with furious anger he sent messengers far and wide to find physicians who could tranquillise her. One after another they attempted to treat her with various nostrums, but she frightened them away with frenzied screams and ravings.

In the meantime, Firouz had set out from Persia in search of the princess. After long wanderings, he heard the strange tale of the mad princess and thought she must be the one whom he sought. He made his way to Kashmir, disguised himself as a physician, and humbly approached the sultan. He said that he specialised in cures for madness but must be allowed to see the patient alone.

The sultan, who was by that time ready to try anything, agreed to this request. At first the princess thought Firouz was only another physician and received him with furious rage and disdain, but this soon turned to joyous acceptance. He told her that she must now pretend to be partly cured, and when he saw the sultan again he explained the problem of the mad princess. She was not mad, but enchanted, because she had arrived on an enchanted horse, and she could be cured only by mounting the horse again and breathing in the smoke of certain magical perfumes.

The sultan delightedly agreed to all the treatments proposed by this new physician, and arranged for the horse to be brought from his treasury and placed in the palace square. He gave orders for the princess to be dressed in magnificent apparel and ornamented with all his most precious jewels, and commanded the entire population to watch the healing of the lady who was to be his bride.

Laden with the sultan's jewels, the princess mounted the horse while Firouz ordered palace servants to place a number of fire pots around the steed. The huge crowd watched as he sprinkled various powders into the flames, uttered strange words, and gesticulated above the rising clouds of vapour.

These emitted a delicious fragrance, but slowly thickened so that they obscured Firouz, the princess, and the enchanted horse. Under cover of this smokescreen he mounted behind her and turned the peg.

As the horse rose above the smoke the young prince and princess smiled triumphantly down at the sultan, and Firouz cried 'Sultan of Kashmir, when you wish to espouse princesses who implore your protection, learn first to obtain their consent!'

A few hours later the prince and princess landed safely in Baghdad, where they were married in a ceremony of great splendour. As for the unfortunate Indian, the Sultan of Kashmir had him beheaded.

Hunting Magic

This type of magic has strong relevance to the uncanny power of drawings, paintings, etc., as previously described. Before setting out on a hunt, one may achieve pre-potency over the prey by drawing its picture on the wall of one's cave or on any other suitable surface. Naturally one would not show the bison, mammoth, or other animal in an attitude of defiance, but pierced with spears and arrows and surrounded by hunters. (The beast should not, however, be depicted as a corpse. This would inspire a kind of reverse magic, releasing the creature's spirit and enabling it to seek ghostly revenge.)

The power of such hunting magic is increased if one of the party, before setting out, pretends to be the desired prey and allows the others to pretend to spear him. Obviously this ritual requires control and caution, because more than one hunter has been transfixed by excited companions at the beginning of a chase. The custom of throwing a member of a fishing party into the sea and hauling him out again, to encourage fishes to take the bait, is also fraught with danger especially in shark-infested waters.

Hunting weapons may be treated according to individual preferences. The blood of mosquitoes, or any other stinging insects, is highly recommended for smearing upon arrows. The blood causes the arrows to seek

their prey with the same accuracy and determination as mosquitoes.

A hunter and his family must observe all the usual taboos before he seeks his prey. He must not indulge in sexual intercourse for several days before a hunt, because this blunts the dagger and slackens the bowstring. While he is away, his family must not eat the flesh of a cockerel or any other male animal. If they do, the hunter may be eaten by his prey.

Finally, the hunters must apologise to any animal they kill, and explain that its death was necessary for the survival of the tribe. This courtesy wards off retaliations by the spirit of the animal. If it is omitted, then the animal will attack the hunters and their families with ghostly horns, teeth, and claws after they have feasted upon its flesh, causing severe abdominal pains or even a fatal convulsion.

Ilya's Honey

A miraculous beverage, possibly a kind of mead, administered to the Russian peasant Ilya Muromyets. Ilya, born to poor parents in southern Russia, remained completely motionless in his cradle throughout his infancy and was not even strong enough to cry. Even when he grew older he lay on his bed too weak to move, with nothing but his breathing to show that he was alive. For the first thirty-three years of his life his parents had to attend to Ilya's every need. They were wondering what would become of him after their deaths when two strolling minstrels called at their cottage to ask for food. The old couple responded generously, and the minstrels repaid them by curing their son with a miraculous beverage made from wild honey.

When Ilya rose from his bed he quickly became a great hero of the Russian people. Having captured a flying horse, and using arrows which would split an oak tree, he led their armies in victorious battles against the infidels. When he had made Russia safe for Christianity he built the great Kiev Cathedral single-handedly, and then turned himself into stone as a perpetual guardian of the Russian people. The proof of this story is that, until recently, the stone figure of Ilya Muromyets might be seen in Kiev Cathedral.

Indian Rope Trick

A feat performed by Hindu entertainers versed in occult lore. The usual accessories are a small boy, a sharp knife, a basket containing a strong rope about four metres long, a large white cloth, and a flute or other suitable wind instrument. The performance is always given in the open air, so there can be no question of deception.

When the entertainer has attracted a suitable crowd, and they have each paid the appropriate fee, he begins to play on his flute. After a few moments, the rope responds to the strange wavering melody by stirring snake-like in its basket and then raising its head. The entertainer plays more vigorously and the rope slowly extends to its full length, until it hangs vibrantly in the air with its lower end a little distance from the ground. At the upper end, a small cloud forms in obedience to the weird notes of the flute.

The entertainer then claps his hands, and the small boy instantly swarms up the rope and disappears into the cloud. The entertainer bows to the plaudits of the crowd, stares upwards, and commands the boy to descend.

But there is no response, and after a few more commands the entertainer loses patience. He seizes the knife, shins up the rope, and also disappears into the cloud.

The crowd looks anxiously up at the cloud, seeing nothing but hearing the sounds of an angry argument. Soon this is followed by a scream of pain, and one of the boy's legs falls bleeding to the ground.

A moment later, the other leg falls out of the cloud. Next come both arms, the head, and finally the torso. The entertainer lowers himself grumblingly down the rope, and gathers these horrid remnants into a bundle wrapped in the cloth.

Once more he plays on the flute, in shrill and piercing notes which cause the bundle to stir, struggle, and then burst open its wrappings. The boy emerges with his white teeth flashing and his slim body wholly restored.

A final note on the flute causes the cloud to disappear and the rope to wind down into the basket, so that the entertainer and his boy may hurry away and leave the crowd to argue about the phenomenon.

So many travellers have described the so-called 'rope trick' that it is hard to doubt its authenticity, but for some reason it is never performed nowadays, although it would prove an enormous tourist attraction.

RUM

Jekyll's Potion

Probably the first of the psychedelic or personality-changing drugs. Formulated by Dr Henry Jekyll, MD, FRS, etc., in about 1884. Jekyll destroyed the formula and constituents of the potion, but it is known to comprise a tincture of blood-red colour and a white crystalline salt. When the salt is added to the tincture it foams, effervesces, and changes first to a dark purple colour and then to a watery green.

Dr Jekyll was a large, well-made, smooth-faced man of fifty, who had inherited a large fortune. Despite his impressive qualifications he does not appear to have practised medicine in his later years, but to have devoted himself to the study of mystic and transcendental affairs. He maintained a large windowless laboratory, lit by a glass cupola, in the garden of his London residence.

Jekyll was a bachelor, but by no means a recluse. His extensive circle of friends regarded him as an able, affable, and genial man and a good judge of wine. They enjoyed regular dinner parties in his comfortable home.

Probably they did not know that their amiable friend had two sides to his nature. One was that of the upright churchgoing citizen, charitable and kind. The other was that of a dissipated rake. And, as a true Victorian gentleman, Jekyll was deeply ashamed of the impulses which sent him on excursions into the seamier side of London society. He wanted to live a virtuous life, regarded his dissipations as 'undignified', and was afraid of discovery.

At last he decided to solve his problem by separating himself into two distinct personalities. The first would be the flawless Dr Jekyll, model bachelor, idol of his servants, and pillar of respectable society. The second would comprise all his evil and carnal desires, and might be set free to wallow in debauchery. After all, nobody would recognise him as the respectable Dr Jekyll.

After lengthy researches, Jekyll worked out the formula for a potion which would separate and release evil from the bonds of good . . . or perhaps the other way round. He ordered the requisite chemicals from a reputable drug wholesaler, Messrs Maw, and locked himself in the laboratory to compound the potion.

When it changed to watery green, he nerved himself to swallow it at a gulp. Instantly he was racked by terrible pangs and a veritable grinding of the bones. He felt a deadly nausea and a dark horror of the spirit, but then these symptoms passed away and he felt younger, freer, and happier than ever before.

A current of disordered sensual images flickered through his mind, he chuckled with heady recklessness, and he knew he had at last thrown off the bonds which confined him.

He found that even his physical appearance had changed, which caused a problem because his servants would see this apparent stranger going in and out of the laboratory. However, he solved this by telling them that a 'friend', whom he named Mr Edward Hyde, must be given free access to the premises.

Dr Jekyll did not make any use of his first transformation into a creature of pure evil, but simply swallowed the antidote (which was the same as the potion) and restored himself to normal. But he soon took advantage of his new freedom, and his servants and even his friends became accustomed to the appearance of Mr Edward Hyde. They did not seem to question the fact that he appeared only in Jekyll's absence, and were too well mannered to make any comment to the doctor about his singularly unpleasant friend.

A lawyer named Utterson, who had known Jekyll for many years and was the executor of his will, later described Edward Hyde as a pale, dwarfish man, who gave an impression of deformity without any definite malformation. He had a displeasing smile, he bore himself with a murderous mixture of humility and boldness, and he spoke with a husky, whispering, and somewhat broken voice. Nevertheless Utterson might have been able to accept all these characteristics if it were not for the inexplicable feelings of disgust, loathing, and fear which he aroused in the lawyer's mind. Utterson later summed up Hyde as 'Particularly small and particularly wicked-looking,' and he certainly did not feel that the horrid little monster bore any relationship to his handsome old friend.

But Jekyll, in his personification as Hyde, had begun to enjoy total freedom from any moral restraints. He dosed himself with the potion at frequent intervals, and set forth from his respectable home to plunge into the vilest debaucheries that London could provide. The days when he had regarded his fairly innocent dissipations as 'undignified' were long behind him, and it appears that he descended rapidly into every type of sadism and perversion. Without thought for the future he broke every law of God and man.

But one night, as the dignified Dr Jekyll, he went to bed as usual and awoke at dawn to see the lean, corded, knuckly and hairy claw of Hyde on the pillow beside him instead of his own well-formed hand. The astonished servants beginning their daily chores saw Edward Hyde scuttling down to the laboratory, and a little while later Dr Jekyll emerged. He now realised that the potion was taking control of his body, and was frightened into an abstinence which lasted for two months.

At the end of that time he could not resist another deadly dose, and this time the evil in his character came raging forth as never before. As he shambled home from a night of debauchery he chanced to encounter the venerable Sir Danvers Carew, and took offence at some mild comment made by the old man. He attacked him with savage delight and beat him to death with his walking cane.

This terrible incident, which was observed by one of Jekyll's maids and caused a hue and cry after Edward Hyde, shocked the doctor into a final resolution to leave the potion alone. He tried to atone for his evil by devoting himself to works of charity, and as the weeks went by he began to find some peace of mind.

But one day, as he sat in the park enjoying the beauties of nature, he changed suddenly into Edward Hyde. He managed to reach his laboratory unseen, and to swallow the antidote, but very soon after that he changed into Hyde yet again.

Now began a fearsome period, made even more awful by the fact that Hyde was wanted for murder, in which Dr Jekyll changed uncontrollably into Mr Hyde and back again. The potion no longer acted as an effective antidote, but in his desperation he thought the ingredients must be impure and begged Messrs Maw to supply the original kind. Unable to show himself to his servants, in case he changed to Mr Hyde before their eyes, he locked himself in his laboratory and strove to compound a permanent cure. His servants, and friends who came to call, sometimes heard him raving behind the locked door and thought they could detect the voice of Edward Hyde.

At last the doctor realised that his flirtations with evil had allowed it to possess his entire personality, and that he would never escape from Edward Hyde. In one of his increasingly brief manifestations as Dr Jekyll he destroyed all traces of the potion, wrote a garbled account of his experiences, and poisoned himself with prussic acid.

Kalvaitis

The mighty blacksmith, skilled in the working of all kinds of metal, who lives in the heavens above the Baltic countries. He makes numerous artefacts for the gods, but his principal responsibility is the daily forging of the sun. Each morning, the eastern sky glows with the great fires of his workshop as he hammers out the golden disc of the sun, and then throws the newly made orb, still radiating the heat and light of metal fresh from a blacksmith's anvil, up into the sky. As the day passes the sun retains its heat until it is cooled down by the chilly breezes of evening. It then vanishes beyond the western horizon, so that Kalvaitis has to forge a new sun every day.

Knots

The tying of a knot automatically creates certain magical powers, which may be greatly increased by witches or other practitioners of the art of sorcery. Newly-wed couples and pregnant women should be very careful not to tie knots, to allow any kind of knotting in their clothes, or even to permit any knotted item to be present in a bedchamber. Knots may prevent the consummation of a marriage or cause delivery problems in childbed.

Knots may also create difficulties in other human affairs, such as councils and conferences. If the people in any conference find themselves unable to agree, the chairman should enquire whether any member is carrying a knot on his person. If this is so, then the knot should be unravelled. This procedure usually results in the unknotting of any argument, and eventual agreement.

An evilly disposed person may cause domestic or business problems by tying knots in any suitable materials, including cloth, cord, or thread, and secreting them upon the premises. The power of the knots will constrict free association between members of a family, between business partners and/or their customers, and in fact everyone using the office, shop, or home.

The appropriate use of a knot is very effective, however, under certain circumstances. A husband who suspects his wife of straying should tie a strong knot in a piece of cord and hide it beneath her side of the marital mattress. The power of the knot will then prevent her straying from his bed. Errant children, servants, elderly parents, and other possible wanderers may be controlled by similar techniques.

In sailing-ship days a certain class of wizards (especially in Finland) specialised in the production of 'wind knots'. These were three complex knots tied in a length of cord or halliard. A shipmaster would buy the knotted cord before sailing on a voyage, and if his ship was becalmed he untied the first knot to release a moderate favourable wind. The second knot released a strong wind, and the third (to be used only as a final resort) released a gale of wind.

In the islands off the north of Scotland, witches sell the wind in the form of knotted handkerchiefs. Fishermen who buy these handkerchiefs may release the wind by slowly loosening the knot, until the wind is blowing at the desired force. The knot cannot be retightened and used again, however, and it is necessary to buy a new knot for each fishing expedition.

Probably the best known of all knots is that tied by Gordius, a peasant of Phrygia. An oracle had told the Phrygians, whose king had died, that their next king would arrive in an ox cart, and when Gordius arrived in the city in his cart the populace hailed him as king. Apparently this is as good a way of choosing a king as any other, because Gordius reigned very successfully. In gratitude to the gods he dedicated his ox cart to Zeus and it was kept in a special temple, but it so happened that the pole of the cart was secured to the ox-yoke by a complex knot which no one could untie. The oracle said that anyone who undid the knot, naturally known as the Gordian Knot, should rule over the whole of Asia. Many aspirants attempted to loosen the knot, but it remained tight until Alexander the Great used the simple method of cutting it with his sword.

Lady Kerith

A warning device used by Harith Ibn Jabala of Arabia, in the days before the Prophet of Islam. Harith allied himself with the Romans against the Persians, who plagued civilisation with their greed and jealousy, and spent much of his reign on leading his armies in the field. He received great honour from the Romans, who made him a Patrician of the Empire, but he longed for peace and especially for the enjoyment of his beautiful palace and city, Khirbat-al-Baidha. Unfortunately he found it was impossible to relax his vigilance, even in his harem, because the Persians often sent disguised assassins to try to kill him.

Then, in a battle with the Persians, his men captured the lifesize figure of a beautiful woman. It was most exquisitely fashioned from various metals, with eyes of emeralds and lips and nipples of rubies. While the Arabs were admiring the figure, it spoke through its ruby lips and said 'I am the Lady Kerith and I warn my owner against treachery.'

This was a great wonder, but the figure would not speak again or answer any questions. Harith took it back to his city and mounted it on a pedestal close to the city gates, as a symbol of his victories over Persia.

She remained silent for many months, until a day when a party of merchants accompanied a caravan into the city. Then the Lady Kerith's lips suddenly opened in a piercing cry of 'Alarm! Alarm!'

She continued this cry, so loudly that it aroused the entire city, until the guards had seized the party of merchants. They were soon revealed as assassins who had come to kill the noble Jarith Ibn Jahala.

Thenceforward, Harith paid great honour to the Lady Kerith and always kept the figure outside his tent or bedchamber. But after the death of Harith, in the time when Mohammed son of Abdullah and Aminah was preaching the true gospel of Allah, the Arabs saw that the figure was nothing but a pagan idol and the Lady Kerith was destroyed.

Lettering

The art of lettering and writing was invented by the Egyptian god Thoth and his principal wife Sesheta. The way in which her name is written, in the hieroglyphs which she helped to invent, signifies 'The Secretary'. Her husband invented all the arts and sciences, from arithmetic and architecture to magic, music, and writing, and it may be said that the last-named invention sprang out of all the others. Thoth was afraid that mortals might forget all the technology he developed, and so he conceived the idea of writing in order to record all his discoveries. Consequently his titles include that of Lord of the Holy Words, while Sesheta is also known as Mistress of the House of Books. She did not by any means, however, occupy a subordinate position. On her own account she developed the measurement of time, she was a skilled architect and mathematician, and as the keeper of the gods' records she became the goddess of history.

The lettering invented by the talented couple, known as hieroglyphs from the Greek words *hiero* = sacred and *glyphos* = carvings, was extremely complicated. It presented no problem to a god and goddess, but humans found difficulty in learning an alphabet in which, for example, the carving of an eagle represents the plural ending of adjectives formed from words ending with the sound 't'.

Possibly Thoth himself understood this problem. In a later manifestation he became the god Hermes Trismogestus, a powerful Grecian deity, who was also an ingenious inventor. It may be that Hermes modified the alphabet into its simpler Grecian form.

Other mysterious beings, in other parts of the world, developed their own interpretations of Thoth's original alphabet. In China it may have been Wen Chang, the god of literature and of stationers. Some peoples, like the Peruvians with their notched sticks and the North American Indians with beads sewn onto wampum, developed forms of lettering which were just as complex as those of the Egyptians and Chinese.

For many centuries, lettering was a closely guarded secret of monks, priests, and other initiates, who were aware that its mysteries should be withheld from the common folk. The ability to perpetuate the intangibility of thought, by marks upon papyrus or parchment, should certainly be reserved for those with a proper respect for the process.

But certain irreverent persons broke through the mysteries and made lettering available to everyone who cares to learn. Whether this is a good thing or a bad one, only Thoth and Sesheta may tell.

Love Potions

As the name indicates, these potions are compounded specifically to attract a subject who is reluctant to surrender to one's carnal desires. They may be administered by males to females, or vice versa, regardless of age, marital status, or position in life.

The potion may be had, at a price, from any alchemist or other person skilled in the preparation of mind-changing compounds. Witches, wizards, and sorcerers, who are generally not interested in love, are sometimes unwilling to manufacture the potions.

The purchaser's only problem may be that of persuading the object of his desire to swallow any of the potion. A recent recipe for a love potion included, among other ingredients, ginger, cinnamon, semen, urine, dried and ground testes from a male animal, extract of human hearts, and any suitable item from the object's person such as hair, blood, or nail clippings. It is hard to imagine a young lady partaking of such a nauseous draught.

Magic

The art or science of persuading supernatural beings to give one power over animate creatures, over the weather and the elements of the earth, and over all things which grow in or on the earth. Magic is older than mankind, because it is a power lent by the gods and spirits, and it is possessed to some degree by representatives of every people of the world. But, apart from such beings as fairies, who are created with magical powers, it is virtually impossible for any individual to have all-encompassing ability in magicology. The body of knowledge required is too enormous for any one person to comprehend in a lifetime, and the gods are so reluctant to co-operate in releasing some of their powers (such as eternal life) that even the most competent magician may be frustrated in his search for total power.

The problem is compounded by the fact that different gods and spirits exert influence in different parts of the world. For instance, the sea god Poseidon is very powerful in certain parts of the northern hemisphere, but a magician of the South Pacific who sought his assistance in nautical affairs would be wasting his time. It would be better to call on Maui or some other of the Polynesian deities.

Magic is not necessarily restricted to practising magicians. They like to surround themselves with dark clouds of specialist mystique, but they simply rely upon their knowledge of the correct spells, rituals, charms, amulets, talismans, and so on for the relevant circumstances. Any intelligent layman, who is not squeamish about such things as plucking out the entrails of a cockerel, may learn the appropriate spells and rituals for obtaining supernatural assistance. He must be careful, however, to repeat every spell exactly and to observe every step of a ritual. Errors in words or actions will infuriate the spirits (who are very touchy about their rights and privileges) and may have disastrous results. The wrong step in a rain dance could cause drought or floods, and even a wrong note in a song associated with fertility rites could cause crops to wither and women to become barren. On the whole it is safer to employ magicians rather than to attempt DIY magic.

The subject of magic is too complex to discuss in a confined space. It affects every human activity and so must be treated with respect and care. The spirits are always listening. They co-operate with properly qualified magicians, but they do not like the subject to be mentioned superficially, or to hear unqualified persons repeat any spells except for such simple ones as 'Touch wood'.

Masks

Man-made coverings for the face, to create a personality different from the wearer's usual character. Probably the power of masks derives from the days when all creatures had a dual existence, both human and animal. These beings were internally human but they wore the masks of various birds and beasts. When they wished to reveal their human aspects they simply pushed up the masks to show the human face within, simultaneously becoming manlike in all aspects of the limbs and body. The human manifestation of such creatures imparted the ability to speak and think, unlike animals which have no speech and simply obey their instincts. As time went by, a number of animals kept their masks up all the time and gradually became totally human.

The use of masks for ritual and ceremonial purposes, over many centuries, has some relevance to the strange origin of these artefacts. A man or woman who dons a mask becomes someone else, whether pleasant, unpleasant, or even terrifying, and must be treated accordingly. If, for some ritual, a man wears the mask of a god or devil, then for the duration of that ritual he assumes the powers of such a supernatural being and should not be held responsible for his actions.

The wearing of masks for any purpose

(commonly called a masquerade) should be considered carefully, lest the wearer should actually turn into the personification of his mask.

Midas Touch, The

The story of King Midas serves as an illustration of the chanciness of gifts from the gods. Midas, king of Phrygia in succession to his father Gordius, was a wise, capable, and charitable ruler. One day, strolling along the banks of the River Sangarius, he found a drunken old man who had been trussed up by peasants and left helpless on the ground. Midas quickly released and looked after him, and discovered that the old drunkard was none other than Silenus, the teacher and boozing-companion of Dionysus the god of wine. Fat, bald, and jovial, Silenus accompanies Dionysus on all his travels, perched precariously on a donkey and propped up by bacchantes and satyrs. The peasants had tied him up because they believed an old story: that whoever traps Silenus when he is in a drunken slumber will hear the future revealed through the old man's mumblings.

When Dionysus returned, he was so grateful to Midas for looking after Silenus that he granted him a wish. Midas asked that anything he touched might be turned to gold, and Dionysus took him literally.

Midas soon discovered the drawbacks of his thoughtless request. He was obliged to go naked because his garments, of solid gold, hung stiff and solid on his body; his wife, children, and favourite horse all turned into gold; he almost perished of thirst and hunger because his food and drink turned into the metal he now abhorred. Gods seldom allow mortals to reverse a wish or prayer, but when Midas prayed piteously to return to normal Dionysus took pity on him. He instructed Midas to bathe in the River Pactolus, which washed away the gold-effect but thereafter flowed with gold dust instead of water.

Apparently this experience did not teach Midas to be wary of the gods. He agreed to judge a musical contest between Marsyas and the god Apollo. When Midas gave Marsyas the prize, Apollo said he must be incapable of hearing properly and changed his ears into a donkey's.

Midas hid these appendages beneath his Phrygian cap, and swore his barber to secrecy. But the barber, like all those of his profession, was a chatty personality and he yearned to tell the secret to someone. Eventually he told it to a hole in the ground, which passed it on to a clump of reeds growing nearby. The reeds told all their brethren, and when the wind blows the reeds all over the world whisper 'Midas has ass's ears.'

Mistletoe

(*Viscum album.*) A parasitic bush which grows in the bark of apples, oaks, willows,

limes, cedars, and other trees in the northern hemisphere. The stalks, leaves, flowers, and berries of the plant are all rich in healing powers, especially if they grow in an oak tree. The mistletoe, however, must not be gathered carelessly, or even cut from the tree with steel or iron appliances. The most effective method is to cut the mistletoe with a golden sickle on St John's Day, and catch it in a white cloth as it falls from the tree. Alternatively, it may be knocked down with a stone or shot down with an arrow.

Mistletoe gathered in the approved manner may be used as a plaster for infected wounds, as a cure for the falling sickness or epilepsy, or as an antidote to poisons. Mistletoe leaves worn close to the flesh will ensure conception in a woman, and as a cattle fodder they will cure barren cows. Bracelets of mistletoe stalks protect warriors against wounds, and amulets of mistletoe leaves protect children against diseases. It is said that an arrow made from a mistletoe stalk always flies straight and is a potent weapon against giants, vampires, and other supernatural beings.

Moon Shots

The American officers who walked on the moon in 1969 were members of a small but select band of space travellers who have flown to the moon during the past three centuries. No doubt the NASA scientists learned a great deal from the construction of earlier space vehicles and from the experiences of such men as Cyrano de Bergerac and Hans Pfaal, who flew hot-air balloons to the moon in the seventeenth and nineteenth centuries. They were followed by such spacemen as Cavor, Stranger, and Atterley, who made individual visits between 1880 and 1900. These gentlemen all achieved lift-off by using various types of anti-gravitational materials. Cavorite, perfected by Mr Cavor in 1900, was applied to the surface of a steel sphere lined with thick glass, and controlled by blinds or shutters operated from inside the sphere. When these were raised, the anti-gravitational effect of cavorite drew the vehicle towards the moon. When they were lowered, terrestrial gravity attracted it back to earth. Careful manipulation of the shutters enabled precise manoeuvring.

The most thoroughly documented of nineteenth-century moon shots is that made by President Barbicane and Captain Nicholl of the Baltimore Gun Club, accompanied by the Parisian gentleman Michael Ardan.

The Gun Club was an association of artillerymen formed immediately after the American Civil War, for the scientific study of artillery and projectiles. The members conceived the idea of casting an enormous cannon, in the pattern known as Columbiad, and firing a manned projectile to the moon. Cambridge University astronomers checked their calculations and declared the project to be viable, and advised on the siting of the cannon and the exact time and date of the moon shot.

Gun Club members, in association with various scientists, designed a cannon 274·32 metres long, with a bore of 274·320 centimetres. The projectile, or space vehicle, constructed to fit this bore, was of cast aluminium with sides 30·480 centimetres thick. The total all-up weight of the projectile, built as a cylindro-conical shell, was almost nine tonnes.

Internally, the projectile was thoroughly padded and equipped with three sleeping bunks. It was heated and lit by coal gas. A Reiset & Regnaut oxygen generating apparatus enabled the crew to breathe in the

stratosphere, by releasing oxygen from potassium chlorate. Containers of caustic potash absorbed the carbon dioxide. The vehicle was provisioned with water, brandy, wine, Liebig soup cubes, dried vegetables, beefsteaks compressed hydraulically, and other comestibles. The specifications mention a gas cookstove, but with nineteenth-century modesty they do not explain the sanitary arrangements.

The propellant charge was 180 tonnes of guncotton (cotton steeped in nitric and sulphuric acid) detonated by an electric charge. This produced six billion litres of gas within the Columbiad and ejected the space vehicle at a velocity of 10,972 metres per second, decreasing to 6,096 m.p.s. after reaching an altitude of 9·656 kilometres.

The enormous shock of this detonation upon the base of the space vehicle was absorbed by a series of compressible sprung partitions and a 'water cushion'. It was expected that this arrangement would also lessen the impact of landing on the moon, but the vehicle also had twenty base rockets which would be ignited, in a style very similar to that used in modern space technology, to provide reverse thrust just before the vehicle touched down on the lunar surface and thus ensure a soft landing.

The projectile, or space vehicle, was, however, remarkably deficient in one respect. With strange nonchalance, the designers failed to provide it with any propellant system to ensure a return to earth. The base rockets were not sufficiently powerful for this purpose.

When the design and specifications were completed, the moon shot was financed by international public subscription. The project caught the imagination of the world and the huge sum of $5 million flowed in almost immediately. The Gun Club wasted no time in casting the enormous Columbiad cannon from cast iron, in a giant mould dug out of the ground. By strange coincidence, the site chosen for the cannon was very close to Cape Canaveral.

Ninety-nine years before the first manned moon shot from Cape Canaveral, a crane lifted Barbicane, Nicholl, and Ardan to the projectile hatch and they were secured inside. Portholes of thick glass enabled them to watch procedures as they were loaded into the Columbiad. They took with them two dogs, Diana and Satellite, to propagate the canine race upon the moon, but Satellite was unfortunately injured by blast-off and died a day or so later.

Otherwise, the first moon shot functioned perfectly. The crew settled down to an estimated flight time of ninety-seven hours, thirteen minutes, and twenty seconds, and apart from a near miss by a huge meteorite it was an uneventful voyage.

Eventually the projectile arrived within 40 kilometres of the moon. The occupants made numerous scientific observations, suffered intensely from the cold of the lunar night, and then realised that their vehicle was off-course. The effect of the meteorite had deflected it just enough to make it miss the moon, and they were in danger of falling into lunar orbit and becoming a 'moon of the moon'.

They solved this problem by skilful use of the base rockets, which knocked the projectile out of moon orbit and began it on a fall of 313,755 kilometres back to earth. The outlook, however, was definitely unfavourable, because they would hit the earth at a velocity of 16,770 metres per second and they doubted whether their compressible partitions would absorb this impact.

Five days later the crew of the cable-laying steamer *Susquehanna*, working off the coast of California, saw a fiery mass plunging out of the atmosphere above them. It came rapidly closer, struck the bowsprit of the ship and broke it off, and fell into the ocean with an enormous splash.

This fortuitous landing meant that the sea cushioned the landing shock and cooled the incandescent casing of the projectile, which soon bobbed up to the surface and floated until the crew could be rescued. The first crew of a moon shot was greeted with enormous acclaim on landing in the USA, where scientists took almost a century to solve the problem of actually walking on the moon.

Nails

All nails, whether metal, finger, or toe, have important supernatural qualities. (The same comment applies to hair, which is related to finger/toenails.) When trimming one's nails (or hair) the clippings should always be hidden or destroyed, preferably by burning. Otherwise an enemy might pass them on to a sorcerer, who could use them as the basis for a charm. A sorcerer may use even such small fragments of the body to gain possession of one's personality.

Metal nails, particularly those of iron or steel, are valuable offensive or defensive weapons against witches, goblins, fairies, pixies, and similar beings. A nail carried in one's pocket provides protection against being led astray by pixies. (Because the nail keeps its possessor fixed onto the right track.) A nail driven into a witch's footprint will cause her such crippling pain that her activities are greatly restricted. Nails driven into a door, especially when several are inserted cruciform, prevents many different types of beings from entering the home. A nail laid on any item left in the open air will prevent the fairies from spiriting it away, because the 'fixing power' of a nail is greater than the levitational powers of fairies. If it is necessary to make a midnight journey, a few nails scattered in one's tracks will discourage pursuit by nightwalkers.

Various theories are advanced to explain the potency of metal nails. Some people say that they represent the nails of the Crucifixion: others that supernatural beings fear their mystic power of securing one object to another. Whatever the reason, a supply of nails provides cheap and easy protection for the average mortal.

Name

The word belonging to an individual and denoting his personality. A name is one's most intimate possession and should be guarded carefully. The repetitive use of one's personal name, by others than those connected by family ties, steadily drains one's persona and has a debilitating effect. The modern widespread custom of using Christian or given names after the briefest acquaintance, by contrast with the more formal usage of previous generations who addressed each other by surnames outside the family circle, probably accounts for many ills of modern society.

Peoples outside the 'western' communities have a much greater respect for names. They know that he who possesses one's name may also possess one's spirit, and they never reveal their names to casual enquirers. This accounts for the fact that many Australian Aborigines assume European names, or endure the absurd nicknames such as Quart Pot or Nose Peg given to them by white men. The Aborigines reserve their true names for use by favoured persons within the tribal group.

In some societies, children are never addressed by their correct names. This is a wise precaution, because a demon hearing a child's name will take possession of its spirit. But if the demon used a child's 'pretend' name as the basis of the necessary spell, then it would be ineffectual.

When travelling with a friend in demon-haunted places, such as a deep forest, down a mine, or by certain types of running water, one should never address him by name. Otherwise the local demon is certain to steal it and use it against him.

The Babylonians did not give their children official names until they became pubescent. Then, during the naming ceremony, the youth or maiden was placed under the protection of an individual god who acted as guardian of the name. If, in later life, the name-owner fell sick, it was then known that he or she had committed a sin, thus prompting the name-god to depart and leave a vacancy which was filled by a demon. It would then be necessary for the priests to discover the name of the demon, so that, by naming it, they could cast it out again.

Some people, including the Nicobar Islanders, the Klamath and Chinook Indians of North America, and certain New Guinea tribes, never mention the name of a dead person. If he heard his name he would think he was being called back from the dead, and reappear to discomfort the living.

Necromancy

This art, practised only by sorcerers, is that of foretelling the future by communicating with the dead.

A sorcerer must endure decades of study, privation, and experiment before he becomes an accomplished necromancer. (The word derives from the Greek *nekros* = corpse, and *mantis* = seer.) One of the basic requirements is prolonged fasting, to rid the body of gross humours so that it may be entered by the spirit of a dead person. Usually it is necessary for the sorcerer to lock himself into a private place, or to go into the wilderness far away from other humans, so that the spirit whom he calls to answer him will not be distracted by the presence of other mortals. The smoke of a small fire, made from aromatic sticks and leaves, is helpful in the process.

The necromancer may have to call upon a chosen spirit innumerable times before it answers him. It may then reply in the form of a dream, in a voice speaking from within the necromancer's mind, or in an utterance from the smoke or any other object on which the necromancer has focused his attention. In some instances the spirit chooses to reply through some totally unexpected medium, such as a tree, bird, or animal.

When the spirit does answer, it is sometimes in such vague and generalised terms that no one but a necromancer could interpret the true meaning.

A more advanced form of necromancy enables the raising of a dead person for the purpose of conversation. This process is fraught with such appalling dangers that it is better not even to mention the elaborate series of spells and incantations which awaken the dead.

Nectar and Ambrosia

The drink and food of the gods. The Greek words *a brotos* simply mean 'not mortal', and no mortal has ever seen, far less tasted, the nectar drunk by the gods and the ambrosia on which they feast. The gods do not, however, restrict themselves to a diet of nectar and ambrosia. Many of them relish mortal foods and some are not averse to wine.

It is possible that ambrosia is a substance resembling cheesecake, but infinitely more delectable. Nectar is believed to be a clear golden liquid, neither sweet nor sour. It is non-intoxicating but nevertheless inspires the drinker into marvellous songs, poesy, and flights of fancy.

Probably the gods need nectar and ambrosia to renew the strength of the ichor which flows in their veins instead of blood.

Omen

An occurrence presaging good or evil. Among the most common omens are the breaking of a mirror, which signifies seven years of ill-fortune; a white cat (or black cat in North America) crossing one's path, which presages bad luck until the following day; a bird entering the house or a picture falling from the wall, both omens of death; and the new moon seen through glass, which portends bad luck for the following twenty-eight days.

The power of omens may sometimes be averted by appropriate actions. For instance, the new moon may be placated by turning around seven times, bowing to the moon, and turning over the money in one's pocket.

There is an unlimited number of omens, and a person sensitive to supernatural influences may detect them in countless everyday happenings. Birds, and all other creatures, are vigorous conveyors of omens. Their behaviour, appearance, and actions should always be observed carefully, although they are not easy to interpret. The omen is often directly contradictory to the action. A bird dropping falling upon one's hat or cloak is the presage of excellent fortune, and a mouse swimming in a pail of water indicates a prosperous sea voyage. But if a seafarer sees a parson immediately before setting sail he is likely to encounter head-winds and bad weather.

Omens generally require skilled interpretation and it is advisable to seek proper advice. Before embarking upon any important project one should take careful note of all the omens and have them interpreted by an augur.

Optics of al Rasheed

An instrument resembling a pair of spectacles of the old-fashioned type, with thin golden frames and with glass so thick that no wearer can see anything through them except in special circumstances.

According to tradition, they were once owned by the famous Haroun al Rashid (or Rasheed), Caliph of Baghdad. They were presented to him by a craftsman of that city who was noted for the manufacture of unusual items. It so happened that the craftsman's eldest son was a scapegrace, and when he was sentenced to be bastinadoed for some offence against the peace his father begged the caliph to be merciful. The caliph said he would pardon the young man if the craftsman could invent some infallible method of detecting an honest man.

Some days later the craftsman returned with the instrument, which he entitled 'optics'. He told Rasheed that the wearer would not be able to see anything through them except for the face of an honest man.

The caliph donned the optics and gazed around at the faces of all the leading citizens of Baghdad, who had assembled to watch the demonstration. But the only face to be seen through the optics was that of a young servant, standing humbly in the background.

The craftsman said that the young servant must be the only honest man among the caliph's followers. When Rasheed looked at the old man's face through the optics he saw him distinctly, and concluded he must be telling the truth.

The caliph pardoned the craftsman's son and promoted the young servant to high office, but a few months later he found he could no longer see his erstwhile servant's face through the optics.

The wise caliph decided it must be impossible for any man to hold high office

and still retain his honesty, and destroyed the optics because he feared they would prevent him from trusting anyone.

Oracle

A place, figure, object or person able to answer mortal queries about the future and to give advice on the appropriate action.

The statue of Hermes at Pharae was a notable example of an oracular figure, although it responded through the mouth of a man or woman. The consultant laid money on the altar before the statue, lit one of the bronze lamps at its base, and whispered his query into the statue's right ear. He then clapped his hands over his own ears and went into a crowd of people. When he uncovered his ears, the statue's answer came in the first mortal words heard by the consultant.

The Talking Oak of Dodona was another famous oracle. This huge tree stood in the midst of a dense forest, and was about 40 metres high with branches spreading over 5,000 square metres. A consultant stood beneath the tree and shouted his query up into the branches, which replied by rustling their leaves. For a small fee, the attendant priests would interpret the answer to the consultant.

In other places, the voice of the oracle spoke through the mouth of a mortal woman. The most famous of such oracles were at Delphi, Argos, Aegae, Claros, and Branchidae, where the oracular spirit dwelt in such natural features as an underground spring or fissure.

The priestesses of the oracle, often mature virgins, prepared themselves in various ways to deliver oracular predictions and commands. A priestess might chew laurel leaves and drink from a sacred spring, drink the hot blood of an animal sacrificed to the oracle, or perhaps only drink sacred water. The Clarian prophet drank from a spring that was said to shorten the lives of the oracle's spokespersons. Usually, several days of fasting preceded delivery of the oracle's predictions.

Such important oracles did not concern themselves with mere personal problems, but would answer only when queried upon affairs of state. Consequently, an oracular prediction was a solemn event, attended by leading politicians and military men and the priestly interpreters of the oracle.

When all was ready, the priestess (known as the Pythia, or Pythoness) seated herself on a tripod before the oracle and surrendered herself to its spirit. As it entered into her, the awed observers saw her face twitch and her eyes roll upwards. Her limbs moved convulsively and she emitted a low babble of sound. Then, as the spirit took full possession of the Pythoness, she writhed in a divine madness. Her tongue protruded, her hair fell about her flushed cheeks, and she might tear her clothes.

At last the oracle spoke through her lips, in long, deep, shuddering groans rising to frenzied shrieks, emitted so violently that some of the terrified observers sank to their knees. The priests listened carefully for the broken words and incomplete phrases mingled with the priestess' moans, cries, and screams, until the oracle left her and she sagged into unconsciousness. The priests then consulted at length upon the meaning of the words and phrases uttered by the oracle through her lips, and solemnly interpreted them to the waiting dignitaries.

The utterances of oracles were of supreme importance, and dictated the national and international policies of Greece for many centuries. Unfortunately the Pythonesses were slowly replaced by charlatans. Some of these descended so low as to conceal themselves in caves or within hollow statues, and to speak oracularly in return for valuable offerings.

Peaches of Immortality, The

The marvellous fruits which grow in the gardens of Hsi Wang Mu, the Queen of the West. Her husband is Tung Wang-Kung, King of the East. Hsi Wang Mu, who embodies the yin or female element of the universe, is more important than her husband who represents the yang or male element. The king keeps a record of all immortal beings, but the queen actually creates new immortals with her gifts of the Peaches of Immortality.

The garden where the peaches grow is laid out around her splendid palace on top of K'un-lun Mountain. The magnificence of her palace, comprising nine storeys of pure jade (or, as some say, of gold and precious stones) is rivalled only by the splendour of her gardens. The peach trees, with their globes of soft golden fruit peeping out from leaves of glossy emerald green, are especially beautiful.

All the immortals, whether gods or ex-humans, spend their time in the gardens in an endless cycle of games, feasts, and entertainments. Occasionally Queen Hsi Wang

Mu adds to their number by presenting a Peach of Immortality to a human who has shown, by the virtue of his life on earth, that he is worthy of such a boon. There are, however, so few virtuous men and women that the Peaches of Immortality ripen only once in each 6,000 years, and it is very rare for a human to taste their delectable flesh.

Prester John's Mirror

The mighty Christian emperor Prester John, who is described earlier in this book, would not have been able to rule over his enormous dominions if he had not possessed a certain instrument known as Prester John's Mirror.

The exact specifications are no longer available, but the instrument appears to have combined the qualities of a computerised periscope and a satellite TV network. The technology of that era could have supplied quartz and glass prisms and lenses and quicksilver reflectors, but the energising cells must have been charged from some transcendental source. Possibly the same source influenced Prester John's Collar, sometimes known as the Great Snake. Possession of this collar of silver and rubies played an important part in the emperor's control of his subjects, and it is said that whoever might find the collar again could unify all the nations of Africa.

Prester John's Mirror must have been portable, because he spent much of his time on campaign with his armies or on moving from one to another of his palaces. The mirror appears to have been part of a two-way communication system, because it enabled him to issue orders to places as far apart as China and Ethiopia.

Prester John used his mirror by looking into it through a vision tube or speculum. Presumably there were various gears for adjusting range, direction, and clarity, because the images seen through the speculum gave a faithful portrayal of everything that was happening in various parts of his dominions. In fact, Prester John's Mirror was a prototype of the 'Big Brother' type of electronic spy system described in George

Orwell's *1984*, and enabled the emperor to dictate every activity in the lives of all his subjects.

Procrustean Bed

An ingenious apparatus used by the robber giant Polypemon Procrustes, which means Polypemon the Stretcher. He lived near Eleusis, on the overland route from Troezen to Athens which was infested by monsters and supernatural beings.

Procrustes had a special technique for eliminating and robbing unwary travellers. His dwelling contained only one bed, an iron contraption with powers of self-adjustment. If a tall person lay upon the bed, it automatically shrank until the occupant's head and legs projected over the ends. If a short person lay down, the bed stretched to excessive length. Whoever used the bed found it was never the right length for his body.

When a weary traveller asked for the giant's hospitality, Procrustes entertained him jovially and then led him to the bedchamber. If the bed shrank when the traveller lay down, Procrustes lopped him down to size by hacking off head and legs. If the bed stretched, the giant seized the occupant by head and ankles and jerked him out to the requisite length. No traveller survived such treatment and Procrustes became rich on his spoils.

But at last the hero Theseus passed through Eleusis on his way to Athens, and asked Procrustes for a bed for the night. Theseus quickly guessed the secret of the unusual bed, and persuaded Procrustes to lie upon it to show him how it was used. The bed shrank in its usual style, and Theseus hacked off the giant's head and legs.

Pygmalion's Wife

Pygmalion was King of Cyprus (or some say of Tyre) in the days when Venus Aphrodite taught mankind the joys of passionate love. Pygmalion's family life appears to have been unhappy and confused. He slew his brother-in-law in a quarrel over the throne and his sister Dido committed suicide.

Pygmalion would have liked to marry but none of the Cyprus ladies measured up to his high standards, especially since Venus had cursed them with immodesty after they denied she was a goddess. The lonely king was, however, a patron of the arts, and may even have been a practising sculptor. He decided to create his own ideal woman, and chose ivory as the medium because it is more like human flesh than cold, hard metal or stone.

It is uncertain whether he actually fashioned his woman out of ivory, or whether he commissioned a sculptor to do so. In either case, the end product was so exquisitely beautiful that he fell in love with it.

The lonely king spent countless hours alone with his ideal woman, gazing entranced upon her beauty and yearning for the embraces of her ivory arms. Often he kissed and caressed her, his hands moving adoringly over the sleek curves.

Venus, who knows every secret of man's desire, knew of Pygmalion's love for his statue and at last took pity on him. One day when Pygmalion was making love to his ideal woman he felt the cool ivory change into the warm silken flesh of a living woman: the carved lips quivered into life and the shapely fingers returned his caresses. The power of his love and the sympathy of Venus had brought the statue to life and he was at last able to consummate his desire.

Pygmalion found his creation to be even more adorable as a living woman than she had been as a statue. He gave her a name, possibly Galatea, and made her his wife and queen. In due course she bore the fruit of their love: the daughter whom he named Paphos, in honour of Venus whom the Cypriots knew as Paphos when they worshipped her as a fertility goddess.

Quaaltagh

The Manx cognomen for the First Foot, or first person to enter a house on New Year's Day. The First Foot is very important because he influences the fortunes of a home for the coming year. If the First Foot is an unlucky or ill-favoured person, a family will suffer the consequences for the next twelve months.

It is wise, therefore, to arrange for the First Foot to be a respectable person of good appearance, and he should bring with him such gifts as a coin, a slice of bread, a lump of coal and a dram of spirits. These will ensure prosperity, food, warmth, and good cheer during the New Year.

Quinquatrus

The five-day festival beginning on 20 March each year in honour of Minerva, the goddess of all arts, crafts, and manufactures. She inspires and guides the hands of craftsmen of every kind, and assists the practitioners of all the arts. Such people should pay homage to Minerva, by feasts and other festivities, during the five days of the vernal equinox.

The goddess is not, however, interested in the sales of objects created under her auspices, or in the rewards received by poets, painters, musicians, actors, and others engaged in the arts. Those who expect to profit from creative activities should also pay homage to Mercury, the god of merchants and messengers. (His name derives from *merx* = merchandise and *mercari* = trade.) He is a capitalistic deity, very interested in profitable commerce.

Rattle

An instrument to produce sharp staccato sounds when it is turned or shaken. A dried gourd, containing a few pebbles or dry seeds, provides an excellent rattle. There are, however, innumerable types of rattles, ranging from hollow containers to strips of wood, caused to rattle against each other.

Rattles are valuable aids to supernatural ceremonies, because their irritating noise provokes the spirits into paying attention. In cases of sickness, a witch doctor uses a rattle to advise the demon inhabiting a patient's body that it is time to depart. By continuous rattling he keeps the demon awake, so that it is forced to listen to the spells which weaken its powers.

Rattles are useful in rainmaking ceremonies, to enliven the spirits of the sky; in hunters' dances to imitate the tattoo of animal hooves; in fertility rites to awaken the spirits of creation; in war dances to attract powerful spirits to the assistance of the tribe; in canoe launchings to advise water spirits that they are about to have a new companion; and in innumerable other ceremonies. Rattles are quickly and cheaply made and may be employed on almost any supernatural occasion.

Mothers find that one of the most important uses of rattles is the protection of babies. If a mother places a rattle within convenient reach of a baby's hand, the infant may shake it when it senses the proximity of evil spirits. The sound attracts the attention of spirits responsible for infant welfare and they soon chase any demons away.

Rhinoceros Horn

A potent energiser for human males perturbed by flaccidity of the generative organ, whether caused by senility or over-enthusiasm. The rhinoceros itself (Greek *rhis* = nose, *keras* = horn) is a dull insensitive pachyderm (Greek *pakhus* = thick, *derma* = hide) which cannot be domesticated and is dangerous and difficult to hunt. The young men of a tribe would not risk their lives in pursuit of rhinoceroses if not for the urging of their elders and the value of the horn. The shape and size of the horn (up to 30·480 centimetres long on the Indian rhinoceros, now almost extinct) provide an enviable exemplar of masculine potency, and it is obvious that powdered rhinoceros horn must restore this quality in those who rely on memory rather than performance. For many centuries, rhinoceros horn has been sought so eagerly that it is now rare and expensive, and can be afforded only by Oriental millionaires.

Rings

Short lengths of thin metal, ranging from approximately 22 mm long and ·9 mm in diameter up to any practicable length and diameter, bent into a symmetrical circle having the two ends bonded together, so that the essential force of the metal cannot escape. Rings may also be fashioned from any suitable material, such as stone, ivory, jade, amber, etc., capable of being carved into a unbroken circlet, so that the inward force of that material revolves continuously within the ring and cannot flow out through open ends.

Rings are generally made to fit the fingers of natural or supernatural persons, but are equally effective in the larger sizes known as bracelets, anklets, and coronets. They may also be worn in the ears.

Rings may be decorated or ornamented according to personal or transcendental taste so long as the body of the ring is unbroken. Rings made of several interwoven circles are especially effective.

The inward power of all such artefacts derives from the function of perpetuity. This is inherent in a ring and is expressed in the saying 'A ring has no end.' The continuously revolving force, spirit, or essence of a ring structure generates a power which envelops the wearer in a protective aura, impenetrable by alien forces because it is perpetually renewed by the power of the ring.

This essential force is made even stronger by impregnation with supernatural influences. Even a simple gold ring, when assumed under the influence of the proper

incantations, is a potent guardian of faith and loyalty.

Some notable rings have much greater powers. The ring Draupnir, made by the dwarfs for the god Odin, had the ability to increase its owner's wealth indefinitely. Andvari's ring (known sometimes as the Ring of the Nibelungen) had similar powers. Rings worn by such dignitaries as kings and bishops bestow a special grace upon supplicants who kiss them.

In England, any person suffering from muscular or internal cramps may obtain relief by wearing a Cramp Ring. It may be made of any material, but must be blessed during a special service attended by the reigning monarch and presented by him or her.

Seafarers have long known the special power of rings worn in the ears. They strengthen a seaman's eyesight and may even allow him to see beyond the horizon.

Round Table

The table in the banqueting hall of King Arthur's castle city, Camelot. Originally, at least 150 knights sat at a single long table, but they frequently jostled each other for the privilege of sitting close to King Arthur at the head of the table. Some knights, by virtue of seniority or ancestry, claimed places at the head of the table. Those relegated to the lower end felt so humiliated they could hardly enjoy their meals. Arthur tried to make his knights take turns at the top, but every feast began with prolonged arguments over the right to sit next to the king. The food grew cold while brave knights argued fine points of nobility and lineage.

The climax came on a Christmas Day. The knights trooped in solemn procession from the chapel to the banqueting hall, but as they walked inside they began an undignified scuffle for places nearest the head of the table. Tempers flared, and in a few moments the hall was filled with struggling groups of knights. Some drew their ceremonial daggers, while others wrestled among the straw and rushes scattered on the stone floor of the hall. They all fought until their Christmas finery was bloodstained and tattered, and several knights had been stabbed or choked to death.

News of the disgraceful brawl spread rapidly through Christendom, and it appears that at least three people offered a solution to the problem. One was the wizard Merlin, another was Arthur's father-in-law King Leodegrance, and the third was a foreign carpenter. Collectively or individually, they said that Arthur should provide his knights with a round table, so that they could all sit around it without any man having precedence over the others.

Arthur accepted the idea and employed the carpenter to build a huge round table, which he finished in six weeks. When it was installed in the banqueting hall it eliminated all the knights' jealousies and created a new sense of brotherhood, so that they referred to themselves proudly as the Knights of the Round Table.

There was, however, still one special seat at the table. Known as the Siege Perilous, from the Latin word *sedes* meaning seat, it was reserved for any knight who had vowed to go in search of the Holy Grail.

Runes

The earliest alphabet used by the Scandinavian and Germanic peoples: probably the ancestor of the Anglo-Saxon alphabet which was corrupted by the Roman invaders of Britain.

Unlike other alphabets, the runes themselves have certain magical powers. These derive from the fact that Odin, chief of the gods, invented the runes. One of his many titles was Lord of the Runes. Originally these powers were beneficial, or at least protective. One well-known example is the rune-sentence engraved on the Bjorketorp monument in Norway, which reads 'This is the secret meaning of the runes; I hid here power-runes, undisturbed by evil witchcraft. In exile shall he die by means of magic art who destroys this monument.'

Similar rune-sentences were used to ward off witches and sorcerers from important places, but the corruption of the alphabet caused runes to fall out of general use. They were gradually taken over by wizards, who learned their special powers and employed rune-writing as a kind of code or cypher.

Rune sentences are now used for the casting of particularly unpleasant spells, almost invariably fatal. The procedure is to write the curse, in runic lettering, upon a slip of paper, and send or give it to the victim. A person who unwarily accepts the paper cannot destroy it by any known method. His only chance of escaping the spell is to discover who commissioned it from a wizard, and then secretly insert the paper into the ill-wisher's garments.

Sa

The magical fluid which runs in the veins of Egyptian gods and pervades them with their superhuman strength and wisdom. Sa-power is not, however, self-perpetuating. At fairly regular intervals a god realises that his ability to work miracles is dissipating, and he must then ask another god with a better supply of sa to lay hands on him.

In the days of the Pharaohs, the god-kings of Egypt, the gods provided a similar service for those rulers. By laying hands on the Pharaohs the gods infused them, alone among human beings, with the supreme powers of sa.

Scarab

The dung beetle (*Scarabeus sacer*) who became the important god Kheperi of the Egyptians. In Egypt, dung beetles lay their eggs in morsels of animal dung, which they push to the top of a slope and allow to roll down again. This has a 'snowball' effect, creating a symmetrical ball of earth and dung. Priestly observation of the process made the Egyptians realise that the sun must be a gigantic ball created by a supernatural dung beetle, which pushes the sun to the summit of the sky and allows it to roll down again. This supernatural beetle is the god Kheperi.

Consequently, the scarab beetle is sacred to the sun, and amulets made in the oval shape of a scarab have a strong influence upon one's powers of creation. The appearance or sighting of a living scarab beetle may be regarded as a certain omen of good fortune.

Sedit's Wings

Sedit is one of the names given to Coyote, the cunning supernatural hero of some American Indians. Sedit embodies both the creative and protective and the adventurous and destructive aspects of human nature. He has some resemblance to Reynard the Fox, having the same talent for getting into mischief and talking himself out of trouble.

On one occasion, Sedit's interfering nature had disastrous consequences for mankind. When the Sky Father decided to create men and women, he told two vultures to build a ladder between heaven and earth so that mortals would be able to pass easily between the two dimensions. Sedit came loping along and saw them working on the ladder, and when he learned its purpose he said it was a foolish idea. In his opinion, men and women would soon grow weary of the eternal life achieved by climbing up to heaven and down again.

The vultures agreed, and abandoned the work. But, before they flew away, one of them remarked that Sedit would also be denied a return to earth from heaven.

Sedit then tried to invent a way in which he alone would be able to commute between earth and heaven. He noticed that the heads of sunflowers always turn in the direction of the sun, and decided they would be the ideal material for a pair of wings. He made the wings, and got himself off the ground, but when the flowers withered he fell back again.

All other attempts to find a way back from heaven to earth have been equally unsuccessful, and Sedit's interference means that mortals are denied eternal life on earth.

Seven-League Boots

A league equals 4·828 kilometres, and seven-league boots enable their wearer to cover 33·696 kilometres at a single step. Little else is known about this footwear, except that it fits anyone who manages to steal the boots from a previous owner. For example, Hop o' My Thumb, the smallest boy of ten who ever wore shoes, stole seven-league boots from a giant and they fitted him perfectly. The boots played an essential part in his subsequent career as a king's messenger.

Spell

The words needed to activate any magical rite, and by association used to mean the effect of the rite on a beneficiary or victim. The words 'He is under a spell' actually mean that a person is the subject of magic activated by a spell. Equally, 'spellbound' means that a person is overwhelmed by spell-energised magic.

Spells may be murmured, spoken, or chanted (when they are known as incantations). They may be uttered by a single person or by several in unison, depending upon the regulations for each spell.

Spells are divided into two categories: traditional and individual. The vast majority are traditional, because the characteristics of men and other animals, and of their surrounding universe, change little from one generation to another. Therefore a spell first formulated in the days of Zeus or Osiris will be equally effective in modern times.

Professional spellbinders such as fairies, gypsies, witches, wizards, and sorcerers learn as many spells as possible, with their accompanying rituals, and use them as required. The spells range from simple, such as those for ridding a child of warts, to terrible. These include spells that alter the weather, cause a man to wither away, or change the destinies of kings. Of course there is an enormous range of spells, for good or evil results, and no spellbinder can learn them all. He or she often refers to encyclopaedias of spells and rituals, which are written in ancient languages such as Sanskrit and Teutonic.

Individual spells are those formulated to aid or afflict a person in circumstances not covered by traditional spells. Considerable expertise is required for compounding individual spells, because a mistake in the wording could have unfortunate results. One well-documented error occurred in a spell formulated for Lady Alysse Conynghame, who paid a witch for a spell against grey hair. Some fault in the wording of ritual caused her to sprout a small pair of horns.

Swords

These fearsome weapons, edged for hacking or pointed for stabbing, have been made in a multitude of shapes and sizes for at least 5,000 years, under countless names from the gladius used by gladiators to the claymore of the Highlanders.

A sword is forged from any suitable metal or metal alloy including bronze, iron, and steel. The hilt, tang, guard, clasp, and blade of a sword may be ornamented as richly as the owner desires, provided that this ornamentation does not detract from the sword's efficiency as an instrument of death. In fact, the ornaments and decorations, in the form of appropriate runes or other symbols or spells engraved on the blade or other components, will improve the sword's ability to release an enemy's life-essence.

Each sword has a spirit of its own, which is extremely sensitive to the spirit of its owner. Ideally, a swordsman should be present during every stage of his weapon's manufacture, so that the spirits of sword and man may blend into perfect empathy. Common swords, mass produced for use by conscripted men, are never as spirited as custom-made weapons wielded by heroic leaders.

The sword of the Albanian hero Iskander Beg is a perfect example of the spiritual relationship between weapon and warrior. When this sword was wielded by a courageous soldier it became automatically sharper, stronger, and more lethal. When it was handled by a man without the true killer instinct, its blade became so blunt it could hardly pierce an opponent's flesh.

The spirit of a sword is infused into it by the forging of the blade, which incorporates the four vital elements of fire, water, earth, and air. Fire enforces the swordsmith's will upon the blade, and as he beats it into shape the blows of his hammer may be reinforced by the rhythmic incantation of a special spell. Air plays its part in the bellows which keep the forge fire ablaze; water in the tempering of the blade; and earth in the sword metal and the grindstone which sharpens it. Fire reappears when sparks fly from the grindstone, and a skilful augur may predict, from the size and direction of the flying sparks, the probable destiny of the sword and its owner.

Naturally the power of a sword is greatly enhanced if it is forged by a supernatural or semi-immortal being, or if it is blessed, dedicated, or consecrated in some specific way. The dwarfs are notable swordsmiths

because of their skills in infusing magic into metal. Probably they forged the famous sword Mistletoe, named after the sacred bush. It was the only sword capable of killing the giant Baldur, whose mother made everything in the universe promise not to harm him but forgot to ask the mistletoe.

Demons and evil spirits are afraid of swords. A man travelling in demon-haunted territory would be wise to carry his sword unsheathed, and to polish it brightly so that demons will be scared off by its flashing menace. A home or other building plagued by demons may be purified by a number of swordsmen engaging in mock swordplay on the premises, emitting loud yells to the accompaniment of bells, drums, and trumpets.

The supernatural powers which support great heroes always give them magical swords, with extraordinary powers over the foe. The Irish hero Cuchulain wielded the sword Caladbolg. Roland, the French warrior who defeated a vast army of Saracens almost single-handed, fought with the sword Durendal. This weapon was so finely tempered that when Roland knew he must die, and tried to shatter Durendal against a boulder, the blade simply bounced off. Roland had to hide Durendal so that it would not fall into enemy hands, and it still lies hidden somewhere in the Pyrenees.

The swords wielded by such heroes were massive straight-bladed weapons, almost 2 metres long, with straight hilts richly ornamented by gold and jewels. The swords were so heavy that the warriors had to hold them in both hands, and create flashing arcs of death as they charged the enemy.

Such swords always came mystically or magically into the possession of those who used them. The great sword of Sigmund Volksung was thrust through a tree trunk by the god Odin, and Sigmund was the only warrior strong enough to wrench it out again. Sigmund wielded this sword until Odin decided he must die, and caused the weapon to break in half during a battle. But Sigmund's son Sigurd (or Siegfried) had the sword repaired by the blacksmith Mime, and wielded it on many gallant adventures, including the slaughter of the dragon Fafnir.

King Arthur's sword, Excalibur, a supreme example of the swordsmith's art, was handed to him by a hand and arm clothed in white samite which appeared out of a lonely lake. Excalibur was so magnificently jewelled and ornamented that when King Arthur was dying, and he commanded Sir Bedivere to throw the sword back into the lake, the knight could not bring himself to do so. All the haft twinkled with diamond sparks, myriads of topaz lights, and jacinth-work of subtlest jewellery, and the blade was strangely and curiously engraved. He hid the sword twice instead of throwing it into the water, but Arthur sensed his disobedience and on the third command Sir Bedivere flung Excalibur over the lake.

The great blade flashed like lightning in the moonlight, whirling and turning until it fell hilt-first towards the dark water. An arm rose out of the water, caught Excalibur by the hilt, and brandished it three times before sword and arm disappeared forever.

Syrinx

A musical instrument invented by the god Pan, as a by-product of his sexual adventures. Pan, like most of the gods, likes nothing better than a fresh young nymph, and a new face in the forest rarely escapes his ardent attention. One day he saw the nymph Syrinx for the first time and set out in pursuit. Syrinx ran fleetly along the riverbank but few nymphs can run faster than Pan's nimble hooves. She heard his lecherous chuckle close behind her, felt the first touch of his horny hand, and screamed to her father, the river-god Ladon, to save her.

Ladon took drastic action by changing her into a clump of reeds on the water's edge, and although Pan watched them carefully for a long time they were never reincarnated as Syrinx. To console himself, Pan plucked some of the reeds and made a new kind of pipe. He fastened them together so that the open ends were in a horizontal line while their stopped ends, formed by the knots in the reeds, slanted down from right to left. When he tried out his new instrument, the music pleased him so greatly that he forgot about the reluctant nymph and capered away into the forest, entrancing every listener with the sound of the new Pan pipes.

Time Machine

A vehicle for carrying its rider backwards or forwards through time as well as space. There is only one genuine time machine, invented by an anonymous gentleman in 1894 and described by the science writer H. G. Wells.

The Time Traveller was a professional inventor, but little is known of him except that he had a pale face and brilliant grey eyes. He conceived the theory that time is simply a fourth dimension, and that men should therefore be able to travel along time as easily as they pass through or across space.

Regrettably, the drawings and specifications of the original time machine appear to have been destroyed. Only the most scrappy description remains, of a 'squat ugly mass'. It looked substantial, but was strangely unstable to the touch. The machine was constructed from quartz rods, brass, ebony, and ivory, with a saddle to be mounted by the operator and a starting lever to activate the forward and reverse gears.

The Time Traveller, who described the sensation of travelling through time as a highly unpleasant experience, made one well-documented excursion back to the very beginnings of the Cosmos and forward into the distant future, but did not return from a second trip. Presumably he perished in some unknown era, whose people could not work out the use of the machine.

Possibly his housekeeper, Mrs Watchett, destroyed the drawings and specifications when she cleared out his laboratory after his disappearance.

Trojan Horse

(Properly known as the Wooden Horse of Troy.) A ruse of war used to capture the city of Troy, probably in the ninth century BC.

Troy was a rich and populous city on the coast of the Aegean Sea, in what is now one of the Asian provinces of Turkey. Poseidon, Lord of the Ocean, built the walls of Troy with the aid of the god Apollo.

The history of the city is long and complicated, full of strife, murder, and teachery. The climax came when Paris, one of the fifty sons of Priam the third King of Troy, visited Sparta and seduced Helen, wife of Menelaus. Helen was the most beautiful woman in the ancient world, perhaps because she was hatched from an egg laid by Leda whom Zeus raped in the form of a swan.

When Helen accompanied her lover on his return to Troy, the Greeks were infuriated by this Trojan impertinence. They built a fleet of 1,000 ships to attack the city and most of the great heroes, including Hercules, sailed with the expeditionary force.

But the Trojans were more than a match for them and the siege of Troy dragged on for ten years. At last the Grecian hero, Odysseus, who was anxious to return to his wife, thought of an idea to gain access to the city. He gained permission from his leader, Agamemnon, to build a wooden horse large enough to contain twenty-three soldiers. Epirus built the horse with the aid of the goddess Athene. When all was ready, Odysseus led his men inside and the Greeks put the ruse into effect. They burnt their camps, boarded their ships, and sailed beyond the horizon, leaving the horse before the walls of Troy. One of them, Sinon, who was

the grandson of a notable thief, stayed behind to work the confidence trick on the Trojans.

They soon sallied forth to see what was happening, and Sinon explained that the Greeks had left the horse behind by way of atonement for destroying the Palladium, a wooden statue of Athene given to the Trojans by the great god Zeus.

Helen warned the Trojans that the horse was a trick, and even knocked on its sides and called out the names of the Greeks whom she suspected to be hiding inside. But Odysseus made them keep silent, and in the euphoria of apparent victory the Trojans ignored Helen and dragged the horse into the city.

Sinon crept away and signalled to the Grecian fleet, which returned under cover of darkness. At the same time, the Greeks slipped out of the horse and ran to all the city gates. They killed the guards, threw the gates open, and defended them until the Greek army swarmed ashore and into the city.

That was the last of Troy, because the Greeks sacked and burned the city and killed or enslaved all its people. As for Helen, her end is obscure. Some say she married the Greek hero Achilles: others that she was killed in the battle for Troy, and became a star alongside Castor and Pollux, the Heavenly Twins. Another story says that she took refuge in Rhodes, whose queen mistrusted the dangerous beauty and had her hanged from a tree.

Tailrings

A horrid artificial cat made by one of the Salem witches to revenge herself against her tormentors. When the Puritans began their persecution of the witches, one whose witchname was Strmantis could foretell her own doom. Before the witch hunters took her, she caught and killed a fine neighbourhood cat and stuffed its skin with a blend of potent herbs mingled with straw. She replaced its eyes with moonstones and its claws with tiny razorsharp blades. When this creation was ready she performed all the necessary rites to bring it to life and spoke all but the last words of the activating spell. She reserved this until the witch-hunters broke into her home, when she screamed the words which energised the cat and sent it scrambling out of the window.

After the death of Strmantis, the cat avenged her by attacking hunters in the nearby woods. Those who saw the cat described its great moonstone eyes glowing in the dusk, the ringed tail that inspired the name of Tailrings, and the fact that no hunter was ever able to hit it with an ordinary musket ball.

Many hunters suffered from the terrible claws of Tailrings, but at last the attacks became rarer and the cat was seen no more. Probably this was because the straw which filled the catskin gradually crumbled away.

Tattoos

The widespread practice of imprinting indelible patterns on the body by rubbing dye into puncture wounds. The art is now degenerate and used only for ornamentation, but traditional tattooing has great supernatural powers. It must be applied only by priests who know the significance of each marking or pattern. As a simple example, a simple type of whorling pattern imprinted in the buttocks has the effect of eyes which enable a warrior to see whether he is being followed. Other patterns protect various parts of the body against disease, increase muscular strength, protect against witchcraft or treachery, and so on. The patterns reserved for chiefs reinforce their powers of leadership and also indicate their rank. Men who submit to the excruciatingly painful process of genital tattooing are consoled by the knowledge that it increases their powers of reproduction.

Seafarers have known the value of tattooing since time immemorial. An anchor tattooed on the arm prevents a man from drifting away if he falls overboard, while the letters H-O-L-D F-A-S-T, individually tattooed on the knuckles, are almost sure to prevent a fall from aloft.

Totem

A real or imaginary creature used as the protective emblem of a nation, family, or tribal group. For example, the lion and the unicorn are the totems of Britons, the eagle of the United States, the cockerel of the French, and the kangaroo and emu of the Australians.

The value of totems is that creatures revered by a tribal group may actually endow the group with some of their own qualities. At the same time, the creature realises that the group has a special claim upon it, and reacts accordingly. A tribe whose totem is the grizzly bear expects the bear to make them brave, strong, stubborn, and enduring, and also hopes that, whenever they go out to hunt a bear, it will not injure any member of the tribe. Totemic dances and ceremonies performed before the hunt should assist the process.

Totemic influences and the associated taboos are multi-layered within the tribe. Apart from the tribal totem, each family and even each individual may have separate totems, each with its own set of taboos. If one belongs to a family of the Snake totem, then one must not marry any person of the same totem. In choosing a spouse, one must pay careful attention to totemic influences. Obviously it would be disastrous for a man of the Fly totem to marry a woman of the Spider totem.

Totemic possession does not prevent one from eating the totem. Many totemic rituals are designed to increase the number of the relevant creatures, such as salmon, buffalo, or witchetty grubs, on which a group survives. And after all one cannot have a more intimate association with a totem than by eating it.

Civilised nations profess disbelief in totems but secretly respect them. Such names as Jaguar and Falcon for motorcars are obvious examples of totemism.

Urbar

The drum carved out of a hollow log, used by the Aborigines of Arnhem Land in northern Australia during rituals to ensure the opening of the rainy season.

In some parts of this territory the drum represents the womb of the female Rainbow Serpent, and the penis of the male Rainbow serpent. These great reptiles, who arch themselves across the sky early in the rainy season, are essential to the fertility of all mortal life.

In other regions, the first urbar drum was made by the python-man Jurawadbad, who was betrothed to the Aboriginal girl Mimaliwu. But Mimaliwu allowed herself to be seduced by a watersnake, and the python-man was so angry that he created an urbar and lay in ambush within it. At last Mimaliwu and her mother came along foraging for food, and they felt inside the urbar to seek honey or any small animal hiding there. When the python-man saw their hands he bit them, so that both of the women died.

The spirits of the three creatures are now associated with the rainy season, and the affair of the first urbar drum is re-enacted during the fertility rituals.

Vail

The coin with which one must pay the ferryman, Charon, for passage across the River Acheron en route to the underworld. Also known as an obolus. Grim old Charon has no pity for the souls of the dead on their final journey, and if a soul cannot pay his fare he refuses passage across the river. The soul must then wander the riverbank throughout eternity, unable to cross to the other side.

To pay the ferryman, a soul must carry the vail or obolus in his or her mouth. A friend or relation must provide this coin as a final duty to the dead, and some people also place honey cakes in the coffin. It is said that Cerberus, the three-headed dog which guards the entrance to the underworld, is fond of honey cakes, and that he may allow souls to wheedle their way back past him to the upperworld if they feed him with the cakes.

Wand, Magic

A tapering rod of any suitable material, possibly tipped with a star or other symbol, used by fairy queens as a sceptre to indicate their sovereignty and by wizards, sorcerers, etc. as a useful artefact. The rod is handy for drawing occult characters in the dust of churchyards as part of magical rituals.

The wand, despite its name, has no integrated magical powers although it may be brandished as part of a ritual. Possibly its principal function is to enhance the mystique of spellbinders, who use magic wands to frighten laymen. As demonstrated earlier in this volume, magic is activated only by specific spells and rituals and not by portable artefacts.

Wax Figures

Figures moulded from beeswax in Britain, Europe, and North America, and from any suitable malleable material in other parts of the world. Usually no more than about 8 centimetres high. Used only for malevolent purposes, especially the infliction of pain or deformity. A witch or sorcerer may make such a figure for personal revenge, or mould it, for an appropriate fee, for an evilly disposed person to employ against an enemy.

The figure must be fashioned to the accompaniment of the correct ritual and incantations, which include the frequent repetition of the victim's name. When all is prepared, the figure must be kept in a secret place.

The operator activates the figure simply by inserting a needle in any desired area. This victim, even if he or she is many kilometres away or even in a different country, instantly suffers a piercing pain in the same region of the body.

The operator may inflict immediate death by pushing the needle through the heart or head of the figure, or prolonged torments by choosing less fatal areas. It is all a matter of malicious ingenuity. The operator must, however, be careful to keep himself advised of the health of his victim. When the victim dies the figure must be instantly destroyed. Otherwise the soul of the departed may enter into it, with hideous consequences for the operator.

Wizards

One of the numerous class of magic workers, which includes sorcerers, magicians, thaumaturgists, conjurers, witches, lamias, warlocks, mages, fairies, enchanters, and mystics.

A wizard is often regarded as the male equivalent of a witch, but this is not totally correct. Witches rely on evil spirits or demons to assist them, whereas wizards usually call on benevolent spirits to activate their spells or at least employ both good and evil spirits. It is probably more appropriate to describe sorcerers, who work their magic with the aid of the souls of the dead, as the male practitioners of witchcraft. Wizards often have good working relationships with fairies (who never associate with evil spirits) and have frequently held respectable positions, such as that of Merlin in the court of King Arthur.

Very few wizards are of supernatural

descent, but are usually men who learn their craft by prolonged apprenticeship to senior wizards and by lives devoted to study and research. Wizards never marry and usually conserve their vital forces by remaining celibate, and so it is not an hereditary profession.

The power of a wizard depends upon the depth of his learning and experience. As a general rule, it may be said that the oldest wizards have the widest abilities in magic. Almost any man who is prepared to accept the rigid disciplines may learn wizardry, but numerous apprentices to the craft are frightened out of it when their masters conjure up apparitions or converse with disembodied voices. Many others baulk at the immense quantity of booklearning. A wizard must be able to read spellbooks written in Aramaic, Celtic, Cornish, Greek, Hebrew, Latin, Old Norse, Old Scots, Slavonic, Teutonic, and many other ancient or obscure languages. The books are never printed or even translated, because this would spread their information too widely, and a young wizard has to copy his own complete set of spellbooks from those in his master's library.

Many wizards abandon the profession even after they have graduated through the first degrees. The idea of casting a spell may seem attractive, but when a young wizard has actually caused invisible hands to prepare his dinner he may think again. He becomes all too conscious of the flimsiness of the curtain which separates natural from supernatural, and of the ghastly creatures ravening for release. Senior wizards are often haggard and haunted men, afraid to sleep because of the fearsome images which leer and gibber through their dreams.

On the whole, a wizard pays a high price for the privilege of wearing the élite uniform of pointed cap and star-spangled robes.

Wu Hsing

The totality of the universe, especially important to artists and craftsmen because it comprises the five natural forces which they must obey, employ, and understand. They are timber; fire in all its powers and manifestations; earth and all that lies within it; metal; and the waters of the earth, sea, and sky.

The five elements exist in an unbroken circle of water-timber-fire-earth-metal, in which each element creates a successor and is consumed by a predecessor. Water creates timber and consumes fire; fire creates earth and consumes metal; metal creates water and consumes timber; timber creates fire and consumes earth; earth creates metal and completes the cycle by consuming water.

Craftsmen who work with all the elements may pay tribute to Wu Hsing as a complete entity, or to each element individually. Each element forms a fifth part of the universe, in which fire is south, metal is west, timber is east, water is north, and earth is the centre. Each region is governed by a celestial emperor, who receives individual tributes or a share of all tributes paid to Wu Hsing.

Yang and Yin

The separate but inseparable dualities of every conceivable object of thought, which by their mysterious symbiosis create a whole. Each is powerless and meaningless without the other.

The concept may be expressed in as many ways as there are objects of thought. Numerically, yin exists in even numbers and yang in uneven. All numbers are separate and yet are useless for calculation without all other numbers, so that yang and yin must work together to achieve an end. If yang is the sun, yin is the sky; if yin is the air then yang is the wind.

In basic terms, yang is generally represented as the male element and yin as the female: action and passion balancing passivity and quiescence; penetration complementing reception; the tree standing upon the earth which supports it; the wave surging across an ocean which will sink back into placidity. And yet the definition of yang and yin must be moulded by one's point of view. There are those who believe that yin represents the deep brooding permanence of the universe, while yang is no more than the convulsions of history passing across its surface. Yang, like a bird, flits overhead and drops a seed onto yin, the fecund bosom of the earth. Without the bird, the seed would not find a home; without the earth, it would have nowhere to grow. Philosophers might argue for centuries about the relative importance of bird and earth, while the seed itself enfolds yet another manifestation of yin and yang and will release them into a new fruition: a new cycle of growth, blossom, and seeding that renews and perpetuates yang and yin yet again.

Zin Kibaru's Guitar

The stringed instrument which belonged to an evil spirit of the Niger River where it flows through Mali and Upper Volta. The spirit, Zin Kibaru, controlled the fish, crocodiles, and other creatures of the river by playing certain chords or tunes upon his guitar.

A farmer named Faran offended Zin Kibaru, and the spirit revenged itself by causing fish to leave the river and eat the farmer's crops. When Faran tried to catch fish instead of growing food, Zin Kibaru caused hippopotami to blunder into his nets.

At last Faran tired of this persecution and tracked Zin Kibaru to its home on the riverbank. He challenged Zin Kibaru to fight, and after a long battle he was conquering the spirit when Zin Kibaru cast a spell which made Faran powerless.

Faran returned disconsolately to his village, but his mother taught him a spell which was stronger than Zin Kibaru's. Armed with this power he challenged the spirit to another fight, and when Zin Kibaru tried to work the spell again, Faran defeated it with his mother's magic.

Zin Kibaru ran away from the river and either took his guitar with him or left it to be destroyed by Faran, so that the river creatures were freed to follow their natural ways of life.

CHAPTER FIVE

THINGS OF WATER, SKY, AND AIR

THINGS OF WATER, SKY, AND AIR

The most important influence on human life is the atmosphere which surrounds us. As fishes live in water so we live in a sea of air, and all its tricks and turbulences dictate our destinies. And, like the sea, it is uncontrollable. Even the most powerful ruler cannot divert a hurricane or save his people from a drought.

The atmosphere, like a capricious lover, is so intimate a friend or enemy that scientific reasoning is too cold an explanation for those vagaries we call 'weather'. Scientists can explain *how* the atmosphere creates weather, but not *why.* Nobody knows why the mighty engine of the universe functions so erratically that a nation may have a year of drought followed by a year of floods; why, in fact, we can never rely on the weather.

But our ancestors knew both how *and* why. Every phenomenon of water, sky, and air is the work of various monsters, spirits, or deities, functioning to reward or punish mankind. Even the stars and planets were once supernatural beings, placed in the sky as the result of some terrestrial activity. Innumerable spirits, each with a special task to perform, occupy water and air. Everything that swims in or on or under the waters, whether ships or fish or men, must pay homage to these beings.

They interfere in the affairs of men and hold mankind at their mercy. When the gods are displeased with mortal behaviour they inflict appropriate punishments, by swamping the world with a deluge or parching it with a drought. When people obey the divine laws, the beings of water, sky, and air reward them with good harvests and prosperous voyages.

As in a human community, these beings range in temperament from malevolent to benevolent and from dictators to minor functionaries. They may be destructive, helpful, mischievous, or capricious: administrators of the elements or mere tormentors of mankind.

And, apart from these potent spirits, there are many other occupants of water and air. They include mermaids and maelstroms, winged horses and Argonauts, sea serpents and krakens, who all exist to perform the essential function of expanding human wonderment.

Acheron, River

The River of Woe: principal waterway of the river system of the Underworld. It was created when the gods won the war against the Titans, and the great god Zeus punished their watercarrier, Acheron, by turning him into a river.

The geography of the Underworld is complex and obscure but it would appear that the Acheron has four tributaries: Styx, the River of Hate, Phlegethon, the River of Flames, Cocytus, the River of Wailing, and Lethe, the River of Forgetfulness. Apparently the rivers run in concentric circles, perhaps crossing or intermingling with each other, and they separate the Underworld into Tartarus and the Elysian Fields.

The ghosts of the dead have to cross all five rivers on their way into the Underworld. Each crossing separates them further from the land of the living, but when at last they drink from the waters of Lethe they forget all about their lives on earth. Their wails and sobs, at separation from all they have loved, finally die away, and they reconcile themselves to the cheerless eternity of Tartarus or a new happiness in the Elysian Fields.

If a mortal can bathe in the waters of the Styx, and somehow find his way back to earth, he will be forever invulnerable to man-made weapons. But he must be careful not to swallow any of the water, which is deadly poison. Alexander the Great was poisoned by Stygian water brought from the river in a hollowed-out mule's hoof.

The gods may, however, drink Stygian water without any ill effects other than sleepiness. They drink the water, brought to them by the nymph Iris in a golden goblet, when they wish to bind themselves to a solemn oath.

Aegir

Lord of the Nordic Seas: the sea-god who commands the seas and oceans in the latitudes of Scotland and Norway. Husband of Ran the Widow-maker, by whom he had nine giant daughters.

Aegir is nicknamed the Ale-brewer, because the white spume of a raging sea resembles the froth of ale working within a brewing vat. It seems, however, that Aegir is a jovial god and that Ran and her daughters cause most oceanic disasters. Aegir is a boon companion of all the other gods, the Aesir, and they often invite him to their feasts and drinking contests in Asgard. From time to time he entertains them in his huge ocean palace, which is brilliantly lit by the reflections from gold salvaged from sunken ships.

It may be that the drunken frolics of Aegir and the Aesir stir up some of the storms at sea, but most of them may be blamed upon Ran and her daughters. Each of the giant daughters is an enormous wave, and on Ran's prompting they all dance so furiously together that ships are wrecked and sailors thrown into the sea. The nine daughters welcome some of the sailors into their seductive white arms, while others fall into the nets with which Ran fishes for the souls of dead seamen. But shipping disasters have happy endings, because the ten ladies escort drowned seafarers down to Aegir's palace and treat them to banquets of seafood and Aegir's ale.

Ahuizotl

A fearsome creature of highland lakes in Central America. No one who sees Ahuizotl lives to tell the tale, and so any discriptions of the monster must be purely imaginary. It is the owner of all fish in the lakes and is made extremely angry by fishermen who steal them with nets and lines. Sometimes it creates great storms over the lakes (some say by lashing its tail) and at other times it grasps the side of a boat or raft, tips it over, and swallows the hapless fishermen thrown into the water. If it is not particularly hungry it allows the drowned bodies to float away. Ahuizotl may occasionally be placated by throwing some of the catch back into the water and hiding the rest in the bottom of the boat, so that the monster is deceived into thinking that the fishermen have not taken any of its property.

Albatross, Great Wandering

(*Diomedes exulans*.) The huge birds beloved by the spirits of both air and sea, which give them special powers of flight and endurance.

The albatross has a wingspan of as much as 3·5 metres. It roams the great circle of southern ocean from 30 degrees south to the edge of the Antarctic ice: the stormiest seas in the world, where the western winds rage eternally around the globe. The supernatural assistance received by the albatross is demonstrated by the fact that it flies above these awful seas, thousands of kilometres from land, without even having to flap its wings. The great bird rides the currents of air with supreme grace and confidence: soaring, swooping, and gliding in total harmony with the wind and sea.

A sailor who kills an albatross is certain to offend the spirits and bring disaster to his ship. The only way to placate the spirits is to tie the dead bird around the offender's neck and lash him to the mainmast, where he must stay without food and drink until the storm has subsided.

Albion

The Patriach of the Atlantic: a benign sea-giant who has a special concern for the people of England. Probably they are his descendants, because early inhabitants of the nation were called Albiones. When the Romans invaded England they thought this name must derive from the white cliffs of Dover, since Albiones resembles the word for 'white' in the Roman tongue. They named the country Albion without knowing that they honoured the Patriach.

Alulei

One of the most powerful sea-gods of Micronesia, the multitude of small islands scattered across the southern Pacific. Alulei was the first to learn how to sail his canoe unerringly between the islands. This amazing ability puzzled all the other islanders, who dared not venture out of sight of land in case they lost themselves on the endless waste of ocean.

Alulei had an unpleasant brother, Faravia, who never lost ar. opportunity to trick or deceive him. But Alulei always forgave Faravai and one day the brothers were reconciled. As a token of this new friendship, Faravai offered to comb out Alulei's tangled hair. When he did so, he found that the dark mass of hair was full of glittering little eyes. Alulei explained that they were the stars, and that they were the secret of his navigational skills.

Alulei taught Faravai how to find his way between the islands by studying the position of the stars, and Faravai passed this information on to all the other islanders. Ever since then, island seafarers have found their way around the Pacific by looking at the little eyes which glisten among Alulei's black hair.

Argo, The

The first fifty-oar war galley: possibly the first ocean-going vessel and certainly the first major warship. Conceived and designed by the goddess Athene, ordered by Prince Jason of Iolchus, and constructed by the shipbuilder Argos. Jason named the ship *Argo* either to honour the shipbuilder or from a Greek word meaning 'swift'.

Jason ordered the *Argo* to be built so that he might discover the Golden Fleece, in order to settle a family quarrel.

This began when his uncle Pelias usurped the throne of Iolchus from Jason's father, Aeson. To protect Jason from Pelias, who might be tempted to murder the rightful heir to the throne, Aeson placed the child in care of the learned centaur, Cheiron.

Another of Jason's uncles, Athamas, was married to the cloud goddess Nephele. She bore him two children, Phrixus and Helle, but discovered that Athamas had taken a mistress named Ino.

Nephele was so angry that she floated off into the sky, but she kept a close eye on the destiny of her children.

Ino hated the boy and girl, and worked out a cunning plot to destroy them. When the time came for sowing the annual crops, Ino roasted all the seeds so that they would not sprout into grain. She blamed the consequent famine upon the wrath of the gods, and persuaded her lover that the only way to placate them was to offer Phrixus and Helle as sacrifices.

Nephele acted promptly to save her children. With the help of the great god Zeus she brought them a flying ram, remarkable not only because of its aeronautical ability but also because it had a golden fleece. Nephele bade her children mount upon the ram and fly away to safety.

The ram soared off on the long flight from Greece to the shores of the Euxine Sea, now known as the Black Sea. But, as it flew above the strait now known as the Dardanelles, Helle lost her grip on the Golden Fleece and fell down into the water. For many centuries, the strait was known as the Hellespont in honour of Helle.

This accident made Phrixus lose confidence in the flying ram. He persuaded it to land and then walked with it overland to the grove of Ares, situated in Colchis in what is now southern Russia. Here, the ungrateful boy sheared the ram and gave the Golden Fleece to the King of Colchis, who hung it in a tree of the grove of Ares under the guard of a sleepless dragon. Phrixus then sacrificed the ram to Zeus, married one of the king's daughters, and apparently lived happily ever after.

In the meantime, Prince Jason had been growing up in exile. When he reached manhood he set out for Iolchus to claim his heritage. On the way to the city he lost one of his sandals while helping an old woman to cross a turbulent river, but she told him it was a sure sign of good fortune and he continued his journey with one foot unshod.

When he confronted Pelias, the wrongful king, he was surprised by the deference which Pelias showed towards him. He did not know that the Talking Oak of Dordona had forecast the king's defeat by a one-sandalled man. Pelias believed that Jason was the herald of destiny.

But Pelias was not prepared to surrender the throne without a struggle. He remained cool enough to debate Jason's claim, and during the discussion he said that he had, in any case, been thinking of leaving Iolchus. He said that one of the gods had come to him in a vision, and commanded him to fetch the Golden Fleece from the kingdom of Colchis. But he complained that he was too old for such an arduous task. He said that if only Jason would bring him the Golden Fleece, he would be glad to step down from the throne.

Jason was too proud to refuse a challenge, and then had to find a way to make the dangerous voyage to Colchis. Fortunately, the goddess Athene had seen him help the old woman (or she may even have been the old woman) and she inspired him to ask the Talking Oak for advice. Then, in the manner of deities, she spoke to him through the Talking Oak and advised him to tell Argus the shipbuilder to construct a fifty-oared galley. This was much larger than any vessel that Argus had built before then, but Athene inspired him with the knowledge of how to create such a mighty vessel.

Also she contributed an invaluable navigational aid to the *Argo*. When Argus and his men were working on the towering bows of the *Argo*, she advised Jason to cut a bough from the Talking Oak and fit it into the prow. The bough, like the tree itself, could talk to men with the voice of Athene, and thus advise Jason on the best route to follow and how to avoid the dangers of the voyage. It may be that Jason had the bow carved into the first-ever figurehead, in the likeness of Medusa the Gorgon.

The great ship took shape on the seashore amid the clamour of craftsmen's saws and hammers, while weavers made the fabric of the huge sail and ropers spun the ropes and cordage of the rigging. When Jason looked at the mighty hull, soon to be launched with the appropriate sacrifices to Poseidon, he wondered how he might find a crew adventurous enough for such a hazardous voyage.

Again the Talking Oak solved the problem. It told him to summon all the heroes of Greece, and enough would answer to make up the crew of the *Argo*.

Jason sent heralds far and wide, and soon the heroes arrived in Iolchus. They included Lynceus, whose eyes were sharp enough to see through a millstone and made him the ideal lookout; Tiphys, who became the navigator because he knew the positions of all the stars; Zetes and Calais, the two sons of Boreas the North Wind, who would be able to blow into the sails whenever the wind dropped; Hercules, the great warrior, who would be able to deal with any giant or monster encountered on the voyage; Orpheus, the musician, whose lyre could give new strength to the weariest oarsman; and the twins, Castor and Pollux, who loved nothing better than combat.

As a gesture to the heroines of Greece, Jason invited Atalanta the fleet-footed to sail in the *Argo*. He knew that her ability to skip lightly from one wave to another would prove useful on the voyage.

When the whole crew had assembled they named themselves the Argonauts, meaning 'Sailors of the *Argo*'. But when they set themselves to launch the ship, it seemed that their venture was over before it had begun. No matter how they all heaved and strained they could not slide the enormous vessel from the shore into the water. Even the strength of Hercules was not equal to the task, and they were looking despondently at the stationary ship when the figurehead spoke up and told Orpheus to play on his lyre. His magical music made the *Argo* slide into the water as easily as a serpent into a bowl of milk.

The splendid ship struck awe into the hearts of all other seamen as she sailed proudly eastwards, with the heroes of Greece plying the great oars that rose and fell as smoothly as swan's wings. The Argonauts had to fight or trick their way through many strange adventures, but at last they reached Colchis.

Here, King Aeetes refused to surrender the Golden Fleece until Jason had tamed two firebreathing bronze bulls, used them to plough a field, sown it with dragon's teeth, and conquered the resultant harvest of armed men. Luckily the king's daughter Medea, a noted sorceress, fell in love with Jason and showed him how to perform these tasks, but Aeetes still refused to give him the Golden Fleece. Jason decided to steal it, and Medea gave him a tranquilliser for the sleepless dragon. As soon as the dragon closed its eyes, Jason snatched the glittering

prize and ran with it to the *Argo*.

Medea and her brother Abstyrus went with him on the ship, urging him to hurry because their father was in close pursuit. The *Argo*'s fifty oarsmen strained at the great oars while Zetes and Calais blew into the sails, so that the great ship leapt through the waves as swiftly and smoothly as a dolphin, but King Aeetes was so furious at his loss that he made his pursuing ship travel even faster than the *Argo*. Medea solved this problem by cutting her brother's throat, chopping his body into small pieces, and dropping them overboard one by one, so that Aeetes had to check his oarsmen in order to pick up all the pieces.

The *Argo* soon left Aeetes far behind, and Jason took further evasive action by taking the ship home by the most roundabout route he could think of. He sailed the ship up and down rivers, across lakes, and across various seas and oceans. At one stage the Argonauts carried the *Argo* for fourteen days across the Libyan desert, with the aid of Medea's magic spells.

At last they took the Golden Fleece to Iolchus, but King Peleas still proved reluctant to step down from the throne. Medea got rid of him by persuading his daughters to cut him up and cook him, so that she might display her magical powers by restoring him to life. The daughters co-operated, but when they had stewed their father Medea claimed that she had forgotten the appropriate spells.

This plot proved ineffective because the son of Peleas took over the kingdom and expelled the Argonauts to Corinth, where they dragged the *Argo* into a sacred grove and set her up as a memorial to their adventures. Jason settled down with Medea as his mistress, but after ten years he arranged a marriage with Princess Creusa of Corinth. Medea pretended to be pleased and sent Creusa a magnificent gown as a wedding gown. When the delighted girl first dressed herself in the garment it burst into inextinguishable flames, cooked Creusa to a crisp, and consumed all the royal family and their palace. Medea then slaughtered all the children she had had by Jason, and flew off to Athens in a chariot drawn by winged serpents.

Jason, mourning his children, wandered into the grove where the hull of the great ship *Argo* still reposed. But her timbers had become dry and rotten, and when Jason lay down to rest in the shade of the overhanging poop it fell and killed him.

Bacabs

The four wind gods of the Mayan people of Central America. During the creation of the Cosmos out of Chaos they played an important part in establishing the final shape of the world, and they now prop up the four corners of heaven. (Or it may be supported by four differently coloured trees planted by the Bacabs.) The breath of the Bacabs creates the four winds from the four quarters of heaven. Their other duties include the supervision of the calendar, with each Bacab being responsible for one of the four seasons.

Bannik

The spirit of the bath house. In earlier days the bannik lived only in Russia and the Baltic countries, where the idea of sauna baths was conceived and brought to perfection. In more recent times the use of sauna baths has spread through much of the western world and the bannik has accompanied the spread of sauna technology. (Like all spirits, it is capable of being everywhere at once.)

The bannik flits amidst the dense steam of the sauna—and possibly that of any other type of bath which emits clouds of steam—and is very occasionally glimpsed through the vapour. It is, however, more likely to be felt than seen, when it touches the back of any person using the bath. The touch of the bannik upon one's naked back is very significant. A caressing stroke is an omen of good fortune, but if the bannik should scratch one's back it is a signal of some unpleasant occurrence.

Boat Blessing, Burial, Burning

The essential ceremonies related to the life and death of a boat and her master. Every boat is imbued with the spiritual powers of numerous objects, persons, and deities, and it is most important for all of these to be in harmony or the boat will never ride easily upon the waters. She embodies the spirits of all materials used in her construction, especially metal and timber; the spirits of all who build her; and the spirit of her master. All these must be reconciled with the local deities of the waters, ships, and boats, so that all work together for the essential purpose of the new-built craft. For example, a boat built on the shores of the southern Baltic should be dedicated to Autrimpas the local god of the sea and Bardoyats the god of ships.

The ceremony of blessing the boat is usually fairly simple, comprising ritual prayers together with the pouring of libations of ale or wine onto the boat and into the water. The launching of a war-boat or war-canoe may, however, require human sacrifices, even to sliding the great craft into the water over the bodies of living slaves.

A properly blessed boat will be lively, willing, and enduring. If the ceremonies are scamped or omitted, she will be sullen and balky—always fighting with the wind and waves instead of co-operating with them.

When the master of a boat dies, it is extremely unfortunate for another person to take command. The spirit of the dead master lives on in the boat and cannot rest until the boat has been taken from the uneasy waters. It is, therefore, advisable to use the boat as a coffin. It may be buried, with the dead master lying in it amidst appropriate tokens and talismans, or used as his floating funeral pyre. With sails set and the corpse lying on the thwarts, she is set afire and sent blazing out to sea, to vanish beneath the waves which were once her path of glory.

Boreas

The North Wind: son of Astareus the Titan and Eos the Dawn Maiden, who gave birth to all the winds. The brothers of Boreas are Eurus, Notus, and Zephyrus: the winds of the east, south, and west. All other winds are children of the four brothers.

Boreas and Zephyrus live in caves of the Rhipaei Mountains of northern Greece, and come rushing or raging forth whenever they tire of other occupations.

Boreas, like most other deities, has wide-ranging sexual proclivities. He has a family in the usual manner but he also enjoys beautiful young men.

Boreas also fell in love with a group of young mares, and changed himself into a stallion in order to mate with them. The offspring from this multiple union are the swift-footed breezes which run across fields of grain and riffle the surface of the waves.

Although Boreas is an uncomfortable companion when he swoops icily out of his mountain cave, he once saved the Greeks from military defeat. The Persian ruler Xerxes attacked Athens with a great invasion fleet, but Boreas came roaring to the rescue and drove all the ships out to sea.

Bunyips

Australian water monsters, also known as Kine Pratie, Wowee Wowee, Tunatabah, Dongus, and by many other names. The monsters are of different species in various parts of the continent. Some have flat faces like bulldogs and tails like fishes. Others have long necks and beaked heads like emus,

with flowing manes like the sea serpent's. Others again have some resemblance to humans, but with terrifying features and feet turned backwards. The difficulty of obtaining precise details about bunyips is easily explained. Most of those who see them never escape to tell the tale, and those who do escape are so incoherent with terror that they can only give garbled accounts of their experiences.

Despite the variations in species, the sound of a bunyip cry is the same in every part of Australia. It is a loud booming roar which reverberates over mangrove swamps, river flats, and the scrub or desert surrounding waterholes. It is heard very strongly during or after long periods of rain, but never during a drought. When bunyip dens dry up in drought seasons, the creatures hibernate by burrowing deep into the mud.

The most perturbing aspect of bunyip infestation, in a comparatively waterless continent, is that they inhabit rivers, billabongs, and other bodies of water, and may thus deny water to the Aborigines. There seems no doubt that bunyip diet consists mainly of Aborigines, especially women and children, although the occasional disappearance of white settlers in bunyip-haunted areas may show that they have developed a taste for European flesh.

The spread of settlement has depleted the number of bunyips, who cannot cope with irrigation schemes, hydro-electric works, water skiers, water pollution, sewerage works, and other disturbances of the water resources of Australia. They react by tipping over fishermen's boats, blocking irrigation pumps, and in other ways, but on the whole they are fighting a losing battle. The improvement of water supplies to Aboriginal communities is depriving bunyips of their natural food supply, and it seems likely that this interesting species will become extinct.

Cavern of the Seas

A huge watery cavern beneath the ocean: the final repository of all ships which vanish without trace. The actual location of the cavern is unknown, but it may move from one ocean to another. Probably the waterspouts which roam the surface of the sea indicate that the cavern lies somewhere beneath them. They may suck up water, and keep it suspended in air, to create the great hollow cavern beneath the surface.

Probably the cavern is connected in some manner with a lake on top of a mountain in Portugal. Many seamen believe that, some months after a ship had disappeared, she will surface again on the waters of the lake and sail there for a little while. If investigators are on the shore of the lake at the appropriate time, the ship's crew will answer their questions and thus solve the mystery of the ship's disappearance. After this brief resurrection, the ship sinks again and possibly returns to the Cavern of the Seas.

Charon

The bad-tempered old ferryman who transports the ghosts of the dead across the River Acheron (or, as some say, the River Styx) on their way into the Underworld. There is some uncertainty as to whether he actually rows the ferryboat, or whether he simply keeps the queues of ghosts in order and takes the fares. It may be that he is bad-tempered because of the endless work of rowing (or poling) the ferry to and fro across the dark waters of the river, or perhaps he is irritated by the jostling crowds of ghosts. He has no mercy on ghosts who try to board the ferry without paying the fare, and drives them away to join all the others who wail eternally at their fate. The ferry fare is one vail or obolus, which relatives of a deceased person must place beneath the tongue so that he or she will be able to pay the ferryman.

Crocodile Gods

Saltwater and freshwater crocodiles (*Crocodylus porosus*, *niloticus*, *cataphractus*, etc.) are usually deities of one kind or another or even the ancestors of certain tribes. In Madagascar, the ancestral chiefs of the Makao and Masombiky tribes live in the bodies of crocodiles and act as intermediaries between gods and mortals, so that any request to the gods must be passed on through the crocodiles. And, at regular intervals, the tribespeople strike a bargain with the crocodiles. They promise not to eat them, on condition that the crocodiles shall not eat any humans.

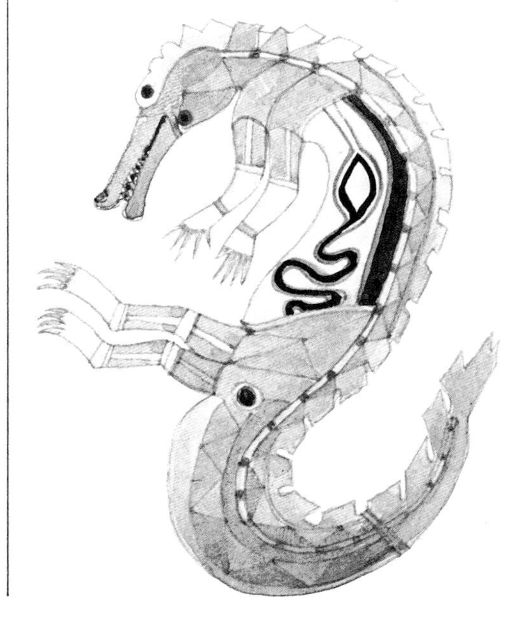

Some other races follow a similar custom, and make sure that the bargain is strictly enforced. If a crocodile does eat a human, then one of its relations must be killed and eaten to warn the whole crocodile tribe that they must stand by the arrangements. By the same token, it is unwise to kill a crocodile without reasonable cause, because its relations will certainly seek revenge.

In some places, crocodiles have been promoted into important gods. Sebek of Egypt is related to the creation gods Neith and Geb, and also to the huge serpent Maka who tries to destroy the sun when it travels underground each evening. Sebek is, however, generally friendly to mankind. He and all his family, who swim in the lifegiving waters of the Nile and lay their eggs on its banks, are deities of water and fertility. In ancient times the city of Crocodilopolis was dedicated to their worship, and the sacred crocodile who lived in a temple pool was richly decorated with jewelled ornaments.

Further to the south, the creation ancestor Nyikang married a crocodile who is now the goddess of birth and babies among the Shilluk people, who live in the swamplands of the upper Nile.

Davy Jones' Locker

Davy Jones was a hardtack, salt horse, sailing ship seaman; a boatswain (or so he claimed) or maybe he was no more than a bo'sun's mate. Nobody can ever pin him down about his origins, like most old seamen he is full of yarns and the one he spins today may be different from yesterday's.

Sometimes he reckoned he sailed in the Phoenician galleys, settled in Cornwall, and took the name of Jones when he married a Welsh woman and shipped out of Cardiff. Now and again, when he's had an extra·

glass or two of grog, he claims he was a seacook in King Alfred's navy, and that he was the one who really burnt the cakes. But he has also said that he was bo'sun of the *Mary Rose*, that he helped Sir Francis Drake to find his way around the world, and that he helped to carry Nelson down to the cockpit of the *Victory*.

Many people believe he was a pirate, and that for some horrid exploit the devil condemned him to live forever in the bottom of the deep blue sea. That's where he keeps his great bo'sun's locker, or possibly sea chest, and stows it with everything that sinks into the deep. Wrecked ships and dead seamen all find their way into his locker and he never lets them go again. Being a deep-sea sailorman he never worries about ships that sink in shallow water, and that's why treasure can be salvaged from the shallows but never from the great ocean deeps.

Deluge, The

The histories of many peoples tell of the time when they were all swept away by a great deluge, and only a few men and women survived to start all over again. This enormous flood afflicted the world at some time after it had been created out of Chaos. When it had taken shape, there was a lengthy period in which gods, giants, demons and monsters all battled for supremacy, with mankind living precariously on the fringes of the cosmic combat. The gods and demons invented such weapons as the thunder and lightning, and some nations were colonised by strange monsters who became the ancestors of the present inhabitants.

After centuries of this global warfare, the world was in such a disastrous condition that the only solution was a clean sweep and a fresh start. Most of the humans were possessed by demons and worshipped monstrous deities, and a few righteous men prayed that the true gods should punish the unbelievers.

The response was a miraculous flood, to cleanse the world of its torments and allow a few survivors to try again. The flood had many different causes. Iceland was deluged with the blood of one of the fighting giants. The great god Zeus swamped Greece with water from the heavens, drowning everyone but Deucalion and his wife Pyrrha, who floated for nine days in a chest until it grounded on Mount Parnassus. In Babylon, the god Ea warned the worthy man Utnapishtim that the gods were going to punish the Babylonians with a flood, and Utnapishtim built a great boat which he loaded with animals, treasure, and craftsmen—including a sailor to navigate the boat. Manu, an Indian, received a similar warning from the god Prajapati, who appeared to him as a talking fish. Manu built a boat and used a serpent as a rope, so that he was able to moor the boat to the summit of Mount Himalaya when the waters covered the whole of India.

The Hebrew god Jehovah issued the flood warning to Noah and his family, who built a great vessel of gopher wood caulked with bitumen, loaded it with male and female animals, and survived for a year until the waters subsided.

In other parts of the world, from Africa to the Pacific islands and the Americas, a great variety of deities and other supernatural beings engineered the deluge. In every instance they spared a very few selected creatures, who had the opportunity of starting again.

Regrettably, a number of the demons and evil spirits were so cunning that they managed to stow away aboard the various ships and boats. When the waters subsided they soon learned how to flourish again and they lost no time in repossessing the hearts of mankind. When the gods again lose patience with men and all their works, they will no doubt send another cataclysm to sweep them from the face of the earth.

Dragons

Monstrous airborne members of the reptile kingdom, classified as serpents (the name derives from the Greek *draca* = serpent) and divided into four orders and numerous families, species, and sub-species.

The four orders of dragon are the European (*Draconis teutonica*), found throughout northern Germany, in Scandinavia, and in numerous islands of the North Atlantic; the Occidental (*D. gallii*) of France, Italy, and Spain; the British (*D. albionensis*) of which the main species is commonly known as the Firedrake and the two principal sub-species are the two-legged Wyvern (*D. bipedes*) and the winged but legless Worm (*D. nematoda*); the Mediterranean or Levantine (*D. cappadociae*) of Greece, Asia Minor, southern Russia, and north Africa; and the Oriental (*D. sinoensis*) of Asia and Indonesia.

A few species of *draconis* have been reported from other parts of the world but they have never been seen in North America, Australia, the Pacific islands, or tropical and southern Africa.

The Greek word *draca* is related to words implying keen vision, which is the common characteristic of every species of dragon. They are all sharpsighted, cunning, shrewd, and wise, but apart from these qualities there are many differences between the various orders, families, and species. Some have more than one head (*D. ladonii* has 100 heads); a sub-species of the Mediterranean dragon never sleeps; the Wyvern and Worm differ from all other dragons which are quadrupeds.

The vast majority are able to fly, although they do not always employ this ability. All except the Oriental dragons propel themselves by membraneous wings, and use a vertical take-off and landing technique. Oriental dragons are distinguished from all other species by their lack of wings, horselike heads, and sharp horns. They fly by a specific mode of balancing between the earth's magnetic field and the prevailing winds.

Most dragons have inflammatory glands, which permit the nasal emission of fire. Usually, dragons employ firebreathing only as a warning or defence mechanism. A burst of fire is normally sufficient to warn off marauders, and it may be that the inflammatory glands contain only enough fire for short spurts before they replenish themselves. There are, however, numerous instances of infuriated dragons punishing a community by burning up all its crops and houses.

It is strange that alchemists, sorcerers, and other magicologists have not carried out more research into dragons (perhaps because of the difficulty of obtaining undamaged specimens). The bodies of these creatures provide potent supernatural resources. Anyone who eats a dragon's heart will be able to understand the language of birds; a meal of dragon's tongue enables the consumer to win any argument; and dragon's blood is a certain prophylactic against stab wounds. The blood of the dragon Fafnir gave the German hero Siegfried immunity from such wounds, but when he bathed in the dragon's blood he failed to notice that a leaf had stuck to his back. This unprotected spot allowed his enemy Hagen to stab him to death.

Before the advent of Christianity, the dragons of the western world lived in an uneasy co-existence with mankind. Their physical powers, awesome appearance, keen vision, and alert shrewdness of intellect made them the ideal guardians of all kinds of treasure, including the Golden Fleece and the Golden Apples of the Hesperides, and they were commonly employed for this purpose. No doubt a special class of wizards and sorcerers had the ability to persuade dragons to act as sentinels. Dragons, like other reptiles, always stay close to their own territory (dragonhaunts); they eat rarely and are content with the occasional ox, sheep, or human; and they mate only once or twice a century. Consequently a dragon which had taken guard over a treasure was almost always at its post, either curled up at the entrance to the hoard or flying above it to keep watch for marauders.

A dragon did not normally pester humans, apart from the occasional snack, but when thieves made an attempt on the treasure then a dragon's wrath was terrible indeed.

A notable example of *drachenstahl* (stealing treasure from a dragon) occurred in Geatasland, South Sweden, in about 512 AD. Some centuries earlier, a Geata king

had been buried in the usual style, surrounded by all his treasure inside a great hollow mound or barrow, and a dragon had been placed on guard. For several hundred years the dragon lived in peace with the Geatas, emerging only at long intervals to eat a bullock or pig. On one of these occasions, a runaway slave entered the barrow and stole some of the treasure.

The dragon was so furious that it ravaged Geatasland, burning orchards, farmhouses, and even the royal palace, and eating most of the livestock. The hero Beowulf was then the king of Geatasland, but he had reigned for fifty years and was a very old man. Nevertheless he girded himself to face the dragon's teeth and claws, and with his henchman Wiglaf he tracked it back to the barrow. When they approached, the dragon rushed out at them with terrible roars and jets of flame. They dodged its first rush and attacked it with their swords, hacking again and again at the tough hide until at last the dragon died from its countless wounds. But Beowulf also was mortally wounded by a slash from one of the great claws, and when he died he was buried with the dragon's treasure.

The prevalence of dragons in the western world is indicated by such place names as Drakelow (which means 'dragon's barrow'), Drakeford, and Dragon's Hill in England; Drachenfels and Drakensberg ('dragon's mountains') in Germany; and Dracha, Dragashani, Draga, and Draconis in south-eastern Europe. There is a strong likelihood that Vlad Drakul (Count Dracula) was in some manner related to a dragon.

The day of the dragon ended during the first few centuries of Christianity, when wandering prophets and missionaries chose to represent these comparatively harmless and useful creatures as emissaries of the devil. They had little difficulty in convincing superstitious knights, yeomen, and peasants that the firebreathing monsters, with their scaled bodies and fearsome claws and teeth, were incarnations of sin and must therefore be destroyed. Unfortunately, a certain number of sorcerers reinforced this belief, by using dragons to guard virgins stolen from the community or to protect themselves against investigation.

Good Christian knights, eager to prove their faith and chivalry, quickly discovered that dragon-hunting was a profitable venture. A young knight could establish his reputation and set himself up for life by killing a dragon and taking its treasure. At the very least, he might ride away from the combat with a beautiful virgin perched on his saddlebow. Improved armour for knights and their chargers, mailed gauntlets, lances up to 4 metres long, and even swords with supernatural strength, took a lot of the danger out of dragon-hunting and the creatures quickly became a rare and endangered species. Many of the noble houses of Europe were founded on the hoards of treasure stolen from dragons. Probably it was at this time that fairy communities moved into the grave mounds and hollow hills of Britain, once occupied by dragons and their treasures.

A British or European dragon is now a highly unusual sight, and the merest hint of a dragonflight is enough to attract mobs of dragonwatchers. Fortunately, the same situation does not prevail in the Orient, where dragons have never been subjected to the remorseless hunting practised in the western world.

Oriental dragons are totally unlike those of other regions. Instead of acting as mere treasure-guards they involve themselves with all manner of human and cosmic affairs. The largest family of Oriental dragons lives in China, and comprises innumerable species ranging in size from a few metres long up to the Great Chien-Tang, who stretches 300 metres from nose to tail. Most of them are of an extrovert nature and they frequently intervene, for good or ill, in the fortunes of mankind.

Chinese dragons are intimately connected with the elements of water and air. Separate Dragon Kings rule the oceans of north, south, east, and west, and each of the great rivers of China. Great Chien-Tang, who is bright red in colour with a mane of fire and eyes that flash like lightning, is commander of all the river dragons. All the dragons of seas and rivers have very uncertain tempers: sometimes placid, sometimes restless, and occasionally raging and destructive. Their mid-air mating, which occurs far more frequently than that of western dragons, results in great storms and downpours of rain.

The Lord of all Dragons is Celestial Lung, who lives in the sky during spring and summer and in the ocean during autumn and winter. Lung has a snake's tail, a horse's head, five claws on each foot instead of the four possessed by other dragons, and, unlike the majority of Oriental dragons, a pair of membraneous wings.

Lung supervises the fertility of the land and all its creatures, and extends this basic responsibility into a generally benign influence upon the affairs of the Central Kingdom. He has numerous relations, each of whom controls some branch of human activities such as music, literature, military ardour, bridge building, litigation, the strength of buildings and the temptations of danger.

The power of an Oriental dragon is not necessarily reflected by its size. Fei Lin, the potent dragon who controls the winds, is not even as large as a tiger.

Apart from the principal dragons there are many less powerful creatures. On the whole they are helpful and beneficial, although dragon temperaments are extremely sensitive and they must always be treated with great respect. The dragon history of China describes many evilly disposed dragons, but it would appear that most of these have been eliminated by gods, heroes, or magicians.

The appearance of a dragon in the sky may usually be regarded as an omen of good fortune, unless its actions demonstrate otherwise. Dragonwatchers may predict the future of any community by studying the quarter of the sky in which a dragon appears, its attitudes and behaviour, and any significant actions such as roaring or fire-breathing.

Ebb Tide

The ocean tides, controlled by silent Selene the amorous moon, have a great effect upon the affairs of men. It is wise to initiate new ventures when the tide is at its flood, because the ebb tide drains the strength from men and as the waters sink they draw the spirit out of the body.

People who live by the sea are well aware of the powers of ebb tide. When anyone is critically ill, they wait anxiously for the turn of the tide because his soul is likely to depart with the ebbing waters. Nor is it wise to sow any seed or plant any tree while the ebb tide is flowing, because the vital essence of the plants runs out with the tide. By the same token, a man who hopes for strong children should lie with his wife only when the flood tide is surging inwards, full of life and vitality.

Eos

Also known as Aurora, the Maiden of the Dawn, who with rosy fingers draws aside the dark curtain of night. Eternally young and beautiful, she awakens both gods and men to overwhelming desire.

Originally she devoted her attentions to the gods of Olympus, but her delicious beauty created many emotional problems. When Ares the god of war fell in love with her, his jealous mistress Venus Aphrodite cursed Eos with desire for men as well as gods.

She had already given birth to the four winds and some of the stars, and by her first human husband, Tithonus, she became the mother of Memnon, King of Ethiopia and one of the gods of Egypt. She loved Memnon best of all her children, and has never ceased to mourn his death at the hands of Achilles. She weeps for him each morning and her tears form the morning dew, but she sets her sorrow aside and performs the happy task of bringing light and love to mankind.

Tithonus the mortal was her favourite husband. She asked the great god Zeus to make him immortal but forgot to ask for the gift of eternal youth, so that her potent young lover slowly became a withered old man, and eventually shrank so small that she had to keep him in a bottle for fear of the rats. After some centuries the gods had pity on Tithonus and changed him into a cicada, the little flying beetle which chirps homage to the sun.

Figureheads

Images carved, painted, or moulded in the bows of a ship, to aid in navigation and/or to endow the vessel with the powers which they represent.

Probably the original figurehead was the bough which Jason cut from the Talking Oak of Dodona and set in the prow of his ship *Argo*. Some accounts claim that he had the oak bough carved into the likeness of Medusa, but it seems unlikely that he would have chosen such an unlucky symbol. And, since the bough could already talk, offer advice on shiphandling and warn against supernatural dangers, there would seem to be little point in carving it into an arbitrary shape.

Other seafarers followed Jason's example, but few if any had the advantage of a talking figurehead. They had to content themselves with such figures as Atalanta the fleet-footed, Lynceus the sharp-eyed, Ares the warrior or Hermes the god of merchants, and hope that the relevant deity would assist their vessel in navigation, trade, and sea warfare. Pecunious ship-owners simply had eyes painted on the bows, a practice still followed by the Chinese. Obviously a pair of eyes helps a ship to see her way through fog or darkness. The Phoenicians carved horses' heads on the prows of their ships, to help them to ride swiftly over the waves.

When the Vikings began their long domination of the northern oceans, their victims were terrified by the 'dragon ships' whose sharp prows were surmounted by the carved heads of dragons. But the dragons were there only to endow the ships with the cunning, keen vision, and shrewdness of the dragon family. They were navigational aids rather than symbols of ferocity.

The great explorers and sea warriors of Polynesia and Melanesia were well aware of the value of figureheads. A canoe prow carved with the likeness of a tribal ancestor, a sea god or sea monster, was of great value in sea combat and navigation.

Floating Islands

Historically, the best-known floating islands are the Symplegades, although there is some disagreement as to whether they were actually islands or merely free-moving rocks.

Jason and the Argonauts had to pass between the Symplegades on their passage through the Hellespont (now the Dardanelles) on their way to capture the Golden Fleece. The great mobile rocks (or islands) were a supreme danger to navigation because they sensed the approach of any vessel, poised themselves, and crashed together as the ship passed between them.

Jason's ship *Argo* would certainly have suffered the usual fate but for the kindly actions of some of his crew. When the *Argo* reached Thrace, the Argonauts found that King Phineus of Thrace had been stricken with blindness and was tormented by three harpies, who either snatched away his food whenever he tried to eat or fouled it with their excrement. Phineus explained that the gods had punished him because he had imprisoned his sons, on the strength of a charge laid by their stepmother Idaea. Zetes and Calais, the sons of Boreas the North Wind who had sailed with the Argonauts, pursued the harpies and threatened them with death if they did not leave Phineus alone, while other Argonauts discovered that Idaea had laid false charges and persuaded Phineus to release his sons.

The gods restored sight to Phineus, and he was so grateful to the Argonauts that he advised them on the way to avoid the Symplegades. In due course, Jason steered the *Argo* cautiously towards the huge rocks, bidding the oarsmen to row in the slowest possible time until the Symplegades sensed the approach of the ship. Then, when he saw them tremble into motion, he released a pigeon which flew between them. The pigeon's flight tricked the Symplegades into thinking that a ship was risking the deadly passage, and they surged towards each other with a great roar of displaced water. But the pigeon soared to safety, the Symplegades paused as though in puzzlement, and then moved slowly back into their usual position.

As soon as Jason saw them begin their recoil, he roared to the oarsmen to strike with all their strength, while Zetes and Calais blew furiously into the *Argo*'s sail. The great ship leapt forward, oars churning the water and the sail bellying taut before the wind, and almost escaped the Symplegades before they sensed they had been tricked and slammed together with explosive speed.

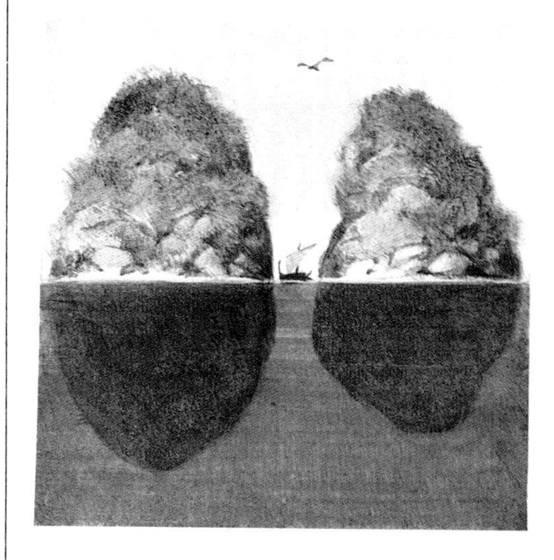

The great rock faces crashed thunderously together, just grazing the *Argo*'s stern and showering her poop deck with splinters and fragments of stone, then recoiled sullenly and rumbled back to their positions on each side of the passage. From that day onwards it seemed that the Symplegades had lost their power, because they never again attempted to smash a ship between them.

Other floating islands have been reported from different parts of the world, but their nature is totally different from that of the Symplegades. They are dreamy and pleasant places, which drift from one hemisphere to another in slow pursuit of the sun and thus enjoy perpetual summer.

The Tir n'an Og, the Land of Youth, is a floating island which occasionally appears off the coast of Ireland. When it appears, the person who swims out to it may be assured of eternal youth. Unfortunately it does not follow any particular schedule, and many a man or woman has waited a lifetime without having a chance to land on Tir n'an Og.

Flying Dutchman, The

A Dutch shipmaster of the seventeenth century, named Vanderdecken or Van Falkenberg, who was becalmed for so long on a voyage to the Indies that he swore he would sell his soul to the devil for a wind. The devil accepted the bargain, and ever since the Dutchman has sailed unceasingly before the devil's wind.

Sightings of the Flying Dutchman have been recorded on numerous occasions during the last 400 years. They usually occur south of the Cape of Good Hope, especially when those huge areas of sea have been flogged into storms by westerly gales.

Sightings occur during poor visibility, when lookouts have to strain their eyes against blizzards of spray and sleet and the winds lash ragged clouds across the tumbling sea. All at once a man aloft will hail the deck and point wildly ahead, and all hands see a storm-driven ship pass so closely across the bows that a collision seems inevitable.

The ship has all sails set even in the wildest weather. Spray bursts over her as she thrusts into the waves, almost obscuring the hull and rigging so that watchers will argue later about her type and nationality. The colours of the tattered ensign are indiscernible: the waves rise so high that the labouring hull vanishes between them, rises again, and then disappears into the storm. The watchers seem to hear a single despairing hail, but they are never certain whether it was a cry for help or the wind shrieking in their own rigging.

Foam-of-the-Ocean

One of two sacred stones brought to earth by the Polynesian god Tane, the other being White-Sea-Mist. The creation ancestor Ta'aroa made Tane the ruler of the tenth and highest heaven, then used him to help in the creation of the earth. Tane performed countless tasks of creativity, and eventually brought all the wisdom of the heavens down to earth in three baskets, to be shared among mankind. Foam-of-the-Ocean and White-Sea-Mist were among the artefacts imbued with this wisdom. When a Maori student has absorbed instruction in various branches of Tane's special knowledge, he graduates by standing on replicas of the two stones so that their *mana*, or spiritual power, may flow into him.

Frogs

This great family of amphibians, which is represented in most parts of the world, contains members of widely varying characteristics. Many are bombastic and vainglorious, given to loud boasting and repetitive arguments, so that the parliament of the frogs rivals any human forum in its output of noise without wisdom. Some frogs are interfering and troublesome creatures, like the West African frog who heard men send a dog on an errand to God, to tell Him that mankind would like to be reborn after death. The frog decided that this was a bad idea, and hopped off on his own account to advise God that men preferred not to have eternal life. Unfortunately the dog stopped for a meal, so that the frog was first to reach heaven on his self-appointed mission.

But some frogs are helpful and benevolent towards mankind. Heket, the Egyptian frog goddess, wife of Khnum who made men and women out of clay, breathed life and spirit into Khnum's creations. The Ching-wa Shen, the frog spirits of China, like to see humans enjoy prosperity and are highly regarded by businessmen. In Australia, where frogs survive long periods of drought by burrowing deep into the mud, they eventually emerge to spout up the water they have stored in their bellies so that it may fall as rain.

One species of Australian frog, the *Litoria caerulea* or green tree frog, enjoys an interesting relationship with the rainforest gnomes of northern Queensland. They apply a special linctus to the frog's tonsils, to prevent croak infection in the humid conditions of its tropical habitat.

Frog communities are democratic but sexist. Only the males, who croak the loudest, are allowed to speak in frog parliaments. These are poorly conducted gatherings in which debate is often drowned by the cry of *brekk-kek-kek-co-ax-co-ax* from members clamouring to be heard. At one time the frog parliament petitioned the great god Zeus to send them a king, but after he sent them first a log, which did nothing, and then a stork which gobbled them up, they voted to return to democratic rule.

Ghost Ship of Loch Awe

A ghost ship of the North Atlantic, which appears in the form of a passenger liner of first World War vintage. There does not seem to be any reason why the ship should be attributed to Loch Awe, which is near Oban on the west coast of Scotland. Probably the loch has never received any ship larger than a coastal cargo vessel.

The ship is seen in northern waters from Scotland to Iceland, but usually within a day's sailing of some rugged coast. She appears only in calm but foggy weather, when the great Atlantic swells roll placidly beneath the dense clouds of vapour. The lookouts on some lonely ship, straining their eyes to see through the fog, are astounded by the sudden silent appearance of a passenger liner with portholes and deck lights blazing and coal smoke pouring from her funnels. She passes so close that one may see the officers on the bridge and passengers strolling on the decks, with the women clad in the feathered hats and long skirts of the early 1900s.

The liner passes at a speed of about twenty knots, and quickly vanishes into the fog astern. It takes a few moments for the lookouts to realise she has passed in utter silence, with none of the sounds of a seething bow wave, threshing screws, and thumping engines one would normally hear from a ship so near at hand.

Catastrophe follows within twenty-four hours of a sighting: a collision at sea, the accidental death of a crew member, or some other disaster.

Even though the apparition is known to seamen as the Ghost Ship of Lock Awe, she has never been identified as the likeness of any known vessel. She does not resemble any passenger liner of her era which was lost at sea.

Grendel

The monster of a Danish lake. Grendel plagued the King of Denmark by assuming human form, forcing a way into the palace each night, and killing some of the king's people. Eventually the monster forced the king to abandon the palace, which remained empty for twelve years until the Swedish hero Beowulf heard about Grendel. The king was glad to accept an offer of monster extermination, and Beowulf sailed for Den-

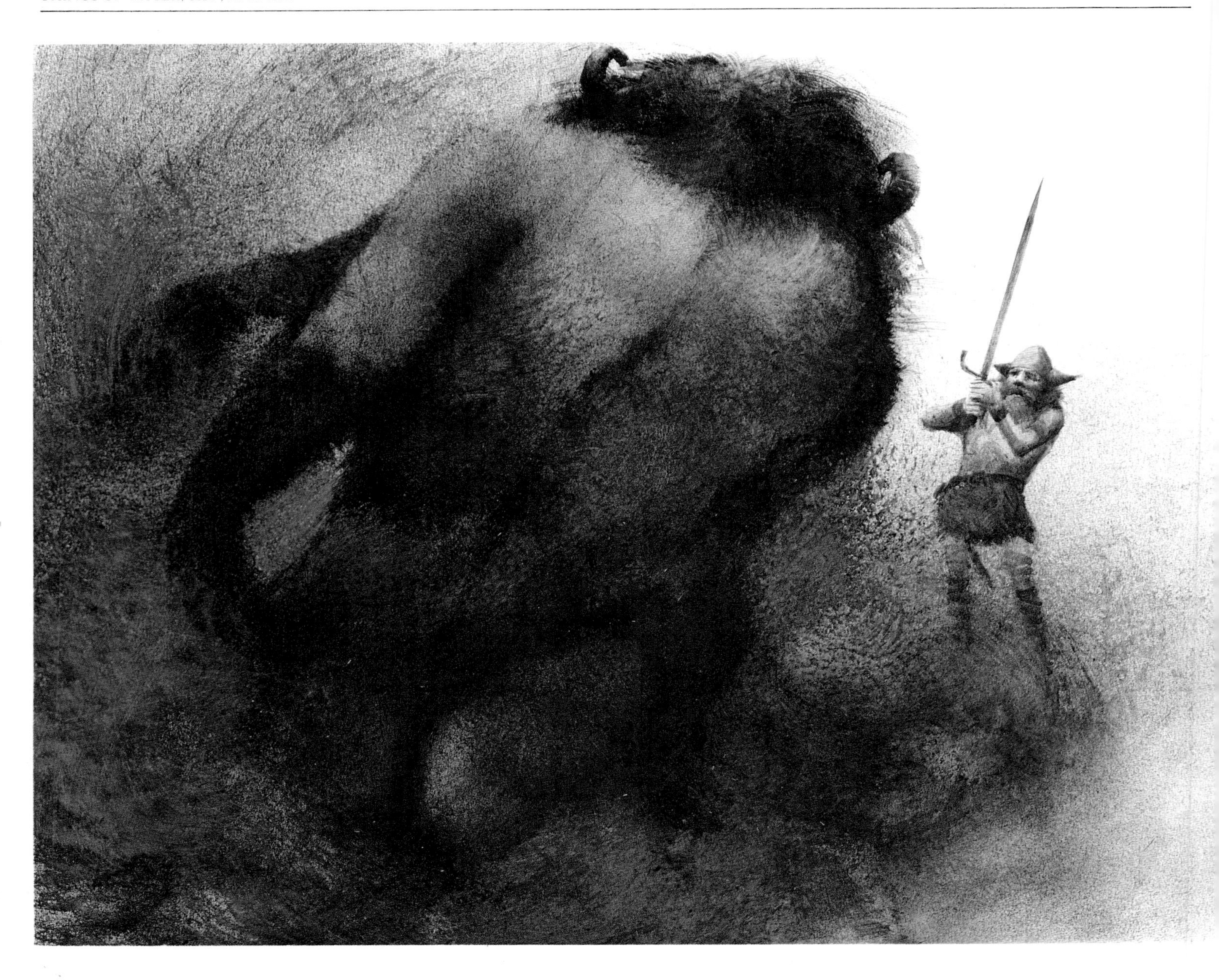

mark with fourteen companions.

They took up residence in the deserted palace, where the king treated them to a feast but hurried away at nightfall. Beowulf kept watch while his companions slept, but the night was so quiet that he had begun to doze off when the monster crashed through the great barred doors of the palace.

Wet and slimy from the lake, and snarling in anticipation of fresh victims, it charged towards the sleeping men. Beowulf leapt to attack it without even taking time to snatch up his weapons, and in a furious struggle he tore off the monster's right arm. Grendel left its bleeding arm in Beowulf's grasp and escaped through the shattered door, with the Swedes in hot pursuit until the blood-stained trail ended on the shores of the lake.

They felt certain the monster would not return, and with great rejoicing the king and his nobles returned to the palace. But on the following night Grendel's mother smashed a way into the palace to seek revenge. She was even more terrible than her son and she killed and carried off one of the Danes, with Beowulf close on her trail.

When she plunged into the lake he dived after her, and found himself in a great vaulted chamber under the water. Grendel's mother attacked him savagely, but he was now armed with his sword and after a bloody duel he ran her through.

The corpse of Grendel lay in the under-water chamber, and Beowulf made doubly sure that the monster would not trouble the king again by cutting off the head and bearing it triumphantly to the palace.

Griffins

Also known as griffons or gryphons. These creatures are the offspring of eagles and lions, and so have the bodies of lions and the heads and wings of eagles, with pointed ears like those of a dog. A griffin has the hind-quarters of a lion, but its forelegs resemble the legs and talons of an eagle. Feathers grow upon its wings, head, and chest, and tawny leonine fur upon the rest of its body. Usually a griffin is eight times larger than a lion and it is stronger than a hundred eagles. Some observers believe griffins to have serpent's tails, but it seems more likely that these caudal appendages are the normal tufted tail of a lion.

Griffin coloration varies considerably between different species. Sometimes they are rather drab, with tawny lion bodies and brown eagle feathers, but the bodies may be pure white, golden, or cream flecked with scarlet. The head and wing feathers may be blue or green and the breast feathers vermilion, while the eagle-like beak and legs may range from horny yellow to brilliant gold. The talons are usually black.

Griffins perform two invaluable functions. One is to draw the chariots of the Sun God and some other gods, such as Jupiter and Nemesis. It is probable that those who draw the chariot of Nemesis, the goddess of certain retribution, differ from all other griffins in having black bodies and feathers.

Their other function is to punish humans for their love of riches. Griffins originated in the desert areas of Turkey, Armenia, Syria, and Iraq, in the days when these regions were lavishly strewn with precious stones. These jewels acted as bait for greedy

humans, who risked their lives for the glittering harvest. A few survived, but most were sighted by griffins patrolling the hot blue skies. The end was inevitable when a griffin pounced and tore the prospector to pieces with teeth and claws.

Over many centuries, enough humans have evaded the griffins to strip the deserts of their bounty. But griffins are still active and they have extended their sphere of operations, so that any man who is too much in love with riches is in danger of being torn apart by griffins.

Griffins hate horses, perhaps because they see them as competitors in chariot-drawing, and are likely to prey on these animals as well as other livestock. A griffin is strong enough to carry off a good-sized horse.

Halcyon, Halcyone, Alcyone

The daughter of Aeolus, Lord of the Winds. She married Ceyx, the son of Atlas. The young couple made such a handsome pair and were so happy together that, in the careless pride of their youth, they likened themselves to the great god Zeus and his wife Hera.

The gods could not forgive such impiety, but there is some uncertainty as to the method of punishment chosen by Zeus. Some say he changed Halcyon and Ceyx into seabirds: others that he caused Ceyx to be drowned in a shipwreck, so that Halcyon's grief made her cast herself into the sea.

Thetis, a kindly sea goddess, then changed the lovers into waterbirds so beautiful that they appeared to be made from jewels. They have glistening blue-green backs and chestnut breasts, and long beaks to fish their food from the waters. When they mated they built a floating nest, and Thetis caused the sea to remain calm during the seven Halcyon Days so that the eggs might be hatched safely.

But as time passed by the descendants of Halcyon took to living on riverbanks instead of by the sea, and spread throughout many parts of the world. They and their relations now have various names such as kingfishers in Britain and America and kookaburras in Australia.

Harpies

Huge predatory birds with the faces of women and the talons of eagles, used by the gods to punish or torment humans. Their name derives from the Greek *harpyiai*, meaning 'snatchers', which indicates their practice of swooping upon a victim and snatching him or her away. In one such exploit they snatched the daughters of Pandareus, who had stolen a golden dog from Olympus, and carried them off to be servants in hell.

Apparently there are two types of harpy. One consists of wind spirits, with such names as Swiftfoot, Stormwind, and Swiftwing. They are ruthless personifications of the wind, but not nearly so unpleasant as the other type. These, with such names as Dark, are violently antagonistic to humans.

The harsh semi-human screams of a harpy as it swoops upon its prey, the thunder of its wings and the foul stench of its unpreened feathers, are signals that it is executing a sentence of the gods from which there is no escape.

Hippopotamus Goddess

The hippopotamus or river horse (Greek *hippo* = horse *potamus* = river) is a huge lumbering creature weighing as much as four tonnes. Despite its size and strength it is a benign personality, generally harmless to mankind unless it is hunted for its flesh or tormented when it emerges from the river to browse on a villager's crops.

The hippopotamus people inhabit most large rivers of Africa, and perhaps because of their portliness they are widely revered as good omens for pregnancy and fecundity. The hippopotamus goddess Taueret is an Egyptian deity of childbirth and maternity, especially benevolent towards women suckling infants.

Her husband, Bes, is a grotesque dwarf with a kindly, helpful nature. He presides over childbirth, protects families against venomous insects and reptiles, and takes a special interest in beauty culture.

Iris

The Nymph of the Rainbow, who is related to air, sea, earth, and sky. She is the daughter of the ocean nymph Electra, and granddaughter of Pontus the sea god and Gaea the earth mother. Zephyrus the West Wind is either her husband or her lover.

Iris is a beautiful young woman with golden wings and winged sandals. Her family connections make her equally at home in or under the earth and water or in the boundless sky. Consequently, she is the ideal messenger for the great god Zeus and his wife Hera, who employ her to carry messages to gods and men.

When Iris has a message for one of the gods, she speeds on the errand on her golden wings. If the addressee is a sea god she plunges into the depths: if the message is for Hades or one of his staff, she darts fearlessly through the gloomy caverns of the Underworld.

But if Zeus or Hera have a message for mortal men or women, Iris runs with it down the rainbow bridge between earth and heaven and her winged sandals carry her swiftly to her destination.

Jonah

The person aboard a ship who attracts bad weather or other misfortunes. When he or she has been disposed of, the ship and crew enjoy fair winds and a prosperous voyage.

The original Jonah was a prophet who tried to evade his responsibilities by taking ship from Joppa to Tarshish. On the voyage, the ship encountered such a fearful storm that the crew were terrified and cast lots to discover who was to blame. The lot fell upon Jonah, who admitted he had offended God by running away and told the sailors to cast him overboard. As soon as he splashed into the raging ocean (where he was swallowed by a sea monster) the wind dropped and the waves became smooth.

Countless generations of seafarers have learned an important lesson from this experience. One should not take an unlucky person or object aboard ship. But, if he or it has found a way aboard, then one should take the necessary steps without delay.

In the opinion of seamen, all passengers are Jonahs because they may be as irresponsible as the well-known prophet. Clergymen are certainly unlucky, because they are in direct line of descent from the prophet Jonah. Corpses should not be carried under any circumstances, and if a crew member dies he should be committed to the deep before the end of the day. Members of the female gender are likely to attract misfortune and it is safer to leave them ashore. The people of certain races, especially Finns who are notorious wind wizards, should not be signed on as crewpersons. Hens may be carried aboard ship but not cockerels, whose crowing will attract contrary winds.

Unfortunately it is not always easy to identify a Jonah. A shipmaster may take every precaution not to accept one in his crew, and then discover that a crewman—perhaps quite unconsciously—carries the affliction. The presence of a Jonah is made obvious by prolonged bad weather or repetitive misfortune, but it may be difficult to identify the culprit. It is then that men begin to mistrust each other and the stage is set for a conclusive disaster.

Juturna

The goddess of pools and still waters. Originally she was a princess of Rutilia, a kingdom of Italy in the days when the Trojans invaded that country. Juturna tried to help in the war against the Trojans, but when her brother was killed she sank weeping into a spring near the battlefield.

The great god Zeus immediately turned her into a water nymph, and then appointed her goddess of still waters. All persons concerned with waterworks, swimming pools, ornamental fountains, and similar water usage should pay homage to Juturna on 11 January each year.

Kappa

A demon dwarf of Japanese waters, resembling a grotesque little naked man with a tortoiseshell on his back and clawed webbed fingers and toes. He has a greenish skin, round eyes, a beaked nose, and smells strongly of rotten fish. On the crown of his head there is a circular depression filled with water.

The kappa's ancestors are the ghosts of people drowned in Japanese rivers, but this semi-human connection does not endow him with pity for living mortals. He lies in wait for people and other animals straying close to the water's edge, drags them into the water, and consumes them from the inside out.

There are, however, two ways to avoid the clutches of a kappa. One is to watch the water carefully for his appearance, and to give him a polite bow when he surfaces. He will return the bow, the water will pour out of the depression in his head, and he is powerless until he has refilled the depression by submerging again. This process gives the human enough time to escape.

The other method is to carve one's name and age in the skin of a cucumber and throw it into the water. Apparently the kappa is fond of cucumbers, and when he eats the gift he will remember the donor's name and spare him from his clutches.

Kelpie

The water-horse of Scottish rivers. The water-horses of the lochs are known as Ech-Ushkya.

Kelpies may appear in either human or equine form. As humans, they emerge from the water in the shape of a hairy and ungainly character who waits for a horseman riding by, then leaps from the heather to mount behind him. The terrified horseman's first knowledge of the unwelcome passenger comes when two hairy arms encircle him, clamping and crushing him in a deadly grip. He loses control of the horse, which gallops madly along the riverbank until the kelpie tires of the sport and slips back into the water.

When the kelpie appears in equine form, it is as a splendid young horse wearing a bridle. It waits by the roadside for a weary pedestrian, but if a man or woman is unwise enough to mount the kelpie it rushes into the river, swims to the deepest part, and disappears. A non-swimming rider will be in dire distress.

A kelpie does not, however always triumph. A person familiar with kelpie activities may carry an ordinary bridle with him, and when he sees the water-horse he should leap onto its back and quickly substitute one bridle for another. He will then be able to make the kelpie work for him, and to use its bridle to work certain magical phenomena. Nevertheless a kelpie-owner should not keep the water-horse and its bridle for too long or make the creature work too hard, or it will curse the human and all his descendants forever.

Some say that kelpies eat humans, but they may be confusing it with the Ech-Ushkya. This water-horse is definitely a people-eater. It appears as a handsome horse or pony which is easy to mount and ride, but anyone who rides an Ech-Ushkya finds it is impossible to dismount. The horse gallops off with him into the loch, and on the following morning a portion of his body drifts ashore as a token of his fate.

The presence of kelpies may be detected by their habit of wailing loudly before storms. During storms, one may see their hooves galloping across the surface of the water.

Kraken

The devilfish or giant octopus seen off the coast of Norway and in the North Atlantic. Like other members of the squid family the kraken can squirt 'ink' by way of a smoke-screen to obscure it from enemies. The Norwegian bishop Pontoppidan, who described the kraken in 1752, commented that all the sea around the kraken was darkened by its defence mechanism.

It is difficult, however, to believe that the kraken needs any defence against other sea creatures—except perhaps Leviathan. It is far larger than sperm whales, which prey upon lesser specimens of the giant squid.

In sailing ship days the kraken was a fearsome menace to navigation. Seamen aboard becalmed ships kept an uneasy look-out for the boiling waters which heralded the ascent of a kraken, but once it broke the surface there was no escape. Its great cold eyes studied the screaming men, as they ran up the rigging in an effort to evade the giant tentacles, but it soon plucked them off one by one and gulped them down its gigantic maw.

Men who ran below decks lived only a little longer. The kraken simply wrapped its tentacles around the ship, squeezed until all her timbers burst open, and then picked out the tasty morsels.

Probably a great many sailing ships and fishing boats which failed to return to port were destroyed by a kraken. One of the theories about the *Marie Celeste*, the ship found drifting in mid-ocean with nobody aboard, is that all her people were taken by a kraken.

The strength, speed, and manoeuvrability of powered vessels protects them against krakens, but the occasional disappearance of a small sailing craft indicates that this monster still roams the deep.

Leviathan

This word is often used as a synonym for the whale or even the crocodile, but the only authentic description of Leviathan (in the Book of Job) shows he is a totally different type of creature.

He is a firebreathing sea monster, of such enormous size that the sea boils when he swims on the surface. He breathes smoke from his nostrils and flame from his mouth, which is rimmed with terrible teeth.

His skin is like a double coat of mail, covered with overlapping scales as big as shields on his back and as sharp and hard as broken pottery on his underparts. Swords, darts, javelins, harpoons, and fishing spears simply bounce off this armoured hide.

Leviathan's character is ruthless and fearless. He has a heart as hard as a millstone and he is unperturbed by any attempts to catch him—not that any human huntsman or fisherman is likely to make the attempt. The sight and sound of this enormous sea dragon, glaring around with fiery eyes as he churns through the waves, strikes terror into the heart of the mightiest warrior.

Loch Morar, Loch Ness, Monsters of

Sometimes supposed to be members of the diosauria, order Saurischia, suborder Sauropoda, species brontosaurus ('thunder lizard') and/or brachiosaurus. It has not been possible, however, to explain why either of these lifeforms should have survived in two Scottish lochs, and nowhere else in the world, during the 200 million years since the Mesozoic Age in which dinosauria stalked the earth. Nor may one know how each of the brontosauri or brachiosauri obtains its daily ration of a tonne or so of soft tropical vegetation, which would be its usual diet. But it is of course possible that, during the two Ice Ages which have elapsed since the Mesozoic Age, the monsters have adapted to a different diet.

Descriptions of the monsters vary so widely as to render scientific identification difficult, if not impossible. A nine-year-old girl, who saw one of the monsters land at Inchnacardoch Bay in 1912, described an elephant-coloured monster with great stumpy legs. This might fit a brontosaurus or brachiosaurus, but later sightings of the creatures indicate that they have long necks, calf-like heads, and 'three humps' following behind. This would not fit the dinosauria, which had bodies curved into a single hump, but might apply to sea serpents. The sea serpent, however, like sea snakes, would travel by a lateral writhing of its body in the same way that a snake does on shore, and not with a caterpillar-like 'humping' action. Furthermore, recent submarine photographs have pictured a great fin or paddle, believed to belong to the monster. Neither dinosauria nor sea serpents possess such appendages.

An alternative is that the monsters are plesiosaurs, great sea creatures of the Mesozoic Age, which did possess 'paddles'. Perhaps they were trapped in the loch 200 million years ago, and they or their descendants have lived there ever since.

The monsters have been seen by so many monster-watchers, and they have tipped so many people out of their boats or astounded them by appearances on the lochside, that there can be little doubt as to their existence. In recent decades an immense amount of scientific or semi-scientific effort, using the latest oceanographic technology, has been devoted to the monsters. It is unfortunate that reputable zoologists and biologists remain unconvinced about this phenomenon.

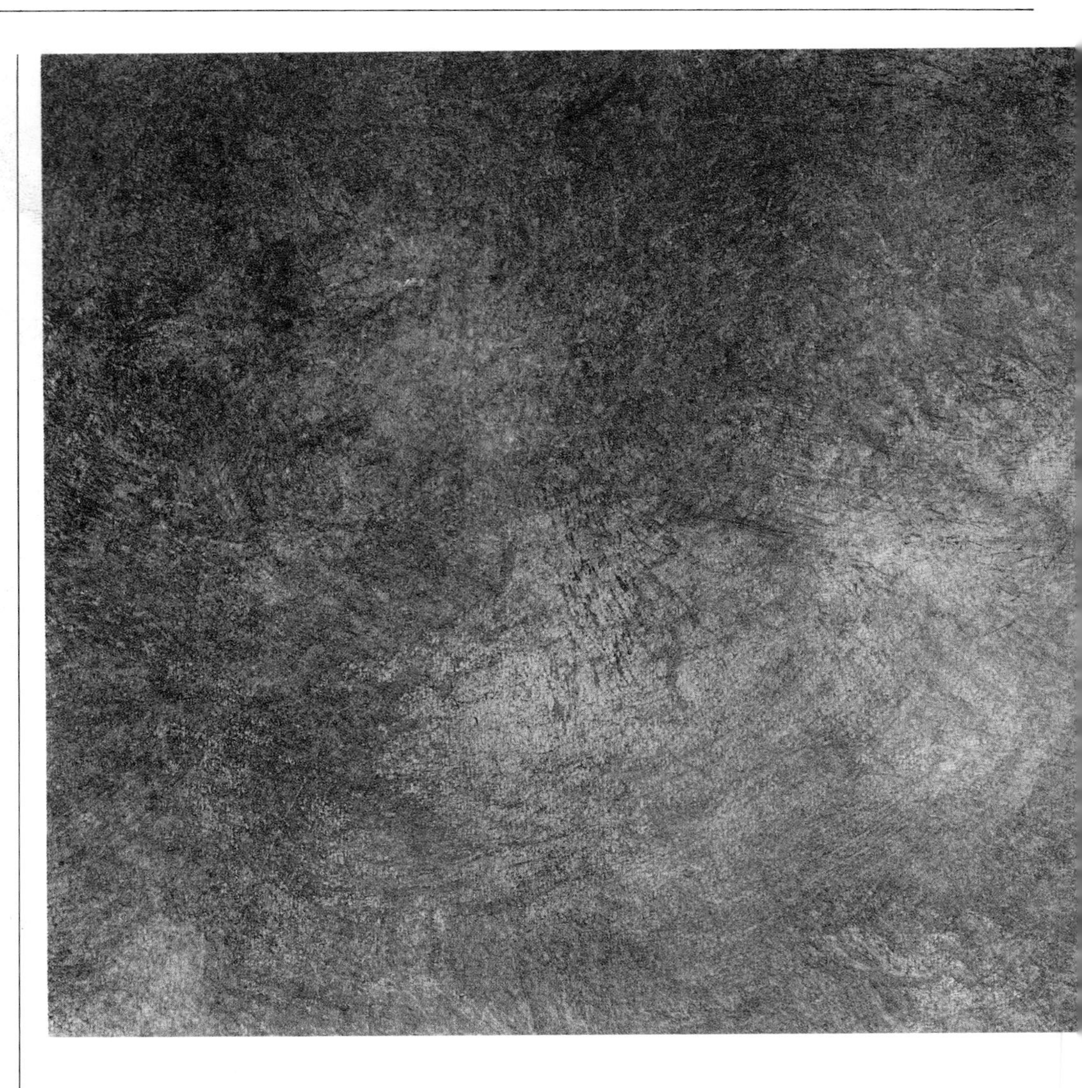

Maelstrom

A huge whirlpool that seizes and destroys ships caught in its sucking inflow. The word derives from the Dutch *malen* = to grind and *stroom* = a stream, and so may be translated as a 'grinding stream'. Possibly this means that a maelstrom grinds ships to pieces on the seabed.

This is certainly the case with the most infamous of maelstroms: that which lies between the islands of Mosken and Amoskenaes, in the Lofoten Islands off the coast of Norway. The tides always race tumultuously between these two islands, but on most days of the year they present no real danger to experienced seamen. It is only when unusually high tides roar between the islands that a fluke of wind may turn the waters back on themselves, and trigger the maelstrom. The surface of the sea begins to revolve, and swiftly gains impetus until it becomes a gigantic basin of tormented foam. The sides of this basin mount higher and higher, emitting a deafening highpitched roar, while the centre probes down towards the seabed. Soon the great pit of waters assumes a funnel conformation, with the spout touching the seabed and the whole process revolving at such enormous speed that the sides of the funnel are as smooth as thick green glass marbled and streaked with foam. The ghastly cry of the maelstrom mounts higher and higher until it is a continuous whistling scream, so loud that no voice could be heard above the noise.

The crew of a ship caught in the vortex of the maelstrom must endure a prolonged agony. Their ship revolves faster and faster as it descends into the funnel of the gigantic whirlpool, until it is whirling round at dizzying speed and at such an angle that they can only cling helplessly to the rigging. They can see great rocks caught up from the seabed, the wreckage of ancient ships, and even the skulls of those who have previously perished in the maelstrom, all sucked up into the glassy hollow column of water which they are descending with every turn of the whirlpool.

The maelstrom does not only move concentrically but also laterally, as the whole mass of water is pressed between the islands by the heaped-up tide. The seamen's last faint hope is that the maelstrom will burst free of the constricting channel between the islands before their ship touches the seabed. If it does, there is a chance that their ship will be thrown to the surface, and perhaps survive the raging tumult of waters as the maelstrom subsides. If not, then they must perish when the whirling waters grind their ship against the seabed and its timbers burst open against the rocks.

Mare Tenebrosum

Literally 'The Sea of Darkness'. An oceanic region, sometimes believed to be the so-called Bermuda Triangle, where the ghosts of lost ships and seamen sail forever in perpetual darkness. The Mare Tenebrosum is not marked on any charts and may even move slowly over the surface of the waters, following the track of such great ocean currents as the Gulf Stream. Seamen never know that they have entered the Sea of Darkness until night has fallen and the sea becomes mysteriously calm, no matter how rough it may have been before the sun went down. There is no moon or stars and the heavens are obscured by solid black cloud. The first indication of other presences upon the water is an agonised hail out of the darkness: the kind of choking, despairing cry that a swimmer might utter in the moment before drowning.

This is soon followed by other sounds and voices: the roar of a cannon, although there are no flashes from the gunfire; the savage yells of men fighting for their lives; the screams of women and children as a ship

sinks beneath the waves; orders bellowed in the language of every seafaring nation since the Phoenicians. Occasionally the sails of a full-rigged ship seem to glimmer through the darkness, or the water is churned into foam by the oars of a war galley or the bows of a destroyer.

At last all the sounds dies away into a bloodcurdling wailing, and ghostly ships loom up and disappear before the bows of the intruder. In sailing ship days, when a vessel might drift becalmed in the Mare Tenebrosum, the experience was so appalling that dawn might find her crew in a condition of near insanity. Powered vessels pass swiftly through the accursed region, but the sights and sounds are still so uncanny that seamen rarely mention them for fear of being disbelieved.

Mermaids, -Men

A race of amphibious beings. Probably they originated on the coast of Brittany and swam across the English Channel to Cornwall, where the inhabitants gave them the Anglo-French name of mermaids and mermen, i.e. sea-maids and sea-men.

From Cornwall they spread up the west coast of the British Isles and around northern Scotland to Scandinavia. Merpersons are occasionally sighted along the other coasts of Europe (although the nereids of the Mediterranean are only distant relations) but they seem to prefer the cold water and rugged Atlantic coasts of Britain and Ireland (where they are known as merrows or merucha) and the cliffs and fiords of Scandinavia.

Merpersons are also sighted on other coastlines of the world, including North America and China, but they often differ greatly in appearance from European mermaids. The theory that they are, however, related to dugongs or manatees is incorrect.

Mermaids and mermen live in and beneath the sea but can make themselves at home on land. They have their own language and customs, but are also able to speak the language of humans living on the nearest coastline. They like to make frequent trips ashore, if only to sit on rocks and comb out their long hair, and so they generally live in soundings rather than in the deep sea.

Fishermen often sight merpersons, especially in rough weather. They say that nothing could be more strikingly beautiful than a school of merpersons of all ages frolicking in the great Atlantic rollers, their silvery bodies glistening amid the tumultuous surf and their green eyes flashing as they glissade down the waves. Contrary to popular belief they are never caught in the fishermen's nets. They are much too sea-wise and agile to become entangled in such obstacles. They live on fish and other seafood but do not resent and never interfere with fishermen—unless of course the humans have offended them in some way.

Most mermaids are strikingly beautiful, even if this beauty sometimes appears a trifle cold. They are blonde, with long tresses ranging in colour from light brown to the tint known as 'strawberry blonde', and possess large green or blue-green eyes. Their skin is an immaculate pearly white, with a silvery sheen when it is slick with seawater. Breasts, arms, shoulders, hips, and waist are all in perfect proportion. The species develops slowly and it is impossible to tell the age of a merperson. The exquisitely beautiful children take a long time to reach adolescence, they enjoy a prolonged maidenhood, and when they reach their prime they retain the appearance of a mature human female for innumerable years.

Mermen are stalwart, swarthy, hirsute, and muscular, but with softer characters than their appearance would seem to indicate.

Both sexes are human in appearance above the waist and fishlike below, with large tail-flukes but no dorsal fins. They are, however, capable of changing their fishlike nether regions into human lower limbs, so that they may walk upon dry land, whenever they so desire. It is even possible that many merpersons spend the greater part of their lives, in or out of the water, with limbs instead of fishtails.

Relationships between merpersons and human beings are exceedingly complex. The two races have a great physical attraction for each other, but their characters are so different that associations between them usually end in disaster. Merpersons do not have souls, they are able to foretell the future, they are vain, jealous, and unforgiving, they have some degree of supernatural power, and they are probably immortal.

There are many accounts of shore-dwelling humans falling in love with merpersons, both male and female. When a woman falls in love with a merman he has the power to make her amphibious, and she goes to live with him under the sea. A mermaid, however, always sheds her tail and goes to live ashore with her human lover or husband.

Initially, such relationships are passionately happy, but the first fine careless rapture soon dies away. A human female starts to long for all her friends and relations ashore, and eventually forsakes her merhusband. A mermaid begins to yearn for the wild freedom of life among the waves, and finds it is very difficult to adjust to the dry dustiness of life ashore. She scandalises the gossips by stripping off on the seashore and plunging naked into the sea, attracting her old companions to join her and sitting with them on the rocks to sing, chatter, and comb her hair.

Mermaids sing very sweetly, but they are hopeless cooks and mermaid beauty soon palls on a husband who arrives home and finds nothing but raw fish for his tea. They neglect the housework, being so vain that they can spend most of the day admiring themselves in the mirror and trying out new hairstyles. When the children come along they have webbed hands and feet, which makes them expert swimmers but ineffective at most other children's games. On the whole it is a relief for all concerned when a mermaid slips away with her children and rejoins her friends in the sea.

Merpersons always know, by their power of foretelling the future, that marriage with human spouses cannot endure, but nevertheless they often show jealous fury when a marriage collapses. They tend to blame the human, and often cast some spell or curse upon the wife or husband. A fisherman who takes a merwife may as well stay ashore after she has left him. He will never catch another fish, and there is even a likelihood that he and his boat will be destroyed.

There are numerous relationships with merpersons apart from marriage. The saddest is when a young mermaid falls in love with a human but he does not respond, so that she pines away from hopeless desire. Sometimes a coastal community befriends a mermaid in order to benefit by her powers of futuresight, which she employs in return for such gifts as golden combs and mirrors. It is very useful for a fishing village to have an infallible weather forecaster, and to be told exactly where to fish for the biggest catch.

Occasionally a mermaid who conceives a passion for a human male will endow him with some of her own supernatural power, such as the ability to find treasure in sunken ships. Or a merperson may take a special liking for a human child, become its self-appointed guardian, and inflict horrible punishments upon anyone who ill-treats the human ward.

Some members of the clergy have caused great distress by attempting to convert merpersons to Christianity, especially when they are beautiful young mermaids. It is, of course, a hopeless endeavour.

Generally it may be said that merpersons are delightful creatures to observe at a distance but uncomfortable on closer association. Their intentions towards human beings are usually amiable, and they are rarely malicious unless they conceive themselves to be offended, but the differences in temperament between persons and merpersons are insurmountable.

Moby Dick

An enormous sperm whale (*Physeter catodon*) about 20 metres long. Probably of great age, because the white markings sometimes seen on old sperm whales were especially noticeable. He had a peculiar snow-white wrinkled forehead, and an unusually large white hump at the point where his enormous head flowed into his body. The rest of his body was so streaked, marbled, and spotted with white that whalers named him the White Whale.

The white markings were distinctive enough to make him instantly recognisable. When he was seen gliding at high noon through a dark-blue tropical sea, leaving a wake of creamy foam, he seemed to be a complete glistening white, totally different from the glossy black or brown of other sperm whales.

But he had other marks of distinction. He had a somewhat deformed lower jaw, studded with great teeth each weighing about 3 kilograms; he was bigger than most other sperm whales; he had three harpoon punctures in his starboard fluke; he always travelled alone, with no harem of cows; and, most of all, he had a maligan intelligence which terrified every whaler who came into conflict with him.

In the days when whalemen hunted whales in small boats, using hand-thrown harpoons, Moby Dick's favourite stratagem was to swim away from the harpooners pursuing him in their six-oared whaleboats and then to turn suddenly and attack them. His huge head smashed and sank the boat and he then crunched up one or more of the whalers struggling in the water.

Numerous whalers suffered death or disablement in the jaws of Moby Dick. He killed the mate of the whaling ship *Town-Ho*, bit off the arm of the captain of the *Samuel Enderby*, drowned the mate of the *Jeroboam*, and caused many other casualties. Whalers saw the White Whale on all the tropical whaling grounds from the South Atlantic to the Sea of Japan, and began to regard him with superstitious awe. Someone gave him the name of Moby Dick, though nobody remembers why.

Sometime in the 1840s, Captain Ahab of Nantucket encountered Moby Dick in the Sea of Japan, and set off in wild pursuit. His three whaleboats pulled frantically after the White Whale, striving to reach him with their harpoons, until Moby Dick attacked them in his usual way. As the three boats sank in a cauldron of churned white water, Ahab stabbed savagely at Moby Dick with a whaling knife. The whale reacted by biting

off one of Ahab's legs, and leaving him half-dead amidst the blood, wreckage, and foam.

Ahab's men rescued him and took him back to the ship, where he lay in his bunk during the long voyage back to Nantucket and developed a venomous yearning for revenge. When the stump of his leg healed he fitted it with a peg-leg made from whalebone, and sent to sea again as master of the whaling ship *Pequod*.

Yankee whaling ships ranged the whole world in their relentless pursuit of 'grease', and whalemen hailed from every port touched at by the ships. The *Pequod*'s crew was a mixture of salt-pickled seamen from places as far apart as Tahiti and the Isle of Man, having only the courage and fortitude of their profession in common. They were led by three Yankee mates of whom the chief was Starbuck: a long lean thirty year old whose flesh seemed as hard as twice-baked ship's biscuit, but who was nevertheless a reasonable and intelligent man.

The crew were used to hardcase skippers but they were awed by their first sight of Captain Ahab. He first stumped out onto the quarterdeck on a stormy winter morning, fitted the tip of his whalebone leg into a hole bored in the deck, and stood there like a great bronze statue balancing itself against the leaping surge of the *Pequod*. His face seemed like that of a man cut away from the stake, scorched and tawny, with a whitish scar threading its way from his grey hair to his neck. Superstitious seamen believed this scar was a brand placed upon him by some fearful experience, and that it ran from his head to his foot.

One of the crew, a man who called himself Ishmael, thought that Ahab's expression showed an infinity of firmest fortitude; a determinate unsurrenderable wilfulness: that he had a 'crucifixion in his face', and all the nameless regal overbearing dignity of some mighty woe.

Some days after his first appearance he assembled the entire crew, and nailed an Ecuadoran gold doubloon (now worth about $500) to the mainmast. In an impassioned speech he said that the first man to sight the White Whale should have the doubloon, and shouted, 'I'll chase him around Good Hope and around the Horn, and round the Norway Maelstrom, and round perdition's flames before I give him up. And this is what ye have shipped for, men! To chase that White Whale on both sides of land, and over all sides of earth, until he spouts black blood and rolls fin out!'

Starbuck protested that the *Pequod*'s mission was not that of wreaking personal vengeance on a dumb brute, but of filling the ship with whale oil for the Nantucket market. Ahab replied that nothing but vengeance would satisfy him, and made his mates drink 'Death to Moby Dick! God hunt us all if we do not hunt Moby Dick to his death!' out of the sockets of their harpoon heads.

The crew did not know what to make of this performance, but for some time the voyage proceeded normally and the ship took several whales. As they sailed down through the South Atlantic, around the Cape of Good Hope and up into the Indian Ocean, Ahab's only sign of abnormality was his questioning of every other whaleship they met as to whether her crew had sighted the White Whale.

But when the *Pequod* entered the Sea of Japan, Ahab ordered her blacksmith to make him a special harpoon. He had collected nail-stubs from racehorse shoes, the finest steel then known, which he said would 'Weld together like glue from the melted bones of murderers.' The blacksmith moulded the steel into the shaft and head of a harpoon, and fitted Ahab's razors into it for the barbs. When the harpoon head was still redhot from the blacksmith's forge, Ahab baptised it 'In the name of the devil' with blood donated by three of the *Pequod*'s harpooners.

Ahab now raved so eccentrically that the crew longed for the voyage to be over. They killed four more whales and rendered down their blubber into oil, but looked wistfully at the whaleship *Bachelor*: homeward-bound with a full cargo, island girls dancing on the deck, and a skipper who said heartily that he didn't believe in the White Whale. But a few days later they met the *Rachel*, which had seen Moby Dick only the day before. One of her boats, with the captain's twelve-year-old son in its crew, was missing and believed wrecked by the White Whale. The captain begged Ahab to join in the search for the boat, but news that Moby Dick was near at hand drove Ahab into a frenzy. He refused to search for the missing men and turned away to hunt for Moby Dick.

For the next four days he stayed continuously on deck or up at the masthead, shouting and raving about his obsession. The *Pequod* met the whaleship *Delight*, which had lost five men to Moby Dick, and after this encounter Ahab seemed to break down. He told Starbuck that he could not understand the force of his own mania. He had much to live for, a young wife and little son awaited him at home, but he felt he could not rest or return until the White Whale's death had released him. Starbuck begged him to abandon the search, but Ahab only raved 'What is it, what nameless, inscrutable, unearthly thing is it . . . that against all natural lovings and longings, I so keep pushing, and crowding, and jamming myself on all the time . . .?'

Starbuck abandoned the effort to persuade him. That night, Ahab sensed the nearness of Moby Dick and at daybreak they saw the White Whale. Ahab armed himself with his special harpoon and took one of the boats in pursuit of him.

The ship and the boats had to chase Moby Dick for three days, in which he wrecked two boats and drowned one of the men. Starbuck made another attempt to calm Ahab's frenzy, but the old man answered '. . . This whole act's immutably decreed . . . I am the Fates' lieutenant, I act under orders.'

Like all men obsessed by hatred and the thirst for vengeance, Ahab at last brought disaster to himself and all round him. In the final act of the tragedy, Moby Dick charged and sank the *Pequod* and sank the remaining boats. Ahab had time to sink his razor-barbed harpoon in the White Whale, but the harpoon line caught him around the neck and dragged him under when the great sperm whale sounded. Ishmael alone survived to tell the story.

Moby Dick vanished into the depths, and perhaps still exists as a symbol of man's self-destructive pursuit of that which he can never overcome.

Nagas

Indian snake-spirits of water and land, which appear sometimes as snakes, sometimes as semihumans with snake tails, and quite often as humans, especially as beautiful maidens. The Nagas comprise an entire nation or perhaps several nations. Their principal capital is Bhogavati, an underground city in the Himalayas, but they appear to have other underground cities. These are all of great splendour magnificently ornamented with precious stones. The Nagas are very fond of jewellery and may steal it from humans.

Nagas have important supernatural powers, including the ability to make human beings invisible in the water.

Nereids

Sea nymphs of the Mediterranean: the fifty granddaughters of Pontus the sea god and Gaea the earth mother. They have some relationship to the mermaids of other seas and oceans, and like them are extremely beautiful, but they do not have fishtails.

Some nereids, such as Galatea and Thetis, occupy important positions among the gods. Thetis is so beautiful that numerous gods sought to marry her, but she avoided accept-

ance until the great god Zeus insisted on her union with the King of Thessaly. Thetis thought that marriage to a mortal was so degrading that she evaded the king's courtship, by turning herself into such shapes as a flame, a wave, and a fish. But the king persisted, and made her the mother of the hero Achilles.

All the other nereids have remained virgins, and they spend most of their time gambolling through the waves with the dolphins and tritons who accompany the chariot of Poseidon, Lord of the Ocean.

Nereids, like the mermaids of other waters, are exceedingly vain. When they heard that Cassiopeia of Ethiopia had boasted of her daughter Andromeda, saying that she was more beautiful than the nereids, they were so insulted that they asked Poseidon to punish the mother and daughter. Poseidon obliged by sending a monster to ravage Ethiopia, and would not recall it until Andromeda had been chained naked to a rock in the sea. Luckily the hero Perseus fell in love with the naked maiden, killed the monster, turned Andromeda's fiancé and his friends into stone by showing them the Gorgon's head, and married the young princess.

Nixies

The water sprites who inhabit the springs and rivers of Germany. They may be male or female, but the male nixies rarely show themselves to human eyes. The female nixies are dazzlingly beautiful, with blue eyes and long fair hair.

Nixy maidens often sit in the sun on the banks of their watery homes, admiring their reflections in the water while they comb their long hair. If they hear a mortal approaching they disappear quickly, and the intruder sees no more than a ripple in the water. But, if he is a handsome young man, he runs the risk of a nixy falling in love with him. If she does then he is lost forever. Her beauty lures him down into the water and he is never seen again.

A different fate awaits those who creep up on nixies to gloat on their beauty. As he watches these watermaidens from the undergrowth, their songs cause him to lose his wits and he is never the same again.

Oceanos, -Us

One of the Titans who took part in the creation of the Cosmos out of Chaos. In the beginning, the creators fashioned a flat world, with the Mediterranean countries in the centre, Ethiopia to the south, Cimmeria, the Land of Darkness, in the north, the Land of Dreams in the west, and Pygmyland in the east. Oceanos then surrounded the whole construction with a great river, named the River Oceanus, and arranged for the stars to rise out of it at nightfall and plunge back into the waters at daybreak. The river waters seeped under the earth and oozed upwards to form the Mediterranean and other bodies of water, together with wells, ponds, lakes, and streams.

With this work done, Oceanos married his sister Tethys. She gave birth to the 3,000 rivers of the world and to 3,000 daughters, the Oceanids, whose task is to supervise all waters and waterlife.

Oceanos and Tethys then settled down in a palace they built beyond the western stars, and lived there contentedly until the gods challenged the might of the Titans. When the gods won the cosmic combat, Poseidon received the ocean as part of the spoils of war.

Pegasus

A winged horse, one of the two offspring which Medusa the Gorgon bore to Poseidon the Lord of the Ocean. (The other was a warrior named Chrysaor.) The horse's name derives from a Greek word meaning 'strong'. It would appear that Medusa was pregnant with her strange children when Perseus struck off her head, because they both sprang fully developed from her headless body.

When Pegasus first appeared it was as a magnificent white stallion with golden wings, but this colouration may have changed later in life. He ignored the man who had slain his mother and instantly took to the air, his golden wings beating steadily as he flew to Mount Helicon, the home of the nine Muses. He repaid the hospitality of the Muses by using his hooves to dig out a spring named Hippocrene, meaning 'horse well', which flows with waters that give poetical inspiration to anyone who drinks them.

Occasionally a god or mortal attempted to catch Pegasus, but he evaded them with contemptuous ease. A single beat of his wings sent him soaring into the blue, where he circled about Mount Helicon with trumpet-like whinnies of triumph.

But eventually the goddess Athene arranged for his capture, to help Bellerophon to destroy the Chimaera. She appeared to Bellerophon in a dream, telling him to catch Pegasus with a magical golden bridle. When Bellerophon awoke he found the bridle in his hand.

Pegasus submitted meekly to being harnessed by Bellerophon, and then flew off with him to seek the Chimaera. This was a great fire-breathing monster with a lion's head, goat's body, and serpent's tail, which was ravaging the country of Lycia. It lived in a cave, but could take to the air and swoop down upon the Lycian communities to blast them with jets of fire.

Bellerophon and Pegasus found the Chimaera hiding in a storm cloud, and in what may be the first recorded aerial combat they pursued the monster through the dark valleys of cloud. The gallant stallion, faster and more manoeuvrable than the ungainly monster, evaded the blasts of flame while Bellerophon fired volleys of arrows, until they literally shot the monster down in flames.

Bellerophon then flew Pegasus to the south-east, so that he might fly the stallion as a kind of gunship against the Amazons. These fierce female warriors were on one of their raiding expeditions along the coast of Syria; but they soon scattered in confusion when Pegasus swooped upon them and Bellerophon showered them with arrows.

Flushed with success, Bellerophon then decided to fly Pegasus up to Olympus and take his place among the gods. But Zeus saw him coming and sent a horsefly to sting Pegasus, who bucked so frenziedly that Bellerophon fell to the ground. When Pegasus recovered from the pain he flew on up to Olympus, where Zeus took him into his stable and thereafter used him to carry his thunderbolts.

Phaethon

One of the many sons whom Helios the Sun God had by his numerous wives and mistresses. Phaethon's mother was the sea nymph Clymene, Queen of Ethiopia, who thought him so beautiful that she gave him the name which means 'The Shining One'.

But Phaethon grew into a reckless and arrogant youth, rather apt to boast of his divine descent. One day an acquaintance scoffed at this claim, and Phaethon asked his mother for proof of his solar paternity. She could only advise him to ask his father, whereupon Helios promised any favour which Phaethon might ask of him.

To the Sun God's alarm, Phaeton promptly asked to drive the Chariot of the Sun on one of its daily gallops across the sky. Helios protested that Phaeton would be unable to control the nine winged firebreathing horses that draw the golden chariot, but Phaethon insisted. He said that everyone would see him at the reins, and know for certain that he was the son of Helios.

Unhappily, Helios kept his promise. He took his son to the eastern stables where the two Horae, the goddesses of the seasons and the calendar, harness the horses to the chariot each morning, and gave his son careful operational instructions. When rosy-fingered Eos drew aside the curtains of the dawn, he handed the reins to Phaethon and gave the starting signal.

Phaethon slapped the reins on the backs of the snow-white horses, they snorted great blasts of flame, and then with a thunderous clap of their golden wings they soared up into the eastern arch of the sky.

Phaethon immediately lost control of the nine immense horses. No matter how he dragged at the reins he was not strong enough to keep them on their appointed track. They veered wildly in one direction or

another, so that terrified mortals saw the sun careering around the sky. At last they swooped down so close to earth that their fiery breath set forests afire, destroyed crops, and made the rivers boil.

This cosmic chaos disturbed the great god Zeus, who looked down from Olympus and saw Phaethon still vainly struggling with the horses. Zeus realised that the foolish youngster might destroy the entire universe, and made a quick decision. He seized a thunderbolt, took careful aim, and fired.

The guided missile knocked Phaethon out of the chariot and sent him tumbling down into the River Eridamus (now the River Po). The nine horses, freed from his clumsy efforts to steer them, resumed their normal course across the sky until they plunged into the sea at evening.

As for Phaethon, the impact killed him and the river nymphs buried him on the river bank. His seven sisters travelled from Ethiopia to mourn his death, and changed into the poplars which now line the riverside, forever sighing and whispering their grief. Their tears turned into the golden amber which may sometimes be dug out of the ground.

Phoenix

A large male bird of the eastern Mediterranean, so magnificent in appearance that the Phoenicians named their country after him. (Or it may be that they named the bird after their country.) It is possible that he originated in Egypt or Arabia and migrated to Phoenicia. He is the only member of his species, although he may have some links with the peacock family, and he is closely related to the sun.

Descriptions of phoenix plumage vary considerably. Some say the bird is an overall reddish-gold, others that he is royal purple with a golden neck and head, and others again that he has a plum-coloured body, scarlet back and wing feathers, a golden head and a sweeping tail of rose and azure. Possibly the bird displays different colouration at various stages of his long life.

The phoenix is friendly to humans, who are enthralled by his gorgeous plumage and sweet singing voice, but does not concern himself with their affairs.

He is semi-immortal, having a lifespan of at least 500 years (some say 1,461 or even 12,954 years) and he uses a unique method of reproduction. At the end of each life cycle he builds a nest of spice tree twigs, settles into the nest, and with a single clap of his wings sets it afire. The mature bird perishes in the conflagration, but as the flames die down a young phoenix emerges from them in all the glory of his pristine plumage.

The first task of the young phoenix is to fly to the Temple of the Sun, at Heliopolis in Egypt, with the mummified corpse of his father. He lays this upon the altar, then flies to Phoenicia and settles down for several contented centuries until his time arrives for immolative self-reproduction.

Pleiades

In the eastern parts of the northern hemisphere these stars are the seven daughters of the giant Atlas, who holds up the sky. The eldest is named Alcyone and her sisters are Asterope, Electra, Kelane, Maia, Merope, and Taygete.

The seven beautiful sisters once attracted the attention of the handsome giant Orion, but although six of them had had passionate affairs with various gods and Merope had married the mortal Sisyphus (a notorious seducer, traitor, bandit, and kidnapper) they all rejected Orion's advances and fled into the woods and mountains of Boeotia.

Orion, with his trusty dog Sirius, followed the sisters to Boeotia, and pestered them for five years without managing to conquer any of them. At last they grew so weary of his approaches that they begged the great god Zeus to succour them. He responded with the ironical trick of changing the sisters into stars and also placing Orion and Sirius in the heavens. The Pleiades, Orion, and Sirius the Dog Star are now fixed in eternal pursuit. Alcyone shines the most brightly, but Merope usually hides her face because she is ashamed of her marriage to Sisyphus.

In North America, where all the Indian tribes had different names for the seven sisters, they were important star spirits with strong influence upon the affairs of men. In the far north they are an Eskimo hunter and his dogs, who once chased a Polar bear so ardently that they followed when it tried to escape into the sky.

In the southern hemisphere, many different stories are related about Orion and the seven sisters. Some Pacific islanders say they are fish which have escaped Orion's net. In southern Australia, they are his wives and daughters. They disappear over the horizon before he does so that they may prepare camp and cook his food. In the centre of the continent, however, Orion is a brutal warrior forever pursuing seven women who flee from his attentions.

Poppykettle

An ancient clay pot made and fired by the Throwers of the Gods, in the now-deserted Inca city of Macchu Piccu in the high Andes. The pot has some resemblance to a teapot or teakettle, used for the brewing of poppyseed tea. (Recipe: Fill poppykettle through spout. Stir in poppyseeds, including the pods if an extra strong brew is required. Place three old brass keys in the bottom of pot, and bring contents to the boil.)

Many years ago, seven Hairy Peruvians or Incagnomes decided to leave Peru, which had been conquered by the Shining Spaniards, and see what lay beyond the horizon. Brown Pelican carried the seven gnomes from Callo, on the seacoast, up to Macchu Piccu, where they found the Poppykettle on a ruined wall and decided it would be the ideal craft for their voyage.

The great Silverado Bird carried pot and crew down to the seashore, where they named it the *Poppykettle*. They made a sail emblazoned with the symbol of the Silverado Bird, loaded the ship with sacks of poppyseed as provisions for the voyage, and ballasted her with two brass keys stolen from the Shining Spaniards.

A silver fish, made by the Incas, towed them out to sea until a fair wind blew them on their voyage. The peaks of the Andes sank beyond the horizon and they were alone on the mighty Pacific, still uncertain about their destination.

First they passed the Iguana Islands, where great dragon-like monsters terrified the sea-going gnomes. They were almost wrecked on the rocky islands, but the fiery breath of the monsters filled the sail and drove them out to sea again.

After that they sailed on for months and months across the Pacific, until the wind and surf carried the *Poppykettle* close to the reefs of a coral island. Their clay pot would have been shattered on the reefs if an island woman had not rescued them and carried the *Poppykettle* ashore.

The gnomes rested on the island for a while, and the islanders showed them a strange chart, made of sticks and cowrie shells tied together with vines, to help them find the way on the next leg of their voyage.

They set off again aboard the *Poppykettle* and sailed through rougher and colder waters until they ran into a great storm. For three days, giant waves tossed the *Poppykettle* so violently that the gnomes could hardly hold on to their reeling craft. When the storm subsided, they found that their ship had cracked and was slowly settling into the water.

Luckily, a friendly dolphin had followed them through the storm, on his way to a family reunion in the waters of the far south. He lifted the *Poppykettle* out of the water and the gnomes lashed it to his head, using a long rope made from the remnants of their sail. When all was secure the dolphin gambolled off on his voyage, and gave the *Poppykettle*'s crew a rough but fast ride all the way to Australia. He tipped the clay pot onto the beach, snorted farewell, and swam off with a flip of his tail.

The Hairy Peruvians left their cracked vessel on the beach and wandered off to make the best of their Unchosen Land. They were the first gnome settlers in Australia.

The proof of this story is that, in 1847, two men were digging for lime in the cliffs near Geelong in Victoria, Australia. One of their shovels clinked against metal and they dug out two ancient brass keys.

Nobody could understand why the keys should be buried so deep in the cliff. The Aborigines did not use keys, and the white people had only been in Australia for a short time. The only explanation is that they were the keys brought in the *Poppykettle.*

Quadriga

Specifically a two-wheeled chariot drawn by four horses, but also a flying chariot used by gods and sorcerers. The flying chariot in which the sorceress Medea escaped from Corinth to Athens, after burning up her lover's fiancée in a self-igniting wedding gown, was doubtless a quadriga although it was drawn by flying serpents instead of winged horses.

Eos, goddess of the dawn, gallops across the sky in a quadriga to herald the arrival of Helios, although her chariot is by no means as magnificent as the great golden vehicle ridden by the sun god. It seems likely that Eos also uses her chariot in order to indulge her taste for beautiful youths, by sweeping down and carrying them off to her home beyond the horizon.

Quadrigas are never self-propelling. They have to be drawn through the sky by various winged creatures, usually horses but occasionally serpents, dragons, basilisks, or even harpies.

The great god Zeus made some use of a quadriga when he fell in love with the delectable youth Ganymede. He changed himself into an eagle in order to snatch Ganymede up to Olympus, and compensated the youth's father by giving him a team of 'stormhorses' to draw his terrestrial quadriga.

Rainbow Serpents

Enormous reptiles known in many parts of the world for their creation and rainmaking activities, especially in North America, Australia, and West Africa. In Africa, the rainbow serpent was the first creation of Mawu the supreme being. The serpent then helped Mawu to create the rest of the world, and when they had finished it wound itself into a great circle under the ocean, to support the weight of the earth. The rippling of its coils may be seen in the movement of the waters, from which it sometimes arises to arch itself across the sky.

North American tribesmen often see the rainbow serpent. In that part of the world it played some part in the creation of man and other animals, and then assumed the important role of providing rain. Occasionally it sleeps for too long between seasons, so that the ground begins to crack with prolonged drought. The serpent's failure to appear in the sky indicates that it is still asleep, and it must be awoken with specially noisy dances and ceremonies.

Rainbow serpents are prevalent in every part of the Australian continent, where they have such names as Karia, Muit, Wulungu, and Yulunggu. Their task in creation days was to carve out creeks, rivers, lakes, and waterholes. The rivers have many curves because they follow the wriggling tracks of the serpents, and the waterholes are round because they are in the shape of a snake coiled up to rest.

Nowadays, the rainbow serpents live in the depths of the waterholes during the dry season. One must be very careful not to disturb them, or they will rear up in fury and create all sorts of disasters by lashing their great bodies through earth and sky.

In the wet season, the rainbow serpents emerge from the waterholes and fulfil their appointed task of bringing lifegiving water to the land. The brilliant arches of rainbows show that the serpents are travelling from one waterhole or watercourse to another, to make sure that they are well topped-up for the dry season.

Rainmaking

This essential art is practised in many parts of the world, to ensure rain during the proper season or to remind the gods that they have forgotten to send enough rain. There are innumerable methods of attracting rain, ranging from the use of items related to water to the performance of elaborate ceremonies. In the desert regions of Australia, the shells of pearl oysters from the north-west coasts are greatly valued as rainmakers. They are traded across the country until they reach the Aborigines of desert regions. The tribesmen polish the nacreous inner surfaces to the accompaniment of special incantations and then show them to the sky. This reminder that rain is overdue will often bring on a downpour. In other regions, the people use a simpler method. They fill their mouths with water and spit it towards the sky, again by way of reminding the clouds of their proper function.

In some areas, the Dreamtime ancestors of the tribal groups are the bringers of rain and must be appealed to with the proper ceremonies. One of them, Irria, is associated with the black cockatoo: the bird which brings the dark rainclouds to the country in the rainy season.

Irria taught another Dreamtime personality, Inungamella, how to make rain by giving him a number of large stones shaped like rain clouds. When the tribal leaders sing the proper songs over these stones they will help to bring rain.

The ceremonies of another Dreamtime rainmaker, Ilpailurkna, are associated with his sacred yamstick. When rain is needed, the celebrants paint a yamstick with red ochre, attach white feathers to the whole length of the stick, and then blow them towards the sky. The feathers then turn into clouds which will bring rain.

Rainstones are important components of the ceremony in many parts of the world. Sometimes they are portable, like those of Inungamella, and they are handed down through countless generations. In other places, including the tribal lands of the Apaches, they are certain fixed stones or boulders which must be thoroughly wetted, to remind the gods that rain is overdue.

Many communities keep special images of gods or saints near to the wells or ponds providing the water supply. When the water level runs dangerously low the people first decorate the image, with appropriate prayers to remind the deity that rain is required. If this has no result then the people either give the image a drenching or dip it into the water, as an unmistakable hint to do its duty. As a final resort, all the adults give the image a good whipping and throw it into the stagnant water, to remain there until it sends down plenty of rain. But if the image has usually been beneficial to the community, it may be enough to give the water a beating instead. The image sees what lies in store for it if it does not do the right thing, and probably responds with a downpour of rain.

It is widely recognised that rain falls only as the result of magical intervention, and there are innumerable ceremonies to beg, force, or inspire the huge variety of rain gods and water spirits into doing their duty. In desperate situations it may be necessary to pound great drums incessantly to awaken the sleeping gods, or to build huge fires whose smoke will make them weep. Sometimes it becomes obvious that a community is being punished by the rain gods, and then the people may have to dismiss their chief or even sacrifice a witch or wizard. On the other hand, a community which enjoys a succession of good rainy seasons must recognise the power of its chief and medicine-men, and reward them with bounteous offerings.

Rukhs

(Incorrectly known as rocs.) Enormous birds which live on certain islands of the Indian Ocean. Their size is indicated by the fact that each feather is as large as a palm frond. The island habitat of rukhs does not provide them with sufficient food, and so they frequently visit the mainlands of India or Africa in search of prey. They carry off all kinds of creatures including elephants.

Sindbad, the merchant adventurer from Baghdad, had two experiences with rukhs. On the first occasion, after he was accidentally marooned on an island, he climbed a tree to get his bearings and saw what he thought to be the white dome of a building. He hastened towards it, but found that the great object had no doors or windows. While he was puzzling over it the sky darkened with an enormous shadow, and he looked up to see a gigantic bird settling upon the dome.

It was in fact a rukh's egg, and the rukh did not even notice Sindbad as she spread herself over the egg and settled down to brood. After some time, Sindbad realised that the bird might be his means of escape from the island. He used his turban to lash himself to one of the huge legs, hoping that the bird would overlook his weight when she took off again. At last she arose, spread her wings, and flapped slowly into the air, with Sindbad fearing that she would snap him up into her massive beak. But his weight meant nothing to the rukh. When she landed on another island Sindbad cut himself free, only to become embroiled in another series of adventures.

Sindbad's second encounter with rukhs came on his fifth voyage, when he and some other merchants landed on an island where they found a rukh's egg. Despite Sindbad's warnings, the merchants chopped the egg open and were devouring its contents when the parent birds returned to the island.

The merchants escaped to the ship, but the rukhs were so furious that they bombarded it with huge boulders. A direct hit sank the ship and all but Sindbad perished. He floated off on some wreckage and landed on Old-Man-of-the-Sea's Island, which is described earlier in this book.

Rusalki

The spirits of girls who have drowned in the rivers of Russia. During the cold winter months they live deep in the water and even survive under the ice. When summer sunshine warms the waters, the rusalki climb the branches of overhanging trees and go to spend a kind of summer holiday in the forest.

There are two species of rusalki: northern and southern. Both are dangerous to humans who venture near the water, but the two species use very different methods of destroying them. The rusalki of the gloomy northern rivers, who look like the naked corpses of drowned women, snatch any innocent wayfarer and drag him down into the depths. There, they bully and torture him before putting him out of his misery. But the southern rusalki, who resemble beautiful girls clad in gossamer garments of water vapour, entice mortals to join them by singing with irresistible sweetness. The man who hears a rusalki song wades into the depths and drowns with a smile on his lips.

Both types of rusalki are extremely mischievous during their summer holidays. They may ruin the harvest with torrential rain, tear up fishermen's nets, damage such constructions as dams and watermills, and steal the garments which women are making for their families.

Anyone who ventures near Russian rivers should protect himself against rusalki by carrying a few leaves of wormwood (*Artemisia absinthum*) in an amulet. Wormwood also protects any article which rusalki might steal, damage, or destroy. In cases of severe infestation one should scatter a quantity of the leaves upon the surface of the river.

Sargasso Sea

A region of the North Atlantic south-east of Bermuda, on the approaches to the West Indies, lying between 25 and 31 degrees North and 40 and 70 degrees West. The tract of ocean is named Sargasso after the floating seaweed *Sargassum Bacciferum* (or Gulf Weed). This tough pale-brown sea-growth is distinguished by the multitude of small air-bladders which keep it afloat, and it is infested by tiny crabs, barnacles, sea lice, and other minor sealife.

North Atlantic storms tear huge quantities of this weed from the coastal regions of America. It then drifts on the ocean currents until it reaches the Sargasso Sea, where the currents move in a huge slow circle so that the weed never escapes. Over the centuries, the weed has accumulated in such quantities that it forms a semisolid carpet on the surface of the sea.

The danger of this natural obstacle to shipping is increased by the fact that it lies within the Horse Latitudes, the great subtropical region of light variable winds. Sailing ships lay becalmed there for weeks on end. Seamen called it the Horse Latitudes because they were forced to slaughter any horses being transported in the ships, in order to save drinking water.

Christopher Columbus, westward-bound with his three ships, narrowly escaped entrapment in the Sargasso Sea. His ships drifted helplessly in the clogging weed for many weeks, until a fortunate breeze gave them enough headway to sail free.

Many other seafarers did not escape so easily. In sailing ship days, a ship becalmed in the Sargasso Sea often lay motionless, while the drifting weed piled remorselessly around her hull, for weeks on end. When the wind at last blew favourably, she could no longer move. Her crew would make desperate efforts to clear the weed away, and even to tow the ship by using her boats, but the weed which held a sailing ship fast had no difficulty in obstructing a rowing boat and clogging its oars. Eventually the ship's crew died slowly of thirst and starvation. The ship herself lasted longer, until her sails rotted and the rigging frayed and snapped so that the masts leaned drunkenly. The teredo worm ate away at her hull timbers and at long last she began to sink.

Countless ships, from Spanish galleons laden with treasure to slave ships with their living cargoes, drifted into the Sargasso Sea and lay rotting there with crews of skeletons. When steamships began to plough the oceans, there was much talk of an expedition into the Sargasso to salvage the money and treasure in this silent fleet. But shipmasters were afraid that their paddle wheels would become entangled in the weed.

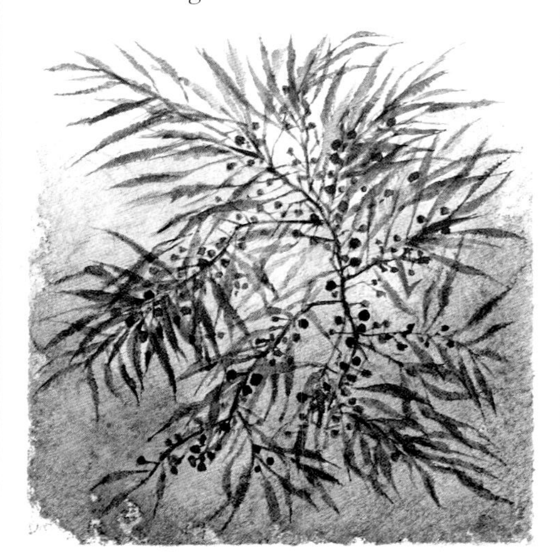

At last, after steamships had grown much larger and more powerful, a proper expedition was prepared. In 1910 it entered the Sargasso Sea in the steamship *Michael Sars*. It was a profitless venture, because the hull timbers of the old ships had long since rotted away and they had sunk below the canopy of weed.

Countless powerful vessels have traversed the Sargasso Sea during this century, with their screws cutting and scattering the weed, but it is still dangerous to small craft which drift into its silent embrace.

Scylla and Charybdis

Two monsters which lay in wait for ships passing between Italy and the island of Sicily. Scylla lived in a cave on the Italian side, while Charybdis still dwells under a rock on the Sicilian side.

Scylla was originally a beautiful young woman, who may have been a daughter of Poseidon, Lord of the Ocean, by one of his many mistresses. When Poseidon himself seduced her, his wife Amphitrite commissioned the sorceress Circe to change Scylla into a monster.

Circe contrived this by steeping magical herbs in Scylla's bathing pool, so that Scylla entered it as a lovely woman and emerged as a monster with twelve legs and six huge dog's heads on long serpentine necks. Her bite was worse than her bark, because the dog's heads only yapped like puppies.

She found a lair in the sea cliffs and lived by snatching dolphins and other seafood from the water, together with passing sailors. Whenever a galley rowed through the straits, she used her six heads to scoop up a whole row of oarsmen.

Any shipmasters who tried to steer clear of Scylla fell foul of Charybdis, who created a monstrous whirlpool by sucking in and regurgitating the waters of the straits three times a day. Nothing is known about her background.

Improvements in ships and navigational methods at last enabled seafarers to evade both these monsters. Nobody has seen Scylla for many centuries, and so she may either have died or sought more fruitful territory. Charybdis, however, still follows her routine of swallowing and regurgitating the seawater thrice daily.

The Sea King's Palace

The palace lies two degrees off the western approaches to sunken Atlantis, equidistant between the eastern column of the Sea Rainbow and the Whale Seaway from north to south. Whale deputations break their world-curving voyages to report on their plight to the Sea King, and hear what has been decided at the Court of the Life Balancers.

The Sea King convenes sessions of this court by sending eel messengers to the River Masters of the world, dolphin couriers to the Ice Sentinels of north and south, albatross emissaries to the Ladies of the Rain, and stormy petrels to summons the Lords of Storm. The times when the court is in session may be known by those periods when the seas of the world lie in glistening repose, with great flocks of seabirds gossiping on their surfaces and flying fish scurrying with the latest news of court decisions. The Lords of Storm allow the oceans an interim of peace.

The River Masters, Ice Sentinels, and Ladies of the Rain sit as a jury while the Sea King listens to the charges laid by his subjects. Whales report on the deaths of their people at the hands of harpooners. Tunas say their families have been decimated by fishermen. Black marlin weep at the passing of their race, cruelly snatched from the depths in the name of sport. Salmon and trout from the rivers tell of the hooks which pluck them from their homes. Lobsters and crayfish recount stories of wicked traps, abalones and oysters of divers wrenching them from the rocks, shark and cod of the bitter substances polluting the waters of their territories.

Representatives of every species have their say. Octopi gesticulate as they tell how they are chopped up for bait, sardines and anchovies whimper their tales of genocide, the brilliant creatures of the tropics tell of the devastation of their homes.

After each complaint, the Sea King asks the jury to pronounce either for or against mankind. The verdict is always the same: Guilty.

The king then passes sentence to be executed by the Lords of Storm. He bids them to arrange typhoons, cyclones, hurricanes, and waterspouts. He nominates the ships to be wrecked and the storms to be whipped up to keep fishermen in port. In extreme cases, he commands a tidal wave. The Ice Sentinels nod silently at instructions to crush ships and build barriers, and the Ladies of the Rain promise to help the River Masters to create floods.

The court then turns to pleasanter subjects. They agree upon the allocation of seawater to the Ladies of the Rain, and the work of the Lords of Storm in fashioning trade winds. They ratify the annual treaty of the Sea King with the moon, to establish the rhythms of the tides. They agree upon the strength of currents, the height of waves, and the amount of ice to be released by the Sentinels.

Every ocean creature from krill to cephalod is administered by the Life Balancers; from the subjects of the Marginal World between sea and shore to those of Utmost Dark. Each one is dealt with fairly, and each one knows that the plan fulfils its needs but demands a sacrifice.

At last the conch horns gurgle the signal that the court is to close, and the Sea King utters the valedictory: 'The Sea is the Fount of Life. Whoever ignores this rule must die.'

The delegates swim or drift back to their territories, and the Lords, Ladies, Masters, and Sentinels depart to do the Sea King's bidding.

Sea Serpents

Gigantic seafaring reptiles with cylindrical bodies, about 70 metres long and 7 metres in circumference, clad with glistening scales which are sea-green on the upper surface of the body and white underneath, and having a flattened snakelike head, with large horny eye sockets and a membraneous 'mane'. Widely seen throughout the world, especially off the coasts of Scandinavia, Denmark, the British Isles, and North America, but also in the South Atlantic and Pacific. Whalers often observe sea serpents locked in combat with sperm whales. The water foams with blood as the whale's great jaws crunch fragments out of the serpent's body, but the monster always wins by wrapping its coils around the whale and dragging it down into the depths.

In sailing ship days, sea serpents often attacked ships in search of prey. Sometimes the monster washed men off the decks and into the sea by surfacing alongside and spouting a hose-like jet of water. More often, it simply snatched them with its huge jaws. On rare occasions it totally destroyed small ships by wrapping its coils around them.

The only certain defence against sea serpents is the gum resin known as asafoetida, obtained from the plant *Ferula foetida* which grows in Persia and Afghanistan. This reddish-brown resin, with its acrid taste and strong onion-like odour, should be ground into powder and scattered on the water around a boat or ship. Sea serpents abhor asafoetida so violently that the merest suspicion of the substance keeps them away.

Sea serpent sightings are so well documented that one may ignore suggestions that the monsters are no more than schools of dolphins, giant squids, or other commonplace maritime occurrences.

Ship Spirits

Ships, like every other object to which humans have devoted the art of hands and minds, each have individual spirits of their own. The character of artefact spirits is formed partly by the materials from which an object is made, but very largely by the amount of human love, pride, art, skill, and imagination devoted to its creation. Our fascination with things of the past springs from the fact that a piece of antique furniture or a veteran motor car was constructed by men who fashioned it with love and pride, so that their spirits flowed into it and created pleasing and responsive 'object spirits'. These spirits have the power of instant thrilling communication with human beings. We respond to them in a way in which it is impossible for us to respond to a plastic bottle, or to a motor vehicle created by automation.

And so it is with ships. For many centuries, sailing ships were the largest and most complicated pieces of machinery built by mankind. Immense skill went into the construction of every ship, and she was built entirely from natural materials from the timber of her hull to the canvas of her sails. A host of proud craftsmen worked on every detail of her construction. When at last she took to the water, she floated there as though with a delight in her own existence.

As soon as she felt the winds and waves of her natural element, her spirit sprang to life in a brilliant manifestation of temperament. She seemed to possess every facet of the human characters which had brought her into existence, somehow blended into something entirely new. She could be willing or wilful: happy, sulky, joyful, responsive, ardent, courageous, or difficult. Like a beautiful woman or a spirited horse, she was never dull but often capricious. Only those who understood her could persuade her to give of her best.

Of course some ships had spirits which resisted every blandishment of those who sailed in her. For some reason their spirits were stunted or warped, perhaps because their designers or builders had skimped their tasks. They were dull, balky, and seemingly bent on self-destruction.

The glory of sailing ships faded slowly into the past, and they were replaced by great metal fabrications propelled by pounding engines. Such ships still had spirits of their own: the spirits of fire and steam which thrust them doggedly through wind and water. Ship spirits no longer chuckled with the sweet rush of water past the bows, nor hummed and sang with the wind through the rigging, but chanted a monotonous song of the thumping machinery.

Then came a new generation of ships: designed by computers, built by machines, navigated by electronic instruments: massive ugly creations fashioned without joy or pride. Their spirits are brutal and sullen, and from time to time they show their contempt for mankind by driving their ship on the rocks and spilling out her contents to pollute the seas.

Sirens

Birds as big as adult humans, having the heads of beautiful women, voices so sweetly seductive that no man can resist them, and a taste for human flesh. There may have been as few as three of them or as many as eight.

Their family history is complex and contradictory. They were originally water nymphs, daughter of a river god named Achelous, but they seem to have been related to Persephone, the Queen of the Underworld. No one knows exactly why they evolved into an avian species. One story is that they did so in order to console humans, by singing to them during their afterlife in the Underworld, but this would not account for their later activities. Another story is that when they were water nymphs they insisted on retaining their virginity, thus exasperating Venus Aphrodite into changing them into birds.

Nor is it known precisely why they devoted themselves to devouring humans, especially seafarers. One account says they were so proud of their musical ability that they challenged the Muses to a singing contest, and when they lost it they exiled themselves to a rocky island (possibly the Isle of Capri) and revenged themselves on passing sailors. Some stories say that they also had the ability to change themselves into mermaids, so that their bare-breasted beauty made them even more seductive to seamen.

Whatever the facts may be, there can be no doubt as to their technique. When they sighted an approaching ship, they posed on the rocks and sang songs of such exquisite sweetness, promising such transcendental delights, that the sailors abandoned their ship and swam ashore. As soon as they landed the sirens pounced, tore them apart with their cruel talons, and added their bones to those which littered the island.

Sirens were a supreme danger to navigation until the crews of two ships managed to evade them. The first were those of the ship commanded by Odysseus, whom Circe the sorceress had warned of the power of the sirens. He stopped up the ears of his crew so that they would not hear the siren songs, and had himself lashed to the mast so that he would not surrender to their seduction.

Odysseus and his men passed safely by, but other crews perished until Jason and the Argonauts came within siren range. They knew nothing of the sirens' dreadful powers, and one of the crew, Butes, actually jumped overboard and swam into their grasp. The rest of the Argonauts might have followed him, but Orpheus, the supreme musician, struck up a tune on his lyre and sang even more beguilingly than the sirens. The crew could not help listening to him instead of to the sirens, who were so infuriated by this second failure that they threw themselves into the sea.

Southern Cross, The

The four stars of this brilliant constellation are the daughters of Mululu, an Aboriginal tribal leader of the Dreamtime.

Mululu had no sons, and when the time came near for him to die he worried about the fate of his daughters. With no brothers to protect them, and to ensure that they received their share of the game killed by tribal hunters, they might find themselves poorly treated after their father had departed.

Mululu thought deeply on this problem and eventually consulted a medicine man. Soon he told his daughters that when he died he intended to become a star, and that for their own sakes they must join him in the heavens.

In due course Mululu died, and the four girls followed his instructions by going to see the medicine man. They found he had plaited a long rope from the hairs of his beard, and that one end of it stretched up into the sky.

He told them to climb the rope, and when they reached the top they found their father waiting for them. He placed them in the sky as the four stars of the Southern Cross, and made himself into the nearby star known to Europeans as Centaurus.

Swans

These splendid creatures of water and air are known in many parts of the world. Their stately beauty, powerful flight, and strong swimming ability have either been accredited to various supernatural beings, or used by such beings to further their own ends. As mentioned earlier in this book, the great god Zeus turned into a swan in order to ravish the beautiful Leda, by swimming up to her while she was bathing in a pool and taking advantage of her unsuspecting admiration. In Java and other parts of Indonesia, the white swans are usually beautiful maidens who want nothing to do with men. They are occasionally captured when a flight descends on a pool, discards their swan's clothing, and frolics in the water in the form of human girls. A man may take one of the maidens by stealing her swan's attire, so that she is left behind when her companions take off. But he will have to hide the swan clothing carefully, because she will spend much of her life with him in a search for the clothing. As soon as she finds it she will fly away, leaving him with any children she may have had by her wingless lover.

Swan-maidens also live in many parts of Europe, especially Germany and Russia. European males seem to be less interested in marrying them than in making use of their ability to foretell the future. A man who wishes to know what the future has in store for him should hide by a pond until a flight of swan-maidens descends. He should then hide the feathered garments of one of the maidens, and refuse to return them until she has told him what he wants to know.

But a man who catches a swan-woman, by mistake for a swan-maiden, will regret that he was ever born. Swan-women are usually witches without souls, adept in sorcery and remorseless towards anyone who offends their dignity.

In Australia, the black swans appeared for various reasons in different parts of the continent. In one region, they were originally Aborigines with very black skins. During the Deluge, which swamped that country as it did so many others in the world, they changed themselves into black swans and swam to safety.

In another region, the swans were originally white and they had very sweet voices. But they lost all their feathers in a great battle with the eagles, and were so exhausted that they could sing no more. Fortunately a family of ravens took pity on them, clad them with some of their own black feathers, and tried to teach them to sing again. The black swans, however, only tried to imitate the ravens, and ever since then they have had strange harsh voices.

Thunder

The reasons for thunder vary greatly from one country to another. In many instances, the sound reverberates through the heavens when various gods are fighting. The thunder is the sound of their great swords or hammers beating against each other's shields, or the hooves of their horses galloping through the sky, while the lightning flashes are spears and arrows which miss their aim and fall to the ground.

No less than eight thunder gods function in Japan, and are associated not only with the thunder in the skies but that below ground, when earthquakes roar horrendously underfoot. Each god is responsible for a different type of thunder and is named accordingly, such as Kami-Nari, the God of Rolling Thunder.

China, however, has only one thunder deity: Lei Kung, the Lord of Thunder, who covers his blue body only with a loincloth and has dragon-like wings and claws. He rides through the heavens in a chariot pulled by little boys, and creates thunderous noise by banging with a hammer on a drum. In his other hand he holds a sharp chisel, used to punish sinners.

Lei Kung is only one member of the heavenly department which controls storms and tempests, comprising twenty-five deities each responsible for a different type of storm. They are all supervised by Lei Tzu, the Ancestor of Thunder, to whom one should pray, rather than to Lei Kung, for the passing of a thunderstorm.

Other thunder spirits and thunder deities include Hino of the Iroquois; the great Thunderbird of the north-west Pacific coasts of America; Pakadringa of northern Australia, Jambuwul of Arnhem Land, and Mamaragan of central Australia, whose tremendous laughter is the sound of thunder. They are all powerful but capricious personalities who must be kept in a good humour. When they are pleased with their people they send down beneficial torrents of rain, but when they are displeased they either hold onto the rain or dump it in such quantities as to cause disastrous floods.

Tritons

The mermen of the Mediterranean. They have some resemblance to the mermen of other waters, but are much less attractive in character and appearance. Apart from a fishlike tail they also have scales on their torsos, sharp fish's teeth, and webbed fingers with long claws. Like mermen of the northern seas, they can change their tails to legs and walk upon the land.

Northern mermen sometimes fall in love with human females, but tritons have no concept of the tender emotion. Whenever they go ashore they behave worse than drunken sailors on a spree. They get disgustingly drunk, ravish any females who stray within their grasp, and vandalise the seaport towns. Landlubbers often have to resort to violence to rid themselves of a gang of tritons. One community suffered so badly from a drunken triton that they cut off his head while he lay snoring on the beach.

Strangely, old father Triton is a peaceful and helpful merperson, quite unlike his delinquent sons. He has often emerged from his home in the depths of the Mediterranean to assist seafarers in trouble, including the Argonauts. He can cause the roughest sea to subside by blowing on his conch shell trumpet.

His sons have no occupation apart from accompanying their grandfather Poseidon on his rides across the ocean. When the dolphins have been harnessed to Poseidon's chariot, and the nereids are assembled to frolic around them as it charges through the waves, the lecherous crew of tritons acts as outriders. Blowing shrill blasts on conch shells, they rampage over the waters to warn everyone to keep out of the way of the stormy Lord of the Ocean.

U-Boats, Ghosts of

So many of the German fleet of submarines or U-boats (*unterseebooten*) were sent to the bottom in both world wars, in circumstances of such appalling pain and terror, that one might well expect a number to reappear as apparitions. It seems, however, that only one or two have been associated with phantom manifestations.

One, believed to be the U-17, was a submarine of World War I. Her second-in-command was drowned, probably because the boat had to crash dive while he was on deck. After that, he reappeared as a ghostly figure in the bows of the U-boat whenever she surfaced after dark. He allowed crew members to approach closely enough to recognise him, but if anyone tried to question him he disappeared. After a few nights, none of the crew of U-17 would go on deck after dark and she had to make a difficult return to base. The crew was dispersed among other submarines, but when a fresh crew took the U-17 to sea, and also saw the ghostly second-in-command, they came close to mutiny. The captain again returned to port and the boat was withdrawn from service.

A U-boat of World War II has been seen as a seagoing apparition in various parts of the Western Approaches. Various stories surround her, including the seamen's yarn that she is the ghost of a boat commanded by Kapitanleutnant (Lieutenant-Commander) Klaus Till. It is said that Till sank a British merchant ship and then shot several of the survivors. Soon after that, a Royal Navy corvette sank the U-boat, but the war crime of Klaus Till has never allowed it to rest peacefully on the bottom of the Atlantic.

Vainamoinen's Ship

Vainamoinen is one of the creation ancestors of Finland. Even though he appeared on earth as an old man he possessed great magical powers, and among other benefits to mankind he invented the art of agriculture.

After many adventures he decided to seek a wife, but his first choice drowned herself rather than marry an old man. His search for a bride then led him to a country of the far north, eternally locked in snow and ice, where the Maiden of Pohja agreed to marry him on condition that he should split a horsehair with a blunt knife, peel a stone, tie a knot in an egg, cut a block of ice without leaving splinters, and build a ship from her weaving loom.

Vainamoinen's magic enabled him to perform all these tasks except for the ship-building. He forgot three words of the necessary spell, and had to venture into the Underworld in search of them.

He outwitted various supernatural creatures before he found the giant Antero Vipunen, the guardian of the magic words. The giant had trees growing from his head, face, and shoulders, and in Vainamoinen's efforts to make him reveal the three words he cut down the trees and pushed his staff down Antero Vipunen's throat. The giant reacted by swallowing Vainamoinen, but the old man hammered on the giant's heart until Antero Vipunen disgorged him and revealed the magic words.

Vainamoinen hurried back and completed his task of shipbuilding, eager to sail away and claim the Maid of Pohja as his bride. But her mother imposed yet another task upon him: that of forging a magical talisman out of iron. Vainamoinen knew nothing of ironworking and regarded the metal as evil, but he persuaded his brother Ilmarinen, who was a blacksmith, to make the talisman for him.

He had to tell Ilmarinen why he wanted the talisman, and when the blacksmith finished the difficult work he thought he would try to take the Maid of Pohja away from Vainamoinen. He knew that Vainamoinen would take eight days to sail to her country and set off on horseback in an attempt to get there first.

Vainamoinen actually won the race, but the Maid of Pohja kept him in suspense for so long that Ilmarinen had time to reach her and ask for her hand. She liked the look of Ilmarinen more than that of his older brother and agreed to marry him, whereupon Vainamoinen consoled himself by kidnapping her sister.

He took this young lady to his ship and sailed back with her to Finland, but the forced marriage turned out unhappily and when she took a lover he turned her into a seagull. After that he stole the talisman back from her mother. The old woman smashed it in a terrible storm, but it was still powerful enough to bring prosperity to Finland.

Vainamoinen decided that his ship had brought him nothing but trouble and that he was too old to bother with any more young women. He abandoned his ship, built a boat out of copper, and sailed away to the land which lies between heaven and earth.

Valkyries

(More correctly spelt *Waelcyrgean*.) The Choosers of the Slain: magnificent young women who ride on great airborne war horses. They have two functions—primarily to attend battles in order to select warriors fit to enter Valhalla, the Hall of the Slain; and secondly to act as waitresses to the warriors feasting in Valhalla. They work under the instructions of the Norse god Odin.

A Valkyry is the archetypal Nordic maiden: tall, strong, and handsome, with icy blue eyes and plaits of blonde hair as thick as the cables of a Viking ship. When Odin learns that a battle is planned he orders the Valkyries to attend, and they don their breastplates and horned helmets and saddle up their flying horses. On the word of command they stream forth from Valhalla to the thunderous skies above the battlefield, where the Valkyry host splits into two divisions to ride above the opposing armies.

With blue eyes flashing they watch the armies charge into battle, and the first savage clash of arms is the signal for the Valkyries to swoop to earth, dismount from their chargers, and stride amidst the opposing ranks to choose who shall be slain in that day's combat. They favour the most heroic fighters: those most highly qualified to join the heroes already in Valhalla. Each Valkyry identifies such a man and urges him into the thickest of the fray, sharpening his blood-lust with her savage cries and bidding him ignore the wounds which sap his strength. At last he falls to the weapons of his opponents, and his attendant Valkyry waits by the bleeding corpse.

When the sun sets over the battlefield, each Valkyry lifts up the spirit of a dead warrior and takes it to her horse, to join all the others who will be carried to Valhalla that night. The host of women falls into a column behind their leader, and then soar back to Valhalla. There, as the dead heroes feast among the slain of countless wars, the Valkyries serve them with roast pork and tankards of mead and ale.

Valkyries sometimes visit the earth in between battles, on errands for Odin. On such occasions they assume the guise of swans, and may be seen sweeping down the storm winds with their great pinions beating the troubled air.

In England, it is possible that some *Waelcyrgean* chose to abandon Valhalla and settle in various parts of the country, where they either began a new existence as witches or acted as witches' consultants.

Vodyanoi

Water-monsters prevalent in many parts of Russia, especially in millponds. (The ponds where water is dammed so that it may pour through a race, and turn the great wheel which powers the grindstones of a water-mill.) The owners of watermills, who depend on waterpower for grinding grain, are very conscious of the influence of vodyanoi and take care not to offend them. Vodyanoi hate watermills because they obstruct the free flow of water, and try to destroy them by floods or put them out of business by droughts, but they perversely spend much of their time in the millponds and may be heard growling, complaining, and splashing about as the millwheel turns. When the water runs low, and there is a danger of the mill grinding to a halt, the owner may try to placate the vodyanoi by drowning some unwary person in the millpond. Obviously the vodyanoi appreciate human sacrifices because they often snatch people into the water.

Vodyanoi have the strange characteristic of living an entire life during each monthly cycle of the moon. They grow old as the moon grows old, but reappear in full vigour with the new moon. It is hard to describe a vodyanoi because they have so many different manifestations. Sometimes the creature may appear as an old man with green hair and beard, which whitens as the moon wanes, or as a beautiful naked woman. It may be a huge fish covered with moss and trailing waterweed, or a snarling monster with fiery eyes, or simply a floating log. It is no wonder that Russian women warn their children to keep away from millponds.

Water Spirits

Apart from the beings already mentioned in this book, a great many spirits of different types live in the waters all over the world. They include Wala-Undayua, who lives in the water even though he is a lightning deity. For several months of each year he inhabits a river in northern Australia. He rarely emerges during the winter months, which are dry in tropical Australia, but in early summer he keeps a keen lookout for the huge thunderstorms which roll in from the sea. When they appear he darts up into the clouds, and spends the wet season stalking among them on his long glittering legs.

Many of the Australian lakes, rivers, and waterholes were created by various Dreamtime creatures, including the Rainbow Serpent. Others were Windulka the bandicoot, who dug out such a deep burrow that he released underground waters; and Mangowa the Hunter, an Aboriginal of southern Australia who chased an unwilling maiden up into the Milky Way. When she still refused to surrender to him, he was so angry that he snatched clusters of stars from the heavens and flung them down to earth. They struck it with such impact that they formed a string of waterholes across the countryside.

Water spirits are often dangerous, and the rivers of many parts of the world are inhabited by serpents or dragons which demand regular human sacrifices to keep them quiet, but there are also benevolent spirits who understand that water is vital to mankind. Egeria, a Grecian water nymph, whose marriage to Numi Pompilius in the sacred grove of Nemi symbolises the fecund union of water and vegetation, is especially well-disposed towards mortals. Her chuckling voice, heard where clear waters run over stones, will forecast the future for those who can interpret her words. Pregnant women find Egeria a kindly deity when they pray to her for an easy delivery. She knows the secret of finding a way through every kind of obstruction.

Another water nymph, Carmentia, also rose to an important position as a deity. When her son Evander emigrated from Greece to Italy she went with him, and like Egeria she became a goddess of water and childbirth. She also taught the Romans to read and write, and changed Greek letters into the Roman alphabet.

There are many water nymphs in Greece, with different names according to the type of water they inhabit. Potamids live in rivers, naiads in streams, crenae in springs bubbling from hillsides, limnads in ponds and pools. All, like Egeria, are friendly towards mankind and play an important role in agriculture, and in their many-toned voices they will foretell the future for those who can understand them. They rarely endanger humans except for handsome young men, whom they may drag down to join them. Probably this is to ensure continuation of their race, because a water nymph lives only for about 10,000 years, although she retains her youthful beauty until the end.

There are innumerable sea spirits and sea deities, especially around the islands of the Pacific. Their stature and influence depend upon the size and power of the sea creatures with which they are associated. Whale gods are the most important and are often the protectors of chiefs and their families. Shark gods are common, under many different names, and should be propitiated before setting out on a canoe voyage. Other spirits concern themselves with fishing and netmaking, the building of canoes, navigation between the islands, and the law of storms.

Japan and China have many important deities of the rivers and seas, who must be treated very respectfully because of their power to help or damage the aspirations of mankind. In China, the water gods and water spirits are invariably dragons.

The European land mass, from the Baltic to the Urals, proliferates with water spirits of which many are unpleasant and antagonistic. Apart from the rusalka and vodyanoi, already mentioned in this book, they include Nakki, who is a lake spirit of Finland and should be asked to leave the water before one dives in for a swim; Vizi-Ember of Hungary and other places, who will drown people if he does not receive regular human sacrifices; and Vu-vozo of southern Russia.

The gypsies who roam Europe have long since discovered a way to control local spirits if one wishes to camp near water. The method is to soak three iron nails in the watercourse for three days, then hammer them into a tree as close to the water as possible. The nails pin down the water spirits until the campers move on.

Wind Gods and Spirits

A multitude of beings, with widely differing characteristics, control the wind and weather of communities throughout the world. In some places, wind control is the prerogative of a principal god such as Quetzalcoatl of the Aztecs, although he delegates the task to lesser deities. In other places a specific god is appointed controller of the winds. Ah-dad of Babylon was one of these, and like many other wind gods he was a two-faced personality. He rode on a charging bull, carried thunderbolts in his hands, and spoke in the voice of thunder, but in softer moods he made up for his destructive activities by sending spring breezes and bounteous rains. Ga-oh the Wind Giant, one of the deities of the Iroquois nation, had a somewhat similar character, although his softer side is represented by the girl Breath of Wind and her husband Master of Winds. Their son Ioskeha is the supervisor of all vegetable and animal foods.

Often a single god is insufficient to control all the winds. The brothers Boreas, Zephyrus, Eurus and Notus are responsible for the winds of the Mediterranean. Three brothers administer the winds of some Baltic coastal communities, and no less than nine gods control the winds of Nicaragua. A number of separate spirits concern themselves with the winds of Australia, from the wandjina, who live in the cyclonic storms of the north-west coasts, to the spirits who dance across the desert in their whirlwind garments of tawny dust. The Aborigines treat the whirlwind spirits very respectfully, because they remember that a young hunter tried to kill one of them with his boomerang and was never seen again. In northern Australia, Bara the north-west wind plays an important role. Each summer he brings rain from the north, together with the spirits of all the children to be born to local tribeswomen during the following year. But he tends to sleep very heavily during the dry season and has to be sharply reminded of his duties. In early summer, the Aborigines use their axes to gash the trees where Bara is sleeping, to wake him up and let him out for another wet season.

The Chinese seem to be rather uncertain about the controllers of their country's winds. Some believe that a celestial dragon named Fei Lin, who appears sometimes as a bird beating the air with his wings and sometimes as a dragon with a bird's head, deer's horn, and a snake's tail, creates the winds which blow over China. Others are sure that wind and weather are provided by the Department of Thunder, which has twenty-five functionaries including Lei Kung the Lord of Thunder, Lightning-Mother, and Little Boy of the Clouds. Wind is controlled by an old gentleman named Feng Po, a mandarin of the second class. He uses two fans to create light winds and occasionally releases strong winds from a leather sack. Some believers maintain that old Feng Po retired some centuries ago and was replaced by Feng P'o P'o, or Mrs Wind, who rides a tiger through the sky.

It seems likely that Haya Ji, the Japanese god of the whirlwind, also carries the wind in a leather sack, to be released whenever he feels that mortals are overdue for punishment. As in China, there are several Japanese gods of wind and weather. The principal wind god, Shina-Tsu-Hiko, is one of the oldest deities of the nation, having been born from the breath of the creation god Izanagi to blow away the primal mists which shrouded Japan. He and his wife, Shina-to-

Be, now occupy the vacancy between earth and heaven and move within it in various directions.

The Japanese wind gods Tatsuta-hiko and Tatsuta-hime, who live in the shrine of Tatsuta, are more closely concerned with the everyday needs of the Japanese people. They help to provide good harvests and good fishing, and favourable winds for seafarers.

Apart from the principal wind gods there is a multitude of wind spirits, with characteristics ranging from benevolent to malevolent. In many parts of Europe the fertilising spirit of the grain is also a wind spirit, with such names as Corn Maiden or Rye Wolf. He, she, or it may be plainly seen running over the standing grain, which bends and sways under the passage of spirit feet. Obviously this type of spirit is benevolent, but malevolent wind spirits stir up the sandstorms of Arabia or live within the terrifying 'twisters' which roar over the prairie states of North America, like huge black serpents with heads in the thunderclouds and tails lashing the ground. Jinni, who are powerful evil spirits of the Middle East, often move across deserts in a whirling column of dust, whipped up by wind spirits controlled by the jinni.

Mortals use countless ways to control wind spirits but are not always successful. On becalmed ships, the sailors may arouse the winds by whistling certain tunes, but on the other hand, a sailor who whistles when the wind is fair may cause it to drop or change. In severe storms, a shipmaster may order his crew to stick their knives into the mainmast and leave them there until the wind subsides, with its power bled away by the knife points.

In some parts of Africa the medicine-men keep the winds bottled up in jars, to be released only as required. A wind spirit should not leave its jar unless compelled to do so by the appropriate spell, but the spirits are so devious that they often escape without permission and have to be recaptured by complex ceremonies.

The wizards of many nations profess the art of wind control, by repeating certain spells or casting charms into the face of the wind. The practice has its dangers because wind spirits delight in tormenting or embarrassing humans. Many a wizard has suffered in reputation by causing an easterly wind to subside, only to find that it blows even more violently from the west.

Windmill Spirits

This subspecies of the wind spirit family infests some types of windmill in Holland and England.

A windmill is a fairly simple but very effective machine. Four or more sails convert windpower into energy, transmitted down a vertical shaft by a basic gearing system of large wooden cogs. (Well-seasoned oak is the most favoured material for the gears.) The shaft turns a large grindstone used for milling grain into flour.

The windpower may also be used to operate such machinery as pumps, lathes, or drills.

It may be thought that once a miller has paid the millwrights to rig the sails, and fit the cogs and grindstones, he is comfortably situated to profit by free windpower. But a windmill is a noisy and demonstrative apparatus, with whirling sails and grumbling grindstones, and this noise and activity are certain to attract a group of wandering windmill spirits. They take up residence in the cupola: the movable dome that may be turned in order to adjust the sails to the wind.

Windmill spirits, like most other spirits of the air, resent anything which impedes the freedom of the wind. Their usual ploy is to arrange for a brisk wind at the beginning of the day's work, so that the windmill sails clatter around gaily and the grindstone growls contentedly. When the miller has fallen into a good working rhythm, pouring in grain at one end and filling sacks with flour at the other, the windmill spirits cause the wind to veer round to another direction.

No sooner has the miller gone through the tedious process of disengaging the main gear, swinging the cupola round so that the sails catch the new wind direction, and starting work again, then the windmill spirits arrange another change in the wind. They may cause it to drop, fluke and flaw through several points of the compass, or blow in howling gusts which make the sails bend dangerously and the grindstone roar angrily at its task.

An infestation of windmill spirits quickly brings work to a standstill, but an experienced miller knows the solution to the problem. He simply throws a few handfuls of flour into the wind. This diverts the attention of the windmill spirits, who spend the rest of the day blowing the flour around and leave the miller to get on with his work.

Yu Tzu, Yu Shih, Ch'ing Sung-Tzu

Names of the Master of Rain, one of the twenty-five members of the Department of Thunder which controls the weather of China. In the days of Shen Nung, the ox-headed emperor who ruled for seventeen generations, there was a great drought which Yu Tzu ended by dipping a branch into a bowl of water and shaking it over the ground. For this feat he was nominated Master of the Rain and he continues to sprinkle rain over China. Some believe that he does this with a watering can: others that he dips his sword into a jar of water and shakes the drops down onto the ground.

Zephyrus

The west wind: brother of Boreas the north wind and Eurus and Notus the east and south winds. The lives of Boreas and Zephyrus are well documented but little is known about their brothers.

Probably Zephyrus was originally a fierce wild stallion, with power to gallop furiously through the air and over land and sea. No doubt he was a stallion when he married the harpy Podarge, who gave birth to two horses named Xanthus and Balius. They could both talk Greek, which proved a useful attribute when the hero Achilles harnessed them into his chariot.

When Zephyrus assumed human form he fell in love with the Spartan prince Hyacinthus, who was already the lover of Apollo. In a jealous anger, Zephyrus blew on a discus thrown by Apollo and caused it to strike and kill Hyacinthus, whose blood spilled on the ground and sprang up into the flowers we call hyacinths.

After these troubled beginnings, Zephyrus became a reformed character. He ceased his furious outbursts and became either the husband or lover of the rainbow nymph Iris. Later he married Chloris, the springtime divinity who causes plants to burst into blossom. Their son, Carpus or Carpos, is the fruit of all trees and vines.

The influence of Iris and Chloris helped to calm Zephyrus and as the west wind he now brings soft airs and beneficial rains.

CHAPTER SIX

THINGS OF THE NIGHT

THINGS OF THE NIGHT

Black as a bat's wing, night brings release to all we creatures who must slither or shuffle away when cockcrow heralds our enemy the sun. People have given us many names: ghouls, ghosts, night wanderers, vampires, werewolves, and so on. But we are all members of the same family; the tormented souls who must return forever to the scenes of our lost humanity. You may hang garlic or a crucifix above your bed, prepare silver bullets to shoot us, call in holy men to exorcise us from your home, but you cannot defeat us. Our name is Legion, and we are too many for you because we are the forces of evil who reflect the evil within your own souls. Even though you run screaming into the darkness we will always catch up with you, because your own evil will always betray you. You know that we live not only in the darkness of the night but also in the darkness within your heart.

Who dares to wander alone through a midnight graveyard? There is no coffin strong enough to contain us; no weight of earth or chiselled stone heavy enough to hold us down. We hate and envy the lifeblood warm within your veins; the love and hope and joy which we abandoned. Locked into an eternity of despair, we find fleeting contentment only when we transform your warm life into an icy terror of the soul. Once you have met one of us you will never be the same again.

Some of us, like the countless folk infected by Drakul's fangs, are outwardly pleasant to the eye. We appear ripe and blooming, fed as we are by a nightly enrichment of new blood. We are plausible and charming, so that you welcome us into your home and never know your error until you awaken one morning wan and exhausted. Of course you can recover your strength by seeking your own victims.

Others of us are not so attractive to the eye. It is not charming to turn a dark corner and confront a living corpse. You believe that is impossible? There are unfortunates, who shiver and whimper each time the sun sets, who would tell you that you are wrong. We live eternally, everywhere, even in your quiet neighbourhood, but show ourselves only when it pleases us to do so. Did you hear that dog howling in the night? No doubt it had seen one of the great company of the grave.

Abiku

An insatiable demon of the night which preys upon the Yoruba people of West Africa. Parents living in the little villages huddled deep in the forest are terrified of Abiku, because his diet consists of children. He relishes nothing better than a plump newborn baby but will satisfy himself with any child up to the age of puberty. As soon as the sun sets, parents hustle their children into the huts, and sometimes hide them under mats or blankets so that Abiku will not find them.

Nobody seems able to give a definite description of Abiku, except that he is as shapeless as smoke and able to filter his way through the densest thicket of thorn bushes. They all agree, however, on his principal peculiarity. He has no stomach, and is therefore obliged to eat continuously because he never knows the satisfaction of a full belly.

Accident, Spirits of

Any Chinese person who dies accidentally is judged to have perished before his appointed time. This means he has broken the cycle of existence and cannot be reincarnated until he has provided the gods of the afterworld with a replacement spirit. For three years after death he must exist as a starving demon on the fringes of the afterworld, and then he is allowed to seek a replacement spirit to stand in for him.

The process is complicated by the fact that he must find the spirit of a person who died in the same way as he did. It is not enough for the spirit of a man who drowned accidentally to take the spirit of a person who fell out of a high window. He must have that of another person who died in the water.

Consequently the homeless demons haunt the places where they died in human form, especially after nightfall. They are quite capable of encouraging similar accidents, and so the Chinese people always avoid the sites of accidental deaths.

Acheri

A female ghost of some Amerindian nations. She is a skeletal squaw-like creature attired in tattered deerskin robes, who sleeps during the day and appears at nightfall to sing her death chant, beat upon her little tom-tom, and shuffle through the ritual steps of her dance. Her voice, as eerie as the wailing of wolves in the depths of winter, floats down from the mountains to the plains and valleys and penetrates even the thickest blanket wrapped around a sleeper's head, foretelling death for the hearer or his family. The only protection against Acheri is to wear garments ornamented with red cloth or beads. The colour protects one against the effects of her death song and anyone dressed wholly in red may listen to it unperturbed.

Adh Seidh

Irish spirits never seen by persons with a clear conscience. They are said to be of terrifying appearance, perhaps somewhat witch-like but with fangs that tear at one's flesh. Other stories say they are like beautiful women who lure one to destruction, or even like animals such as shining black horses, with fiery eyes and terrible teeth.

Fortunately, those of us who live an upright life have nothing to fear from the adh seidh. They appear only to such people as blackmailers, seducers, corrupt leaders, maltreaters of children, tellers of harmful lies, and others who have managed to evade mortal justice. To such people the adh seidh are terrible indeed, and the fear of their midnight visits may destroy the sinner's sanity.

Altebar, Baroness Russlein Von

A female ghost who appears only to descendants of Count Johannes Rathenau. During the religious wars, Rathenau captured Schloss Altebar in Bavaria and slaughtered the whole Altebar family with particular savagery.

Baroness Altebar appears to Rathenau men as a seductive and beautiful woman. She chooses her victim at night, at a ball or some other happy occasion, and displays such charm and promise that he is unable to resist her. What happens after that will vary according to her whim.

In Vienna in 1896, a cab driver picked up Walther Rathenau and a beautiful woman late one night. He heard the couple laughing and talking in his cab, but suddenly smelt an appalling odour of rotting flesh. His horse stopped and refused to move, and when he opened the cab door he found the woman had vanished and that Walther was speechless with terror. He died three days later.

At Baden Baden in 1938, Major Helmut Rathenau was enjoying a successful evening in the casino in the company of a woman later described as 'More beautiful than Hedy Lamarr'. At midnight, he strolled into the garden with her and his winnings. At dawn, a gardener found his corpse under a lilac tree. It appeared to have been immersed in water for many weeks.

The baroness always makes sure that the Rathenau men know the reason for their fate. In 1703 she transformed Carl-Heinz Rathenau into an object resembling a mummy, which lived long enough to croak out the story she told him.

One would think that Rathenau men would be on their guard against strange women. But the rich and scented beauty of the baroness, with dark eyes promising untold delights, always makes them forget the old story as they follow her into the night.

Ankou

Silent walkers of the night, whose appearance on the roads of Brittany presages death for those who see them pass by.

They manifest themselves as a tall gaunt man, driving a cart drawn by a pale boney horse, accompanied by two silent figures who walk beside or behind the cart. All have bowed heads so that one may not see their features.

They appear at dusk, at the time when it is just possible to distinguish black from white, and pass silently by. The unfortunate observer does not realise that the horse's hooves, the cartwheels, and the feet of the walkers make no sound upon the rough road until they have passed him. When he turns to look after them they have vanished into the darkness, and he knows that he, or one whom he loves, must soon follow the same road.

Azeman

A rare example of a vampire actually appearing in the form of a vampire bat. Fortunately the azeman is restricted to certain regions of north-eastern South America, especially the part once known as Surinam or Dutch Guiana.

The azeman is invariably a woman, who has been infected with vampirism by the blood contact of another azeman. During the day she appears to be perfectly normal, but after dark she changes into a bat and flits around the village in search of prey. In normal vampire bat style she seeks for a sleeper whose foot is exposed, and with exquisite care uses her fangs to scrape away a fragment of flesh from the big toe. When the blood trickles she laps it up until she is engorged, and flaps heavily back to her own hut. In the morning her victim is drained and weak whereas the azeman is in hearty good health.

Luckily it is easy to prevent an azeman from entering one's hut, simply by propping a broom across the doorway.

Banshee

A female spirit of the Gaelic and Celtic peoples, rarely seen but often heard. She is said to be a woman with straggling black hair and eyes red from weeping, and dressed in a green robe and grey cloak. She has an appalling cry, described by some who have heard it as a blend between the howling of a wolfhound, the cry of wild geese, the screams of an abandoned child, and the groans of a woman in labour.

Those who have heard a banshee say that this dreadful semi-human sobbing, screaming, and wailing will awaken the soundest sleeper and rise above the wildest gale. It is especially awesome when it echoes over the moors and lakes in the twilight of a grey summer's day.

The wail of a banshee has only one meaning—that a member of the family which hears it is doomed to die. The man or woman may be far from his home, but the banshee warns the family in the homeland.

The word 'banshee' derives from the Celtic words *bean seidh*, meaning 'Woman of the Fairies'. Numerous ancient families of Eire and of the Scottish islands and highlands claim to have their personal banshees, which only attend families of pure Celtic or Gaelic descent.

Bassarab, Vlad Drakul

(Also known as 'Count Dracula'.) The sole survivor of the Bassarab dynasty of Walachia, which is now a province of Roumania. For many centuries, this country of the Vlach people was torn by wars and invasions until the great warrior Ralph the Black consolidated Walachia as a nation, and established the Bassarabs as the ruling family. Reigning under such titles as Vlad I, Vlad II, Vlad III, and Vlad IV, the Bassarabs still had to fight off invasions by Mongols, Turks, and Hungarians, however, and these perpetual wars gave the Bassarabs an unquenchable lust for blood.

One was so horrifyingly cruel that he became known as Vlad Dracul or Drakul, meaning either 'dragon' or 'devil'. The Walachians said that a man so appallingly evil must have been sired by Satan or a dragon. Also, he bore all the marks of vampirism and seemed to flourish on human blood.

His successors, Vlad Tepes and Vlad Tsepesh, were equally cruel. Vlad Tepes, known as 'The Impaler', liked to have prisoners of war impaled on pointed stakes, and enjoyed eating his dinner in front of a group of impaled prisoners groaning away their lives. In between wars, he indulged this taste for torture by having Walachian men, women, and even children impaled for his pleasure.

Slowly the nation became more civilised and the Bassarabs presented the appearance of learned and cultured aristocrats—although the Turks drowned one of them as the result of a family intrigue. By 1658 the dynasty seemed to end with the death of Constantine Bassarab, but there was one survivor of the tainted line.

He was another Vlad Drakul, who had bought a great estate in Transylvania. It is uncertain whether he was a Bassarab descendant or simply a continuing reincarnation of the original Vlad Drakul and of Vlad Tepes and Tsepesh—in fact a vampire maintaining immortality by regular engorgement with human life essences.

This Vlad Drakul lived in Transylvania for about three centuries, but in the 1890s the peasants of his estate were almost exhausted by his continuous blood tax. He decided he must venture further afield, and arranged with a firm of London estate agents to buy property in England.

They sent a young representative, Jonathan Harker, to Drakul's castle in Transylvania in order to negotiate the deal. He saw Drakul (whom he named 'Count Dracula') as a tall gaunt old man with sharp teeth, pointed ears, hair in the palm of his hands, and a foul breath—all the symptoms of vampirism. One of Drakul's three female companions manifested herself in Harker's bedchamber, and in a scene of near-sexual seduction enjoyed a feast of fresh young English blood.

In a complex series of events, Drakul made his way to England and attached himself to a young lady named Lucy Westenra. After draining her blood he turned to Harker's

young wife Mina, but was eventually foiled by Harker and a group of friends. They chased him back to Transylvania, where Harker cut his throat and another man stabbed him through the heart. These are not, however, the prescribed methods of dealing with vampirism, and there can be little doubt that the last survivor of the Bassarabs still prowls in search of human blood.

Baykok

A night spirit of North America, restricted to Indians of the Chippewa nation. The baykok has some resemblance to a walking skeleton, except that its bones are covered by a thin translucent skin. A fearsome red light glows out of the eye sockets of the skull.

The baykok only preys on warriors, who receive some warning of its approach because its bones creak and rattle as it walks. There is, however, no escape from the baykok, which either smites with its club at close quarters or kills with invisible arrows.

Bedclothes

The intimate embrace of one's bedclothes provides evilly disposed persons with an ideal opportunity for unpleasant spells. The impression on the mattress, and the shape of the bedclothes after a sleeper has arisen, provide a kind of invisible mould of the occupant's body. It is therefore possible for a spellbinder to cast influences which affect a person next time he or she lies in the bed. These influences may range all the way from bad dreams to actual bodily anguish, and any sleep disturbances may be attributed to bewitched bedclothes.

In extreme instances, a sorcerer may pervert the life essences which have seeped into the bedclothes and cause the sheets and blankets to assume a life of their own during the night, to stifle or at least terrify the sleeper.

It is, of course, easy to foil such bewitchments, simply by giving the bedclothes a good shake each morning and smoothing out the mattress, to rid the bed of one's lingering personality.

Bodach

A malicious house spirit of the Scottish Highlands, having the form of a shrivelled little old man who lives up in the chimney during the daytime. He survives quite comfortably in the fumes of the burning peat, and keeps a sharp ear open for troublesome children who make a fuss at bedtime.

When all is dark, the bodach slithers down the chimney to tweak the naughty child's toes, ears, and nose, pull its eyelids open and look into the terrified eyes, and inflict horrid nightmares.

If the child's behaviour improves then the bodach will leave him alone, but it is said that if a cunning child drops a pinch of salt on the fire it will keep the bodach in his lair.

Chuang Kung

The Chinese immortal who occupies every bed, together with his wife Chuang Mu, and has some influence on every bed activity including sleep, lovemaking, sickness, and childbirth. (Although there are, of course, other deities who play separate parts in such activities.)

Probably Chuang Kung's principal function is to provide a peaceful and unobtrusive bed environment, so that (for example) persons making love on a cold night are not distracted by the bedclothes sliding to the floor. The extent of the powers of Chuang Kung and Chuang Mu is not fully understood, but it is wise to placate them by placing a cup of tea on one side of the bed and a cup of tea on the other. The deities may then refresh themselves during the night and will not become restless.

Domovoi and Domovikha

The Russian household spirits who crept into the first human habitations and have lived there ever since. On the whole they are benign spirits, who live beneath the stove or doorstep or in the cellar. When a family moves into a new home it is wise to place a piece of bread beneath the stove to attract Domovoi. His wife accompanies him but takes up residence in the cellar.

Domovikha never speaks, but one may often hear Domovoi during the night. When he chatters and murmurs softly, the family may be sure that nothing unpleasant is likely to happen. But when he sobs or groans loudly it is a sign of misfortune, and Domovoi weeping is a sure sign of a death in the family.

Humans rarely see Domovoi and never see Domovikha. It may be that he resembles a small man covered with silky hair, who may be mistaken for a dog or cat. A Domovoi-sighting is extremely unfortunate, and if he does appear it may be better for the family to seek a new habitation.

Duppy

A type of ghost raised by people of the West Indies to perform some service, usually of revenge. A duppy is raised by calling the name of a dead person continuously over a grave until the duppy arises through the earth and awaits instructions. Ideally, a duppy should be a relation of the caller, because non-related duppies may attack him instead of doing his bidding.

A duppy does not seem to be capable of performing useful tasks, and even when ordered to attack someone it can only cause vomiting by breathing on the victim or convulsions by touching him or her. When it has performed the task it should be rewarded by placing rum and tobacco on the grave.

Anyone who has reason to fear duppy-attack may keep them away by sprinkling tobacco seed around the house.

Forso

Ghosts of the islands off northern Australia, including some parts of New Guinea. One very rarely sees a forso but often feels the effect of forso activities. Death is a very tedious occupation, and the forsos become bored in their lonely graves or in the trees where corpses have been placed to rot away, and they pass the time by pestering their living relations. When anything goes wrong in human affairs, one may be fairly sure that a forso is reminding mankind of its presence in the universe.

The best way to keep forsos calm and reasonably contented is to make frequent visits to the abode of corpses, or to keep the skulls and bones of one's ancestors on display in the village. These practises give the dead plenty of company and the forsos do not become bored and restless.

Ghosts

The spirit of a dead person appearing in visible form, usually because of some tragedy suffered during life on earth. Most human tragedies begin with a lost belief, because we are nothing if we do not believe in something, and the loss or betrayal of a belief wounds us so deeply that even death will not heal the trauma. Those who carry these unhealed wounds beyond the grave are known as ghosts.

The most common ghosts are those of betrayed lovers, deserted children, and men or women murdered by false friends. All have known the betrayal of belief and the abandonment of love.

The ghosts of murdered lovers are the most pathetic of all, because murder is the ultimate betrayal. They return forever to the scenes of their lost happiness, bewilderedly seeking the reason why their love was so betrayed. The broken-hearted sobbing and wailing of such a ghost is a hair-raising sound.

Ghosts of this character are quite harmless. They are wistful creatures who have no reason to harm you. If you should see the spectre of a weeping child, or the misty form of a woman dressed in the garments of the past, you should feel pity rather than fear.

People who lived a normally contented life, and died from natural causes or even from violence, never return as ghosts. They did not suffer the betrayal of belief which creates a ghost. But, if some danger threatens those whom they loved during life, they may make a supreme effort to re-appear in their once familiar form. If you should see a beloved relation or friend in this manner, you should take instant warning that danger lies ahead.

The most dangerous ghosts are of those who practised some treachery during life. They may have been murderers, cheating friends, callous lovers, cruel parents, or treasonable retainers. They betrayed those who trusted them. Their sins deny them rest, and they seek perpetual revenge on those who still know love and life.

Exorcism will help any ghost to find eternal rest, and it may be a kindness to have this ritual practised even for harmless ghosts.

Golem

An animated clay figure whose name derives from that given to Adam before Jehovah breathed life into him. In about 1590, Rabbi Low Ben Bezalel made a golem to protect the Jews of Prague against attack by the Christians. The rabbi approached his task with great reverence, using pure water and clay from a newly opened pit. He blessed each portion of the golem's anatomy as he fashioned it from clay, and eventually brought it to life by inserting a slip of paper, bearing the sacred word *shem*, under the clay tongue.

The golem proved not only an effective sentinel, but also a useful domestic servant. It scared away Christians prowling around the ghetto after dark, and did the heavy housework in the rabbi's home. But on one Friday night the ponderous creature ran amok, because the rabbi forgot to remove the slip of paper at sunset, when all Jews should cease work until sunset on Saturday. The golem rampaged through the dark streets of the ghetto until the rabbi and his friends could catch it, remove the slip of paper, and cart the clay figure off to the cellars of the Great Synagogue. According to tradition, the golem still lies there awaiting re-animation.

Ghouls

Ghastly creatures of the night, originating in Arabia, who lurk around places of burial and keep watch for the interment of fresh corpses. They may resemble demons, with fiery eyes and breath, but it seems more likely that they are horrid jelly-like grey creatures which become invisible by standing still, and move in complete silence on large feet which make no impression in the dust. Despite their amorphous bulk they are extremely strong, able to wrench away piles of stone covering a grave, and possessed of sharp fangs so that they may rend corpses apart for a ghoulish feast.

As a precaution against ghouls it is best for funerals to be carried out quickly, quietly, and simply, without any rich display, interment of jewels or money with the deceased, or any other activity likely to arouse ghoulish interest.

Hallowe'en

The night of 31 October: the eve of Hallowmass (Holy Mass). The night on which the spirits of the dead visit their living relations in search of comfort.

The multitude of spirits abroad on Hallowe'en creates an ideal atmosphere for every kind of occult happening. Goblins seize their last opportunity, before they are frozen in for the winter, for wreaking all kinds of mischief on human beings. The shrieks and cackles of witches fill the night sky, as flocks of them fly to the final Sabbat of the year. Fairies spirit away young wives, whom they return dazed and amnesic 366 days later, and snatch babies from cradles. Werewolves howl and prowl; every kind of ghost gibbers and moans around windows and doorways; skeleton hands reach up out of ancient graves.

All these supernatural tensions create a splendid ambience for divination and fortune-telling. Crystal-gazers are busier than at any other time of year, while palmreaders drive a thriving trade. The best fortunes are those told by gypsies in church doorways.

Mortals should not cower inside their homes on Hallowe'en. They should light great fires on hilltops to frighten the witches away; throw riotous parties and dance around houses and barns to scare off goblins and fairies; stone witches' cottages; and give plenty of food and drink to children and poor people in the name of charity. The community which stages an uproarious Hallowe'en will drive away all the prowling creatures of the night.

Herne the Hunter

The figure of a shaggy man or forest spirit, horned with antlers like a great stag, which rides a firebreathing horse through the woods of Windsor Great Park in the vicinity of Windsor Castle. Numerous stories explain

this apparition of the dusk and darkness, last seen as recently as 1964. The most believable account says that Herne was one of the Royal Huntsmen of King Henry VIII, and that he offended the king in some now-forgotten way. Herne was either hanged by royal command, or he hanged himself in the forest out of despair and remorse. Probably his silent gallop through the forest, which has been witnessed many times over the centuries, portends ill-fortune to any observer.

Imandwa

The ghosts of certain folk heroes and tribal leaders of the Tanzanian region. Even though they played important parts in tribal life during their mortal existence they are jealous of living people, and revenge themselves for their deaths by troublesome activities during the night.

Incubus

A male spirit or demon which visits women in their sleep. Its name derives from the Latin *incubare*, meaning to lie upon, in, or with, because an incubus lies with a mortal woman in ghostly sexual intercourse. The woman does not awaken during the peculiar embrace although she may experience it in a dream.

A woman impregnated by an incubus becomes pregnant in the normal way, and eventually gives birth to a child of supernatural capabilities. Possibly it will grow into a person of evil intent or possibly, like the magician Merlin who was born of the union between an incubus and a nun, it will become a powerful wizard of strongly moral character.

Inua

The inner spirit of a person of the Indian and Eskimo nations of North America. An inua may be regarded as a spirit of both life and death. It inhabits a person during mortal existence, and then reappears in some other form after the death of its physical host. Each of the stars and other heavenly bodies which shine down on the Arctic ice was once the inua of a human being.

An inua never reveals itself until the time comes near for it to depart from its human habitation. Then it appears as a flickering light in the darkness, and the host human knows that the tribe will soon be singing his death song.

Kasha

Malicious ghoul spirits of Japan. Unlike the ghouls of Arabia, who disinter corpses, the kashas have to steal a corpse before it is cremated. Sometimes they are so eager and greedy that they even carry off the coffin in which a corpse reposes. Consequently, it is necessary to keep a tight guard on corpse and coffin until they have been cremated, and to make a lot of noise during the night before cremation in order to scare the kashas away.

K'uei

The undead of China: the souls of persons who have not earned sufficient merit during their lives on earth to warrant promotion to the afterworld, and must continue a miserable existence on earth. This fate makes them angry and evil, always on the lookout for sinners on whom to take their revenge. They resemble skeletons except that their skulls are fronted with demonic faces. K'uei always move in straight lines, and so they are easily frustrated by setting a screen just inside the doorway of a room. They cannot move around the corner of the screen and so must go elsewhere in search of prey. It is also advisable to build roofs with upward-curving gables, so that k'uei cannot slide down them and pounce on anyone standing below.

Lilith

The Queen of the Night, but also known as Lili or Lilu which means 'monster of the night'. Jehovah created her out of mud to be Adam's first wife, but her soul was marred in the making and she gave birth only to evil spirits. Eventually she deserted Adam to join Satan's henchmen, and Jehovah created her replacement by fashioning Eve out of one of Adam's ribs.

Lilith is a woman of ageless sinister beauty, marred by the coarse black hairs smothering her otherwise shapely legs. She is so ashamed of these that she always keeps them covered. By the time any man discovers the reality it is too late for him to be repelled by this flaw.

Probably Lilith is the original vampire, whose tainted touch has been passed on from one unfortunate to another during countless centuries. She has the vampirish ability to pass through any kind of obstruction and manifest herself on the other side, either for a feast of blood or to seduce sleeping men into somnambular intercourse, from which they awaken as exhausted as though they had been drained by a vampire. Also she has an unpleasant habit of acting as a invisible attendant on couples making love during the night, so that she may steal some semen which she will conjure into new demons.

She hates children because her own were so repulsive, and often tries to pervert their nature or even to destroy them.

Any man who fears midnight seduction by Lilith should follow the simple practice of writing 'Adam and Eve may enter herein but not Lilith the Queen' upon the door or wall of his bedroom.

Lycanthropy

(From the Greek *lukos* = wolf, *anthropos* = man.) The phenomenon in which a human turns into a beast during the night and reverts to human form at sunrise. The were-beast may be as harmless as a rabbit or as dangerous as a wolf, crocodile, or tiger. In Africa, where whole tribes may be affected by lycanthropy, a white hunter once shot hyaenas wearing golden earrings.

Lycanthropy occurs internationally and always follows the same course. An apparently normal human, usually quite inoffensive in everyday life, changes at sunset into some kind of wild animal. During the night the were-person indulges a taste for human flesh or for the raw flesh and blood of other animals. Were-persons are appallingly dangerous in their bestial form and may even eat their own human children or other relations.

The only exception to this rule is that of were-persons who change into vegetarian creatures such as squirrels, rabbits, or hares. Probably these are witches or wizards who wish to spy on people for the purpose of blackmail.

The causes of lycanthropy are obscure. It may be that a human deliberately learns the necessary magical powers, or he may be under a spell cast by a magician (St Patrick of Ireland changed Veretius, King of Wales, into a wolf). Or he may become infected with lycanthropy by physical contact with a were-beast in human or bestial form. Some researchers believe that even the consumption of food prepared by a lycanthropist is

enough to carry the infection. Lycanthropologists are still uncertain whether a were-person makes an involuntary transformation at nightfall, or whether he/she aids the process by smearing the body with ointment made from the fat of the relevant animal.

Sometimes a were-person reveals himself or herself involuntarily, as in the case of the Indian were-tigress caught in a trap. At sunrise, the villagers found the trap contained a naked woman. On other occasions a hunter shoots at some beast spotted during the night, and on the following day a villager is seen limping from a wound.

Apart from such obvious revelations, a were-person is easily detected when there have been night-time attacks in a neighbourhood. He or she has no appetite, because of the feasts of raw meat taken during the night; and is always tired and stiff in the daytime because of the vigorous nocturnal activities. If the lycanthropist co-operates then the condition may be cured by any accomplished witch or wizard. If not, then the were-person should be shot with a silver bullet.

Menahune

Night spirits of the Hawaiian Islands. They are unusual spirits of the night because they are helpful rather than dangerous. Like the brownies of the British Isles, the menahune appear when the household is asleep and do all the housework. It seems, however, that the menahune are very particular about their employers. They do their work only for families which they feel to be especially pleasant and kind. Very few people have seen the menahune, which are believed to have pointed ears, shaggy black hair, and tiny agile bodies.

Min Min Light

A phenomenon of the Min Min region of Queensland, Australia. Midnight travellers across the plains are often followed or accompanied by a large flickering luminescence which appears suddenly, stays for varying periods, and disappears as abruptly as it came. Some travellers have described the Min Min as no more than a glowing amorphous light, while others claim that it assumes the shape of a horse or man. Modern travellers often confuse it with the lights of an approaching vehicle and take violent evasive action. Many people have been badly frightened by the Min Min Light although it does not seem to have harmed anyone so far.

Moon, The

Most people agree that the moon is a lady, either the wife or sister of the sun. The Babylonian moon was, however, a god named Sin, who sailed across the heavens in his moon boat, and the Japanese moon god, Suki-Yoki, shows himself as a rabbit on the face of the moon.

The moon goddess has many names. The Romans knew her as Luna, and the Greeks as Selene, sister of Helios the sun. Each evening she bathed her white body in the ocean and set off across the sky in a silver chariot. Selene has an especial liking for lovers, and on many nights she caresses her own sleeping lover, Endymion, with her soft rays.

Cheng O, the Chinese goddess of the moon, is also a beautiful young woman. She stole the elixir of immortality from her husband, fled to the moon, and now lives there comfortably in a splendid palace. Hina, the Polynesian goddess of life and death, also chose the moon as a refuge. She retired there when she had completed her cosmic tasks on earth, and now spends her time making tapa cloth from the bark of a great banyan tree.

The stars over Russia are the children of the sun and moon, whose marital relationship has sometimes been turbulent. In some parts of Africa, the moon once had a shining immaculate face until her husband the sun splattered it with mud. In other regions they were once two suns, until the wife washed herself white in a river.

The moon, like all beautiful and intelligent ladies, has many sides to her personality. She changes a little every day and regularly goes on long journeys. In the Algonquin nation of North America she disappears each month to summons the sun back from his hunting trips, and in some parts of Australia she wearies of lovemaking with her companion and goes away for a few days rest and recuperation. But on the whole the moon is more faithful than the sun, who is sometimes hot and sometimes cold, whereas she smiles down on us in both winter and summer.

Nightingales

Small rather drab birds of England and parts of Europe, Asia, and Africa. Noted for their exquisite song heard during the nights of late spring-early summer.

Originally the nightingale was Philomela, whose sister Procne was married to King Tereus. But Tereus fell in love with Philomela and pretended to her that Procne was dead. They enjoyed a passionate affair until Philomela discovered the truth. Tereus cut out her tongue so that she might not reveal it to others, but Philomela managed to find where Procne had been imprisoned by Tereus and to convey the story to her.

The two sisters planned a terrible revenge, by cooking Tereus' son Ithys and serving the king with roast boy for his dinner. When they did this, the gods were so horrified that they changed the two sisters, the king, and his son into different types of birds.

Philomela became the nightingale, forever singing the sad sweet song of Tereus' betrayal of her love.

Owls

Nocturnal birds of prey found in many parts of the world. One of the best known is *Athene noctua*, the Little Owl of Great Britain. This owl, once the companion of the all-wise goddess Athene, is noted for its wisdom and knowledge.

Owls are favoured friends of witches, wizards, sorcerers, and other practitioners of black arts. Anyone who keeps a pet owl may be regarded as some kind of magician. The silent nocturnal flight, all-seeing night vision, and supernatural wisdom of the owl family are invaluable to magic-makers, and anyone acquainted with an owl is certain to absorb some of these qualities.

Unfortunately it is not uncommon for such people to cook owls, in order to extract their essences for use in spells and potions. Elixir of owl is commonly prescribed for sleepiness, poor vision, mental incapacity, and fear of the darkness.

Pretas

The ghosts of Hindu men who have died by violence, and whose corpses have been disposed of without the proper ceremony. They may also be the ghosts of men slain by violence whose parents or relations neglected to perform, or instruct them in, the correct rites for male Hindus when they were alive.

The pretas appear as naked males of diabolical aspect and are remorseless towards living humans, especially their surviving relations. They may strangle them, strike them dead, frighten them out of their senses, or afflict them with crippling illnesses. Probably there is no protection against a preta determined on revenge.

P'ang Che, P'ang Chiao, P'ang Chu

The three goddesses of corpses. They live in a corpse during the Chinese mourning period between death and burial, and are important functionaries in the spirit's difficult and dangerous journey from this world into the next. It is important, therefore, to prevent them from leaving the corpse, which they may do during the night. A nightwatchman must be set over the corpse, but if he nods off into sleep the goddesses will certainly depart, in order to report his neglect of duty to the other gods. These are sure to punish him, and the whole occurrence will have unfortunate results for the family of the deceased.

Quicksilver

The name of a particularly mischievous female poltergeist (German *polter* = noisy, racketing, *geist* = spirit). Poltergeist activities are well known and extensively documented—the smashing of crockery and windows, noisy crashes and rappings, furniture falling over, and so on. Modern researchers tend to believe that poltergeists always work through the agency of an adolescent girl. It is true that poltergeist manifestations are rare in families which do not include a teenage girl or at least a pubescent boy, but Quicksilver may be the exception to the rule.

She has pestered people in various parts of the English-speaking world, and always leaves her 'trademark' in the form of a large Q scrawled in soap, lipstick, or crayon on a wall, mirror, or window. Her other characteristic is a tinkling laugh, loud enough to disturb a sleeper but intriguing rather than frightening.

Unlike other poltergeists she visits families without teenage children and is mischievous rather than destructive. She plays such pranks as slamming every door in the house at midnight, turning on all the lights, turning all the clothes in a wardrobe inside out, and filling baths, sinks, and washbasins to overflowing. Luckily she never stays long enough with a family to become a real nuisance.

Rakshashas

The appalling 'unholy family' of Hindu India. The lord of all rakshashas is Ravana. He has ten heads and twenty arms which grow again as soon as they are cut off, and a body hideous with the myriad scars and open wounds of his endless battles with the gods.

Rakshashas are dedicated evildoers who strive continuously to defeat the gods, sometimes winning and sometimes losing, but they also war against mankind and devour great quantities of men, women, and children. Naturally they hate holy men, whom they snatch away from their prayers

and gobble up with shrieks of demoniac glee. Mortals are helpless against rakshashas and must rely on the gods to keep them under control, even though the terrible Durga, a rakshasha with the body of a man and the head of a bull, once conquered all the gods and forced them into exile.

A host of lesser fiends supports these dominant demons, and plagues both the living and the dead. Pishacas, which are goblin-like creatures but even more repulsively hideous, live in cemeteries and torment the dead but also affect living humans. They are vampires and creators of such foul diseases as leprosy.

Bhutas, their kindred spirits, also infest cemeteries. They are the evil spirits of the dead, probably aroused and spurred on by the pishacas, and they can actually force the dead to arise from their graves and attack humans.

Grahas, another branch of this unholy family, are demons of disease. They too inhabit cemeteries, and lie in wait for an unwary human who passes by after dark. As soon as he comes within reach they enter his body by its various orifices and settle down to destroy it from within.

Revenants

Literally 'returners', from the French word *revenir* meaning 'to come again'. They are the restless ghosts who return eternally to the scenes of deadly crimes, of which they were either victims or perpetrators. The victims return to bewail their untimely fates: the perpetrators because their bloody deeds deny them eternal rest. Revenants of murderers can be very dangerous to the living and should be dismissed by the rites of exorcism.

In Haiti, the voodoo island of the West Indies, revenants are of a different character. They are the ghosts of dead persons who feel they are fading out of living memory, and return to give vigorous and sometimes unpleasant reminders that they still exist in another dimension. A revenant may jolt a relation's memory with such actions as overturning a boiling pot into the fire, inflicting skin diseases, or leading a child away to become lost in the jungle.

Rona

The moon-woman of New Zealand. Originally she was a Maori girl who forgot to bring water from the stream during daylight and had to fill her waterpot after dark. The moon was shining brightly as she walked down the rocky path from her village to the stream, but it suddenly hid itself behind dark clouds so that Rona tripped on the rocks and fell over. She was so angry that she called out insults to the moon, which also lost its temper and came down to earth to carry her away. Rona resisted violently and clung to a tree, but the moon tore up the tree by the roots and carried it off with Rona still attached. When the moon is full, it is possible to see Rona, the tree, and her waterpot on the face of the moon.

Sakarabru

The God of Darkness who reigns in those regions of Africa now known as Guinea and Senegambia, where he is worshipped by the Agni peoples. He lives in the fetish house at the entrance to every village, together with all the gods who look after such important matters as fertility, the weather, and the magical arts.

Sakarabru is a two-sided personality. In some moods he prowls through the village and snaps up any person foolish enough to leave his hut after dark, and crunches him up with its terrible teeth. But he also guards the village against night attack by wandering demons, and when he receives the proper offerings he will heal the sick and fight off disease spirits. On the whole he is a just god, and if anyone is eaten by Sakarabru, or dies from disease despite prayers and offerings, one may be reasonably sure that it is a punishment for some sin.

Sleep

The mysterious process which immobilises the physical body so that the soul may rove freely upon its own adventures. The god Hypnos causes sleep by touching mortal eyelids with his soft fingers or fanning a person hypnotically with his dark wings. Hypnos (known to the Romans as Somnus) has three sons: Morpheus, Phoebetor, and Phantasus. Their duty is to occupy the sleeper's mind while it is empty of the soul, and entertain, warn, or punish the sleeper with the fantastic activities we know as dreams. In the personalised dramas, Morpheus takes the form of human beings while his brothers assume the forms of animals or objects.

Dreams are extremely important, because the gods may employ Morpheus and his brothers to advise or warn human beings about their destines. It is essential, therefore, for a dreamer to consult an oracle or augur each morning, so that the purpose and meaning of a dream may be correctly interpreted.

No living person has been able to pursue the adventures of the errant souls who escape from a sleeper's body, and rove unchecked through space and time. Some people, including the Transylvanians, say that the soul exits through the sleeper's mouth in the form of a white mouse or white bird, but no one has actually seen this phenomenon and so it is probably no more than a fable. No doubt the soul has methods unknown to mortal man. Its transcendental journeyings may include visits to the afterworld, to consult with the ancestral beings of its mortal host.

One should never wake a sleeper abruptly, or the soul may not have time to return to the body before he or she awakens. It then has to hover helplessly until the owner goes to sleep again. In the meantime, the lack of a soul may allow a mortal to engage in uncharacteristically foolish or violent activities. On the other hand, one should not allow a sick person to drift off into sleep. This allows the soul to escape on its usual adventures, and it may not care to return to a body weakened by illness.

Succubi

Lascivious female spirits or demons, probably descendants or relations of Lilith, Queen of the Night. They are ardent for masculine embraces but their equivalent male demons, the incubi, are interested only in mortal women. Succubi are too hideous to appeal to human males, but they find a way around this problem by seducing men into lustful intercourse during their sleep. The succubi, however, being incapable of true love, have to seduce men in strange phantasmal forms and lure them into all manner of nocturnal perversions, from which the sleeper awakes exhausted, dissatisfied, and ashamed. Probably the name of the succubi derives from the Latin word *sugo* meaning 'I suck', because they suck the strength from human males during the hours of darkness.

Succubi take a particular delight in tormenting holy men under vows of chastity, who believe that fleshly contact with women will deplete their spiritual powers. The female fiends visit such ascetics while they are asleep, drag them into phantasmal orgies, and seduce them into the very ecstasies they have sworn not to enjoy.

Taxim

An Eastern European name for the walking dead or 'undead': the ambulant physical remains of mortals whose souls cannot rest in peace. Usually a person afflicted in this way finds a way out of the grave because he (a taxim is invariably male) is determined to extort revenge for some evil suffered during his mortal existence.

There is an essential difference between the undead and ordinary ghosts. The latter appear in shadowy or even transparent form, whereas a taxim may have the appalling appearance of a person who has been buried for some time. In fact the dreadful stench of corruption often precedes a taxim and gives warning of his approach. This is not, however, invariably the case, and a taxim may manifest himself in comparatively fresh condition. It all depends upon how long the taxim needs to gather up the supernatural strength required to burst out of a vault or grave. Sometimes this is sufficient to enable it to achieve a kind of ectoplasmic condition, pass through any solid obstruction, and reassemble itself on the other side.

A taxim moves only during the hours of darkness, because it is dazzled by daylight, and has a fairly limited range. Naturally it cannot use public transport or hitch a ride, and so it must travel on foot over the ground. It is, therefore, comparatively easy to escape a taxim seeking revenge, simply by fleeing immediately to some other part of the country. One may be reasonably sure that a ruined or abandoned house has been deserted because its occupants were threatened by a taxim.

Usually a taxim has no desire to hurt people unknown to it during life, but it cannot help inflicting icy fear upon them as it shuffles through the night. It seeks only the person upon whom it desires revenge, and until it succeeds in this search it must arise from time to time, usually at the dark of the moon, and set off on its stumbling journey through the night. Naturally it looks and smells worse on each expedition.

Anyone who has sufficient courage (and such people are few indeed) may set a taxim at rest by confronting it as it follows its midnight track, and explaining that revenge is the prerogative of the Supreme Being, who will ensure that divine justice is done.

Vampire

A bloodsucking ghost or undead person. Vampirism and vampirology have been practised at least since the days of the ancient Egyptians and probably since much earlier centuries. Modern vampirologists believe that the original vampire was Lilith, Queen of the Night and Mother of Demons, who was Jehovah's first flawed attempt at making womankind. The tainted touch of her lips upon the throat of some hapless mortal of the Middle East, and the razor-sharp incision of her teeth so that she might suck her bloody feast, began the line of vampires which has proliferated internationally.

The greatest concentration of vampires is found in Magyarorszag or the Country of the Magyars, which covers portions of modern Hungary and Roumania. Our own word vampire derives from the Magyar *wampyr* or *vampyr*. Possibly the vampires of the Middle East drifted into the region in search of fresh blood, or they may have entered Magyarorszag during the Turkish invasions. The rapid development of transport facilities during the last century or so has enabled vampires to spread widely through the First, Second, and Third Worlds, even though it is said that vampires cannot cross the sea. In fact, they may do so quite easily if they fill their pockets with grave soil.

There is no relationship between vampires and the so-called 'vampire bat' (*Desmodus rufus*) of South America. The bloodsucking bats were named after vampires and not vice versa. The true vampire always appears in the form of a human male or female.

Vampirism is contracted only by blood contact with an existing vampire, who enters a sleeper's bedroom and with exquisite delicacy presses a vampire kiss against the throat above the carotid artery. Then, with supernatural surgical skill, the vampire's scalpel-sharp teeth pierce through to the artery, and release the life essences which ensure a vampire's horrid immortality.

The vampire drinks its fill of hot blood and then, using a process which scientists cannot understand, seals the wound so that it is no more than a faint red mark. Now that a victim has been selected the vampire returns to the blood feast again and again. The involuntary blood donor wanes, becomes feeble and skeletal, and eventually dies.

But now the tainted kiss shows its eternal effect. The victim himself becomes a vampire and in due course rises from the grave to seek his own victims, thus continuing the dreadful cycle.

It must be noted, however, that a vampire's victim does not always die. Often the effect of a vampire kiss is so powerful that the victim is vampirised while he or she is still alive, and seeks his or her own blood supply in the community.

It is sometimes said that vampires appear as bats or other animals, to creep or climb into the victim's bedroom, but this is unlikely. A vampire combines the attributes of ghosts and mortals and so is able to pass freely, in ghostly or ectoplasmic form, through any obstacle, and manifest himself or herself as a 'human' on the other side. Jonathan Harker, who was a vampire victim, has left a clear description of a female vampire manifesting herself, through what he thought was a strange whirling of dust in the moon rays entering his chamber, and then transforming into a voluptuous young woman.

The symptoms of vampirism are easily detected. If it is believed that a 'dead' person is responsible then the grave or vault must be opened and the corpse inspected. A vampire corpse, even if centuries old, will probably have the appearance of a healthy human being or at least will not show any signs of corruption. If it has not had a blood feast for some considerable time, it will look pale and weak but will have a slowly beating pulse. If it has fed recently, it will have flushed cheeks and ruby-red lips, abundant glossy hair, and soft pliable skin. If it should open its eyes, then it will look up at the investigators with a brilliant hypnotic stare of cold intelligence. The only way to deal with such vampire corpses is to remove them instantly from the original place of interment to a new grave, preferably dug at a cross-roads. When the corpse is laid in the raw earth, it must be pinned down by a stake driven through the heart. The corpse will remain inert throughout the operation if it is carried out between sunrise and sunset, but not otherwise.

'Living' vampires, that is, those infected this side of the grave, always develop long sharp white incisors, pointed ears, hairs in the palms of the hands, and a foul breath. Their diet of the life-essence of other humans gives them an appearance of abounding vitality, with red cheeks and lips, although this may fade from time to time if there are long intervals between blood feasts. As a final check, one should sprinkle a suspected vampire with a few drops of holy water. He or she will scream as though burnt with acid.

The elimination of such a vampire is inevitably a messy affair, because the heart must be cut out of the body and burned.

Vampire-infested communities should follow a preventative programme to check the spread of the problem. When burying a person who has died from the vampire kiss, the attendants must sprinkle poppyseeds within the coffin, secure it with a rope tied in many knots, and place the branch of a thorn tree on the lid before the grave is filled. Each householder should place a crucifix and a string of garlic bulbs above each bed in the house, and encourage a 'vampire garden' to grow close to the windows and doorways. This garden consists of wild rose bushes, garlic, wolfsbane, hemlock, and wormwood. Vampires abhor the smell and touch of these plants and will not venture near a home protected by such a garden.

If these precautions are carried out then the vampires will move away and inflict themselves on some other community.

Vetala

The Indian breed of vampires. They appear to be very similar to those of other nations although they may have more 'ghostly' characteristics. They live in corpses, which remain incorruptible for as long as they are vampire habitations, but it may be that the corpses stay motionless in tombs etc. while the vampires leave them in search of prey.

Voodoo

The cults of black and white magic and sorcery practised by the black peoples of the West Indies, especially Haiti. The word derives from the Creole French *vaudoux* = sorcerer or witchdoctor, probably applied by early Haitian slaveowners to black magicians.

Voodoo originated in the ancient religions and magical arts of western Africa, from Gambia in the north to Angola in the south. When African chiefs sold huge numbers of their tribespeople into slavery, the crammed slave ships carried many priests and wizards of the ancient beliefs across the South Atlantic. The slaves were eager for the support of such magicians, who quickly established themselves in the New World.

All magic depends upon the co-operation of spirits, demons, and deities with the magicians, and in the West Indies the massed spiritual forces of the great slave communities created a whole new assemblage of such beings. They are known as loas, and like the spirits of every other part of the world their function is to help, comfort, or torment human beings.

The wizards and sorcerers founded a whole new cult, popularly known as voodoo, upon the worship of loas. Probably its real name is unknown except to the trained practitioners of the cult.

The priests of voodoo, known as houngans, and the sorcerers, who are called zobops, may be either male or female. They have to undergo prolonged training and initiation, in absolute secrecy, before they are qualified to perform voodoo rites and formally accepted into the order of zobops. Fully-initiated houngans and zobops possess powers similar to those of witches, wizards, and sorcerers of all other parts of the world. They can raise the dead, fly through the air, appear in a variety of forms, and supply all the usual spells and charms ranging from love potions to death spells.

It appears, however, that the male practitioners may be more powerful than the females. It is said that a male zobop may voluntarily turn himself into a loup-garou, a kind of ghost mosquito which sucks the lives out of children, whereas a female may change into a loup-garou against her will.

There is a huge assemblage of loas, led by Papa Legba and Maitre Carrefour. They have such names as Amelia, Bazo, Danger Mina, Gangan, Ogoun, and Wangol. Many, like Erzilie, the loa of erotic love, help humans in special ways when the houngans ask them to do so. Others perform more generalised tasks, and may torment men and women unless the houngans hold them at bay. Some are new manifestations of ancient tribal deities, but many, known as the proto loa, are those which sprang into existence in the New World. The houngans also maintain that a number of Christian saints, including John the Baptist, has joined the ranks of the loas, and even that Christian angels (known in voodoo as zanges) play their part in voodoo rituals. The zanges, and the loas with saints' names, act as messengers to the God of Christianity, to ask Him to help with whatever may be required.

Houngans and zobops contact the loas in order to perform their magic, whether helpful or harmful. They dominate Haitian communities because of their ability to manipulate the spirits and deities. Voodoo rituals for contacting the loas are shrouded in secrecy, but people speak in whispers of fearsome ceremonies using the blood of white children and of the appearance of loas in the form of venomous serpents.

Some voodoo ceremonies involve whole communities, so that the total force of many mortal minds and souls may be concentrated into an irresistible power. When the beat of voodoo drums is heard through the jungle night, and distant firelight flickers through the trees, it means that every man and woman of some village is dancing in a frenzied ritual. Anyone not directly concerned should keep well away, because the night will be full of loas answering the zobops' call.

Walpurgisnacht

The eve of St Walpurgis' Day or May Day, which in many parts of the northern hemisphere is the first day of summer. On the night of 30 April, covens of witches gather for their second great Sabbat of the year, to worship Satan and draw renewed vigour for all their evil activities. The soft spring night is besmirched by their horrid rituals, which attract every kind of evil spirit to hover around human habitations.

On May Day, the taint of such vile infestations should be disspelled by ceremonies dedicated to St Walpurgis. She was an English nun who emigrated to Germany in about 750 AD, founded a religious community renowned for its holiness, and became a notable performer of miraculous cures. The very name of St Walpurgis is a protection against witchcrafts. Dances, processions, and other May Day celebrations offered in her name will protect a community throughout the summer months.

Watchers, The

Mysterious beings glimpsed at night in many parts of the world. Usually they sit or stand in some commanding position such as a hillside, a church steeple, or the top of a tree, which gives them an overview of nocturnal human activities. Their dark forms, more or less human in outline, sit or stand motionless, as though they were gazing intently through the darkness.

A watcher will allow a human to approach quite close to it, but does not move or give any sign of recognition. If the human speaks, or attempts to touch the watcher, it simply disappears.

Nobody has been able to explain the purpose of the watchers. They do not seem to do any harm or foretell any kind of disaster. It can only be surmised that they report to some superior being on the sins and follies committed by humans after dark.

Witches, Black or White

Persons, usually female, who practise magical arts activated by association with supernatural powers. Black witches enter into a compact with Satan and cast spells with the help of demons and other evil spirits. White witches dedicate themselves to the Supreme Being and derive their mysterious powers from saints, angels, and the spirits of the faithful departed. Male witches, generally known as warlocks, tend to be white rather than black.

The English word witch derives from the Anglo-Saxon 'wit', meaning 'to know'. Witchcraft is therefore the seeking of knowledge and wisdom, approached by the path of good or evil. A witch, like a scientist, is devoted to study and research for their own sakes, regardless of their efforts upon human beings.

A principal difference between black and white witches is that the latter adheres to a reputable form of religion. In some communities, a white witch may actually create and lead a branch of such a religion and administer it for the good of the populace. But a black witch worships Satan and is devoted to the whole assemblage of demoniacal creatures such as Lilith, Queen of the Night. Black witches seek a more complex knowledge than the simple truths revealed in the sacred writings of acceptable religions, but if they are left alone they may never use this knowledge except in a purely experimental form. A witch who casts a spell upon a farmer's cattle, causing them to speak in Latin, may do so purely to satisfy her own curiosity.

But even a black witch has to make a living, and she does so by selling spells and charms. It is the effect of these, in the hands of bloody-minded human beings, which has brought witchcraft into ill repute. Like an armaments manufacturer, a black witch does not see why she should be held responsible for the uses made of her products.

A white witch usually works for the good of the community, in such ways as the preparation of folk medicines. White witches limit their communication with the other

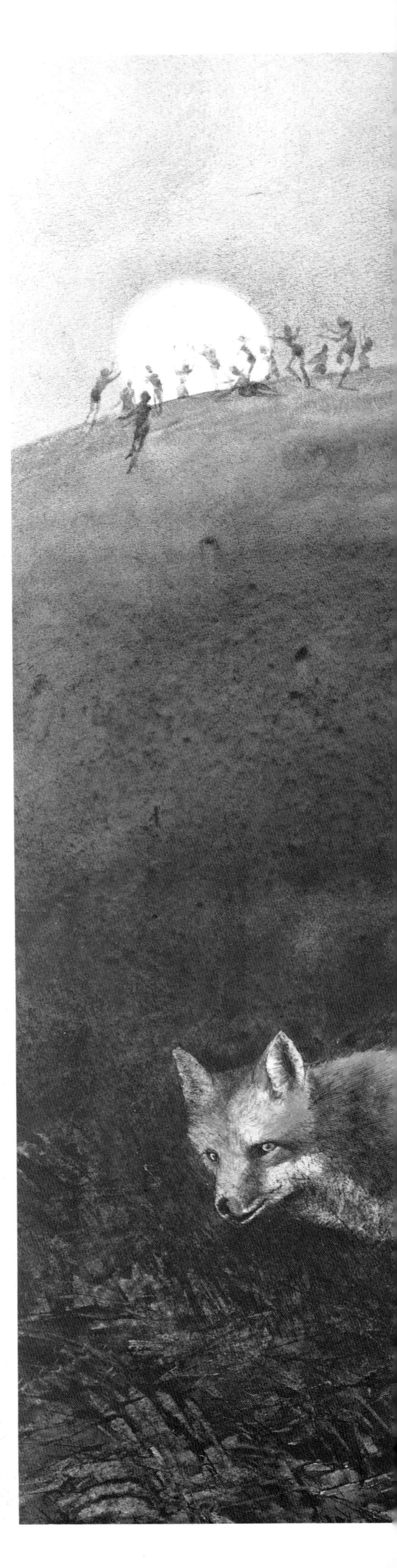

world to acting as mediums, and to such straightforward activities as crystal-gazing. They never attempt to conjure up the dead, or to affect natural forces in such ways as bringing down thunderbolts upon their enemies. In times of trouble they may find themselves condemned as black witches, but at least they escape the eventual fate of a black witch. The latter carries such a burden of illicit knowledge that she cannot ascend to heaven and must be snatched by Satan.

White witches are usually self-taught. They gain their knowledge from a close study of nature and the sacred books, and reading in herbals and other approved documents. Occasionally a white witch accepts a pupil, but she generally tends to keep her knowledge to herself.

On the contrary, black witches are quite willing to accept students in the long and difficult craft. They offer the initial rewards of physical beauty and irresistible sexual attraction, with the side effect of inability to reproduce. A black witch cannot produce offspring. Other rewards include that of prolonged life, because a black witch may live a century or more. The witchmistress does not, however, tell a pupil that the early beauty fades quickly and that a witch's destiny is not appealing. Satan may return her to earth in some form after death, but this is likely to be a toad, viper, or earthworm.

A witch may commence her studies at any age after puberty and proceed through numerous degrees of achievement. The aspiring witch commences with relatively minor witchcraft, such as the mixing of love potions and the casting of blights and murrains, and proceeds slowly to the final degrees. These include the gift of prophecy with the aid of a familiar; levitation, or flying through the air with or without the use of a broomstick and flying ointment; lycanthropy, or transformation into the form of an animal; and the casting of runes to gain power over human beings.

Witchcraft is taught by word of mouth. The only written instructions have long since been burnt by the public hangman. An aspirant witch spends a great deal of time in learning spells by heart, but cannot actually make them work until she has sworn her soul to Satan.

Isobel Dowdie, a beautiful young red-headed Scottish witch of the seventeenth century, told her prosecutors much of what we know about the induction of young witches into the craft. An aspirant must stand naked before witnesses, place her right hand on her head, raise her left foot and place her left hand on its heel, and vow to surrender to Satan all that lies between her hands.

The young witch becomes an associate member of a coven of thirteen witches, but cannot gain full membership until one of the other witches has been exorcised, snatched by Beelzebub, burnt at the stake, or otherwise robbed or witchly powers.

Covens assemble once a month at the full moon, and organise Witches' Sabbats four times a year; on Candlemas in February, Walpurgisnacht or May Eve, Lammas in August, and Hallowe'en or November Eve. Those who fear witches may easily avoid them by staying indoors during the full moon or on Witches' Sabbats, although witches often welcome outsiders to these assemblies. The only rules are that all attendants must strip themselves naked, worship Satan, and join wholeheartedly in swinish guzzling, public fornication, the defilement of maidens, and congress with goats.

Despite the fear and disgust which many well-meaning people feel towards witches, an accomplished witch may be an asset to the community. It is useful to have a source of such staples as 5 centimetres or so of hangman's rope to cure skin blemishes, graveyard mould gathered at midnight to silence a nagging mother-in-law, or the pubic hairs of a mummy to bring home an errant wife.

Witches do not presume to judge community morals. If you have an enemy, then a single gold piece will buy you a *mannequin gris*: a wax doll fashioned in the form of your enemy, so that you may torment him mentally and physically by thrusting needles through the doll. The thirteenth needle brings death.

Regardless of your age or character, a witch will sell you a love potion guaranteed to make the most modest maiden surrender. If you believe that a seducer has administered such a potion to your wife, you may purchase an antidote which will cause his vital parts to shrivel and your wife to devote herself to you with renewed ardour.

A witch is also willing to cast beneficial spells, ensuring a good harvest, increased milk yields, success in business or public affairs, or other advantages. The only drawback is that the price is a tiny portion of your soul, and that such witchboons are addictive. The temptation to succeed in every venture becomes overwhelming, and you sell fragment after fragment of your soul until it is entirely in the witch's possession. She, of course, will pass it on to her master Satan.

A witch's great problem is the jealousy and prejudice of her neighbours. She has no spells efficacious against these superior powers of evil. Many male members of the community enjoy nothing better than tormenting women, and they use the Biblical injunction 'Thou shalt not suffer a witch to live' as the excuse for an agreeable programme of persecutions including stoning, ducking, flogging, and preaching against from the pulpit.

This persecution turns the witch against the community and she becomes actively dangerous. She causes epidemics, storms in harvest time, and infestations of flies, weeds, frogs, and toadstools. She turns strong men weak and maidens reluctant, forces babies to cry all night and dogs to howl at the moon, curdles the milk and sours the butter, and inflicts rheumatism upon the elders of the village.

Soon, the villagers decide to settle all their problems at one stroke. They set out on a witch hunt to pull in all likely and suspected witches in the neighbourhood, and haul them before a summary trial. Usually there is ample evidence, even if it is no more than the possession of a 'familiar' such as a dog or cat. If an old woman possesses a cat to which she talks at all hours of the day or night, it is obviously a familiar spirit which helps her in witchcraft.

When the witch hunters have satisfied themselves then their duty is clear. They must burn the witch on a fire of seasoned oak, carry her ashes outside the parish, and scatter them to the four winds. This of course leaves a vacancy in the local coven, to be filled by one of the student witches.

Xenoglossia

'The tongue of a stranger' (Greek *xenos* = stranger, *glottis* = tongue.) The voice of a demon speaking through the mouth of a human. An accomplished sorcerer may throw a human into a trance, and summon up a demon who will speak through his or her mouth, to give the sorcerer any information he desires. It may also be possible to persuade a spirit of some deceased person to speak through the same medium. This midnight practice, performed with complex spells and rituals, is appallingly dangerous for the human who acts as the 'tongue of a stranger'. The demon may either refuse to leave its mortal host, or snatch his/her mind and soul away when it departs.

Yama Uba

A Japanese witch of mountainous regions. Little is known of her except that she may cause avalanches by throwing stones down

at those who attempt to approach her, and that she can catch children by lassoing them with her hair. This drags a child towards her so that she may gobble it up.

Yowie, Whowie, or Wowie

An Australian creature of the night, which probably assumes a form midway between a reptile and an insect. Those who have glimpsed it say that it has six legs like an insect, the head of a great lizard, a body scaled either like a beetle or a reptile, and the tail of a snake. Apparently the yowie lives in deep caves and only ventures forth after dark in search of prey. Some of the livestock losses blamed upon dingoes may in fact have been caused by prowling yowies.

Zombies

Persons brought back from death by voodoo rituals, so that, as living corpses, they may be programmed to work for the houngans or zobops who have resurrected them. Sometimes a voodoo practitioner will actually kill a person, in order to resurrect and enslave him in the form of a mobile corpse.

Zombies only move around after dark, so that anyone seeing one from a little distance away during the hours of darkness might not know it to be dead. It is easy, however, to distinguish a zombie from a living person. It can 'see' in the dark, so that it avoids obstacles which might trip a living person, and it never moves faster than a slow shambling walk. If it should confront a human being, it will not raise its head to look him or her in the eyes.

A zombie is obedient to all human commands and will do the heaviest work without protest or wearying, although it must return to its grave before sunrise. The owner does not have to feed or care for it in any way, but must make sure that it never touches salt. Even a few grains of salt will make a zombie realise it is dead, whereupon it will dig itself back into its grave and ignore any further attempts at resurrection.

It may be assumed that any prosperous farmer, who does not exert himself unduly, is the owner of zombies who do all the work for him during the night. A zombie-owner does, however, lead an uneasy existence. There is always the possibility that some rival or enemy may use the appropriate spells to re-programme one of his zombies, so that it will turn upon him during the night.

There is another class of zombies known as 'errant zombies'. These are the bodies of people who have died in accidents instead of living out their natural lifespan. They arise from their graves and wander around during the night, but do not seem to do any harm. Eventually, when they reach the end of the period for which they would have lived but for the accident, they settle peacefully into their graves.

Zashiki Warishi

A Japanese poltergeist, probably the spirit of a little boy. Like all little boys he can be very mischievous and he will often disturb a family by his activities during the night. One should not, however, resent his appearance because he often brings good fortune, and it is unwise to try to scare Zashiki Warishi away.

Zorya Vechernaya

The goddess of the dusk, whose father is Dazhbog, the sun, god who rides over eastern Russia. Each morning, her sister the goddess of the dawn opens the gates of Dazhbog's palace, so that he may ride through the skies in his golden chariot. In the evening, when he drives the great white chariot horses back into the palace stables, Zorya Vechernaya closes the palace gates after him. As the gates close softly together, so evening falls and night brings a peaceful end to the activities of another day.

BIBLIOGRAPHY

Countless dreamers, researchers, tellers of tales and spinners of yarns have created an enormous reservoir of material concerning Things That Never Were. The following bibliography, listing the books to which the writer referred while preparing the text, represents only a few drops from that reservoir. They may help your own exploration into unknown territories and new dimensions, and when you venture forth you will find innumerable books to help you.

In this listing, the original dates and places of publication are shown against books written many years ago, while the actual editions to which the writer referred are shown in brackets.

ANDERSEN, HANS CHRISTIAN *Fairy Stories* Copenhagen: 1835 (Cassell's edition, undated)

BACON, J.R. *The Voyage of the Argonauts* London: 1925

BAINTON, ROLAND H. *The Story of Christianity* London: 1964

BARKER, RICHARD *Living Legends* London: 1980

BENNELL, EDDIE *Aboriginal Legends from the Bibulmun Tribe* Adelaide: 1982

BERNDT, R.M. and C.H. *The World of the First Australians* Sydney: 1964

BIBLE, THE HOLY (Collins Revised Standard Edition, 1952)

BIRCH, CYRIL Chinese Myths and Fantasies Oxford: 1961

BORD, JANET & CYRIL *The Bigfoot Casebook* Harrisburg, Pennsylvania: 1982

BRANDON, VICTORIA *Understanding Ghosts* London: 1980

BRASCH, R. *The Supernatural and You!* Stanmore, New South Wales: 1976

BREWER, E. COBHAM *A Dictionary of Phrase and Fable* Boston: 1870 (Avenel Books edition, New York, 1978)

BRIGGS, KATHERINE An Encyclopaedia of Fairies, *Hobgoblins, Brownies, Bogies, and other Supernatural Creatures* New York: 1976

BUNYAN, JOHN *The Pilgrim's Progress* London (?): 1678, 1684 (J.M. Dent edition, 1958)

BURLAND, C.A. *Secrets of the Occult* London: 1972

BURTON, SIR RICHARD *The Thousand Nights and a Night* (Now known as 'The Arabian Nights'). Ten vols., London, 1885-88. (Note: The writer used several 'condensations' of Burton's work, which give varying interpretations of the original stories).

CARROLL, LEWIS (C.L. DODGSON) *Alice's Adventures in Wonderland* London: 1865 (Consolidated Press edition, 1935)

CANNING, JOHN *50 Strange Mysteries of the Sea* London: 1979

CAVENDISH, RICHARD (ed.) *Mythology, An Illustrated Encyclopaedia* London: 1980

COLERIDGE, SAMUEL T. *Kubla Khan* London: 1816 (*Poetry of the English-Speaking World,* Heinemann, London: 1947)

COLT, JONATHAN (ed.) *Beyond the Looking Glass: Extraordinary Works of Fairy Tale and Fantasy* London: 1973

CORLEY, EDWIN *Sargasso* New York: 1977

DAVIDSON, H.R.E. *Gods and Myths of Northern Europe* London: 1964

DAVIDSON, H.R.E. *Scandinavian Mythology* Feltham, U.K.: 1969

DAVISON, RONALD C. *Astrology: How to Cast Your Horoscope* London: 1963 (Granada paperback 1979)

DEFOE, DANIEL *The Life and Strange Surprizing Adventures of Robinson Crusoe* London: 1719 (Consolidated Press edition, 1936)

DIAGRAM GROUP, THE *The Complete Book of Predictions* London: 1983

DOWNING, C. *Russian Tales and Legends* Oxford: 1956

DRISDALE, TIM *Project Waterhorse: The True Story of the Monster Quest at Loch Ness* London: 1975

DRYDEN, JOHN (trans.) *Plutarch's Lives of the Noble Greeks and Romans* (University of Chicago edition, 1952)

DRURY, NEVILL, AND TILLETT, GREGORY *The Occult Source Book* London: 1978

EDWARDS, GEORGE *The Pyramids of Egypt* (Penguin edition, 1961)

EVERY, GEORGE *Christian Mythology* Feltham, U.K.: 1970

FRASER, G.M. *Flashman and the Redskins* London: 1982

FRASER, SHELAGH *Strange Tales of the Highlands of Scotland* Glasgow: 1933

FRAZER, SIR JAMES *The Golden Bough* London: 1922 (Penguin edition, 1978)

FARR, FLORENCE *Egyptian Magic* London: 1890 (Aquarian Books edition, 1982)

FARSON, DANIEL *The Hamlyn Book of Horror* London: 1977

GRAHAME, KENNETH *The Wind in the Willows* London: 1908 (Methuen paperback, 1961)

GRANT, MICHAEL *Myths of the Greeks and Romans* London: 1961

GRAVES, ROBERT *The Greek Myths* (Penguin edition, two vols., 1959)

GREEN, ROGER LANCELYN *A Book of Myths* London: 1959

GUIRAND, FELIX (ed.) *New Larousse Encyclopaedia of Mythology* Feltham, U.K.: 1959

HAGEN, WOLFGANG VON *The Gold of El Dorado: The Quest for the Golden Man* London: 1974 (Collins New Classic edition)

HAGGARD, RIDER *King Solomon's Mines* London: 1885 (Collins New Classic edition)

HAGGARD, RIDER *She* London: 1887 (Collins New Classic edition)

HAGGARD, RIDER *Ayesha: The Return of She* London: 1905 (Collins New Classic edition)

HAINING, PETER *Ghosts: The Illustrated History* London: 1974

HAINING, PETER *An Illustrated History of Witchcraft* London: 1975

HAWTHORNE, NATHANIEL *Tanglewood Tales* Boston: 1840 (?) (Dent/Dutton C.I.C. edition)

HAWNTHORNE, NATHANIEL *Wonder Book* Boston: 1841 (Dent/Dutton C.I.C. edition)

HENDRY, ALLAN *The UFO Handbook* London: 1980

HOLE, CHRISTINA *A Dictionary of British Folk Customs* London: 1976

HOPE, ANTHONY *The Prisoner of Zenda* London: 1894 (Nelson Sevenpenny Library, undated)

HUXLEY, FRANCIS *The Invisibles* London: 1966

INGPEN, ROBERT *Australian Gnomes* Adelaide: 1979

INGPEN, ROBERT *The Voyage of the Poppykettle* Adelaide: 1980

IONS, VERONICA *Indian Mythology* London: 1983

JACKSON, K.H. *A Celtic Miscellany* (Penguin edition, 1971)

JONG, ERICA *Witches* New York: 1981

KING, TERI *Love, Sex, and Astrology* London: 1972

KINGSLEY, CHARLES *The Heroes: Greek Fairy Tales* London: 1856 (Dent/Dutton C.I.C. edition)

KOUTSOUKIS, A. (trans.) *Indonesian Folk Tales* Adelaide: 1970

KREIGER, LEONARD (ed.) *Time-Life Great Ages of Man Series* New York: 1965, 1968. Including *Ancient Egypt* by Lionel Casson; *Imperial Rome* by Moses Hadas; and *Classical Greece* by C.M. Bowra.

LAMB, CHARLES & MARY *Tales founded on the Plays of Shakespeare* London: 1807 (Dent/Dutton C.I.C. edition)

LANG, ANDREW *Adventures of Odysseus* London: 1883 (?) (Dent/Dutton C.I.C. edition)

LANG, ANDREW *Blue Fairy Tale Book* London: 1889

LAWRENCE, P. & MEGGITT, M.J. *Gods, Ghosts, and Men in Melanesia* Melbourne: 1965

LURIE, ALISON *Fabulous Beasts* London: 1981

MACKAL, ROY *The Monsters of Loch Ness* London: 1972

MACKENZIE, D.A. *Myths of China and Japan* London: undated

MANGUEL, ALBERTO, & GUADALUPI, GIANNI *The Dictionary of Imaginary Places* New York: 1980

MAC CANA, PRINSIAS *Celtic Mythology* Feltham, U.K.: 1970

MAPLE, ERIC *Supernatural England* London: 1977

MAZZEO, HENRY (ed.) *Hauntings: Tales of the Supernatural* New York: 1968

MELVILLE, HERMAN *Moby Dick or The White Whale* New York: 1851 (Macmillan edition, 1972)

MORE, SIR THOMAS *Utopia* (in Latin) Louvain: 1516. First English translation, by Ralph Robinson, published in 1551 as *A fruteful and Pleasant Worke of the best State of a Publyque Weale, and of the newe Yle called Utopia.* (Dent's Everyman edition, undated)

MUNTHE, AXEL *The Story of San Michele* London: 1929

PAGE, MICHAEL *Weird Tales of Land and Sea* (unpublished ms.)

PARKER, K. LANGLOH *Australian Legendary Tales* London: 1896 (Brolga Books paperback, 1969)

PARRINDER, GEOFFREY *African Mythology* London: 1982

PARRINDER, GEOFFREY (Advisory ed.) with BARKER, MARY & COOK, CHRISTOPHER (eds) *Pear's Encyclopaedia of Myths and Legends* (4 vols.) London: 1977

PLANER, FELIX E. *Superstition* London: 1980

POIGNANT, ROSLYN *Oceanic Mythology* Feltham, U.K.: 1967

PSYCHIC RESEARCH SOCIETY, THE *Proceedings* London: various dates from 1890

RIDEOUT, P.M. (ed.) *Larousse Ecyclopaedia of Astrology* New York: 1980

RHYS, JOHN *Celtic Folklore, Welsh and Manx* Oxford: 1901

ROBERTS, AINSLIE & MOUNTFORD, C.P. *The Dreamtime* Adelaide: 1965

ROBERTS, AINSLIE & MOUNTFORD, C.P. *The Dawn of Time* Adelaide: 1969

ROBERTS, AINSLIE & MOUNTFORD, C.P. *The First Sunrise* Adelaide: 1971

ROBERTS, AINSLIE & MOUNTFORD, C.P. *Dreamtime Heritage* Adelaide: 1975

ROBERTS, AINSLIE & ROBERTS, MELVA JEAN *Dreamtime: The Aboriginal Heritage* Adelaide: 1981

ROGO, D. SCOTT *The Poltergeist Experience* New York: 1979 (Penguin USA edition)

SHELLEY, MARY WOLLSTONECRAFT *Frankenstein* London (?): 1818 (New English Library paperback, 1966)

SHULMAN, SANDRA *Nightmare* Stanmore, New South Wales: 1979

SIMPSON, COLIN *Adam in Ochre – Inside Aboriginal Australia* Sydney: 1962

STANTON, ROBERT *The Unexplained at Sea* London: 1982

STEVENSON, R.L. *Treasure Island* Edinburgh: 1883

STEVENSON, R.L. *The Strange Case of Dr Jekyll and Mr Hyde* London: 1886

STEVENSON, R.L. *Island Nights' Entertainments* (story 'The Bottle Imp'.) Edinburgh: 1893

STOKER, BRAM *Dracula* London: 1896 (Arrow paperback)

STORY, RONALD *The Space Gods Revealed* New York: 1976

SWIFT, JONATHAN *Travels [illegible] Several Remote Regions of the World, by Lemuel Gulliver, first a Surgeon and then a Captain of Several Ships* Dublin: 1726 (Hurst & Co. edition)

TENNYSON, LORD ALFRED *Poems* London: 1842 Including 'The Lotos Eaters'; Morte d'Arthur'; 'Camelot'; 'Idylls of the King' etc. (Macmillan edition, 1893)

TWAIN, MARK (SAMUEL CLEMENS) *The Adventures of Tom Sawyer* Hartford, Conn.: 1875 (Nelson school edition, undated)

TWAIN, MARK (SAMUEL CLEMENS) *The Adventures of Huckleberry Finn* New York: 1884 (Harrap edition, undated)

UNDERWOOD, PETER *Dictionary of the Supernatural* London: 1978

USHER, GEORGE *Dictionary of Plants used by Man* London: 1974

VERNE, JULES *A Journey to the Centre of the Earth* Paris: 1864

VERNE, JULES *From the Earth to the Moon* Paris: 1865

VERNE, JULES *Around the Moon* Paris: 1870 (All above in Dent/Dutton C.I.C. editions)

WALSH, JOHN W. *Tales of the Greek Heroes* London: 1949

WARRINGTON, JOHN (trans.) *Aesop's Fables* London: 1955

WATSON, LYALL *Supernature: The Natural History of the Supernatural* London: 1973

WELLS, H.G. *The First Men in the Moon* London: 1901 (Heinemann/Octopus omnibus)

WELLS, H.G. *The Time Machine* London: 1895 (Heinemann/Octopus omnibus)

WHEATLEY, DENNIS *The Devil and All his Works* London: 1971

WHITE, SIR HAROLD (ed. BOARD CHAIRMAN) *Australian Encyclopaedia* Sydney: 1977

WILDE, OSCAR *The Picture of Dorian Gray* London: 1896 (Penguin paperback)

WOLF, LEONARD *Monsters* New York: 1974

WRIGHT, H.W. AND M.H. *Richards Topical Encyclopaedia* New York: 1959

YUST, WALTER (ed.) *Encyclopaedia Britannica* (1955 edition) London: 1955

INDEX

A note on the illustrations

The ardent student of Things Out of this World, who has read widely in the wondrous literature of the imagination, will notice that some of the illustrations pay homage to the styles and techniques of earlier artists in the field. The unmistakable stamp of such illustrators as Howard Pyle, Arthur Rackham, and the ancient School of Classical Sculptors has been imposed here and there to remind the reader that this volume follows a long and honourable tradition, and to acknowledge the pioneering work of adventurers into the regions of fantasy. Apart from these illustrations, a few others have deliberately developed out of possibly familiar scenes, figures, and situa-ations, with the intention of showing that the real can be unreal and vice versa. The majority, however, spring from the same source tapped by the original tellers of the tales recounted in this book.